SAILOR-SCHOLAR

Admiral Sir Herbert Richmond 1871-1946

BARRY D. HUNT

Admiral Sir Herbert Richmond was "a unique phenomenon in the Victorian-Edwardian navy—a professionally competent and successful officer who was also an intellectual," writes the author. "This was enough to ensure that his progress would be stormy."

This thoroughly documented biographical study of Richmond's professional career reveals a fully experienced, clear-thinking officer with a profound understanding of naval history, "a restless and uncompromising personality," and a passionate concern with naval strategy, the art of war, and the most effective training programme for officers. Richmond persistently challenged the accepted practices and prejudices of the naval profession. He and his small group of disciples, the "Young Turks," found themselves in the thick of the most crucial controversies in the British Navy. In spite of frequent official displeasure, however, Richmond became an influential naval historian and educator, responsible for the creation of the modern naval staff and the Imperial Defence College.

The volume rests on extensive research in the official records and the private papers of Richmond and his close associates. It will interest not only naval historians, but also those with a general interest in the impact of one man's thought and actions on Britain's defence policy and the outcome of two World Wars.

Barry D. Hunt received the Ph.D. degree from Queen's University and is presently Associate Professor of History at the Royal Military College, Kingston, Ontario. He has published several essays on British and Canadian maritime affairs, and is co-editor of War Aims and Strategic Policy in the Great War, 1914-1918.

SAILOR-SCHOLAR

**Admiral Sir Herbert Richmond
1871-1946**

BARRY D. HUNT

SAILOR-SCHOLAR

Admiral Sir Herbert Richmond
1871-1946

BARRY D. HUNT

Wilfrid Laurier University Press

Canadian Cataloguing in Publication Data

Hunt, Barry D. (Barry Dennis), 1937-
  Sailor-scholar

Bibliography: p.
Includes index.
ISBN 0-88920-104-8

1. Richmond, Herbert, Sir, 1871-1946. 2. Admirals −
Great Britain − Biography. 3. Great Britain. Royal
Navy − Officers − Biography. 4. Great Britain −
History, Naval − Historiography. I. Title.

DA89.1.R52H86   359.3′31′0924   C82-094117-4

Contents

Abbreviations

(Official and Common Service Usage)

A.C.N.S.	Assistant Chief of Naval Staff
A.D.N.O.	Assistant Director of Naval Ordnance
A.D.O.D.	Assistant Director of the Operations Division
A.S.W.	Anti-submarine warfare
B.E.F.	British Expeditionary Force
C-in-C	Commander-in-Chief
C.I.D.	Committe of Imperial Defence
C.I.G.S.	Chief of the Imperial General Staff
C.N.S.	Chief of the Naval Staff
C.O.S.	Chief of Staff to a Flag Officer Commanding. Also, prior to May 1917, Chief of the Admiralty War Staff. After 1923, refers to the Chiefs of Staff Committee
D.C.N.S.	Deputy Chief of Naval Staff
D.M.I.	Director of Military Intelligence, War Office
D.N.I.	Director of Naval Intelligence (from 1912-1918, known as D.I.D., Director of the Intelligence Division)
D.N.O.	Director of Naval Ordnance
D.O.D.	Director of Operations (Division), Naval Staff
D. of P.	Director of Plans Division
D.T.S.D.	Director of the Training and Staff Duties Division
G.F.B.O.	Grand Fleet Battle Orders
I.D.C.	Imperial Defence College
N.I.D.	Naval Intelligence Division
R.A.F.	Royal Air Force
R.F.C.	Royal Flying Corps
R.I.M.	Royal Indian Marine
R.I.N.	Royal Indian Navy
R.N.A.S.	Royal Naval Air Service
S.N.O.	Senior Naval Officer

In the Notes

Add. MSS	Additional Manuscripts, British Museum
Adm.	Admiralty Papers (Public Record Office)
Air.	Air Ministry Papers (Public Record Office)
B.M.	British Museum
Cab.	Cabinet Papers (Public Record Office)
CP	Julian S. Corbett Papers
DEW	K.G.B. Dewar Papers, National Maritime Museum
HEN	W. H. Henderson Papers, National Maritime Museum
H.M.S.O.	His Majesty's Stationery Office
LHP	Liddell Hart Papers, States House, Medmenham, Bucks (now deposited in King's College, London)
R.C.N.	Royal Canadian Navy
RIC	Richmond Papers, National Maritime Museum
N.M.M.	National Maritime Museum, Greenwich
N.R.	The *Naval Review*
N.R.S.	Navy Records Society
P.R.O.	Public Record Office, London
R.U.S.I.	*Royal United Services Institute*
W.O.	War Office Papers, Public Record Office

Acknowledgements

This book has been published with the help of a grant from the Social Science Federation of Canada, using funds provided by the Social Sciences and Humanities Research Council of Canada. Research over several summers in the United Kingdom was made possible through the generous financial assistance of the Royal Military College Arts Research Fund and, during a sabbatical in 1973-1974, by a Canada Council Leave Fellowship.

This is the appropriate place to acknowledge my deep gratitude to Professor Donald M. Schurman. In addition to sharing generously his own extensive knowledge of Admiral Richmond and Sir Julian Corbett, he has extended the wise counsel and inspiration of a gifted teacher and, most of all, the faith of a valued friend.

All students of modern British naval affairs are indebted to the many outstanding works of Captain Stephen W. Roskill, Professor Gerald S. Graham and the late Professor Arthur J. Marder. My own reliance on their scholarship is acknowledged in the bibliography and notes that follow. Here also I want to express my personal thanks for their advice, for access to certain of their papers and for other encouragements without which this book could not have been completed.

Captain Sir Basil and Lady Kathleen Liddell Hart very graciously welcomed me to States House where, shortly before his death, I enjoyed access to Sir Basil's extensive private papers and intimate knowledge of Richmond and other personalities of the inter-war period. I am especially grateful to Lady Liddell Hart for her continuing friendship and moral support which I value deeply.

My thanks are due also to Mr. J. A. Pollen of London who in addition to granting access to his family's papers also allowed me to read the manuscript of his biography of his father, Arthur Hungerford Pollen. Mr. Jon Sumida was especially helpful in bringing these papers to my attention and in patiently explaining the intricacies of Pollen's computers and gunnery fire control system.

I wish to thank the Trustees of the National Maritime Museum, Greenwich, for permission to make use of archival materials under their jurisdiction. Mr. Alan Pearsall, as Custodian of Manuscripts, was unfailingly helpful during my extended visits to Greenwich and through many months of trans-Atlantic correspondence. As always, Mr. John Spurr, Mr. Clifford Watt, and the other members of the Royal Military College Massey Library staff have gone out of their way to make the researcher's task much easier. For permission to consult various collections of private and official papers, I wish also to thank the following institutions: the Churchill College Library, Cambridge; the Douglas Library, Queen's University, Kingston; The Naval Library, Ministry of Defence, London; the Redpath Library, McGill University, Montreal; the Directorate of History, National Defence Headquarters, Ottawa; the Public Archives of Canada, Ottawa; and the Public Record Office, London. Crown copyright materials in the P.R.O. appear by permission of the Controller H. M. Stationery Office.

A word about references to the _Naval Review_ is in order here. Until fairly recently, it was accepted practice to make use of articles in this privately circulated journal but without citing it by name. This presented some difficulties in view of Richmond's leading part in the _Review_'s creation and early development. Although the decision to remove the ban on citations has solved these problems, I nonetheless have based my analysis of the _Review_'s history mainly on materials contained in the private papers of Richmond and his closest associates and, as much as possible, restricted citations of specific articles to those with which these men were directly involved.

Finally, I extend my appreciation to my students and colleagues at the Royal Military College for their tolerance and assistance in so many ways, most especially Professor Frederic F. Thompson and Dr. Ronald G. Haycock; to Dr. Ernest Gilman (now of the Operations Research Analysis Establishment in Ottawa); and to Mrs. Karen Brown, Secretary to the History Department R. M. C. who typed most of the manuscript. I owe the greatest debt of all to my wife Betty who in addition to typing portions of the manuscript has also lived with it longest and endured it best.

Barry D. Hunt

The Royal Military College
of Canada

Introduction

Admiral Sir Herbert William Richmond (1871-1946) is remembered mainly for his work as a naval historian. His first book, *The Navy in the War of 1739-1748* (3 vols., Cambridge, 1920), established his reputation as a serious scholar and in 1926 won him the Royal United Service Institution's Chesney Gold Medal—a distinction previously accorded to only one other naval officer, the American Captain Alfred Thayer Mahan. Probably the most widely read today of Richmond's books is his classic *Statesmen and Sea Power*. Published shortly before his death in 1946, it is in itself sufficient justification for placing him in the Colomb-Mahan-Corbett tradition of naval historians. In this sweeping analysis of British policy from Elizabethan times up to the end of the Second World War, Richmond's purpose was to educate politicians and sailors alike on the abiding realities of naval greatness, the inter-relationships of political and military strategy, and the connections between Britain's developing overseas influence and the utilization of her maritime strengths. These were the matured thoughts of a man nearing the end of a long and incredibly active life, the conclusions of one who, in the course of two highly successful careers—first as a Royal Navy officer who rose to the rank of Admiral, and then as a professional historian at Cambridge—had personally experienced the workings of British defence politics during the half century that spanned the steam and nuclear naval revolutions.

Students of modern British defence and foreign policy will also recognize Richmond the defence critic and prolific writer of books, articles, and letters-to-editors on most aspects of inter-war naval affairs. Though virtually nothing has been written about his influence in shaping public opinion and policy, few accounts of the period fail to invoke some fragment of his wisdom or reference to his strictures

on contemporary policy development. Most of this activity followed
his retirement—more accurately, his dismissal—from the Navy in
1931 when, no longer hemmed in by the requirements of service
discipline, he was free to express openly ideas he had nurtured and
fought for all his life. Thus, his success as an historian and publicist
was all of a piece with his record as a regular naval officer long
committed to the idea that reform of the Royal Navy was both necessary and possible.

Richmond was a unique phenomenon in the Victorian-
Edwardian Navy—a professionally competent and successful officer
who was also an intellectual. This was enough to ensure that his
progress would be stormy. Professor Arthur Marder's publication of
excerpts from Richmond's diaries (*Portrait of an Admiral*)[1] covering
the years 1909-1920, clearly reveals the intolerance he had for less
gifted contemporaries—a certain prickliness of character that coloured most of his personal relationships. Yet the picture that emerges
of a highly censorious, ambitious, and impatient young captain of the
Dreadnought era is inevitably incomplete and must be balanced
against the one contained in his other private letters, and his Admiralty and other official papers. These portray an officer eminently
capable of clear thinking, with a sense of moderation and sanity, and a
decided flair for the use of persuasive logic; a man who by virtue of an
outstanding intellect, a restless and uncompromising personality,
and the depth of his grasp of historical realities became the foun-
tainhead of British naval thought in the twentieth century. Above all,
Richmond worked to cure the intellectual retardation which characterized the pre-1914 Royal Navy and accounted in large measure for
its less than inspiring record in the First World War and its myopic
approach to policy development in the years following.

World War I revealed that in a number of vital areas the Royal
Navy's adjustment to modern conditions was surprisingly incomplete. Deficiencies in *materiel* and mentality, of doctrine and system
of command, underlay the Navy's disappointing operational record.
Reactions to the Dardanelles and Jutland both exemplified a general
sense of opportunities lost and potentials somehow unfulfilled. For a
public long conditioned to judge naval success in terms of Trafalgars
and Tsushimas, it was difficult to understand how the Royal Navy had
failed to achieve results commensurate with its apparently unpre-
cedented superiority in 1914. The lack of a well-organized and competent Naval Staff at the Admiralty, together with the long neglect of
naval education and training of officers in the higher aspects of their
profession, help explain this paucity of wartime success. The lack of a

1   Arthur J. Marder, ed., *Portrait of an Admiral: The Life and Times of Sir Herbert
    Richmond* (London: Jonathan Cape, 1952).

fully integrated Staff prior to 1914 also severely crippled the Admiralty in its struggle with the War Office and Army for a position of primacy in the formulation of overall strategic policy. When war came, the system of Admiralty control proved inadequate and totally unsuited to the conduct of operations in the face of unpleasant enemy surprises.

The virtual atrophy of the Navy's intellectual apparatus had its roots in the revolution in technology which, since the mid-nineteenth century, had kept naval thinkers' minds occupied almost exclusively with questions of ship design and weapons performance. Admiral Sir John Fisher's prewar "reforms" accelerated and intensified these materialist tendencies. His brilliant measures and ruthless methods were undoubtedly the main reasons for the Grand Fleet's numerical superiority in September 1914. However, they were also the basis of serious defects. "The brain of Jupiter had indeed produced an Athene fully armed," one of his many critics suggested. "It was no one's business to be sure that the poor lady could ever use her spear."[2] Thus, prior to 1914, naval thinkers and reformers who worked to encourage a broader, more intellectual approach to problems of tactics, strategy, and national policy were dealing with a service whose recent history and whose current sense of urgency were geared to a materialist ethic.

Of the naval officers who took issue with this preoccupation, Richmond proved to be the most persistent and formidably intelligent. His career provides evidence of the state of intellectual development regarding sea warfare in the Royal Navy of his day. He focussed his mind on the rules of thumb that passed for naval thought amongst his contemporaries, both service and secular, thus providing shape and form to many serious problems. His overriding purpose was to prevent any repetition of the near-disaster which 1914-1918 had been for Britain. All his postwar writings bear witness to his conviction that the First World War represented failure. Like Liddell Hart and Fuller, and for motives akin to those of a Sassoon or Graves, he protested the horror, waste, and mistakes. But Richmond, unlike these men, was not only reacting to personal experiences of those terrible years. His commitment to naval reform predated the War by several years. His leadership of an "intellectual revolution" within the Navy had started in 1912 with the founding of the Naval Society and the publishing of the Naval Review. From that point, Richmond and his disciples—the so-called "Young Turks" of the Grand Fleet—worked to bring about major changes in naval strategy, policy, and organization. The record of their successes and failures and their impact on the personalities and events of these important years is the subject of this study.

2 Naval Review, 18 (1930), 168.

Apart from Professor Marder's book, the only other important analysis of Richmond's work is that contained in Professor Donald M. Schurman's *The Education of a Navy*.[3] Here, however, the author's main interest was to set Richmond's major works within the wider context of the British naval historian-strategists of the late nineteenth, early twentieth centuries. Of other published biographical notes and articles, none have been based primarily on Richmond's extensive papers or those of his closest associates, most of which have never been published. This study is an attempt to fill that need.

It is not a "life and times" of the modern Royal Navy, though given the amazingly catholic range of Richmond's interests, the temptation to extend its focus has had to be resisted by concentrating on those issues which he judged to be the most important. This has involved discussing those issues in ways which may appear to inflate their significance. Still, a sense of proportion has been sought. Historical figures must of course be explained in terms of their own environment. This is all the more important in Richmond's case for it is in his written work and participation in public issues that his mind and personality are most clearly revealed. His family life, though happy and secure, was straightforward and conventional and, judging from the very limited amount of documentation related to his private existence that has survived, does not seem to have had any appreciable effect on his career one way or the other. The "private" Richmond must therefore remain a somewhat shadowy figure, though perhaps this examination of his handling of the problems of his day will go some way towards resolving the paradoxes both of his own personality and of the workings of British defence politics in the post-Fisher era.

3   D. M. Schurman, *The Education of a Navy: The Development of British Naval Strategic Thought, 1867-1914* (London: Cassell, 1965), pp. 110-46.

1

The Fisher Era: The Education of a Reformer

Herbert William Richmond was born at Beavor Lodge, Hammersmith, on September 15, 1871, the third child and second son of Sir William Blake Richmond and Clara Jane Richards. In 1885, at age thirteen, he entered the Royal Navy as a cadet in the training ship *Britannia*. His first appointment as a midshipman of fifteen was in H.M.S. *Nelson*, flagship of the Commander-in-Chief on the Australian Station, one of the Navy's first twin-screw battleships which was also fully rigged as a sailing ship. Thus, his career began at a moment when the last vestiges of the great sail navy upon which Britain's imperial fortunes had rested for so long had all but disappeared. It was to be a career of exceptional promise for a gifted young officer who recognized where the best avenues of advancement lay.

In 1892, he joined the Hydrographic Branch and served in the Mediterranean as a Sub-Lieutenant and Lieutenant in the survey ship *Stork*. But the prospects in this service were too restricted—only one of some sixty assistant surveyor lieutenants could expect promotion in any year—and when in 1893 an attack of Malta fever temporarily invalided him back to England, he took the opportunity to transfer to the more promising torpedo branch. That he was one of the very few lieutenants selected to qualify in this specialty was evidence of his above-average abilities. It was also significant that Admiral Sir John ("Jacky") Fisher, himself a torpedo expert, was then in Portsmouth. Following graduation in 1897 from the Torpedo School, H.M.S. *Vernon*, Richmond returned to the Mediterranean as Torpedo Lieutenant in the *Empress of India* (1897-1898), H.M.S. *Ramillies* (1899), flagship of Admiral Sir John Hopkins, and H.M.S. *Canopus* (1899-1900), then the most modern battleship in service. In 1900, he joined *Majes-*

5

tic, flagship of the Channel Squadron, where he served under Vice-Admirals Sir Harry Rawson and Sir Arthur Wilson. As a result, by 1903 when he was promoted to Commander and brought to the Admiralty as assistant to the Director of Naval Ordnance (D.N.O.), Richmond had earned a reputation for outstanding technical expertise and, equally important, had made himself known to influential personalities at the very centre of naval affairs. For over a year during his Admiralty stay, he served on a committee investigating the training of executive warrant officers. This was followed by almost three years (1904-1906) as Executive Officer in *Crescent*, flagship of the Cape of Good Hope Station. In December 1906, he was recalled to the Admiralty to serve as Naval Assistant to Fisher, then First Sea Lord.

Richmond's prospects were amongst the brightest in the Navy. Fisher had marked him as a coming man. His promotion to Captain in 1908, at age thirty-five, and appointment the following year to command H.M.S. *Dreadnought*—flagship of the Home Fleet and the first of Fisher's revolutionary all-big-gun battleships—accorded entirely with the way members of the so-called "Fish Pond" were treated. That Richmond was definitely a member of that elite is worth emphasizing in view of his later estrangement from Fisher and everything that he represented. For all the high hopes which this his first seagoing command held open, there were elements in Richmond's personality which caused him to question his evident progress and hasten the process by which his reputation as a "young comer" began to fall to pieces.

He had been born into a family of sensitive and accomplished men and raised in an environment congenial to a boy of his capacities and apparent independence of spirit. His great-grandfather Thomas and grandfather George Richmond were eminent portrait painters. His father, Sir William Richmond, K.C.B., R.A., who from 1879 to 1893 was Slade Professor of Fine Arts at Oxford, was also a distinguished artist whose many friends and connections encompassed a wide circle of Victorian notables. The result was that the family home, an old house which at that time was still surrounded by hayfields, became a favourite retreat of artists, academics, and political figures, as well as a reputedly melancholy lady ghost which most of the Richmonds seem to have encountered at some point. It was a happy, close-knit family of four other brothers and an older sister with whom Herbert always retained strong ties. He adored his mother, a gentle and intelligent woman who instilled in her children a love for beauty in all its forms and encouraged this sophisticated environment which nurtured the young Herbert's self-assurance and intellectual precocity.

Sir William Richmond evidently took some pains to encourage his son's considerable artistic gifts although these were mainly confined to caricaturing his messmates and contemporaries, a talent which won him some repute in the Navy of the 1890s. For many years, a large scrapbook of these were preserved by H.M.S. *Vernon* until they were misplaced or stolen. Many of his sketches and watercolours illustrating his midshipman's logs and recording his early experiences survive in the Richmond Collection at Greenwich. But art was never more than a recreational pastime for Herbert. His restless disposition was attuned to more active pursuits. From his early childhood, he would be remembered as being always cheerfully high-spirited, often impetuous, and possessed of great personal courage and loyalty to the Navy.

His decision to embark on a naval career was prompted apparently by a casual sighting, during a visit to Portsmouth when he was nine or ten, of some warships and a boatload of bluejackets commanded by a midshipman. That plus an unhappy existence at St. Mark's School in Windsor, to which he and his older brother had been sent, confirmed the decision. He cried when he failed the entrance examination in 1883 at the age of twelve. His second attempt, the next year, was successful. The Navy was an escape from the school work he disliked so intensely, though not a complete one, as his brother Arthur Richmond later recalled:

> the career of a naval officer alone would never have satisfied him. He was possessed throughout his life by a creative urge. Even as a midshipman he would not just keep a log-book. He had to illustrate and decorate it. And even at that time of life he was a great letter-writer. I think he always had to write. It was a necessary form of self expression to him, and he wrote excellent and vivid letters. By nature he had to seek perfection . . . wherever he touched life in a practical form and found what seemed to him defects he had to try and remedy them. For that reason he could have been anything. Essentially his interests and sympathies were liberal. He hated injustices and if the circumstances of his life had brought him into touch with social problems he would have been an ardent social reformer. Perhaps as a result of his early training in the Navy, which in some ways was a hard one, he developed a superficial attitude of sympathy with conservative and traditional ideas and methods, but in fact he spent his life fighting against established ways of thought in his profession and championing ideas which were often regarded by his superiors as revolutionary. Indeed the liberalism of his instinctive outlook constantly broke through the conservatism of a partially super-imposed personality.[1]

1   As quoted in G.M. Trevelyan, "Admiral Sir Herbert William Richmond 1871-1946," *Proceedings of the British Academy*, 32 (reprinted, 1946), pp. 326-27.

Richmond's reactions to his early training reflect what was probably a fairly common professional disdain for excessive technical and mathematical values and preference instead for "all-roundedness" and "general ability." He had his share of the typical "snotty's" prejudices and displayed the usual fondness for ward room pranks whether it was challenging visiting officers to guest night duels with tomahawks or leading them in a game of "follow my leader" through the ship's upper works and over the side. What did, however, set him apart from his contemporaries was his artistic temperament which eventually emerged as an unusually deep commitment to the study of history.

By age, temperament, and background, Richmond was a highly receptive medium for the ideas of Captain Mahan, Sir John Laughton, the Colomb brothers, Julian Corbett, and others whose works formed such an important part of the outburst of public interest in naval affairs and historical writing in the latter decades of the nineteenth century. He had read the lives of Napoleon and Nelson as a cadet, but his serious study of history began during his Mediterranean tour. He began, as Professor Marder has suggested, in reaction to the limitations of his training: "the fear that exclusive concern with the technical and routine side of the naval profession might get him into a rut."[2] In a more immediate sense, the 1898 crisis in Anglo-French relations opened his mind to the wider issues of war and naval preparedness. Years later he explained to Captain Basil Liddell Hart:

> Fashoda had brought the country very close to war, and, speaking for myself, I felt there was neither strategical nor tactical clarity in our minds. How should we fight France if war came? We asked each other: and no one had an idea. . . . None of the questions were new: but none had been answered. There was no doctrine.[3]

The search for answers to these questions through the research and writing of naval history thereafter became the dominating drive in his life.

The most powerful influence in this respect was the gifted naval historian Julian Corbett who, until his death in 1923, was Richmond's teacher, mentor and, to the extent that the difference in their ages allowed, his close friend. It was Corbett who first inspired and then later advised the young author in his first major writing venture—a three-volume history of *The Navy in the War of 1739-1748*, of which more will be said presently. Richmond had known Corbett through a long-standing family friendship, but their personal relationship began in connection with Admiral Fisher's campaign to introduce sweeping reforms of the Navy's education system (the Selborne or

2   Marder, *Portrait of an Admiral*, p. 168.
3   LHP, Richmond to Liddell Hart, September 1934.

"New Scheme" of 1902) and their efforts, after 1905, to interest Fisher in the creation of a naval war staff. Richmond's involvement in both of these important issues earned him a place high on the list of Fisher's favourites. It was also the basis for his subsequent alienation.

Richmond's contribution to the origins of the Selborne Scheme was that of a coordinator and collator of ideas and intermediary in transmitting them to those in a position to push them through. Aided by Admiral William H. Henderson—himself a veteran campaigner for educational reform, and later to be intimately associated with Richmond as editor of the *Naval Review*[4]—Richmond pressed his own ideas and those of others directly on Fisher.[5] He fed information to Corbett ("I gave him copious notes to shew how things stood at present")[6] who in turn used it to write three powerful *Monthly Review* articles (March, April, and June, 1902) condemning the existing system and offering suggestions for improvements. The whole exercise was a tribute to Fisher's methods of manipulating public opinion, though his success in this case owed as much to Richmond's basic arguments as it did to the writing skills of men like Corbett and J. R. Thursfield, *The Times* naval correspondent.

When the Selborne Scheme was eventually promulgated on Christmas Day, 1902,[7] Richmond had misgivings about some of its provisions. As early as 1894, he had commented on the inadequacies of the training he had himself survived. He accepted the need to tighten up old ideas, to de-emphasize cramming methods and learning by rote, to broaden the educational approach through a greater emphasis on the humanities, and to stop attempting to combine practical sea training for midshipmen with academic instruction afloat. The "New Scheme" provided for the common entry and training

4   See below Chapter 2, pp. 33-39. Also, RIC/14/2, Letters to and from Admiral W. H. Henderson concerning the Training of Naval Officers, June-December, 1902.
5   Note the ideas of Commander Carlyon Bellairs in the *Monthly Review*, "The War Training of Naval Officers" (October 1900); "The Navy and the Engineer" (April-June 1902). Bellairs and Richmond established their friendship as shipmates in the 1890s. Failing eyesight resulted in Bellairs' early retirement in 1901. A Member of Parliament (Conservative) until 1931, he became a well-known and voluble critic on naval affairs in the House, and source of support and information for Richmond. His private papers are deposited in the Redpath Library, McGill University, Montreal. See also the ideas of Admiral E. R. Fremantle, "Training of Naval Officers," *Monthly Review* (March 1901), and those of J. R. Thursfield, Correspondent to *The Times* (Fisher to Thursfield, July 12, 1902), in A. J. Marder, ed., *Fear God and Dread Nought: The Correspondence of Admiral of the Fleet Lord Fisher of Kilverstone*, vol. 1 (London: Jonathan Cape, 1952), pp. 254-55.
6   RIC/1/6, Diary April 13, 1902.
7   For a full description of the Scheme see A. J. Marder, *From the Dreadnought to Scapa Flow: The Royal Navy in the Fisher Era, 1904-1919*, vol. 1 (London: Oxford University Press, 1961), pp. 28-32, 46-52; and also his *Fear God and Dread Nought*, vol. 1, pp. 243-47.

of Executive, Engineer, and Marine officers for two years at each of the newly established Royal Naval Colleges of Osborne and Dartmouth. The most contentious feature of the system, the so-called "interchangeability" of Executive and Engineer Officers, was "too Utopian" in Richmond's view and he was pleased when Fisher deferred to widespread opposition by downplaying its importance in the final Memorandum. Otherwise, Richmond accepted the Selborne Scheme as an important and useful initial step: "The corners will be rubbed off with further consideration and the whole scheme a success." The fact is he supported Fisher's "broad big idea."[8] Corbett was unstinting in his praise of Richmond's and Henderson's contributions and, on learning that the Scheme had been adopted, wrote to the latter:

> all I can say at present is to congratulate you on the fruition of your crusade.... to you belongs much if not most of the credit of providing the service with a sound Scheme of education. Anything I have been able to do is solely due to you and Richmond and I can't honestly feel I had much share in it.[9]

Richmond had been useful to Fisher. Shortly after he joined the Admiralty as Assistant Director of Naval Ordnance (A.D.N.O.) in early 1903, he made a point of calling on the Second Sea Lord to express his thanks for his recent promotion to Commander. In the course of their conversation, Fisher expressed interest in some of Richmond's suggestions for the training of navigation officers. These were part of a proposal which he and his friend Commander (later, Admiral of the Fleet, Sir) Henry F. Oliver had worked out while serving together aboard the *Majestic*. Uncertain as to how to push forward their ideas, Richmond had suggested a direct approach:

> I asked Oliver if I might take them and give them to J. Fisher as they stood. He agreed: and this bundle of papers I gave Jacky. He thanked me and said he would read them and let me know what he thought; and next day I was sent for—told they were exactly what he wanted.[10]

The outcome was the Navigation Education Committee to which Oliver and Richmond were appointed with their plan as the basis of discussion.

These were heady days for Richmond, and the high point of his admiration for Fisher. "Oliver is delighted, naturally," he confided to his diary. "It really is wonderful to have a man at the Head of Affairs who can take up a matter as Fisher has, who is absolutely approachable and ready to listen to suggestions and act on them." Fisher also accepted Richmond's advice for at least two other members of the

8   RIC/1/4, Diary October 30, 1894; RIC/1/6, March 26, May 3, 1903.
9   HEN/5/2, Corbett to Henderson, December 27, 1902.
10 RIC/1/6, Diary March 26, 1903.

Committee; namely, Captain H. D. Barry, who as D.N.O. was Richmond's immediate superior; and Commander A. Hayes-Sadler navigator H.M.S. *Empress of India*. The other members were Commander F. S. Miller, navigator H.M.S. *Revenge*, and P. Dale Russell, Private Secretary to Rear-Admiral John Durnford as Committee Secretary. At the same time, Fisher appointed Richmond to an executive committee which was then supervising the implementation and progress of the Selborne Scheme.[11]

By early May, with Richmond and Oliver carrying out most of the staff work themselves, the Report of the Navigation Committee was completed. Fisher immediately announced the establishment of the new Navigation School (H.M.S. *Dryad*) with Oliver as first Commandant. "As Jack said," Richmond noted, "we want this school to be a success and Oliver is the man to start it well."[12] Oliver's future was assured. He would become Fisher's Assistant and, like most of the bright captains who also filled that position—including Scott, Jellicoe, Madden, Bacon, and Jackson—was later moved to posts of real responsibility as Director of Naval Intelligence (D.N.I.), as Naval Secretary to Churchill in October 1914, and a month later, as Chief of Staff (C.O.S.) where he remained until January 1918. In recalling those early days, Oliver credited Richmond for the Navigation Committee's creation and its very pleasing personal consequences.[13]

Fisher also went to some lengths to reward Richmond's "missionary work," first with an offer to join an expedition to the Antarctic, then command of a second-class cruiser (H.M.S. *Iris*), and finally, an attachment to the U.S. Naval Academy at Annapolis. However, by July 1903, when Fisher left the Admiralty to become Commander-in-Chief (C-in-C) Portsmouth, Richmond had declined all his patron's offers. His subsequent bids for command of either of the battleships *Prince George* or *Albemarle* were blocked by superiors resentful of his precociousness. Fisher was sympathetic; this was "not the way to encourage officers to come to the Admiralty." For the moment, however, he was powerless to intervene. But he did promise Richmond "I will take care you don't suffer eventually and in some ways it will do you good."[14] The result was his appointment as Executive Officer of the *Crescent*, Flagship on the South African Station.

11 It is interesting to note that Captain Rosslyn E. Wemyss, M.V.O. (1864-1933), was also a member of the New Scheme Committee. Despite his opposition to many features of the Scheme, he was appointed Commandant of Osborne, November 25, 1902. As First Sea Lord (1917-1919), his views on officer education would cause many difficulties for Richmond. See Chapter 5, pp. 91-96.

12 RIC/1/6, Diary May 27,1903.

13 Ibid., Diary enclosure, Oliver to Richmond, April 9, 1935. For Oliver's later career see Admiral Sir William James, *A Great Seaman: The Life of Admiral of the Fleet Sir Henry F. Oliver* (London: Witherby, 1956).

14 RIC/1/6, Diary May 27 and June 16, 1903; enclosure, Fisher to Richmond, July 6, 1903.

The next three years were happy ones for Richmond. Professionally, his reputation for unusual ability, intelligence, and energy was
confirmed. His private life also took an important and pleasing turn
when, after his return to the Admiralty in December 1906, to become
Fisher's Assistant, he began courting Miss Elsa Bell, daughter of the
industrialist Sir Hugh Bell. Their marriage in 1907 introduced an
entirely new focus. In the words of his Cambridge historian friend
George Macaulay Trevelyan (brother of Sir Charles Trevelyan who
was to marry Elsa's sister Mary):

> [The Bell] house in 95 Sloane Street and their Yorkshire house of
> Rounton were centres of a great society of cousins and friends, with
> whom Herbert was very soon a favourite. He much enjoyed the social
> life in London, and in Yorkshire he threw himself with zest into
> whatever was going on—the hunting and shooting, the dancing, the
> skating on the ice however rough, acting in village plays, and all the
> round of country activities. It was a side of English life he had not
> known intimately before, and he loved every bit of it. . . . Like many
> sailors too, who have lived for years in officers' messes, he relished
> the seclusion and comfort of home life, and as time went on, he was a
> devoted and delightful father and companion to his family of four
> daughters and one son.[15]

But the joy of marriage was not the only new departure. In 1907 he
also began, under Julian Corbett's prodding, to write his first book.

He had passed his time on the South African Station through
steady correspondence with Corbett[16] and by exercising his mind on
naval history and problems of British strategy and the need for further
reforms in education and organization to ensure these matters received systematic study. Lady Richmond recalled: "When he was
courting me, the chief thing I remember about our conversations was
his outlining with fervour his plans for a Naval General Staff!"[17] By
then, he had formed strong views on the need for a war staff—a
question to which he, Corbett, and others increasingly turned their
energies. Fisher's seeming disinterest in the question then became a
primary reason for Richmond's estrangement from him. Though
unable personally to influence events which, over the next few years,
culminated in Winston Churchill's appointment as First Lord in 1911
and the creation of the Admiralty War Staff early the following year,
Richmond was nevertheless in a position to witness them at close
range. What he observed provided the basis for his personal revolt
that followed.

Generally, Fisher has carried most of the blame for the failure to
create a naval staff system similar to the Army's General Staff. He

15 Trevelyan, "Richmond."
16 CP, B13a, Letters Richmond (Cape Station) to Corbett, 1904-1906.
17 Marder, *Portrait of an Admiral*, p. 18.

mistrusted any structure which might restrict his personal powers or diminish the established authority of the Board of Admiralty. Both he and his immediate successor, Sir Arthur Wilson, crushed all suggestions for changes which could remove the preparation of war plans from the hands of the First Sea Lord alone. Other factors, including the service's own deep-rooted aversion to change, contributed to this inertia. Fisher himself encountered serious difficulties in cutting through the prejudices of the Victorian navy whose essential conservatism cast innovators of any kind in the role of dangerous cranks. But the most important aspect of the Naval Staff question was the manner in which it was argued, not on the basis of the Navy's needs but in the context of an Admiralty-War Office power struggle in which the main determinant was a rapidly changing strategic and political environment. In this very complex process, the Committee of Imperial Defence (C.I.D.)—established in 1905 as an advisory body to the Prime Minister to ensure that the joint planning and executive functions of British strategy were realized—was removed from the mainstream of defence policy formulation. This sidetracking of the C.I.D. in its early years was both a result of, and contributed to, the Navy's intellectual retardation by 1914.

It has been generally accepted that the steady growth of the C.I.D. and its affiliated sub-committees provided the machinery for Britain's strategic planning and decision-making prior to 1914; that by 1911, its early growing pains had been overcome and the Committee pushed steadily forward in developing the general principles of Britain's preparations for war. This view needs qualification, however. Even Franklyn Johnson, in one of the first thorough analyses of the C.I.D., pointed out that despite the undeniably important achievements of the Committee (particularly its advisory and coordinating responsibilities in Empire defence arrangements, preparation of the War Book, and other technical functions), it did display serious deficiencies as a centre of strategic planning especially in the mobilization of manpower and industrial resources, and the provision of a "planned higher organization for War."[18] More recent research even suggests that the C.I.D.'s involvement with Grand Strategy was so limited as to render the country an actual "disservice"; that prior to 1914 it was "far more of a failure" than has been recognized:

> A failure due essentially to the alteration of that strategic environment which it had been designed to control, and its own contribution to the continuation and enlargements of the chasm between capability and policy, between naval materiel and military influence.[19]

18 Franklyn A. Johnson, *Defence by Committee: The British Committee of Imperial Defence, 1885-1959* (London: Oxford University Press, 1960), pp. 134-35, 161-62.
19 Nicholas J. D'Ombrain, "The Military Departments and the Committee of Imperial

Created by a "Blue Water" Prime Minister, Arthur Balfour, at a time when navalist writers and historians were at the zenith of their influence, and in the wake of the Boer War when the Navy enjoyed an unquestioned ascendancy over the discredited Army, the C.I.D. reflected the unquestioned primacy of maritime thinking in the formulation of general empire defence policy. Not surprisingly, the Admiralty accepted the new Committee, viewing it as an extension of its own machinery. Indeed Fisher's use of the C.I.D. to press home his fleet concentration and scrapping reforms suggests his confidence about controlling the Committee's work. This attitude is clearly revealed by the attempts in the summer of 1905 to give life to what was known as the Combined Operations Strategic Sub-Committee[20] through which it was hoped the C.I.D. would evolve as a *de facto* joint general staff for the Empire. But the Sub-Committee was stillborn and, as a result, so too were the Admiralty's chances of preserving its primacy of control in policy formulation. For from this point on, Britain's isolationist policy and Imperial-maritime focus became increasingly circumscribed by the diplomatic revolution of 1904-1907 with its gradual military commitment to France. Having failed to force the ailing Balfour government into adjudicating between a maritime or a continental strategic emphasis, Fisher seems to have dropped the Sub-Committee idea altogether and with it any further interest in joint studies of possible amphibious schemes.

Maurice Hankey, Secretary of the C.I.D. from 1912, blamed the failure of the Strategic Sub-Committee on "subtle influences" which he had never fully identified. He wrote to Richmond in 1914:

> They were due probably in part to the pacifist tendencies of Campbell-Bannerman, who was disinclined to carry out the policies of his Unionist forbears; partly also to J. F.'s [sic] objections to working in with the War Office in these things; and partly due to the personal equation of the War Office team at the time.[21]

Admiralty domination was undoubtedly a major factor in the General Staff's antipathy to the Sub-Committee and the whole concept of joint operations from which it had grown. The new men—"the personal equation"—at the War Office were looking toward a specific role for the Army and more direct cooperation with France in the event of a war against Germany. Because its preliminary studies of amphibious operations on the north German coast were rejected virtually out of

Defence, 1902-1914" (D. Phil. dissertation: Oxford, 1968), p. 327; revised and published as *War Machinery and High Policy: Defence Administration in Peacetime Britain, 1902-1914* (London: Oxford University Press, 1973).

20 Add. MSS, 49711, pp. 64-69, "Formation of a Permanent Sub-Committee of the C.I.D. to Consider and Elaborate Schemes of Joint Naval and Military Expeditions."

21 RIC/7/4, Hankey to Richmond, April 3, 1914. See also M. P. Hankey, *The Supreme Command, 1914-1918*, 2 vols. (London: Allen and Unwin, 1961), vol. 1, p. 62.

hand by the General staff, the Sub-Committee never took shape. The
result was that when in December 1905, international tension surrounding the Algeciras Conference moved the French to seek Britain's reassurances, the machinery for deciding the issue of future
British strategic policy was non-existent. With Balfour gone and the
new Government preoccupied with general elections, Sir George
Clarke, Secretary of the C.I.D., took it upon himself to make at least
some preparations. A long-time advocate of amphibious operations
himself, he called together a small group of like-minded naval and
military officers for informal discussions. But when it became clear
that even this group was prepared to consider (if not entirely admit)
the logic of direct support of the French, Fisher withdrew the naval
representative, Captain Sir Charles Ottley (D.N.I.).[22] The Admiralty's
boycott of Clarke's meetings, when linked with the secret Anglo-
French military conversations initiated by the War Office in January
1906,[23] thus marks the point from which the C.I.D.'s work became
increasingly tangential to the mainstream of prewar strategic policy
formulation.

Denied the patronage of a sympathetic government, and sensing
the Admiralty's growing disadvantage in the C.I.D., Fisher's attitude
became increasingly negative, amounting virtually to a naval boycott
over the next few years. He became preoccupied in a rearguard action
against War Office assertiveness and what he regarded as the "snip-
ing" of dissidents and their attacks on Admiralty policy and the Navy
generally. The idea of a naval staff had been suggested by Admiral Sir
Charles Beresford as early as 1866 and was still one of the principal
demands of the so-called "Syndicate of Discontent." The open erup-
tion of the famous Fisher-Beresford Dispute of 1909[24] would ensure
that the question of war plans and the naval staff no longer remained
an internal service issue but became instead the subject of widespread
public agitation and, above all, an instrument of political leverage to
force Fisher's hand. Given this kind of environment and opposition,
and the need to protect his earlier reforms in personnel and materiel,
Fisher's reluctance to throw open to public or even service debate
such prickly questions of policy and staff organization is understandable. But because he did not, he also became increasingly divorced
from those of his closest supporters who wished to push naval reform

22 D'Ombrain, War Machinery, pp. 81-87. R. F. MacKay, Fisher of Kilverstone (Ox-
    ford: Clarendon Press, 1973), pp. 350-54. The other members were Lord Esher, and
    General Sir John French, Commander at Aldershot.
23 G. W. Monger, The End of Isolation: British Foreign Policy, 1900-1907 (London:
    Nelson, 1963), pp. 236-56; also, Samuel R. Williamson, The Politics of Grand
    Strategy: Britain and France Prepare for War, 1904-1914 (Cambridge: Harvard
    University Press, 1969), pp. 59-88.
24 A summary of the Beresford Dispute and the subsequent inquiry is given in Marder,
    Dreadnought to Scapa Flow, vol. 1, pp. 71-104, 186-204.

into these broader areas of strategy, tactics, and planning—areas to which his own intellectual powers were much less finely attuned.

His own Director of Naval Intelligence, Captain Edmond Slade, was a case in point. He became one of Fisher's most bitter critics, in secret at least, over what he regarded as the First Sea Lord's growing obstinacy and estrangement from the C.I.D.[25] Even Lord Esher would complain of Fisher's "Achillean attitude" in this regard. Richmond underwent a similar transformation; and as he became more and more an outspoken advocate of a naval staff, the gulf widened. But neither Slade nor Richmond was fully aware of the extent to which the C.I.D. was being by-passed by those favouring a continental policy. Both, somewhat naïvely, condemned Fisher for refusing to push combined operations. Even as late as 1914, Richmond would continue to complain of the lack of joint planning for what he felt would be a "largely Colonial War."[26] Yet, as Fisher had recognized, combined operations as a basis for British planning were acceptable to neither the War Office nor the Government.

How well Fisher genuinely understood the need for a naval war staff needs some explanation. During his command of the Mediterranean, he had drawn up a paper "On the Increasing Necessity for a General Staff for the Navy to meet War Requirements." In 1902, as Second Sea Lord, he submitted it to Lord Selborne urging the expansion of the existing Intelligence Department and its affiliated War Course College at Greenwich:

> We have a magnificent model to work upon and to guide us! The Great German General Staff, the admiration of the world and the organiser of the greatest victories of modern times is absolutely applicable in its ideas and its organisation to meet all the needs of the Navy.[27]

Yet, for all this adulation of the German example, his comprehension of the functions of that elite seems to have been as superficial as his enthusiasm was short-lived. In reality, Fisher preferred a much less formalized and purely advisory system. To that extent, he encouraged the development of the War Course College (after 1907, the Royal Naval War College).

The College had been established on a permanent basis in 1900 as an eight-month course for commanders and captains. Three years later it was divided into two courses each of four months' duration in order that more officers could attend. It was an outgrowth of the

25 Slade Papers, MS 66/073-1, Diary November 12, 13, 1908. Also CP B13, Slade to Corbett, January 11, November 16, 1908.
26 RIC/1/9, Diary August 5, 1914. Along with Corbett and Ottley (then D.N.I.), Slade had been involved with the original initiative for the stillborn Combined Operations Sub-Committee. RIC/1/7, Ottley to Corbett, July 1 and 3, 1905.
27 Mackay, *Fisher*, p. 256.

lectures given at Greenwich by Sir John Laughton in the 1870s and later take over in 1887 by Vice-Admiral Philip Colomb. After 1895, these were delivered by Captain H. J. May who became the first commandant in 1900.[28] From that point, May struggled to concentrate the College syllabus on the "study of the art of war" in the widest possible sense by emphasizing instruction in strategy, tactics, history, and international law and, to a lesser extent, navigation, meteorology, and foreign languages. But this emphasis ran counter to Fisher's and, following May's death, he exerted a strong influence on the College's character to bring it more in lines with his clearly more constricted view:

> There are a great many things we want our naval Von Moltke to tell us when you have started him at the head of the Naval War College! What distance shall we open fire? How near shall we approach the enemy in view of the gyroscope? If not within 2,500 yards, what is the use of fighting tops weighing tons and tons?[29]

It was to offset this tendency that May had originally approached Corbett in August 1902, to present a series of lectures on maritime strategy.[30] This was a significant move, as it turned out, for Corbett's annual lectures proved to be the inspiration for his own work as well. Later extended and presented as his Ford Lectures at Oxford in 1903, they formed the basis of his two-volume masterpiece, *England in the Mediterranean*, which was published the following year. Moreover, Corbett's association with Captains Slade (who succeeded May as Commandant in the spring of 1905) and Ottley (D.N.I.) and their work with the War Course students constituted the only source of independent naval strategic thinking in Britain prior to 1911.

Corbett was aware that the work of the college could not entirely replace that of a properly constituted staff system, but his attempt, in December 1905, to impress this fact on Fisher's thinking clearly revealed the limits of his support. Fisher replied:

> I do not see my way as yet to dis-associate the First Sea Lord from the present way of doing the business but there is force in your remark (*not written but implied*) that an effete First Sea Lord would be the very devil! I will think more of it![31]

By spring 1906, he clearly had thought more and sent Corbett a suggestion for widening the War College's functions making it, in effect, the basis of an ad hoc staff system, or rather, the basis from which a staff might gradually evolve.[32] Corbett and Slade took the

---

28 For Fisher's assessment of May's brilliance, see Marder, *Fear God and Dread Nought*, vol. 2, pp. 229, 240, 264-65.
29 Ibid., p. 234.
30 CP B13, May to Corbett, August 22, 1902.
31 Ibid., B12, Fisher to Corbett, December 22, 1905.
32 Ibid., Fisher to Corbett, May 12, 1906; Corbett to Fisher, May 13, 1906.

opening and, with Fisher's blessings, prepared two articles on the College which were published in *The Times* of June 5 and 9. Specifically, they outlined the need for a body of qualified officers "whose function it is to thrash out systematically all sorts of war problems, quite independently, and unhampered by the routine work of an Admiralty department such as the N.I.D. [Naval Intelligence Division]" The War Course was a beginning, they suggested; a great deal had been achieved already and much more was possible without extensive restructuring. The War Course Director, working closely with the N.I.D., could be kept well informed on current developments and, by tapping the brains of his students and staff, could provide useful analyses and commentaries.

Fisher was delighted and from this point did use the War College as an ad hoc general staff. He explained Slade's transfer in 1907 from Greenwich to the Admiralty as D.N.I. as part of a gradual process: "by thus calling to its counsels the Staff of the War College, the Intelligence Department was wisely stepping towards the inauguration of a Naval General Staff."[33] The following year, Slade was authorized to open direct communications with the College whose functions were expanded to include the study of specific problems as determined by the D.N.I.[34] This suggests that Fisher was paying something more than lip service to the "vital importance" of joint planning, though it is unlikely he was prepared to go much further. Richmond, for one, doubted the First Sea Lord's sincerity. He was convinced that Fisher had "no inclination to accept the principle" of a properly constituted naval staff.[35] Fisher's failure to support Slade's later efforts on behalf of a maritime strategic policy before the C.I.D. seemed to confirm this judgment.

Slade had been a member of a small committee which, under the chairmanship of Captain G. A. Ballard (until July 1906, Director of Naval Operations), met from December 1906 until early 1907 at the War College under conditions of considerable secrecy and haste to draw up a series of plans for a war against Germany—the so-called Admiralty War Plans. Julian Corbett wrote a lengthy scholarly introduction while Slade, working from one of his own previously prepared papers,[36] contributed a general review of the international situation. The remaining papers were developed by the whole Committee whose other member was Maurice Hankey, then a captain, Royal Marines (R.M.), recently appointed to the War College. Ottley, as D.N.I., was not a member but was kept fully informed of the Commit-

---

33 Marder, *Fear God and Dread Nought*, vol. 2, pp. 411-12, Fisher to Leyland.
34 CP B6, Slade to Corbett, June 3, 1908.
35 RIC/1/7, Diary, General Entry, April 1907.
36 Adm. 116/1036-B, "War with Germany," Captain E. J. W. Slade, September 1, 1906.

tee's progress. The final report was printed in April-May 1907, as "General Remarks on War with Germany: A Preamble for Reflection and Criticism." Slade's plan argued that the defence of Holland and Belgium was the only justification for Britain's participation in a war against Germany (the possibility of a German attack against France curiously was ignored), and therefore prescribed a solution which envisioned the taking of a North Sea island (preferably Borkum) followed by the destruction of the enemy's coastal and naval defences and the opening of his territory to seaborne attack. The other members of the Ballard Committee were much less sanguine about the increasing risks to naval covering forces from mines and torpedoes under modern conditions and expressed serious doubts about close blockade operations, including coastal landings for which they doubted Britain possessed an expeditionary force of sufficient strength in any case.[37] The latter consideration depended, of course, entirely on the extent to which Britain might be committed to France—the one scenario Slade's personal proposal had not included.

As D.N.I., Slade reiterated his combined operations ideas during the C.I.D.'s Second Invasion Inquiry (1907-1908). The seemingly receptive response of the War Office representatives gave him hope that joint planning was, after all, still possible. During the Casablanca Crisis when he joined Foreign Office-General Staff discussions, he was aware that the Army representatives' outward politeness notwithstanding, his joint operations schemes had been the subject of much private criticism.[38] He felt betrayed by Fisher. There is little reason to doubt that the Ballard Committee had worked under Fisher's general guidance and that the War Plans reflected much of his own thinking. Given the obvious discrepancy between Slade's contribution and the rest, it is difficult to believe Fisher ever seriously considered them anything other than a basis for further discussion. Still, they were the only war plans worked out during this time, and he certainly made use of them against critics like Beresford who doubted the existence of any plans.

Richmond's disenchantment with Fisher was also evident by this time. His contacts with Corbett and growing preoccupation with historical-strategic questions convinced him that the absence of a properly constituted staff was symptomatic of a widespread malaise of naval organization generally which accounted for the amateurism and wastefulness he had seen everywhere since becoming Fisher's Naval Assistant.

37 A complete set of the "War Plans" is contained in Lieutenant Commander P. K. Kemp, ed., *The Papers of Admiral Sir John Fisher*, 2 vols. (London: Navy Records Society, 1960-1964), vol. 2, pp. 316-468.

38 Slade Papers, MS 66/073-2, Diary February 20, October 8, November 4, 1908. Also, RIC/1/7, Slade to Corbett, December 16, 1908.

He summed up his private criticisms in a lengthy diary entry of April 1907. Admiralty organization, which he characterized as being "beneath contempt," made the development of war plans virtually impossible. He opposed the concept of using the War College as a *de facto* planning group. It was after all an instructional institution and the officers there were only students beginning to learn "the strategic side of their profession." The D.N.I.'s office did not exercise any executive function: "The Commander sitting in Foreign branch, for instance, spend their [sic] time cutting extracts out of foreign papers." Far from being a planning body, the D.N.I.'s office was really an information centre which fulfilled the important role of assisting the Naval Board in its scrapping and building policy. "M" (Military) Branch, which did deal with war preparations, was staffed entirely by civil servants. A war staff would mean the suppression of this well-entrenched source of civilian influence. This alone was a major source of Admiralty inertia. And so, Richmond complained:

> nothing is being done. Fisher makes no move . . . we have no one
> trained to think of the problems of war, the organisation required and
> the multitudinous details. I know only too well how ignorant we are
> not only of modern wars but even of wars in History . . . Fisher, clever
> as he is, has not made a study of it, and in reality has no knowledge.
> He is a genius, and a genius may do things not within the compass of
> an ordinary man: but his predecessors have not been, nor may his
> successors be geniuses.[39]

Here Richmond was formulating the essential features of his own concept of a naval war staff and its purpose; that is, its responsibility for independent initiation, investigation, and formulation of plans whose acceptance would not depend on the interests or personality of any one man. But he also touched upon the broad educative roles which staff organizations should fulfill. This was an important point which few critics at the time, including Corbett, had really grasped. As to any direct analogy between the Army's and the Navy's staff needs, it had to be recognized that the powers of the Admiralty Board were far broader that the Army Council's and more direct in the sense of controlling the service as a whole. A naval staff would produce active war plans, acting, in effect, as the brain and central nervous system of the whole structure. Yet, at this point in his career, Richmond's ideas were still in a formative stage. He was only partially aware of Fisher's situation and of the forces taking developments along other lines. He could only watch and chafe at what he saw.

In October 1909, as a result of the findings of the Beresford Inquiry,[40] Fisher was forced to announce the formation of the Admi-

39 RIC/1/7, Diary, April 1907.
40 Cab. 16/9, "Report and Proceedings of a Sub-Committee of the C.I.D. appointed to
    inquire into certain questions of Naval Policy raised by Lord Charles Beresford."

ralty War Council. At best, it was a face saving device; an attempt to silence criticism with minimal effort. In no sense was it a proper staff, since it was a purely advisory body and sat at the discretion of the First Sea Lord. During Fisher's last three months in office, it met only four times, and over the next two years under Sir Arthur Wilson, only seven times. In no way did the Council satisfy those who wanted a real, thinking staff. Richmond was especially sceptical:

> the most absurd bit of humbug that has ever been produced for a long time. It pretends to be the basis of a General Staff, but its constitution shows that whoever devised it has no idea of what a staff is wanted for, or the particular functions of such a body. The result of the Committee of Enquiry has therefore merely been to produce an absurd anomaly called a War Council, which means nothing. The study of war forms no part of its work. The First Sea Lord remains supreme and imposes his crude strategical ideas on the nation.[41]

Wilson was even less interested in fostering war studies and planning within the service or through any inter-departmental body including the C.I.D. His testimony before the Beresford Inquiry had made clear his absolute conviction that the drawing up of precise war plans in peace-time was not "practicable or desirable." Such plans as might be necessary would be kept secret, reserved for the eyes of the First Sea Lord alone, and divulged only at the outbreak of war!

The Agadir Crisis of 1911, and Admiral Wilson's wretched performance before the famous C.I.D. meeting of August 23 laid bare the weaknesses of the Admiralty's position. While a final decision in favour of the General Staff's continental policy was not made at this time, the meeting did climax the process by which War Office ascendancy was assured. Winston Churchill was brought in to replace McKenna as First Lord with instructions to set up an Admiralty Board that could work in closer harmony with the War Office and to begin the work of creating a proper naval staff.[42] Richmond was hopeful, though not without reservations: "Churchill's appointment fills me with hope—that he may do something towards staff work. I distrust him intensely but I think there's a chance he may take the line. And in that case his tenure of office may be of benefit."[43]

On November 28, 1911, a month after taking office, Churchill made a clean sweep of Wilson's Board. Only the Third Sea Lord, Rear-Admiral Charles Briggs, was retained. Admirals Bridgeman and (Prince Louis) Battenberg were recalled from the Home Fleet as First and Second Sea Lords respectively. Callaghan and Jellicoe were

41 RIC/1/8, Diary October 27, 1909.
42 Randolph S. Churchill, *Winston S. Churchill*, vol. 2: *Young Statesman, 1901-1914* (London: Heinemann, 1967), pp. 535-39. Also Peter Gretton, *Former Naval Person: Winston Churchill and the Royal Navy* (London: Cassell, 1968), chap. 4.
43 DEW, 6, Richmond to Kenneth Dewar, November 8, 1911.

posted to key commands in the Home Fleet, and Beatty was brought in as Churchill's Naval Secretary. Wilson's refusals to cooperate with the War Office and C.I.D., and his open opposition to a naval staff and Churchill's notions of "Admiralty Power" had made such drastic action unavoidable.[44]

As to the naval staff, Churchill first outlined his views in a lengthy memorandum of October 28. This impressive document, based largely on a paper prepared by Battenberg, justified the staff in terms of removing policy formulation from the exclusive control of the Sea Lords who might not be competent strategists and whose differing views in the past had resulted in an "absence of continuity" in naval policy. Moreover, there was a need for a body of staff specialists who should be treated for promotion and other preferments on a basis of full equality with other branches. To that end, he suggested the establishment of a special twelve-month staff course for junior officers.[45] These ideas were extended into a paper which, when released on January 6, 1912, brought into being the Admiralty War Staff. The central figure in this new organization was the "Chief of the War Staff," who reported directly to the First Sea Lord and was responsible for the work of three Divisions—Intelligence, Operations, and Mobilization. Overall, the new War Staff was charged with undertaking special studies of the operational side of war as distinct from the purely technical:

> It is to be a brain far more comprehensive than that of any single man, however gifted and tireless and unceasing in action, applied continuously to the scientific and speculative study of naval strategy and preparation. It is to be an instrument capable of formulating any decision which has been taken, or may be taken, by the Executive in terms of precise and exhaustive detail.[46]

All these changes were strongly backed by the Cabinet and C.I.D., and were greeted with general press and public approval. Yet, as Churchill himself later noted, it would take time to make good these beginnings. But war came too soon.[47]

All the same, the new War Staff did achieve some major advances prior to the summer of 1914. Of these the more important included the adoption of a "distant blockade" policy, the creation of an Admiralty department for arming merchant vessels, the fortification of Cromarty

---

44 Vice-Admiral Sir E. E. Bradford, *Life of Admiral of the Fleet Sir Arthur Knyvet Wilson* (London: Murray, 1923), pp. 231-35. Also N. J. D'Ombrain, "Churchill at the Admiralty and the C.I.D., 1911-1914," *R.U.S.I.*, 115 (March 1970), 40.

45 Cab. 37/108-135. Also Admiral Mark Kerr, *Prince Louis of Battenberg: Admiral of the Fleet* (London: Longmans, 1934), p. 236.

46 R. Churchill, *Young Statesman*, pp. 542-44.

47 W. S. Churchill, *The World Crisis*, 5 vols. in 6 (London: Butterworth, 1923-1931), vol. 1, p. 70.

Firth, the establishment of a trawler minesweeping organization, and the restructuring of East Coast Command. But it was in the areas of education, planning, and executive control that the War Staff fell short, and insufficient time was not the sole or major reason.

The lack of properly trained personnel militated heavily against the War Staff's chances of success before 1914. The R.N. Staff Course for junior officers was set up at Portsmouth as part of the War College in 1912. It was closed two years later for the duration of the war and then transferred to Greenwich as a separate institution. During its prewar existence, the Staff Course enjoyed only limited success; the nominations of candidates suggest that service opposition to the idea of specialist staff officers would not be soon overcome. An Admiralty "History of the Naval Staff," written in the 1920s, pointed out the major defects of Churchill's organization which the strains of war laid bare. On this point, it added:

> The idea of a staff was by many still regarded with indifference, if not with distrust. The Navy had no use for the word "staff' in the Army sense, in which the staff was regarded as a system of machinery indispensable to the conduct of operations of war . . . Mr. Churchill had not the whole body of Naval opinion behind him.[48]

A further serious weakness was that the Chief of Staff (C.O.S.) had no executive authority. Nor did he sit on the Board. He was, in fact, only a responsible adviser, though with direct access, to the First Sea Lord. Wilson had warned Churchill of this flaw, but Battenberg's opposition to combining the offices of First Sea Lord and C.O.S.—as Slade later suggested to Richmond, his refusal to "lower the position of his office by becoming the C.O.S. to a civilian First Lord"—ensured that the two functions were kept separate. For Battenberg such a union was wrong in principle: "he was the Executive head of the Navy, and he could not mix up Staff duties with executive work."[49] As will be seen, the two offices would not be finally merged until May 1917.

But these shortcomings aside, Churchill's new Board and War Staff were a beginning and they satisfied at least those who had sought to bring the Admiralty into line with general strategic policy. Nurturing the Navy's intellectual apparatus and breaking down professional resistance to modern planning procedures would take much more time and effort. Finally, Churchill's encouragement of officers to study history, strategy, and tactics, and his support of the *Naval Review* which was founded in 1912, helped to stimulate a naval intellectual revival that was just beginning to take shape under Richmond's leadership.

48 Admiralty, Training and Staff Duties Division, Monographs (Historical), *The Naval Staff of the Admiralty: Its Work and Development* (1929), Admiralty Library.
49 RIC/1/8, Slade to Richmond, September 26, 1913.

Richmond, however, had hoped for more from Churchill. His earlier doubts seemed justified and he felt disappointed, even "disgusted" by the actual results.[50] In his opinion, Churchill had not consulted a broad enough spectrum of expert opinion, nor satisfied the need for a true "thinking division" at the Admiralty. In reality, the War Staff question had been settled as a political issue only.

These, then, were some of the important political and high-level service attitudes which shaped naval policy development prior to 1914. Richmond, a perceptive but minor figure, appears as exhibiting a chafing discontent at the minimal achievements which were made in those areas that did not involve purely technical appreciations. It is clear that these attitudes, which a man of his rank could only dimly appreciate from the sidelines, blocked acceptance of his ideas. This is not to say that his views were wrong, but that he was, practically speaking, confined by his rank. He had the advantage of a clear, logical mind, rendered more profound by his contacts with historical reality. He had the disadvantage of being driven to criticism while he lacked real responsibility or power. At times, his diary entries seem self-righteously ludicrous, and his often unrestrained criticisms make him appear as an indiscreet crank. What was really happening, however, was that a mind of great imagination and surprising force was being trained to recognize the requirements of naval greatness. An intellectual was at school in these years, learning through the brushes with custom that his impatient temperament made inevitable. Richmond did not alter the Royal Navy in the Fisher era. But against the background of that age, and through his growing historical knowledge, he tempered his mind which, by the early 1920s, was to become the most formidable of any naval officer's since Mahan's days.

50 DEW, 6, Richmond to Dewar, November 18, 1911; April 26, 1912. Also, RIC/7/4, King-Hall to Richmond, August 17, 1912; Dewar to Richmond, n.d., 1912.

2

The Naval Society and Review

Richmond was promoted to Captain at the end of 1908. The following March he joined the staff of Admiral Sir William May, C-in-C Home Fleet, and shortly afterwards assumed command of the flagship H.M.S. *Dreadnought*. Then three years old, she was the controversial first of her kind and the choice berth in Fisher's new navy, especially for a young Captain's first sea command. Richmond's prospects were never brighter; it appeared he was to become a naval person of the highest consequence. Yet, as his diaries reveal, Richmond began to dispel these hopes himself as he discovered within the Home Fleet symptoms of that same malaise of method and mentality he had seen at the Admiralty. His unsuccessful attempts to provoke critical appraisals of accepted Fleet doctrine only increased his impatience and disillusionment. Unfortunately, he did not always hide his annoyance. His intolerance and intellectual arrogance caused him to be regarded as an unsettling gadfly, increasingly isolated and mistrusted by his superiors.[1] Consequently when he left *Dreadnought* in March 1911, he was relegated to the command of second-class cruisers—H.M.S. *Furious* (until March 1912) and *Vindictive* (until October 1912), which were attached to the torpedo school at Portsmouth.

However much he resented this obvious turn-around in his expectations, he accepted the appointment as the best alternative to half-pay or an unwanted course at the War College or the Gunnery School. "It looks rather like a loaf," he confided to his diary:

> but if I am in *Furious* I get my sea-time, I go to sea occasionally, and I
> have time to work at history and things that interest [*sic*], besides

1   RIC/1/8, Diary, March 4, 1911.

being handy to the War College and so able to attend all the lectures without going through the stereotyped course. Altogether it would suit me well. I see no chance of another good real sea-going ship, so the wisest thing is to take what is offered.[2]

He was usually able to come ashore each day to his house at Alverstoke where he spent his afternoons on historical research and editing, for the Navy Records Society, a volume of *Papers Relating to the Loss of Minorca in 1756*.[3] He also wrote the bulk of his first major historical work, *The Navy in the War of 1739-1748*. It was finally completed in 1914, though publication was delayed by the outbreak of war.[4] This was particularly unfortunate, for Richmond's descriptions of the complex interplay of events, personalities, and ideas that govern war, and his original interpretations of the major strategic concepts of eighteenth-century maritime warfare, contained a great deal that was relevant to an understanding of the forces at play in the North Sea after August 1914. Not that his conclusions could be applied directly to current practical problems, nor was it really likely that practising admirals and captains would make such distinctions. As Professor Schurman has suggested in his study of Richmond the naval historian:

> This was so because Richmond's utilitarian bent was never allowed to dominate his highly developed sense of the need for strict attention to the facts . . . . His was not the handy compendium approach . . . . Although it was apparent that *The Navy in the War of 1739-48* reveals how conditions and even actions of past wars have a relevance for the present day, the author was much too sophisticated a writer to allow this fact to dominate his recording purpose.[5]

Of all of Richmond's books this was the most detailed and comprehensive, demonstrating literary ability and analytical skill all the more remarkable in that it came from a serving officer of the *Dreadnought* era. In recent years, Richmond has been criticized for ignoring important external documentary sources, such as the Spanish records, with the result that his perspective was too exclusively British. Yet, given the limitations under which he worked, he might be forgiven this shortcoming. The fact is Richmond was the first to tackle the war as an organic whole. It was a pioneering effort which, because of his meticulous attention to detail and careful use of an impressive collection of government documents (both British and French) and contemporary private papers, remains the authoritative work on the subject. Corbett's verdict that "it's your war" still stands. It may well be that if Richmond, with a sharper eye for the predilictions of his

2 Ibid., Diary, November 12, 1910.
3 London, 1913.
4 Richmond, *The Navy in the War of 1739-1748*, 3 vols. (Cambridge, 1920).
5 Schurman, *Education of a Navy*, p. 134.

potential audience, had taken a more polemical approach, his book might have had a wider impact on professional thinking than it eventually did. The real problem, however, was that there were too few officers in the prewar Navy so equipped as to understand what Richmond was about. This solitary experience of writing a learned book was probably the most important formative experience in Richmond's own education and it shaped much of his thinking in relation to the major strategic issues of the First World War. The book also undoubtedly improved his own powers of application and analysis; whether other officers were capable of gaining as much from reading it is less clear.

Richmond did not confine himself to academic pursuits in these prewar years. He excelled as a practical seaman and ship's captain and was highly respected for his energy as a leader and manager of men. *Dreadnought*, under his command, was regarded as a model for efficiency and high crew morale. Less concerned about routine details of "spit and polish," he prepared his men for the war he knew must come. Even the young midshipmen were encouraged to read German and learn something of the German Navy. Indeed, it was this fatherly encouragement of younger officers to use their brains and take an interest in the wider questions of their profession that set him apart. Kenneth Dewar (later Vice-Admiral), whose friendship with Richmond began aboard *Dreadnought*, wrote in 1939:

> He was a type of naval officer I had never met before. Besides being an extremely competent executive officer, he was that rare phenomenon in the Navy—a student of war. I had served under very good Captains but H. W. Richmond was more than that. He encouraged one to think and look far beyond the narrow limits of ship life. . . . History is a powerful talisman in the investigation of any large question, and like Moltke, Richmond developed a sound strategical and tactical instinct by studying the actual happenings of war.[6]

This "instinct" led Richmond to look at the broader implications of contemporary naval policy. The Home Fleet exercises of 1909, 1910, and 1911 allowed him to focus directly on prevailing tactical doctrine which he was appalled to discover was as devoid of realistic ideas as the Admiralty War Plans. He observed the absence of detailed plans for the offensive employment of cruisers and destroyers, the reluctance to exercise these classes as part of a homogeneous fleet, the cumbersome signalling techniques and, above all, the lack of special training for Fleet commanders.[7] Admitting that he could be "damned

6 Kenneth Gilbert Dalmain Dewar: born 1879 to Dr. James Dewar of Edinburgh, entered Britannia 1893. See his *The Navy From Within* (London: Gollancz, 1939), p. 115.
7 RIC/1/8, Diary, December 13, 1909. Also, May 2, June 22, July 8, 1909; and February 22, April 24, May 4, 1910.

dogmatic" in argument, he began to work out his ideas more fully on paper. In particular, he challenged the twin fetishes of prewar tactics; namely, the rigid single line-of-battle formation, and centralized command and control of the Fleet. Eventually, on the basis of one of these papers, the C-in-C initiated experimental Fleet exercises in which divisional attacks and decentralization of command were featured. "Tactically I think we have scored a triumph," Richmond noted.

> A twelvemonth ago, Willy [Admiral May] pooh-poohed the idea of dividing a fleet and fighting in squadrons. But he had never given the thing a moment's thought. We have now given it some thought. I have written a long argument showing what advantages such a method of fighting possesses, and he is becoming less dogmatic on the virtues of the single line as the only sound basis of tactics. But oh how slowly ideas take root![8]

These promising results were not followed up, however, by May's successor, Admiral Bridgeman. In the absence of an accepted comprehensive tactical doctrine, the single-line-ahead concept simply persisted as dogma.[9] Many years later, Richmond recalled the results of the 1910-1911 Fleet exercises to Captain Basil Liddell Hart:

> "Safety First" was the cry. If we get into line no one can make a mistake. All we have to do is follow the leader and keep the guns trained on the enemy. We were preparing to fight a "soldier's battle" the result of which would not depend on the skillful placing of the ships but on the skill of the gunner alone. Our ablest men, therefore, were up to their eyes in technical artillery and torpedo work—designing instruments for fire control, torpedoes that ran farther and faster, ships that had thicker armour than those of other nations, or bigger guns. *Strategy—how we would make war—*received no real attention. It didn't "pay" an officer to study it: indeed, it definitely paid badly, as he became known as a theorist: whereas to produce some gunnery or torpedo gadget was a sure recommendation for advancement. It would have been far better to make a development in Wireless Telegraphy than to make one in tactical thought.[10]

This denigration of material genius could easily be written off as a stimulus to vanity to which Richmond, no less than many other historical writers with a non-technical bent, was vulnerable. But he was correct in highlighting the contrast between the naval profession's obsession with materiel and the general lack of interest in the manner of its use. The absence of a staff system whose function it was

---

8   Ibid., January 25, 1911.
9   Prior to 1914 the only work on tactics available was a book compiled by May. It was based on the 1910-1911 Exercises and issued to Captains of the Fleet. For a summary of prewar tactical developments, see Marder, *Dreadnought to Scapa Flow*, vol. 1, pp. 305-404.
10 LHP, Richmond to Liddell Hart, September, 1934.

to show how the results of technical advances might be played into strategic and tactical policy was one more legacy of Fisher's obstinacy on this question.

These frustrations aside, Richmond's experiences in these years did bear fruit in other ways. The free reign he gave to his own mind and the way he taught his subordinates to think things out forged bonds of sympathy and friendship which would become increasingly important. Under his guidance, Kenneth Dewar began his own serious studies of tactics and strategy which he expanded during his tour as an instructor at the War College (1911-1913).

When Dewar had first joined Richmond's ship in January 1910, he was already recognized as one of the gunnery elite's more exceptional members. The coveted appointment as *Dreadnought's* Gunnery Officer and First Lieutenant testifies to that. His outstanding record at Whale Island, where he had trained under the renowned Sir Percy Scott, had earned him accelerated promotion upon graduation and his first independent command, the destroyer *Mermaid*. That same year Dewar joined the staff of the Gunnery School at Sheerness. A succession of gunnery appointments followed: in 1907, the armoured cruiser *Kent* and the battleship *Prince George*; in 1909, H.M.S. *Commonwealth* and a stint on the staff of the Inspector of Target Practice. But while Dewar's talents for originality and improvisation and his devotion to efficiency brought professional, and indeed public, acclaim—as in 1907 when *Kent* led the Fleet in battle-firings and gunlayer's test—they also earned him a reputation as an outspoken individualist known to despise the very training system he had topped so easily.

Dewar's status as a minor naval celebrity probably had something to do with his being invited, in 1909, to lecture to the War College on the Japanese Navy which he had visited two years earlier. The occasion was unique not so much because he was a young lieutenant lecturing commanders and captains, but because he took it as an opportunity for criticizing current British practices. He portrayed Admiral Togo, the hero of Tsushima, as the kind of intellectual, independent-thinking senior officer the Royal Navy needed, and the Japanese Navy as one in which common sense prevailed, where juniors were given responsibility and allowed to learn from experience. Not surprisingly the College President abruptly terminated his lecture.[11]

With the help of Richmond and his older brother, Lieutenant A. C. ("Archie") Dewar,[12] Kenneth won the Royal United Services Insti-

11 Dewar's paper was later printed, after a few deletions, and circulated throughout the Fleet. Dewar, *Navy from Within*, pp. 105-106.
12 Alfred Dewar had made thorough study of the German Staff system. Following his retirement from the Navy in 1910, he wrote several articles on the need for a Naval

tute (R.U.S.I.) Gold Medal Essay for 1912 on the subject of the influence of overseas commerce on naval policy and the operations of war
past and present. The final section of the essay was suppressed by the
Admiralty, supposedly because of its references to the specific situation of a war against Germany.[13] Dewar and Richmond, however, were
convinced that the real reason was his advocacy of a "distant" blockade strategy; that is, control of the North Sea by holding the
Orkney-Norway line with the main fleet, while submarines and older
battleships kept the English Channel. This was surprising in view of
the fact that the then accepted ideas of Close Blockade were subsequently dropped in favour of the so-called Observational Blockade
(1912-1913), and finally, the Distant Blockade (1914).[14] As Dewar
himself later recalled: "In the light of later events, the opposition
aroused by my proposals may seem extraordinary, but they marked a
complete break with tradition and were far from obvious at the
time."[15] But such events were not unusual, and Richmond warned his
protégé that the path he had chosen would never be an easy one:

> I rather feel that I had done you a somewhat ill turn in that being by
> nature a mutineer, and impatient of hidebound methods and of
> restraint, I have rather encouraged you to express heretical opinions:
> but do remember that heretics are the exception, and that the fate of
> the heretic is often an unfortunate one.[16]

During 1911 and 1912, Richmond gave occasional lectures at the
War College on naval history and strategy. Exposing his ideas to the
rigours of student criticism probably helped to sharpen up his own
thinking. But equally important was the effect he had upon the students. For it was from this group that he and Dewar drew their
immediate and, as it turned out, their lasting centre of support—most
notably Commander (later, Admiral Sir) Reginald Plunkett Ernle Erle
Drax, and Lieutenant Commander (later, Rear-Admiral) Roger M. Bellairs. Many years later, Drax could still remember how Richmond's
knowledge and force of character quickly dispelled the students'
initial doubts about the relevance of "ancient history" to contemporary problems:

War Staff. See his "Naval Strategy and the Crisis of 1911," *United Service
Magazine*, 44 (March 1912) 585-89. He was also acquainted with R. B. Haldane
"who in later days," Kenneth Dewar recalled,' "used to ask us to his house at Queen
Anne's Gate where we had some interesting conversations on education and organisation." *Navy From Within*, p. 40.

13 DEW, 6, Richmond to Dewar, March 5, 1912. This date should read 1913. Dewar
    worked on the paper from April to October 1912. The Essay was awarded the Gold
    Prize and appeared in the April 1913 *R.U.S.I.* Notification of the award appeared in
    The Times, March 5, 1913. The suppressed Chapter (9) is printed in full as Appen-
    dix 1, *Navy From Within*, pp. 371-81.
14 Marder, *Dreadnought to Scapa Flow*, vol. 1, pp. 370-77.
15 Dewar, *Navy From Within*, p. 149.
16 DEW, 6, Richmond to Dewar, April 29, 1912.

> his judgement on matters of policy or strategy was never unsound and usually well ahead of his contemporaries .... At the Naval War College, and later at the Imperial Defence College, he dispensed sound principles with a mature wisdom that was recognised by all. He was always ready to listen to the opinions of others and, if he disagreed, could always counter them with compelling arguments.[17]

In some respects, these lectures were an extension of Corbett's earlier efforts. But Richmond was neither a regular member of the College faculty nor did he enjoy the support of a President who actively endorsed his approach to officer education.[18] Moreover, since 1907, significant changes in the course curriculum had been introduced including, notably, a downgrading in emphasis on tactics, strategy, and command. And the usefulness of what little time was allocated for exercises in these areas was seriously undermined by the lack of fully qualified instructors.

Similar weaknesses plagued the new Naval Staff Course set up by Winston Churchill in 1912. In the months preceding its creation, Dewar campaigned for a syllabus emphasizing history, strategy, tactics, and the principles of command, and employing tutorial instructional methods to encourage students to teach themselves and develop their critical faculties. In practice, however, emphasis was given to the more routine duties of the junior staff officer. Looking back on all this in later years, Dewar admitted that a major obstacle to the adoption of the approaches he and Richmond wanted was the serious lack of qualified personnel. "We had the opportunity but not the intellectual capital to float a staff."[19] These experiences of 1911 and 1912 confirmed Richmond's long-standing scepticism of the War College's value. Convinced that the whole spirit of the College was hostile to creative work, he and Dewar turned their crusading efforts in another direction.

Up to this point, Richmond had attempted to alter the mind and habits of the Navy by force of argument—by presenting "good" ideas. That had failed. With Fisher gone, there was no way to get at the top where real power lay. He would have thought it disloyal to go to the politicians; in any case, he mistrusted Churchill. Instead, he decided to apply pressure through the pages of a professional journal, hoping to create an intellectual climate where criticism would not be mistaken

17 Drax Papers, "Admiral Richmond," unpublished MS fragment by Drax, February 5, 1957.
18 The President then was Vice-Admiral Sir Henry Jackson, a clever and gifted officer. His previous appointments had been mainly technical. His Fellowship in the Royal Society came as a result of pioneering research work in the field of wireless telegraphy. He later became First Sea Lord in succession to Fisher until December 3, 1916, when he was replaced by Jellicoe.
19 Dewar, *Navy From Within*, p. 154.

for treason and where non-materiel ideas could pass as the products of careful, practical thought.

The publication in February 1913 of the first number of the *Naval Review* thus marked the beginning of the most ambitious of Richmond's prewar attempts to influence naval policy and officer education. It was the first printed challenge to the dominance of the materiel school in naval affairs and to the convention that questions of strategy and the higher conduct of war were the exclusive preserve of senior admirals. It testified also to the beginnings of an intellectuals' revolt which, under Richmond's leadership, brought together many of the more fertile minds in the Royal Navy.

The idea of forming a Naval Society was first suggested by Richmond, Dewar later recalled. "I was walking with him on Southsea Common discussing the apathy of officers on tactical and strategical matters, when he suggested that a few officers (about twelve was the number mentioned I think) should circulate articles on such subjects in order to encourage thought and discussion."[20] By beginning modestly and relying on the contributions of fellow enthusiasts, Richmond hoped to create a "Correspondence Society." He invited Dewar together with such officers from the War College as he knew might be interested to his house at 55 Bury Road, Alverstoke, on Sunday, October 27, 1912.[21] Besides Richmond and Dewar, those attending were: Commander R. Plunkett (Drax), Lieutenants T. Fisher, H. G. Thursfield, R. M. Bellairs (all would become Flag Officers), and Captain E. W. Harding, R.M.A. Bound together by what they saw as an urgent need for the fullest discussion and spreading of ideas which alone would encourage the evolution of a sound doctrine of naval warfare, they agreed to form the Naval Society. In Drax's words, they were going to "undertake the regeneration of the British Navy." In 1946, his marginal comment on this diary entry was: "No doubt at the age of 32 one was inclined to think big!"[22] Somewhat more soberly perhaps, Richmond had noted in his Diary:

> We are going to have a try to stir up interest in what Kempenfelt called the "sublime" parts of our work—strategy, tactics, princi-

20 As quoted in Admiral W. H. Henderson, "The Naval Society: An Account of the Foundation and Development of the Naval Society and the Fortunes of the Naval Review During the War," unpublished MS, dated June 1916. From Papers Relating to the Origin and History of the Naval Society, in possession of A. B. Sainsbury, London, England.

21 DEW, 6, Richmond to Dewar, October 24, 1912. The actual date of this first meeting is open to question. Richmond's diary entry (RIC/1/8) is October 19, 1912. Richmond himself later queried this date on the basis of a letter from Custance, dated October 12, in which the latter rejected an offer to become secretary. Richmond to Thursfield, July 7, 1941, in papers belonging to A. B. Sainsbury. All other correspondence indicates October 27 as the actual date.

22 DEW, 9, copy of letter Drax to Richmond, August 28, 1946. This also contains excerpts from Drax's 1912 Diary, entry October 31, 1912.

ples . . . . What I hope to develop is the mental habit of reasoning things out, getting at the bottom of things, evolving principles and spreading interest in the higher side of our work. I wonder what the authorities will say when it reaches their ears![23]

Fear of what the authorities would think accounts, in part, for the decision to make the *Review* a "private" journal, with a restricted or controlled circulation and containing mainly unsigned articles. Anonymity of authorship, in addition to discouraging self-advertisement and overriding the obstacles of seniority and rank, would offer some protection from victimization and hopefully lead to freer discussion as well as encourage contributions from all levels within the Navy. Discussions and formal meetings were therefore rejected as impractical and even antagonistic to these aims. Dewar claimed that it was his idea to expand on Richmond's original concept of a correspondence society and to publish instead a quarterly journal under the direction of a regular editor.[24] As *pro-tem* Secretary of the new Society he canvassed some forty officers for their support together with a £2 contribution to underwrite the costs of the first issue. He also approached Reginald Henderson (later, Admiral Sir Reginald), then Senior Lieutenant of H.M.S. *Excellent*, to invite his uncle, retired Admiral W. H. Henderson, to become the Society's Treasurer and Editor.[25] Thus began a relationship which proved vital to the *Review*'s very survival. Serving continuously until his death at eighty-five in 1931, Henderson performed yeoman service both as editor and, as will be seen, the organizational focus for the "Young Turks" various "political" activities throughout the war years.

"Busy William" brought to the new Society the acquired wisdom of one who knew well the frustrations of an earlier generation of reformers. His enquiring mind, first whetted by reading Hamley as a junior lieutenant, had been sharpened by direct contacts with the major naval thinkers of his own era. In 1885 he had served under Admiral P. H. Colomb, as Commander of the *Duke of Wellington*. "I knew him well for the rest of his life and realized the struggle he had always to maintain, even to get a hearing." Similarly, from 1888, he kept up a regular exchange of letters with Mahan. These contacts, Henderson wrote in 1916, "strengthened my views and determined me to make a move whenever opportunity offered."

In 1886-87, as a student at the Royal Naval College, Henderson had suggested that instruction in tactics and strategy be introduced. However, apart from Colomb's appointment to give a series of six lectures, the results of his efforts were disappointing. In 1888, he was

23 RIC/1/8, Diary, October 19 [27], 1912.
24 DEW, 5, Dewar to Admiral Sir G. C. Dickens, February 3, 1954.
25 Ibid., 6, Richmond to Dewar, February 16,1936.

reprimanded by the Admiralty for expressing his personal views of
Beagle class ships at an R.U.S.I. lecture. Undeterred, Henderson
turned his reforming zeal toward the whole question of officer education and training for war, and it was this which had first brought him
into contact with Richmond and Corbett at the time of the Selborne
Scheme.

Henderson also brought to the Naval Society some practical experience which helped shape the *Review*'s publication and editorial
policy. He was one of the few surviving members of the Junior Naval
Professional Association which had been founded in February 1872
by Herbert Grenfell (then Senior Lieutenant of H.M.S. *Excellent*).
Though similar in the sense that it was the only previous attempt to
form a society and journal within the service, the Association differed
from the new Naval Society in two important respects. Its scope was
wider, concentrating less heavily on the more "sublime" aspects.
More significantly, its membership was limited to officers of lieutenant rank. Senior officers received honorary membership only. After
two years and twenty-eight issues, the Association collapsed, a victim
in Henderson's opinion of over-ambition and lack of support—the
latter a consequence of the Admiralty's discountenance of the whole
scheme.[26] The lessons were clear. Discussion had to come from all
quarters within the Navy, and careful editorial guidance was needed
to ensure acceptance by a naturally suspicious Admiralty and service
tradition.

Initially, membership in the Naval Society was restricted to officers in the Royal Navy and Royal Marines. By March 1913, however,
invitations were also extended to officers of the Royal Australian
Navy and the Naval Service of Canada. In the interim between the
Society's founding and publication of the first issue of the *Review*,
membership rose to almost sixty. Within two months the total was
282. By January 1914, these figures had climbed to 596; by September
1914, to 722; and by Christmas 1915, to 1,260.[27]

26 Membership in 1872 was seventy-two and included such names as Lieutenant
    (later Admiral Lord) Charles Beresford, Lieutenant (Vice-Admiral) H. W. S. Gibson,
    Lieutenant (Admiral Sir) T. S. Jackson, and Lieutenants (later all Admirals)
    A. MacLeod, W. F. S. Mann, and (Admiral of the Fleet Sir) G. H. U. Noel. By 1874,
    membership was 300. Henderson, "Naval Society" (1916), p. 18. E. J. Reed, editor
    of *Naval Science* which also came into existence in early 1872, noted with respect
    to the formation of the Junior Naval Professional Association: "It has been
    alleged—we know not with what truth—that the Admiralty had discounted this
    movement . . . such an Association would probably do more harm than good even
    in matters of Naval Science, while the open discussion by very young officers of the
    works and acts of the Admiralty—for they would inevitably come under
    discussion—might injure to a very great degree that discipline and sense of subor-
    dination which are absolutely essential in the Naval Service."
27 Henderson, "Naval Society" (1916), p. 23. The earliest membership list after the
    October 27, 1912 meeting shows the following names in addition to Richmond and

If these early membership figures suggest that the *Review* was welcomed by the service they also belie the very real anxieties the founders suffered. The following excerpt from a letter to Basil Liddell Hart, written by Richmond in 1934 to explain the prewar atmosphere in the Navy, gives some indication of how much they felt they were Davids tackling Goliaths:

> you could not have known all this turmoil that was going on, this internal argumentation and hostility between the small and feeble school of thought to which I and others belonged and the great powerful and dominating school which had all the patronage, all the power, in its hands. It was that school which began the increase in [battleship] size which has been so utterly disastrous to the Navy: which set the preservation of the ship above the destruction of the enemy: which would spend any amount of money on a dreadnought and grudge a ten pound note for books or study, or for a proper organization for consideration of war.[28]

Consciously working to overcome the natural reluctance of naval officers to participate, and anxious to disarm as quickly as possible any hostile Admiralty reaction, Henderson circulated copies of the first number to Churchill, Asquith, and others "in high places" with a view to publishing such favourable replies as might come in: "such support [Richmond had suggested] would be invaluable and turn the case of many waverers who fear joining."[29] Copies were also sent to the Admiralty Library. Henderson personally contacted the First Sea Lord, Prince Louis of Battenberg. The best approach to him, in Richmond's view, was to point out the advantages of the *Review* as a means of gauging the opinions of the younger generation. "They don't hear the ideas that are simmering among the younger men. A great wave is at present in progress, due largely to the writings of Corbett, and to the discussions at the War College. A new view of what war really means is taking shape."[30] Battenberg's response was sympathetic and encouraging: "I discussed yesterday with the First Lord how Admiralty could further the spread or assist pecuniarily, the admirable Review." Henderson also canvassed every flag officer he knew and was successful in bringing in such men as Jellicoe, Beatty, Chalmers, and also Carlyon Bellairs.[31] A very generous offer of private

Henderson: From the War College—Commanders K. G. B. Dewar, A. V. Vyvyan, R. Plunkett, Sir C. Blane, and Lieutenants Fisher, Thursfield, Bellairs, A. Gilbert. From Whale Island—Commander E. A. Rushton, Lieutenants R. Henderson, G. Blake, H.M.S. *St Vincent*, Lieutenant A. H. Taylor. Also Lieutenant A. C. Dewar and Captain Harding. RIC/7/1, Richmond to Henderson, November 4, 1912, and March 3, 1913.
28 LHP, Richmond to Liddell Hart, September 1934.
29 RIC/7/1, Richmond to Henderson, February 17, 1913.
30 Ibid., July 23, 1913.
31 Drax Papers, "Richmond," February 6, 1957.

financial support from Sir George Warrender was gratefully refused (in spite of Richmond's initial willingness to accept), on grounds of maintaining the *Review's* complete independence.[32] Despite these encouragements, however, the suspicions of the majority of senior officers were not overcome so easily. The Fisher-Beresford row had amply demonstrated what happened to the careers of men marked as dissidents. Frustrated by the timidity of those who balked at the *Review's* unofficial status, Richmond complained bitterly to Dewar:

> Damn these fellows with their whine for "Official Sanction." What some of them will do in war when they have to disobey orders I don't know. But besides that we *have* official sanction. Battenberg has cordially approved and joined, Churchill has ordered it to be taken in at the Admiralty: what more do these people want?[33]

Dewar was quick to point out that although "Prince Louis was an exceptionally able and intelligent officer, it did not do to confuse his approval with that of the Admiralty."[34]

Still, Richmond made a point of encouraging the cooperation of senior personnel hoping to avoid charges that they were being ignored or left out. An attempt to get Vice-Admiral Doveton Sturdee, Chief of the War Staff, to contribute an article on the "functions of Cruisers etc." brought the all-too-common reply that pressures of time and fear of leaking confidential information to the world precluded his participation. Richmond's frustration was predictable:

> These futilities make me sometimes so angry I can hardly contain myself. At other times they appear to me only ludicrous. But at all times they impress upon me how painful a travail we have to go through if we want our officers to know anything about war. I fully expect that many a Captain and Admiral will shake their heads gravely when my new history comes out.[35]

Just how suspect the *Naval Review* was became obvious with the first sudden shocks of war, and this despite the high calibre of the early issues. The 1913 and 1914 volumes merited far more serious attention than they apparently received. Almost one-quarter of the space was devoted to questions of officer training and education. Several articles on submarines and air-power tempt the present-day reader to conclude that had they been seriously considered by the authorities, a great deal might have been achieved in averting the subsequent stalemate at sea. But it was the introduction, in the November 1914 number, of a new series of articles entitled "With the

---

32 DEW, 6, Richmond to Dewar, n.d. "I am not disinclined to consider Warrender's offer. In an infant industry Protection does no harm to enable it to weather its years of delicacy."
33 Ibid., Richmond to Dewar, n.d.
34 RIC/7/4, Dewar to Richmond, n.d.
35 DEW, 6, Richmond to Dewar, October 14, 1913.

Grand Fleet" that interested the Admiralty most. These were followed by the first of a long series of personal narratives on operations from the opening months of the war at sea.

Henderson's first indication that the *Review* was publishing undesirable material was a letter of May 14, 1915, from Sir William Graham Greene, the Permanent Secretary to the Admiralty. Since the Admiralty's attention had been drawn "to certain passages in the May number which contained matter which it was considered should not have been published," it had been decided that all future articles would be subject to censorship.[36] As a result, the August and November issues for 1915 had to be passed by the Chief Naval Censor. Of the articles submitted for the November number, only seven dealing with general subjects were passed. Eight were rejected; these included personal narratives of wartime operations at Konigsberg, the Dutch Shoals, the Dardanelles, Falkland Islands, and Dar es Salaam as well as one on international law and sea-power.[37] That it was the First Sea Lord, Sir Henry Jackson, who personally awarded the "not passed" certifications suggested to Richmond that control of the *Review*'s activities had assumed a surprisingly high priority at the Admiralty: "what a state things must be in when a person of the standing of the 1st S.[ea] L.[ord] thinks it his job to do censorship! A European war upon his hands and he wastes his time in that way. It is preposterous."[38]

From all of the lengthy correspondence and negotiations that followed and resulted in the *Review*'s complete suppression, several points are worth noting. The offending articles or passages were never specified by the Admiralty. Henderson's carefully reasoned pleas were met only with indirect references to the dangers of security leaks and implied criticism of Admiralty policy. The original source of complaint was never revealed. Richmond and Henderson initially blamed Sturdee, while Dewar suspected Jellicoe. Eventually, however, it became obvious that the real opposition was of a far more limited and petty nature than first suspected. Graham Greene was the prime mover and his motives had little to do with a sense of propriety or concern for security. In Richmond's opinion, the Secretary of the Admiralty had engineered the whole business to save himself additional work:

> I quite imagined that perhaps *after* the appearance of the August number, Sir H. J. found in it something he disliked, sent for Censor, and asked why it was left in; difference of opinion between 1st S.L. and Censor. Censor says "well, best thing will be to stop it al-

36 Admiral Richard Webb, "Suspension of 'The Naval Review' in 1915 and 1919," unpublished MS, September 11, 1939. Papers in possession of A. B. Sainsbury.
37 RIC/7/4, Henderson to Richmond, October 14, 1915.
38 RIC/7/1, Richmond to Henderson, October 15, 1915.

together." I can see such a scene: the method of getting over difficulties by avoiding them is a common one in Governmental Establishments.[39]

It was no accident that Graham Greene was one of the first casualties
of Lloyd George's sweep of the Admiralty in 1917. He would be
sacked without explanation. By then, as we shall see, Richmond had
the Prime Minister's ear.[40]

But the censorship and suppression of the *Review* had much
wider implications particularly as a symptom of what was to go
wrong with the Admiralty's whole handling of the war. In
Richmond's words:

> The whole episode is rich in the causes which have made our failures
> in the war. The lack of clear ideas, the dislike of even a hint of
> criticism, the confused notions as to what "secrecy" really means,
> the idea of keeping your own people in the dark, the stifling of
> interest, the suppression of a movement tending to make officers
> think and discuss matters—all these are evident in the events con-
> nected with the suppression.[41]

In his opinion, the Admiralty's refusals to offer concrete reasons for
suppressing the *Review* had more immediate causes as well:

> The fact is that they want to suppress the Review somehow because
> they are afraid they may get bowled out in some of their stupidities [a
> reference to the Dardanelles operation]. They want to keep officers in
> ignorance of what is going on and they don't want a new school of
> thought to grow up. They are behaving as reactionaries have be-
> haved, and they will lose in the end by their stupidity.[42]

In the end, Richmond and Henderson were careful not to push
their resistance to suppression too far. They were looking to the future
and the possibility of resuming publication once the war ended. A
prolonged and bitter struggle at this point would prejudice that
chance as well as discourage officers from joining the Society.
Richmond's prediction that "as reactionaries . . . they will lose in the
end" proved all too accurate. Denied their one means of in-house
debate, the naval reformers turned their energies into other channels.
As the war progressed and as public and Service disenchantment
with the Admiralty's direction of operations developed, the Naval
Society provided a framework around which Richmond and his

39 Ibid., September 29, 1915.
40 Ibid., September 21, 1915, and September 26, 1915. Richmond referred here to the
    importance of "The G.G. correspondence" and that it "should be included in the
    sealed library copies. It is most important that it should remain on record." Unfor-
    tunately, none of these appear to have survived in either Admiralty files or the
    Graham Greene Papers, National Maritime Museum.
41 Ibid., September 2, 1915.
42 Ibid., October 26, 1915.

supporters—the Young Turks of the Grand Fleet—preserved a sense of group identity. Without this structure, their ideas might have remained unheard; because of it, they became a vital element in the organizational and leadership changes that overtook the Admiralty in 1917 when the crisis of the war at sea was reached. The "Young Turks' Revolt," like other intellectual movements before and since, drew much of its vitality and staying power from the attempts of established authority to deny its existence.

3

At the Admiralty: The First Years of War (1914-1915)

The *Naval Review*'s misfortunes were not the only indication that Richmond's and his disciples' ideas irritated the Navy's senior officers. As World War I progressed official antipathy solidified, jeopardizing both their cause and their personal careers. Of course, Richmond and Dewar were their own worst enemies. Outspoken and abrasive, uncompromising and intolerant, they were branded as "difficult men" and shunted away from what today's sailors would call the "career-enhancing" billets. Not that their ideas were wrong. Generally, their assessments were sound and on many critical issues they were well ahead of their contemporaries. No doubt this was a reason for much of the mistrust and ostracism they met. Richmond's habit of having his forecasts proved right by events was particularly annoying. As Assistant Director of Operations (A.D.O.D.) from February 1913 to May 1915, he was in a position ideally suited to his unique qualifications and through which he might have infused a greater sense of strategic rationality into the opening moves of the war at sea. That he failed to do so had very little to do with his own personality defects.

When Richmond returned to the Admiralty, the War Staff had been in existence for over a year. But it was an organization whose junior members were still given little real responsibility. It remained a misused and mistrusted organization until the later stages of the war, its potential circumscribed by senior officers who had little appreciation of modern staff methods and who clung to the ancient tradition of individual responsibility.

Vice-Admiral Doveton Sturdee was a case in point. As a former Chief of Staff to Beresford and, reputedly, a serious student of history

40

and warfare, he was seen as an obvious candidate when appointed
Chief of the War Staff in the summer of 1914. The choice was disastrous. Sturdee lacked the imagination and leadership qualities necessary to the appointment. He did nothing to tap the brains of his juniors
or encourage their sense of initiative. As Richmond discovered, he
took "any suggestions as personal attacks to his own intelligence, so it
is hopeless trying to do anything through him." Moreover:

> He is stubborn, as many stupid people are, but he is not firm, nor can
> be make up his mind on a new thing. One or two old shibboleths,
> such as the one of wanting to bring the enemy out and not keep him
> in, are his whole strategical stock in trade. As to strategems or
> anything of that kind, being unable to imagine them and having
> never read anything, he fears he will look foolish if he adopts them![1]

Beatty went further, rating Sturdee as "one of the curses of the
Navy . . . . He was principally responsible for all our disasters afloat,
and Fisher showed his acumen by turning him out."[2] Fisher also
blamed Sturdee for most of the Navy's mistakes in the first weeks of
the war. This, plus the fact that Sturdee was a member of the Beresford
camp, was reason enough for Fisher to replace him immediately after
his own return to the Admiralty.

Vice-Admiral Henry Oliver, who became C.O.S. on November 5,
1914, held similar views about Sturdee although, unfortunately, this
very capable and level-headed officer proved as prone to over-
centralization as his predecessor. Richmond was soon lamenting his
old friend's propensities for involvement in virtually every detail of
daily operations leaving no time for wider strategic problems. "The
principle of decentralization and trusting subordinates has as yet
gained no ground; so seniors are worked to death and juniors find no
use for their brains."[3] Richmond's immediate superior, Rear-Admiral
Arthur Leveson, Director of Operations Division (D.O.D.), was no
better: he "refuses to do anything." Fisher would also remove Leveson, though only to replace him with Captain Thomas Jackson who, in
Professor Marder's words, turned out to be "a real disaster." Given
such leadership, there was little Richmond could do to influence
operations at sea, and he was reduced to sitting by, recording in his
diary the disasters which a policy of extemporization inevitably produced.

Germany's vigorous naval efforts in the opening weeks of the war
and the Admiralty's hesitation in countering them angered many
active officers. Especially frustrating was the policy of "limited response" to the enemy's mining activities which, in Richmond's

1   RIC/1/11, Diary, October 19, 1914.
2   Marder, *Dreadnought to Scapa Flow*, vol. 2, pp. 92-93.
3   RIC/1/12, Diary, February 14, 1915.

words, were making the North Sea a "German Ocean." Those in the Grand Fleet and the Admiralty who favoured aggressive responses in kind found themselves at odds with the First Sea Lord and Sturdee who felt that large-scale mining would only restrict British movements, forestalling their basic object of enticing the High Seas Fleet out to fight. Richmond's correspondence with Drax (then a member of Beatty's staff in H.M.S. *Lion*, flagship of the Battle Cruiser Squadron), and with Dewar (Commander of *Prince of Wales*, Channel Fleet) in these early weeks clearly reveals their confidence in Jellicoe and Beatty as opposed to the "timid" people in London.[4] But this difference of views as to what was possible or desirable was only the first of many which brought Richmond into direct conflict with his immediate naval superiors.

A full year before the war began, Richmond had submitted proposals for a fully developed plan defining the Grand Fleet's principal strategic object in the North Sea and the need for immediate and concerted offensives against Germany's trade, including her overseas bases and colonies.[5] The Admiralty's reluctance to face the implications of supporting the British Expeditionary Force (B.E.F.) in France also prompted him to suggest the establishment of a Joint Naval and Military Committee to develop a "comprehensive scheme of offensive action" which would immediately put the High Seas Fleet on the defensive. This proposal was eventually sanctioned by Sturdee and approved by Battenberg and Churchill. A letter for the C.I.D.'s direction was even drafted.[6] But opportunities for further action were overtaken by the German invasion of Belgium. "Now we have our war," Richmond recorded Churchill as saying in private: "The next thing is to decide how we are going to carry it on! What a statement! The Duke of Newcastle himself could not have made a more damning confession of inadequate preparation for war."[7] Just *how* inadequate became obvious all too quickly. The absence of comprehensive plans for covering the crossings of the B.E.F. was especially unnerving. Fearing an incursion by High Seas Fleet elements, Richmond bombarded Leveson and Sturdee, and even Churchill, with proposals for quickly reinforcing the Channel Fleet, for counter-mining operations backed by destroyers, torpedo-boats, and submarines, and even for an emergency deployment of units of the Grand Fleet in the Western

4   RIC/7/4, Plunkett (Drax) to Richmond, November 15, 22, 1914; December 18, 24, 30, 1914; January 14, 21, 1915.
5   RIC/1/9, Diary, August 6, 1914. Also RIC/14/3, "North Sea Strategy," Remarks by A.D.O.D., August 1913; "Considerations Affecting the Capture of Tsing-Tau," September 1913.
6   RIC/1/9, Richmond's "Notes for C.O.S.," June 1914. Adm. 1/8386, "Plans for Combined Offensive Action on the Outbreak of War," War Staff Admiralty; July 21, 1914; also Minutes of July 24 and 25, 1914; Draft letter for Secretary C.I.D., n.d.
7   RIC/1/9, Diary, August 5, 1914.

Approaches. In the event, his fears were premature; thankfully, the German Naval High Command was as blind to its opportunities as was the British.

Elsewhere, however, such oversights did take their toll. Richmond's proposals for arming disguised merchant vessels ("Q" ships, or "special service vessels") to counter German U-boats were not taken seriously at first. His warnings about the obvious dangers of dispatching ships on regular and predictable patrols if heeded might have averted such disasters as the tragic triple sinking of the cruisers *Cressy*, *Aboukir*, and *Hogue* on September 22. Other examples could be cited, but perhaps Richmond's prescience was most evident when it came to analyzing the options open to Germany's Far East Squadron should Japan enter the war, and their likely effects on Admiral Cradock's force on the South American Station. His repeated recommendations for the dispatch of three, and preferably four armoured cruisers to intercept the Germans were vetoed by Sturdee. That it would later be Sturdee, "this consequential blunderer," who received a baronetcy for his victory at the Falklands (December 8, 1914), in effect avenging the tragedy of Cradock's destruction at Coronel a month earlier (November 1), which he had helped to put in train, would always be supremely and bitterly ironic in Richmond's mind.[8]

But if some of Richmond's ideas were sound, the means and opportunities for putting them forward were not. Leveson, Richmond complained,

> neither consults me, nor refers any question of any kind to me, nor allows me to take any action, nor acknowledges any suggestions I make ... I am now a cypher and my position is unbearable. There is no ship for me to go to, so I must sit here and accept such bones as he chooses to throw me.

The solution, he soon realized, was to circumvent his immediate superiors; "to try and shew Winston the madness of it all." This was no easy task, however, for although Churchill was frequently in the War Room and could always be approached, it was quite another thing to get him to listen. Churchill, he noted, "is absorbed in naval brigades, the defence of Antwerp, and the Flying Corps, and high sea-strategy is a thing he does not understand—not any sea-strategy for the matter of that."[9] In a fundamental sense, Churchill's concepts of naval strategy clashed with those of most of his naval advisers. He was obsessed with the idea that the Fleet must "do something," and his fertile imagination grasped at the possibilities of a wide variety of

8   RIC/1/11, October 10, November 3, 4, 13 and December 13, 1914. Also, DEW, 13, Diary (1914-1915), May 30, 1915. See Marder, *Dreadnought to Scapa Flow*, vol. 2, pp. 101-28; and Captain Geoffrey Bennett, *Coronel and the Falklands* (London: Batsford, 1962).
9   RIC/1/10, September 17, October 9, 1914.

schemes which usually ignored the very real problems involved. In almost every instance where Richmond tried to "shew Winston," he achieved little beyond a lowering in value of his own stock.

As early as February 1913, Churchill had expressed his disappointment with the Admiralty's decision to scrap even the pretence of a close blockade of Germany. He preferred an offensive posture designed to keep the Germans constantly on their toes, and to this end, he suggested strikes at their home bases. The B.E.F.'s passage to France would then be covered, not by blocking the Dover Straits, but by a vigorous ten-day offensive against the Elbe, to be followed up on a recurring basis. 'We must so conduct ourselves [he wrote] that the sea is full of nameless terrors for him—instead of us." The impracticability of such a scheme had been previously well demonstrated, a fact not lost on Churchill's advisers at the time.[10] Richmond went further in his private condemnation of the First Lord's amateurish thinking.

> Merely to steam about at sea is not taking the offensive. To bombard the defences of Wilhelmshaven, to attack Wilhelmshaven with an army and attempt to destroy their fleet in the harbour, or to drive it out to destruction by a superior force, *would* be taking an offensive. But merely to do what the old seamen and others used to call having a Spithead Review is not an offensive . . . . What the First Lord loses sight of is the real function of a fleet or squadron of battleships. It is because he fails to see where our real offensive powers lie that he propounds these fantastic measures—for such I call them. Sweeps, hustling the enemy, getting him into a jumble—all these are words only. They mean *nothing*. They will not affect well-considered plans of a thinking enemy any more than beating drums or waving flags would do.

But warnings as to technical problems or the dangers of underrating German abilities had little effect. Close blockade remained a possibility in Churchill's mind as late as June of 1914. His continuing resistance to his professional advisers says a great deal about his sincerity in espousing the War Staff concept in 1912.

Richmond had always doubted Churchill's motives in this respect and his misgivings were confirmed. Even after Fisher was recalled as First Sea Lord in November and Sir Arthur Wilson was added to the War Staff Group as an unofficial special adviser, it was obvious that Churchill had no intention of being reined in. According to Mrs. Richmond, Hankey informed her husband about the War Council's discussions of a proposed attack against the German island of Borkum during which Fisher and Wilson "sat absolutely mum only

10 Adm. Mss, Churchill to Battenberg, February 17, 1913, "Remarks on War Plans and on the First Lord's Notes on the Subject," March 11, 1913, by Jackson (C.O.S.); also, remarks on Churchill's letter by D.O.D. (Ballard), n.d.; remarks on Churchill's letter by A.D.O.D. (Richmond), n.d.

looking grumpy, while Winston dilated on his plan . . . and allowed Winston to persuade everyone else." In Richmond's opinion, "Fisher talks very big in his own room about putting his foot down and not having it, but when it comes to the point, he says nothing and lets Winston have [it] all his own way."[11] Oliver also confided to Richmond that he was able to keep Fisher, Wilson, and Churchill in line only by playing them off against one another. Most of his time was devoted to managing "two stupid old men and one raving lunatic,"[12] and preventing their wilder schemes from being put into operation.

Richmond also condemned Churchill as a "shouting amateur" in strategic matters and, on occasion, doubted his sanity too.[13] All the same, he sympathized with the First Lord's concern over mounting public doubts about the Navy's ability, even willingness, to take decisive action against Germany. As a result, when Churchill—knowing that Richmond was offense-minded—approached him for personal advice, he was faced with the dilemma of how to counterbalance the First Lord's notions without himself being counted among the Admiralty "do nothings." "I did not argue," Richmond noted after Churchill showed him a plan to violate Dutch neutrality and occupy Born Diep near Ameland as an advanced base for British flotillas. "He was vehement in his desire to adopt an offensive attitude. I saw that no words could check his vivid imagination and that it was quite impossible to persuade him both of the strategical and tactical futility of such an operation. So I have busied myself . . . in such rare moments as I could snatch to argue it out."[14] Similarly, in January 1915, he characterized the scheme for an attack on Borkum as "quite mad." "The reasons for capturing it are NIL, the possibilities about the same. I have never read such an idiotic amateur piece of work as this outline in my life. Ironically enough it falls to me to prepare the plans for this stupendous piece of folly."[15]

These were private diary fulminations, however, and quite unlike the balanced and closely reasoned arguments he marshalled as A.D.O.D. to discourage Churchill's Baltic and North Sea projects. This is not to say that Richmond exercised a monopoly on strategic sanity within the Admiralty; but rather, that his careful assessments did reflect a spectrum of sound expert opinion which Churchill could not entirely ignore. Ultimately, the final arbiter of the Baltic schemes was Jellicoe, who as Commander-in-Chief Grand Fleet, had vetoed all

11 RIC/1/17, Lady Richmond's Diary, January 9, 1915.
12 Ibid., January 14, 1915.
13 RIC/1/9, August 20, 1914.
14 Ibid., August 9, 1914.
15 RIC/1/11, January 4, 1915; Enclosure, "Attack on Danzig" (code name for Borkum), by H. W. Richmond, January 19, 1915.

such plans since July 1914.[16] In later years, Churchill blamed Fisher for not whole-heartedly supporting the Borkum ideas thereby deny-ing any possibilities of a full exploration of the subject.[17] Still, his obsession with offensive action was not always successfully con-tained, as the Antwerp expedition of October 1914 illustrates. And Richmond was not alone in his condemnation of Churchill for this fiasco, or in his suggestion that much of the madness these schemes involved stemmed from the First Lord' peculiar sense of heroism and glory on the one hand and, on the other, the War Staff's inability to control and shape it to real advantage. "No Board of Admiralty with twopenny-worth of knowledge and backbone would have allowed marines to be used in such a way . . . . It is a tragedy that the Navy should be in such lunatic hands at this time."[18]

The Dardanelles operation, and the processes by which it was conceived and executed, provides the best illustration of how Church-ill's determination and eloquence could override all objections, both technical and conceptual, which expert opinion and the lessons of history could muster. The decision to attempt a naval attack on the vital Turkish straits without troops was, in Richmond's view, the ultimate expression of how "very very ignorant" the First Lord was of the potentials and the limitations of sea-power. He warned that the operation would be tactically costly, if not impossible. More impor-tant, it offered none of the strategic advantages which a properly executed combined offensive applied to the Eastern Mediterranean theatre could. "The bombardment of the Dardanelles, even if all the Forts are destroyed, can be nothing but a local success, which without an army to carry it on can have no further effect."[19]

The root cause of the Dardanelles disaster lay with the system which placed such decisions in the hands of men whose expertise was insufficient for the task. The War Staff, underdeveloped as it was, was never properly consulted. Operational preparations were so de-partmentalized that even technical considerations were never thoroughly incorporated into the overall planning. The War Council's deliberations focussed on political ends while naval and military means were insufficiently discussed. Indeed, the most striking fea-ture of the entire process was this by-passing of professional and expert opinion.

At the end of August 1914, following the escape and passage through the Dardanelles of the German warships Goeben and Breslau,

16 Admiral Sir Reginald Bacon, The Life of John Rushworth, Earl Jellicoe (London: Cassell, 1936), pp. 188-89.
17 Churchill, World Crisis, vol. 2, p. 41. Fisher's Baltic ideas are summarized in Marder, Dreadnought to Scapa Flow, vol. 2, pp. 191-98.
18 RIC/1/10, Diary, October 4, 1914.
19 RIC/1/12, February 14, 1915.

Churchill and Kitchener agreed that staff officers from the Admiralty and War Office should meet immediately to study the rapidly changing Turkish situation. Specifically, Churchill suggested on September 1 that this joint group should examine and formulate "a plan for the seizure by means of a Greek army of adequate strength of the Gallipoli peninsula, with a view to admitting the British Fleet to the Sea of Marmora." At six o'clock that same evening, Richmond together with the Fourth Sea Lord, Captain C. F. Lambert, and the Director of Transports, Graeme Thompson, met at the Admiralty with Major-General Charles E. Callwell and Colonel M. G. Talbot of the War Office.

Callwell's participation was significant for he was not only the Director of Military Operations, but also the recognized British authority on combined operations theory and an ardent advocate of inter-service cooperation.[20] Equally important, he was also the author of a memorandum which had formed the basis for the C.I.D.'s unequivocal rejection in 1906 of any such operations against the Dardanelles. Indeed, his earlier conclusions had been so convincing that his memorandum and much of the correspondence relating to it had been destroyed or removed from the C.I.D.'s files by prime ministerial order to avoid possible security leaks which would utterly destroy the usefulness of even a threat of British action against Turkey in the future.[21] Thus, in September 1914, copies of the 1906 "missing memorandum" could not be found. Nevertheless, Callwell did recall his own conclusions and these, reiterated to the new joint committee, were formalized into another memorandum whose tone was intended to be "decidedly discouraging."[22] As in 1906, the impossibility of guaranteeing absolute secrecy meant that landings would be opposed. Turkish improvements and reinforcement of the Gallipoli defences since that time only strengthened these conclusions. It was also doubtful that the Navy had the requisite expertise and materiel for fully effective fire support against land targets.

The committee met again on September 2, this time with Churchill and Battenberg present. The result was another report submitted by Callwell to Kitchener on September 3 which, though continuing to emphasize the extreme hazards involved, went on to suggest that, with a force of 60,000 men, an attack on Gallipoli might be justified.

20 C. E. Callwell, *Military Operations and Maritime Preponderance: Their Relations and Interdependence* (Edinburgh: Wm. Blackwood, 1905) and *Small Wars: Their Principles and Practice* (London: H.M.S.O., 1906) rated at the time as the definitive work on small-scale operations.

21 Cab. 2/2, C.I.D. Minutes of 93rd Meeting, November 13, 1906; and 96th Meeting, February 28, 1907.

22 Callwell, *Experiences of a Dug-Out, 1914-1918* (New York, 1920), pp. 88-90. Also W. O. 106/1463, Note by Colonel Talbot, September 5, 1914, summarizing events, September 1-3. Also Cab. 19/28, "Summary of Proposed Evidence."

Just how Callwell was induced to modify his views is not known. As Churchill's biographer suggests: "How far Churchill had prevailed on Callwell to reverse his opinion by the weight of evidence, how far by an assertion of his authority, is not clear."[23] What is clear is that the First Lord made no further use of the joint committee in his continuing search for strategic justifications and resources. Callwell later recalled that the committee was "almost the only occasion—if it was not the only occasion" when representatives from responsible positions in the War Office and Admiralty met jointly to discuss the Dardanelles attack.[24]

Callwell and Richmond did keep in touch though both were largely by-passed in subsequent Dardanelles planning. Richmond also tried to follow up on the joint talks by suggesting alternatives to the Dardanelles. On September 27 he submitted outline plans to Sturdee for combined operations and demonstrations along the coast of Syria. But nothing was done. "When Turkey came in on November 1st—nearly five weeks after this paper—my report had been lost and none of the points in it had been considered."[25]

In the months that followed, Richmond was only peripherally connected with the events that eventually led to the decision to attempt the Dardanelles by naval units alone. He was aware, at least, of some of the forces in play and of the alternatives debated in the War Council and the highest levels of the Admiralty. But his own energies in this period were concentrated mainly on investigating Churchill's Borkum and North Sea proposals. By mid-January 1915, he had reason to feel hopeful that his efforts, backed by Oliver, had finally "squashed" these schemes. Ironically, they were too successful perhaps, for Churchill never gave any indication that he accepted the merits of their arguments. Quite the contrary, it probably only strengthened his conviction that without strong political leadership, the sailors would do very little on their own—a conviction that affected not only his use (or non-use) of the War Staff in the Dardanelles situation, but also his whole approach to civil-military relations in later years as Prime Minister in World War II.[26] In any case, by mid-January 1915, Churchill's gaze had already turned away from Borkum, and only then did Richmond learn of the plans being developed for a major attack on the Dardanelles.

These plans were based on a Staff Appreciation of January 15 prepared by Admiral Sir Henry Jackson who had studied the results of

23 M. Gilbert, *Winston S. Churchill*, vol. 3: *1914-1916* (London: Heinemann, 1971), p. 203.
24 Callwell, *Experiences*, pp. 90-91.
25 RIC/1/10, Diary, September 26, 1914; also November 1 and 3, 1914.
26 A. J. Marder, *From the Dardanelles to Oran: Studies of the Royal Navy in War and Peace, 1915-1940* (London: Oxford University Press, 1974), p. 178.

the earlier November 3 bombardment of the outer forts. Richmond seized the opportunity to resurrect his own proposals for operations along the Turkish coast. "I spoke again to General Callwell about it at lunch today," he noted in his diary for January 16, "he said Kitchener couldn't or wouldn't make up his mind. The French naval attaché is very keen to do something there—preferably to force the Dardanelles. This Oliver has proposed, and Sir H. Jackson has I believe prepared the outline of a plan. So have I." There was something to be said for the idea: "With our modern long heavy guns we can outrange the Turkish forts, and a useful bombardment can be carried out. If we can force the passage, we have Constantinople open, and the result will I hope be a revolution in Turkey." But, he cautioned, the Dardanelles were not the whole answer. "The two things must come to-gether—an attack on the Dardanelles and a landing in Syria. The joint effect would be fatal to Enver Pasha and his German advisors." This was a critical qualification to add, especially at a time when other minds were turning exclusively to the Narrows.

On February 9, Richmond wrote to Hankey in the hope that he could influence "someone to seize this psychological moment and sling the Egyptian troops into Alexandretta." He urged the occupation of Aleppo, or the isolation of Haifa by cutting the Damascus railway, to be followed up by raids, feints, and "solid attack" all along the Palestine coast. Anxious that the full potentials of the moment should not be lost, he also approached Fisher. Cornering him in an Admiralty passageway, he reminded the First Sea Lord of a cartoon he had drawn in 1903 to illustrate a speech in which Fisher had said "the soldier couldn't go anywhere or do anything unless the sailor carried him on his back." Fisher's genial response provided the opening and Richmond passed him another of his papers entitled "Remarks on Present Strategy" which Fisher agreed to read. "So I, very pleased, left him," Richmond wrote. "I hope it may touch a sympathetic cord in his heart. It ought to, with his views, and if it does, if only he takes it up and shoves it before the War Council, *something* might be done."[27]

The "Remarks on Present Strategy" paper is especially interesting because it represents Richmond's first attempt to apply his own broad historical and theoretical knowledge to the realities of war on the grand scale. His wife noted that he called it "a scheme . . . for *nothing less than the whole strategy of the war in the Spring* [sic]."[28] Also, because Julian Corbett and Edmond Slade assisted in preparing the final draft, the paper directly reflects the ideas of those who, since 1905, had worked consistently to prevent a too exclusive commitment of Britain's military resources to the Western Front. In the sense that it

27 RIC/1/12, enclosure, February 14, 1915, "Remarks on Present Strategy."
28 RIC/1/17, Lady Richmond's Diary, February 10, 1915.

was a plea for the Navy to have a bigger voice in the overall management of the war ("that will get Jacky's shirt out"), it was hardly
original. But as a concise and eloquent expression of the so-called
"Easterner" strategic mentality, it merits some examination.

Countering the critics who argued that the utility of any combined operations or raids policy had been obviated by the Central
Powers' use of military railroads, Richmond pointed out that sea-
power was the British Army's only means of outflanking the enemy's
advantage in the central theatre. The sea was Britain's strategic railway, in effect, and unless she was prepared to capitalize on the
advantages it conferred, she would be playing directly into Germany's hands. "We are conducting the war on purely Continental
lines, trying to beat them at their own game, at which we can develop
only half our peculiar strength, and the enemy can develop the whole
of theirs. We are fighting Germans with German weapons and con-
forming like sheep to their strategic plan."

Amphibious operations were impractical in the North Sea and
the Baltic. They were possible in the Mediterranean theatre because
there the Allies exercised effective command of the sea. The Mediterranean offered "an ideal theatre for the use of our old method of
working fleet and army together to increase the power and reach of
both and gain direct access to the vital continental theatre." This
recognition of the Eastern Front as the "vital" theatre in Europe was
the primary consideration. Any moves designed to augment Russia's
striking power there would constitute the best use of Allied resources
at this point in the war. Turkey's defeat would give Russia more
freedom of action and might also encourage the smaller European
Powers to cooperate in the destruction of enemy forces in south-
eastern Europe. On this latter point, Richmond was undoubtedly as
over-optimistic (even ignorant) as Hankey and other Easterners about
the motives and possible actions of Greece, Bulgaria, and Roumania.
In any case, he emphatically denied that any of these effects were
possible through naval action alone. He suggested a two-pronged
combined forces offensive—one based on strong British forces backed
by Russian and perhaps Greek formations aimed at Constantinople;
the second, in a "distinct zone of operations," would employ the
Egyptian garrison striking out along the Palestine-Syria coastal reg-
ions supported by the Navy. Ultimately, both elements might be
shifted to Salonika or Montenegro to strengthen any advance into the
Danube from the south.

Here then was Richmond's grand view of an amphibious strategy
aimed at the invasion of Turkish outposts as a means of destroying the
Central Powers and covering Britain's imperial and central Asian
interests. Contrary to what his critics subsequently assumed, Rich-

mond was not advocating here some "peripheral" strategy as an *alternative* to the "Continentalists" or "Westerners." Nowhere, either in his general historical writings or in the specific circumstances of early 1915, did he advocate a maritime strategic mentality as being an exclusively naval option. Nor did he deny that Britain's commitment of the B.E.F. to France was necessary, even unavoidable—the subsequent total mobilization and commitment of British resources to the Flanders front was another thing, of course, in which the failure of the Dardanelles-Gallipoli strategy and Britain's doubts about her Allies' willingness to persevere in the struggle were major determinants. What concerned Richmond in early 1915 was that the Royal Navy's extensive (and very expensive) resources were not being fully exploited. The fact is, strategic options of the Dardanelles type were not beyond Britain's materiel means. Whether or not the Army's and Navy's lack of expertise and equipment for such specialized operations could be surmounted in the circumstances was a question which Richmond was not the only one to ignore.

Fisher's reaction was encouraging: "YOUR PAPER IS EXCELLENT!" Similarly, Hankey replied: "Your memo is absolutely A1 and is most opportune. In sending it to Jacky you are preaching to the converted, but it may ginger him up."[29] These replies are especially interesting both as a commentary on Fisher's and Hankey's methods, and also as an indication of how small a part the Admiralty War Staff played in the Dardanelles planning. The fact is, events had already outdistanced Richmond; both men knew that the major decisions on the operation had been taken up to a month prior to his submission. Indeed, the preliminary bombardment of the outer forts began only four days after this exchange of letters. That Richmond, as A.D.O.D., was so out of step in his timing suggests the extent to which he and his junior colleagues had been ignored. It was especially galling, in view of his own efforts to strike some balance between the Admiralty's defensive proclivities and Churchill's more extreme offensive ideas, to discover that the Dardanelles expedition had been launched with such inadequate preparation. He had no doubt that "the First Lord's personal vanity" had been the vital factor:

> [Churchill] could not understand that the capture of the Dardanelles was a joint operation, or else he wanted all the glory himself. Result, an attempt to do with the Fleet what is beyond the power of the Fleet. I hope this has opened his eyes to the foolishness of his Borkum proposals![30]

Churchill had understood the need for a large military force from the beginning. However, since troops were not available, he had

29 RIC/1/12, February 15, 1915.
30 Ibid., March 26, 1915.

chosen to exploit Admiral Carden's view that ships alone could force the straits. Then, on February 15, Sir Henry Jackson submitted a memorandum which corroborated Richmond's contention that such action would be futile unless followed up immediately by troops. Early the next day, Fisher also warned that 'Not a grain of wheat will come from the Black Sea unless there is a military occupation of the Dardanelles, and it will be the wonder of the ages that no troops were sent to cooperate with the Fleet with half a million soldiers in England." Churchill recognized the force of these arguments. That same day, at an emergency meeting of the War Council, it was agreed that the Twenty-ninth Division would be dispatched to assist the naval attack. This formation had been assigned to a projected expedition to Salonika, but the Greek Government's rejection of this operation only the day before freed the Division for use on the Gallipoli peninsula, and Churchill was instructed to prepare for its transport from England and the transport of the Australian and New Zealand Corps (ANZAC) from Egypt. Thus, his biographer writes, Churchill "was relieved that troops would be used in conjunction with ships, and that the doubts of Hankey, Richmond, Jackson, and Fisher were thereby set to rest."[31]

But this eleventh-hour change in the whole nature of the undertaking raised more problems than it solved, not the least of which was the fact that no joint planning whatsoever had taken place for what was now truly a combined Admiralty-War Office operation. Hankey, for all his earlier enthusiasm, sensed that only tragedy could follow. On March 15, he wrote to Esher:

> Although on general principles this operation is brilliantly conceived, and quite correct, I am not at all satisfied that it is being carried out in the best possible manner. Troops ought to have been there, or at any rate within a day or two's reach, when the bombardment began. There ought to have been no blatant press announcement at the outset, and the bombardment ought to have been announced merely as a demonstration. While the bombardment was commencing the transports ought to have appeared at some entirely different point on the Turkish coast, such as Alexandretta or Haifa . . . . Then the troops ought to have come in as a bolt from the blue, and closely supported by the fleet (and ought?) to have captured the plateau overlooking the forts of the Narrows by a *coupe-de-main* . . . . Now we have given the Turks time to assemble a vast force, to pour in field guns and howitzers, to entrench every landing place, and the operation has become a most formidable one. Please burn this.[32]

In private at least, he now worked to rouse opposition to the operation's continuance.

31 Gilbert, *Churchill*, vol. 3, pp. 287-88; Also *Winston S. Churchill: 1914-1916: Companion*, no. 1 (London: Heinemann, 1971), pp. 506-16.

32 S. W. Roskill, *Hankey, Man of Secrets*, vol. 1 (London: Collins, 1970), pp. 167-68.

At Hankey's suggestion, Richmond approached the First Sea Lord directly once again. This time he advised Fisher, in view of Italy's pending decision to enter the war, to consider carefully the effects of a British setback at the Dardanelles. Postponement of further efforts there, or at least a temporary diversion of force to Haifa or the Syrian coast seemed advisable until Italy's position became clear. Fisher was impressed. Churchill, however, was not. Richmond was informed "it was not my business to interfere in proposals that had been approved, and that I would be required no longer in the Adty [*sic*]."[33] Churchill's sensitivity to criticism and his personal hostility was apparent as Richmond noted:

> I can't help thinking that he now has such an antipathy to me, owing to various of my remarks on his schemes, that I have only to put my name at the bottom of a proposal to ensure its defeat....
> My proposal as to Italy appears to have interested Fisher enough to make him take [it] to 1st Lord, who was furious at it (so Bartolome later [told] me), and as F. told him *I* was the writer, I suppose I am more unpopular than ever. All the same, something *has* been done.

When Asquith also suggested a short postponement in view of the delicate Italian situation, Churchill understandably had grounds for suspecting that Richmond had got at the Prime Minister. In reality, it was Hankey who planted the idea. In Richmond's words, "it has been a little plot between Hankey and me."[34]

Whatever satisfaction Richmond drew from this, he had clearly outlived his usefulness and took no further part in the Dardanelles-Gallipoli disaster. He had hoped for a post on Carden's Staff at the Dardanelles. Oliver had also suggested that he might succeed Jackson as Director of Operations at the Admiralty. But he was also aware, through Commodore Charles de Bartolomé the Naval Secretary, that Churchill was "furious" with him because of his Baltic and Holland papers. The Italian suggestion was the last straw.

It is worth emphasizing at this point that it was not the Admiralty permanent staff, but rather the political leadership that banished Richmond into exile. The admirals of the War Staff Group understood how very dangerous, if not suicidal, it was for any officer to seriously oppose the First Lord on anything to which his mind and instincts were committed. And it is partly for this reason that they must share in the formidable indictment against Churchill's leadership in the entire Dardanelles debacle. For one of his junior rank, Richmond's obstinate interference was foolhardy and tactless in the extreme; perhaps to the point of implying personal courage and professional integrity of a kind even Fisher might well have considered worth preserving.

33 RIC/1/12, Diary, April 8, 1915.
34 RIC/1/17, Lady Richmond's Diary, April 11, 1915.

In May Richmond was transferred from the War Staff to the Italian
Navy as Liaison Officer to the Duke of Abruzzi aboard the flagship
Cavour. He accepted the appointment with relief and some enthusiasm, noting on his arrival in Taranto: 'My first impressions are
distinctly good. The Duke, young and vigorous; his Chief of Staff
able .... I feel we are at the beginning of a prodigiously interesting
campaign."[35] But even this forced optimism vanished as it became
obvious that the Italians were reluctant to pursue vigorous offensives
against Austria in the Adriatic. By mid-August, he was seeking relief
and within another month had left Taranto for a short period of
half-pay before assuming command of H.M.S. *Commonwealth* of the
Third Battle Squadron. Clearly, official hostilities had not diminished
appreciably during his absence in the Adriatic. Originally, in fact, he
had been offered another choice of postings—as Senior Naval Officer
(S.N.O.) French Coast, or transport officer at Salonika—both of which
would normally be given to older and less "promotable" officers.
Equally disturbing was his discovery, through talks in London with
Balfour and Hankey, that his reports on the Italian situation had been
virtually ignored by the Admiralty.

From then until the spring of 1917, Richmond remained opera-
tionally sidetracked. The Third Battle Squadron, comprised of eight
pre-dreadnought *King Edward VII* battleships (the "Wobbly Eight"),
was detached from the Grand Fleet and based at Sheerness. Not
one round was fired in action by the Squadron during Richmond's
period of attachment. Confined to harbour in the Thames from May 2,
1916, they even missed the Battle of Jutland, a point about which
Richmond would always be sensitive:

> The only point I regret beyond the intense disappointment of taking
> no active part in a war which I have thought about for twenty years is
> that nothing that I say will ever have any weight afterwards—"What
> the devil does *he* know about anything? Why he never saw a shot
> fired!"[36]

Disgusted, frustrated, bored beyond measure, Richmond con-
soled himself with still further submissions to stir up ideas for offensive action.[37] But he knew only too well that he had been shelved,
particularly after Jellicoe's appointment as First Sea Lord in December 1916 failed to bring any immediate change in his fortunes. By
then, however, other forces were at work. The political revolution of
that month which brought Lloyd George to power also brought an end
to the Balfour-Jackson regime at the Admiralty. The domestic politi-

35 RIC /1/13, May 24, 1915.
36 DEW, 6, Richmond to Dewar, August 9, 1916.
37 RIC/13/1, Various Memoranda, 1913-1915; RIC/14/3, Various War Papers, 1915-
    1918.

cal crisis of the war had arrived while the naval one at sea was fast approaching. Whether the Admiralty under the new leadership of Carson and Jellicoe was up to that challenge was the question which then faced the nation.

4

Crisis at Sea: The Young Turks' Revolt (1916-1917)

By April 1917, the war at sea reached its most critical phases. The ambiguous outcome of the Battle of Jutland of May 1916 appeared to confirm earlier trends against any adventurous naval strategy and, by autumn, an atmosphere of seemingly inescapable stalemate settled over the British and German battle-fleets. Public disappointment grew into uneasiness and alarm as Germany's unrestricted U-boat offensive, launched early in 1917, began to take its toll exposing as it did defects in organization and leadership which crippled the Royal Navy's potential. Richmond and his associates experienced the same restlessness. United by their shared experience of official mistrust, they set out in the summer of 1916 to educate the Service and the politicians on the need for sweeping reform; to "cause an outcry and an insistence upon it ... [through] ... the press, a book, or whatever else may be agreed upon."[1] Richmond, Dewar, Drax, Bellairs, and R. G. Henderson became the nucleus around which a steadily widening spectrum of discontent within the navy gravitated.

The Naval Society's role as an organizational focus for Richmond's "New School"—the Young Turks of the Grand Fleet—has already been mentioned. From this point, the Society's editorial office became the central clearing house for their expanding missionary work in the field. Admiral Henderson's contacts with London's newspaper editors,[2] particularly the Northcliffe empire, provided openings to informed opinion outside of the Navy and ultimately to

---

1 DEW, 6, Richmond to Dewar, June 2, 1916.
2 HEN/2/1, 2/2, 2/3. Personal correspondence with various editors, 1914-1916. HEN/3, correspondence mostly of a public or semi-public nature, outside his *Naval Review* work.

56

the highest political leaders including the Prime Minister. Richmond's correspondence with Julian Corbett[3] (then heading the C.I.D.'s Official History of the War) reinforced his own connections with Hankey who, by early 1917, had become Secretary of the Imperial War Cabinet. The Young Turks thus had access to information which few of even their superiors could claim. Their willingness to use it, in defiance of accepted codes of service discipline, loyalty, and procedure, was justified—at least in their view—by the crisis brought about by Germany's submarine menace and the Admiralty's hesitation and ineptness in responding.

The introduction of mercantile convoys as the ultimate response to the U-boat threat has been the subject of a continuing debate in the history of World War I civil-military relations. Proponents of the civilian leadership, led by Lloyd George himself, have argued that it was only as a result of his personal intervention—the threat implied in his famous April 30 visitation—that the objections of a "palsied and muddle-headed Admiralty" were finally overcome.[4] Jellicoe and the Admiralty, on the other hand, have been defended on the grounds that opposition to convoy was both unavoidable and necessary until conditions such as America's entry into the war made it practicable.[5] Recent research, most notably by Professors Marder and Temple Patterson, indicates that the truth lies somewhere between these extremes; that the Admiralty's objections were honestly felt and that Lloyd George's role was at best anti-climactic.[6] By April 1917, the combined effects of America's entry, the disastrous losses in shipping and, most especially, the discoveries by Commander Reginald Henderson (Anti-Submarine Division) and Kenneth Dewar that the escort numbers problem was not as unmanageable as had been assumed,[7] had pushed the War Staff to accept experimental convoys some five days before the Prime Minister's intervention. The significance of all this Professor Marder has concluded from his analysis of the relevant factors—including the supposed shortage of ocean-escorts, and the

3   RIC/9/1, Papers belonging to the late Sir Julian Corbett (wartime), sent to Admiral Richmond by Lady Corbett.
4   Lloyd George, War Memoirs of David Lloyd George (Boston: Little, Brown and Co., 1934), vol. 3, pp. 70-136. This view has generally been supported by Churchill, Thoughts and Adventures (London: Butterworth, 1932), and The World Crisis; Dewar, Navy From Within; and more recently by A. J. P. Taylor, English History, 1914-1945 (Oxford: Clarendon Press, 1965).
5   Admiral Sir Reginald Bacon, The Life of John Rushworth, Earl Jellicoe; F. C. Dreyer, Sea Heritage (London: Museum Press, 1955); Jellicoe, The Submarine Peril (London: Cassell, 1934); Sir Henry Newbolt, History of the Great War, Naval Operations, vol. 5 (London: Longmans, 1931).
6   Marder, Dreadnought to Scapa Flow, vol. 4, Chapters 4, 5, and 6; A. Temple Patterson, The Jellicoe Papers, 2 vols. (Navy Records Society, 1966, 1968); and Jellicoe: A Biography (London: Macmillan, 1969).
7   DEW, 13, Diary (1 buff notebook), "Anti-Sub Campaign 1917: Dewar's Work with R. G. Henderson on Shipping Figures, and Notes on Admiralty Methods."

misgivings of the Admiralty, merchant marine, and shipowners—is that Naval opposition to convoys was largely "unconscious" in its motive. Preoccupation with the "big battle idea" had obscured the question of commerce protection. To a service which worshipped the gunnery crowd as its *elite*, that question was of secondary importance. Nor was it an exclusively British prejudice. When Jellicoe concluded after Jutland that the Grand Fleet could not move without an extensive destroyer escort, Admiral Scheer similarly refused to deploy the High Seas Fleet without sufficient submarine support. Once they were removed from his control and committed to their own offensive, he refused to move his surface units at all. The German High command at least seems to have sensed that by its gamble on U-boat commerce raiding, Britain could be brought to her knees without a major surface fleet action.

An insufficient study of war among naval officers was one reason for this distortion in perspectives. Serious historical study might have softened professional indifference to "lesser" naval functions including the continuing need for convoying, and might have at least short-circuited many of the specious arguments raised against its introduction before 1917. The retarded development of a naval staff also accounts for the Admiralty's initial ignorance of the facts and its early problems in administering a convoy system once it was adopted.[8] But the convoy question, to place it in perspective, was only one element in a much wider public debate concerning sea-power generally and the proper employment of the Fleet.

Fundamentally, the naval strategy debate of 1917 was an expression of public uneasiness about the stalemate in the North Sea. The "Victory" or "Sea-Heresy" school, led by Admiral Sir Reginald Custance and Winston Churchill, argued that preoccupation with the protection of Britain's sea communications diverted naval minds away from what they believed was the primary object of naval strategy; namely, the decisive destruction of the enemy battle-fleet. Only this would open the way to solutions for other problems, including the U-boats. Doing a double-reverse on his earlier positions, Churchill came down heavily once more on the side of "digging out" the Germans and attacking them in their home bases.[9] Only a few

8   Ibid., 5, "The Defence of Shipping," n.d. Writing during World War II, Dewar remarked on the already overworked Admiralty's reluctance to assume extra burdens. "In the case of independent sailings, that Admiralty had merely to issue instructions as to routing and further responsibility fell on the Master. Convoy on the other hand, placed much great responsibilities on the Admiralty. It also meant a great deal of administrative work which the existing organization could not undertake and which eventually involved the creation of new departments and to some extent, the eclipse of those divisions which had opposed the convoy system."

9   *The Times*, May 7, 1917. "The Real Need of the British Navy," *Sunday Pictorial*, June 24, 1917.

months earlier, in October 1916, he had sparked the first Sea-Heresy debate by suggesting that the search for unnecessary battle was risky, and that until the Germans themselves decided to come out, Britain's best policy was "our silent attack [i.e., the blockade] upon the vital interests of the enemy."[10] He had been strongly endorsed by such well-known journalists as Leyland, Bywater, Hislam, Hurd, and Fiennes, together with the influential *Army and Navy Gazette* and the *Naval and Military Record*, as well as a number of retired Admirals including Sir Nathaniel Bowden and William Henderson.[11] Now, they were quick to challenge Churchill's *volte face* and reaffirm their faith in the blockade as the decisive instrument of Britain's options, especially against an enemy fleet so well protected and unwilling to fight as the High Seas Fleet appeared to be. Although both schools favoured a more offensive Admiralty mentality, the distance otherwise separating the schools was too great to ever be overcome. The efficacy of decisive fleet action regardless of the costs was something the "Defensive School" and most naval professionals—including the Young Turks—simply could not accept.

This was the reasoning which Richmond, in response to a request from Drax (H.M.S. *Blanche*, with the Fifth Battle Squadron) and Lieutenant W. S. Chalmers (who with Roger Bellairs was a member of Beatty's staff in *Lion*), offered as his assessment of the "correct policy" in 1916. The starving and crippling of Germany was the primary strategic object. The destruction of her Fleet was only one means. "If in endeavouring to destroy the German Fleet we run risks which may prejudice our success in the greater object of the destruction of Germany, those risks are too great . . . . Take no risks with the G. F. [sic]. The whole operations all over the world depend upon it."[12] He was angered and bewildered by the "Sea Heretics" influence. It made him "utterly sick" that Custance, as a retired Admiral, could argue that the destruction of the High Seas Fleet would permit the imposition of a close blockade.

> He must either be ignorant of the number of bolt holes in the Frisian coast, or of the potentialities of the modern submarine . . . . He talks as if a naval victory involved the destruction—the entire destruction—of the enemy's fleet. Such a victory has never occurred in history and is far more improbable today.[13]

10 "The War by Land and Sea," *London Magazine*, October 1916.
11 Sir Archibald Hurd (Naval Correspondent, Daily Telegraph), "Sea Heresy, Invasion, and Other Matters," *Fortnightly Review*, December 1916. Gerard Fiennes, "Conditions of a Naval Offensive," *Nineteenth Century and After*, August 1917. Also HEN/2/4, Correspondence with various editors and with A. J. Balfour (First Lord) concerning Admiralty communications with the Press; Henderson to Balfour, November 13, 1916, Balfour to Henderson, November 5, 22, 1916.
12 RIC/1/14, August 29, 1916, in reply to Chalmers and Drax, August 22, 1916.
13 DEW, 6, Richmond to Dewar, May 12, 1917.

Richmond's resentment of the "Victory School" went beyond the
sailor's natural suspicions of journalists. Sydenham's and Custance's
articles were also part of their personal vendetta against Julian Corbett
whose prewar teachings they blamed for the Admiralty's over-
cautious mentality. He was uneasy too about the public attacks on
Jellicoe led by Arthur Hungerford Pollen, the Naval Correspondent to
the *Westminster Gazette* and military feature writer (along with Hil-
laire Belloc) for the influential specialist weekly, *Land and Water*.
Pollen had been one of the Admiralty's most steadfast and respected
supporters. In the immediate aftermath of Jutland, when the Government's ambiguous public announcements had stirred up serious
doubts about the real extent of the British "victory," it was Pollen who
led off a national press campaign in defence of the Grand Fleet's and
Jellicoe's performances. But by April 1917, even he had come to doubt
Jellicoe's ability to continue in office and in company with Custance
had joined the growing chorus of critics.[14] When the Censor stopped
publication of his May 3 *Land and Water* article demanding the
immediate removal of Jellicoe's regime, the result was an immediate
press outcry in which Pollen was backed by the *Telegraph*, *Daily
Sketch*, the *Star*, *Truth*, *New Statesman*, and the *Sunday Times*.
Richmond was disturbed by all this anti-Jellicoe publicity, but he also
recognized that it could be useful if channelled in the right directions.

He had, of course, been searching for a means of exposing naval
deficiencies for some time—through the *Naval Review*, a book, or
perhaps even a postwar public enquiry or Royal Commission.[15] In
June 1915, he had written a series of articles entitled "The Need for
Enquiry" which he instructed his lawyer to release to *The Times* in
the event of his death. The 1917 "Sea Hersy" debate offered a more
immediate opening provided he and his friends could set out a constructive reform programme. Dewar suggested that if he, Richmond,
"and a few others could come to a definite agreement on this point
then we would know the direction on which to write and work. . . .
The first thing that is required is a gospel and apostles to spread it."[16]
The "gospel" they chose was Admiralty organization. Here was an
issue on which all elements concerned with the naval crisis—

14 *Land and Water*, April 17, 1917. Pollen interviewed Jellicoe and Duff on the convoy
    question in early March. Almost a year later, according to Richmond, Pollen
    recalled that Jellicoe had considered convoys to be "impossible" since merchant
    vessels could not keep station. Richmond noted, "Duff shrieked when the word
    'convoy' was mentioned and said he wouldn't listen to any suggestion or give any
    reason for not adopting it." RIC/1/15, Diary, February 28, 1918; also entry July 3,
    1918.
15 DEW, 7, Dewar to Richmond, May 9, 1917. RIC/9/1, Corbett to Richmond, Decem-
    ber 7, 1916; May 23, 30, 1917.
16 DEW, 7, Dewar to Richmond, n.d.

including those not prepared to attack Jellicoe personally—could and did focus.

On April 30, the *Daily Mail*, followed a few days later by *The Times*, launched a theme which Admiral Henderson had contributed: "The present board is a collection of heads of departments all so fully occupied with departmental work that they have no time for the hard thinking that is required in war." The existing difficulties would be overcome by freeing the Sea Lords from their overwhelming administrative responsibilities and reconstituting them as a Board of Strategy, and by assigning supply functions to an entirely separate organization.

These were Richmond's ideas, first expressed to Henderson in private correspondence, and subsequently expanded into a paper entitled 'The Admiralty'' which was widely circulated including a copy to the War Cabinet on February 28, and another to the Prime Minister on May 20, 1917.[17] Stated simply, Richmond favoured restructuring the Admiralty Board as a "real Imperial Board whose duty it is to prepare for war and not be absorbed in administrative work." The existing arrangement whereby virtually everything was channelled through the Chief of the Staff to the First Lord and First Sea Lord made decentralization difficult and operational planning for the future impossible. His remedy was to form a separate Board out of the departments of the Second, Third, and Fourth Sea Lords (Personnel, Materiel, and Supply respectively), "as the Navy and Victualling Boards did in the past." For the operational side, he recommended the appointment of three separate officers, responsible for the main areas of the North Sea and cruiser blockade, the "Outer Seas," and local defence. Each of these officers should be a Lord of the Admiralty. Overriding all of them would be the First Sea Lord as his own Chief of the Staff. Together they would constitute the Board.

It was no coincidence that many others in the Grand Fleet were expressing similar, if not identical, views. Few sea-going officers had much to say for the existing regime at the Admiralty. During the course of their proselytizing, the Young Turks discovered that on this issue they had the sympathies of many senior officers including Roger Keyes, Reginald Tyrwhitt, and Reginald Hall. Beatty criticized the Admiralty for its lack of a planning body and an executive authority capable of rapid decision-making and action. He deplored Jellicoe's resistance to new ideas and his refusal to select bright, capable men. As will be seen, it was with Beatty's encouragement and assistance that the Young Turks managed to press forward some of their ideas for

17 RIC/7/1, Richmond to Henderson, February 14, 1917. H. W. Richmond, "The Admiralty"; copy in DEW, 6, February 22, 1917. The original, in RIC/1/15, is dated February 17, 1917.

offensive operations in the summer and autumn of 1917. In the spring, however, their more immediate concern was the question of War Staff and Admiralty reorganization.

Apart from Richmond's "Admiralty" paper, and Commander Reggie Henderson's briefings about convoys and shipping figures, no *direct* contacts were made between the Young Turks and Lloyd George prior to the latter's Admiralty "visitation" of April 30. Three days earlier, however, while dining with his friend Philip Kerr (then one of the Prime Minister's private secretaries), Admiral Henderson did arrange for Arthur Pollen to prepare a lengthy letter (delivered April 28) urging Lloyd George to acquaint himself with the views of these younger officers.[18] The main purpose of his meetings with Jellicoe was to examine the question of changes in Admiralty organization first hand, particularly the set-up of the War Staff and its effects on the anti-submarine campaign, and also to examine the question of mobilizing the nation's ship-building resources for the production of more anti-submarine vessels. The reorganization scheme,[19] as approved by the War Cabinet only three days after this visit, did bear a direct resemblance to Richmond's principles. Jellicoe, in addition to being First Sea Lord, became Chief of the Naval Staff (C.N.S.), thereby giving the Staff executive as opposed to purely advisory status. He was to be assisted by Oliver as Deputy Chief of the Naval Staff (D.C.N.S.), responsible for the Operations, Mobilization, and Intelligence Divisions and a new Signal Section; and Duff as Assistant Chief of the Naval Staff (A.C.N.S.), who was responsible for the Trade, Anti-Submarine, and Minesweeping Divisions and the Convoy Section (later, Mercantile Movements Division). Both joined the Board as additional Sea Lords. Sir Eric Geddes was also given a seat on the Board as Controller and made responsible for the country's entire ship-building and production resources, both naval and mercantile. Theoretically, his appointment would free the Sea Lords from all problems of administration and supply; a revival, in effect, of the old Navy Board which had been disbanded in 1832 as a result of Sir James Graham's reforms.

Press and public reaction to the changes was generally favourable. But few naval critics were misled especially so long as it was Jellicoe, Oliver, and Duff whose titles were altered. Their attitudes would not change. "The same as before, but with new labels," Beatty noted, "but it seems to please the Critics, which is apparently all that is desired. It is not the system that is wrong, but those that run it."[20] Similarly, as Richmond later pointed out to Lloyd George, "No reor-

18 A. H. Pollen Papers, Pollen to Admiral W. H. Henderson, April 28, 1917; Pollen to
     Philip Kerr (delivered by hand, April 28, 1917).
19 Adm. 1/8489, Order-in-Council, May 19, 1917.
20 Marder, *Dreadnought to Scapa Flow*, vol. 4, p. 179.

ganization . . . can make the smallest difference without changes in the personality."[21] This, indeed, was the crux of the problem, as the Prime Minister was fully aware. But these reforms were only a first step in his wider campaign to revitalize the entire British war effort. The significant point was that the changes announced by Carson in the House of Commons on May 14 had resulted from outside prodding from Lloyd George and public and service criticism, and not, as Jellicoe later claimed, from the Admiralty's self-appraisal.[22] Jellicoe's growing pessimism about the U-boat menace and persistent lack of enthusiasm for convoys convinced Lloyd George that the only effective course was a clean sweep of the whole regime in favour of more energetic men. In this campaign, the primary targets were first Carson, and later Jellicoe.

The Prime Minister's penchant for "sucking the brains of the best men he could get" (Hankey's phrase) inevitably increased friction and Admiralty suspicion. But as he wrote in his memoirs, the urgent situation and the eventual results fully justified his jumping of normal channels:

> freedom of access to independent information is quite compatible with order and due respect for the hierarchy, if that liberty is tactfully and judiciously exercised . . . . There must be no appearance of flouting the men at the top. On the other hand, they must not make it impossible to act without forcing an open disregard for their authority.[23]

His first direct contact with the Young Turks was with Lieutenant-Commander Joseph M. Kenworthy (later, Tenth Baron Strabolgi), a young officer then serving under Richmond in H.M.S. *Commonwealth*. He was brought to the Prime Minister's notice by Sir Herbert Lewis, Parliamentary Secretary to the Board of Education, a mutual friend who had earlier passed Richmond's "Admiralty" paper to the War Cabinet. Personal audiences were arranged by Lord Northcliffe as a result of three conversations with Kenworthy, during one of which Sir Edward Hulton of the *Daily Sketch* was also present. In two private interviews with Lloyd George (May 14 and 20), Kenworthy laid out the complaints of the officers he claimed to represent.[24] Though he later denied being a "mere messenger," there can be little doubt he was really his Captain's mouthpiece. His detailed criticism of organization, ideas, and specific personalities was pure Richmond. His exceedingly frank endorsement of Richmond and Dewar and recounting of their treatment during the war corroborated reports the

21 RIC/1/15, Diary, May 12, June 5, 1917.
22 Jellicoe, *The Crisis of the Naval War*, vol. 2 (London: Cassell, 1920).
23 Lloyd George, *War Memoirs*, vol. 3, p. 115.
24 Lieutenant-Commander J. M. Kenworthy, *Sailors, Statesmen and Others: An Autobiography* (London: Rich and Cowan, 1933), pp. 69-83.

Prime Minister had evidently already heard. They may also have had a double-edged effect. Richmond himself had little real respect for Kenworthy's mind or abilities, then or later. He therefore ensured that Kenworthy was suitably armed for his second meeting with some "carefully drawn up memoranda" including another copy of the "Admiralty" paper.[25] But aside from these important interviews and several private conversations with the editors of the *Daily Mail* and *Daily News*, Kenworthy's role in the Young Turks' revolt was limited. He was later appointed to the new Plans Division for a period of five months.

One immediate result of the Lloyd George interviews was Dewar's recall from the wilderness. Since leaving the *Prince of Wales* in late 1915, he had languished in a series of backwater commands—the *Marshal Ney*, a monitor in the Dover Patrol, and then the *Roberts*, another monitor more or less permanently fixed at Gorleston as part of the Yarmouth defences. Richmond's fall from grace at the Admiralty had also killed off his hopes of a War Staff berth. Now Dewar was assigned to the Operations Division to write weekly Appreciations of the Naval Situation for the War Cabinet. The summons to come to the First Sea Lord's office on May 18 came as a complete surprise, though in offering Dewar the new post Jellicoe made his personal feelings clear: "I hear you are a person with strong views and if your views do not agree with mine, of course yours will have to give way." As Dewar explained to Richmond, it was obvious "there is a mystery surrounding the appointment. I do not believe Jellicoe wants me there but that I have been foisted on him in some peculiar way."[26] Richmond and Henderson were both very pessimistic about Dewar's chances of being fully used. Whatever Jellicoe thought of Dewar personally, he resented even more this irksome innovation in Cabinet-Admiralty relations. Not surprisingly, the weekly Appreciations were carefully supervised to guard against "independent" opinions.[27]

Richmond's own audience with the Prime Minister was arranged by Admiral Henderson who approached Lloyd George, Milner, and Northcliffe during the last two weeks of May. What transpired at a meeting in Milner's office on May 25 is unknown; however, Henderson obviously made full use again of Richmond's criticisms of the new Admiralty structure and Jellicoe's shortcomings as a strategist,

25 RIC/1/15, Diary, May 15, 1917. RIC/7/14, Kenworthy to Richmond, June 20, July 27, September 15, October 16, 1917.

26 RIC/7/14, Dewar to Richmond, May 19, 1917. Dewar notes in his *Navy from Within*, pp. 212-13, that he was ordered to report to Jellicoe on May 10 and was interviewed the next day. His papers show, however, that the meeting occurred sometime between Kenworthy's two audiences of May 14 and 20.

27 RIC/7/1, Richmond to Henderson, May 25, 1917; RIC/7/4, Henderson to Richmond, May 23, 29, 1917. Also, DEW, 13, Diary, "Admiralty Staff Work—Notes for Cabinet Appreciations, Summer, 1917."

tactician, and administrator.[28] It was agreed that Richmond himself should be made available to both the Prime Minister and the First Lord on Tuesday and Wednesday, June 5 and 6, for frank discussions, including "specific proposals both as to the reconstitution of the Admiralty and the changes in its principal personnel."

Anxious to exploit fully this rare opportunity, Richmond took leave from his ship (H.M.S. *Conqueror*, Second Battle Squadron Grand Fleet, to which he had transferred in late April) and spent the weekend of June 2 and 3 in London carefully preparing his case with Dewar and Henderson. Ideas which they had previously discussed were expanded, and together with specific recommendations for changes in key senior positions, were incorporated into a detailed scheme for Admiralty reconstruction.[29] They aimed at the "absolute" separation of Operations from Administration. Only this, Richmond argued, would counter the tendency for over-centralization which had resulted in a heavy overloading of the First Sea Lord and C.O.S. and encouraged the retention of less than qualified staff officers at the lower levels.

> Matters have thus come to such a pitch that young officers with ideas are in despair, and yet, still hoping to get their schemes considered, they send them to the Commander-in-Chief of the Grand Fleet, where they receive sympathy from that broad-minded officer. But this is most improper. He has other work to do in commanding the Fleet, and it is the duty of the Admiralty Staff to deal with these things.[30]

Turning to personalities, Richmond delivered an unrestrained attack on Jellicoe whose defensive and unimaginative mentality made him totally unsuitable to be First Sea Lord. He "had failed at Jutland. This has surely impressed itself upon him by now. It has not made him bolder. And while he was a defensive tactician, he is now a still more defensive strategist." This was patently unfair, as Richmond knew only too well. But perhaps he felt obliged to overstate the case for the benefit of his audience. A reading of Richmond's correspondence in the immediate post-Jutland period, while revealing a personal dislike of Jellicoe and obvious admiration of Beatty, also clearly indicates that he was prepared to blame the Grand Fleet's performance on factors over which he knew Jellicoe had no control.[31]

28 HEN/2/5, Henderson to Lloyd George, May 16, June 3; to Milner, May 20; to Northcliffe, May 27; C. Smith (Secretary to Lord Milner) to Henderson, May 22, 1917. RIC/7/1, Richmond to Henderson, May 19, 25, 1917.
29 RIC/1/15, Diary, June 8, 1917.
30 Ibid., June 5, 1917. "Notes prepared and used in conversation with Mr. Lloyd George on June 5. Repeated on June 6 and expanded considerably in conversation with Sir E. Carson."
31 RIC/7/1, Richmond to Henderson, June 21, 1916.

In a similar vein, Richmond also attacked his old friend Admiral
Oliver who, worn out by two and a half years as C.O.S., was even more
cautious and unwilling to trust his subordinates. "He burnt his fin-
gers at Gallipoli and is, I should imagine, averse from any further
operations involving risk."

The solution, Richmond concluded, with all the boldness he
could command, was to replace the lot, "re-organize the office on
fighting lines," and open up "the channels of thought of the officers at
sea." This could be done by creating a Board of Admiralty (Operations) and a Navy Board (Administration). The former could be
headed by the First Sea Lord (Admiral Rosslyn Wemyss) aided by an
Assistant C.O.S. responsible for plans. There would also be three Sea
Lords (Richmond called them First, Second, and Third, actually
meaning Second, Third, and Fourth); the First (Duff) responsible for
Local Defence of trade; the Second (Hope) for the Grand Fleet and all
North Sea Squadrons including Dover, Dunkirk, and the Tenth
Cruiser Squadron; and the Third (H. Sinclair) for overseas trade, mili-
tary operations in the East, etc. Administration would be handled
exclusively by the Navy Board, headed by a First Commissioner
(Browning) who would be aided by eight other Commissioners.
Should Sir Edward Carson hesitate to make such a clean sweep, he too
could be replaced as First Lord by Roch or Smuts. As for his own
future, Richmond immodestly added:

> Relieve me and let me work with Hankey for a time until the change
> comes, to get *au fait* with political situation, etc. Put me in your
> office for the time, but not near the Admiralty, nor in any connection
> with them. Let me have Dewar's assistance and that of the officers
> whom I w^d name.

These same ideas, suitably modified, were put to Carson on the
morning of June 6. This time, Richmond bid for command of an active
force, preferably one operating off the Syrian coast. However, he
added, if he was needed at the Admiralty, he would be of most use as
Deputy Chief of Staff.[32]

How much Richmond's brand of frank speaking was appreciated
can only be guessed at. Little of his message was new to Lloyd George,
though it did corroborate other opinions and confirmed feelings already well developed in his own mind. Corbett reported that when
questioned by Hankey as to whether he had been impressed with
Richmond's testimony, the Prime Minister had replied, "Partly yes
and partly no." Carson's biographer does not mention the Richmond
interview though the First Lord's slighting reference to another young
officer's visit (probably Kenworthy) and his comment "I thought him

---

32 RIC/1/15, Diary, June 8, 1917. Reference is to Walter F. Roch (Lib. MP, Pembroke-
     shire, 1908-1918), a member of the Royal Commission on the Dardanelles.

rather a fool" suggests that Richmond's forwardness and presumption was seen as just that! Richmond was not overly optimistic, although he did inform Corbett that the Carson interview "had been very satisfactory."[33]

On his return to the Grand Fleet, Richmond wisely advised Beatty of his two visits, only to discover that the Commander-in-Chief had himself talked with Carson and was fully aware of what had transpired. He too, Richmond noted with satisfaction, was pushing for similar reforms.[34]

In one important respect, Lloyd George was directly influenced by Richmond's thinking, namely, the formation of a special Admiralty section to investigate and formulate long-range plans for offensive operations. Like Churchill, he had seen his own pet projects—such as offensive actions in the German Bight, and bombardments of the Flanders harbours—cut to pieces by expert naval opinion. He did not contest these judgments, but now recognized that so long as the Operations Staff was swamped by the minutiae of day-to-day activities, there was no possibility that more realistic schemes would ever receive systematic study. Shortly after Richmond's visit, Carson made the same point to Jellicoe. It was clear, from his conversations with the Prime Minister and other Cabinet members, that the Admiralty's weaknesses on this point were the source of much of the evident public dissatisfaction.

> Without entering into the question how far such criticism is justified, if at all, it is clear . . . that we ought to be in a position to silence it by being able to state positively that the possibility of taking the offensive at sea is continually under review by the Naval Staff, and that Staff plans worked out in detail are constantly being put forward and considered. . . . I am so impressed with the amount of labour that day-to-day events impose on the Naval Staff, that I am now convinced that there may not be some truth in this idea.[35]

Carson therefore recommended the creation of a special planning section under the Director of Operations made up of "officers who have shown special capacity for devising and working out plans for the offensive." His further suggestion that the notices to senior officers concerning the new section should include the encouragement of junior officers to submit plans and propositions for study bears the unmistakable imprint of Richmond's influence.

33 Ibid., June 15, 1917. Also, CP, Diary, June 8, 1917.
34 RIC/1/15, Diary, June 27, 1917. Beatty's thoughts on "Admiralty Organization" are printed in Marder, *Dreadnought to Scapa Flow*, vol. 4, pp. 180-81. These "Notes for Conference" were probably drawn up for his talks with Jellicoe on or about July 19. Also Bellairs Papers, "Notes for Conferences, July 1917—March 1918," (Marder Papers, selections from notes, Directorate of History, National Defence Head Quarters, Ottawa, M.62).
35 Adm. 1/8489, Carson to Jellicoe, June 7, 1917.

Predictably, Jellicoe opposed both the idea of the new section and the suggestion that Richmond head it. His reply to Carson clearly illustrates his scepticism and resentment:

> I have been informed that the Prime Minister sent for Captain Richmond (I presume in connection with this proposition), and I presume that this was done at the instigation of Colonel Hankey. I do not make any comment on this interference with Admiralty administration by Colonel Hankey if I am correct in my assumption, but if Captain Richmond is likely to be suitable in other respects, I think that he would probably be useful at the Admiralty, and I therefore suggest his appointment as a preliminary step.[36]

But Richmond was not recalled. Not until April 1918 did he return to the Admiralty, and then it was as Director of Training.

Jellicoe was even less enthusiastic about the whole principle of a planning section. He opposed the use of younger minds because of their inexperience and lack of detailed knowledge about current operations and availability of resources. Such officers' proposals "would merely waste the time of the more senior members of the War Staff." Instead, he suggested to Carson that "the Operations Division should be strengthened by the appointment of the officers you suggest, leaving the D.O.D., the D.C.N.S.and myself more time to study the possibilities of offensives." An additional remark that he had "been considering possible offensives ever since the commencement of the war and I am fairly certain that there is no possible operation . . . which has not been considered a great many times" clearly reveals his myopic view of the new section's potential.

Not surprisingly, when the Planning Section was formed on July 16, it became in Dewar's words, "the Cinderella of the Naval Staff." Headed by Captain Dudley Pound,[37] its membership was limited to Dewar and Major Halliday, R.M.L.I., V.C. In practice, Dewar could contribute only a few days' work each week since his responsibilities for the Weekly Appreciation continued into late August. Jellicoe's hostility had effectively crippled the new section, giving further credence to his critics' claims that meaningful reform could only come from a clean sweep of the naval high command, beginning with Carson and Jellicoe.

The move to ease Carson out of the Admiralty forced Lloyd George to draw heavily on all his reserves of political courage and cunning. The First Lord had powerful friends in Parliament, many of

---

36 Ibid., Jellicoe to Carson, June 9, 1917; and Jellicoe's "Remarks Attached," n.d.
37 Formerly Captain of H.M.S. *Colossus* (4th Battle Squadron) and later (1939-1943) First Sea Lord. "Not an ideal choice" in Marder's view. He had great capacities for hard work and good judgment, but he was also "too rigid, too methodical, too much a master of detail . . . a supreme centralizer." *Dreadnought to Scapa Flow*, vol. 4, p. 197,

whom saw the criticisms of Admiralty inefficiency as a roundabout attack on his position as leader of the Ulster Unionists. Moreover, Carson refused to desert Jellicoe. He stood firm on his previous declaration to protect the Admirals from "amateur strategists" and, at a luncheon on May 17 honouring the U.S. Navy, publicly reaffirmed his confidence in Jellicoe. The danger was that continued hostilities with Carson might well fuse the naval and Irish questions.[38] It was this fearsome prospect which led Lloyd George into his temporary alliance with Field Marshal Sir Douglas Haig who was then in London for discussions on the forthcoming Flanders offensive (the Battle of Third Ypres).

Lord Beaverbrook has suggested that the "real motives" behind Haig's London intrigues against Carson and Jellicoe in June 1917 ("a well-organized, thoroughly considered and widespread campaign") lay "mainly in diverting the lightning from striking at himself." But there were genuine grounds for Haig's concern about Jellicoe's ability to carry on and this, as much as anything else, drew him together with Lloyd George. Jellicoe's astonishing performance at the June 20 meeting of the Committee on War Policy played directly into their hands. His utterly pessimistic prediction about Britain's ability to even continue the war in 1918 because of the U-boat campaign was, in Marder's words, "a first-class gaffe," and his refusal to sanction naval attacks against Ostende and Zeebrugge in support of the planned Paaschendaele drive (justified though he was in this case from a purely naval viewpoint), only discredited him further.[39] Haig's subsequent talks with senior political leaders on June 25 and 26, including the celebrated Downing Street breakfast party at which Lloyd George, Milner, Haig, and Eric Geddes discussed Admiralty inefficiency, resulted in the decision to replace Carson. Just who should succeed him, however, caused difficulties. Lloyd George considered several possibilities including Hankey and General Sir William Robertson, the Chief of Imperial General Staff (C.I.G.S.). The latter was approached by Haig that same day, but not surprisingly he refused.[40]

38 Beaverbrook, Men and Power, 1917-1918 (London: Hutchinson, 1956), pp. 145-46 et seq; A. M. Gollin, Proconsul in Politics: A Study of Lord Milner in Opposition and in Power [London: Blond, 1964], pp. 420-23.

39 Robert Blake, ed., The Private Papers of Douglas Haig, 1914-1919 (London, Eyre and Spottiswoode, 1952), pp. 240-41. Jellicoe Papers, vol. 2, memorandum "Attacking Ostende and Zeebrugge," June 18, 1917; also Jellicoe to Beatty, June 30, 1917. See also Captain Stephen Roskill, "The U-Boat Campaign of 1917 and 3rd Ypres," R.U.S.I. (October 1959).

40 Blake, Haig, p. 244. A month earlier, Robertson had highly recommended Richmond to Lloyd George's attention: "He is evidently a keen student of naval history and warfare, and is described to me as 'the first naval officer who seems to have a General Staff mind.' I gather that he would be a great asset at the Admiralty—on the War Staff—and probably far more use than in a ship." Beaverbrook, Men and Power, p. 167. A summary of the main talks, June 10-25, is given

The solution finally came from Lord Milner who also provided the necessary force of character to drive it through.

The so-called "Milner Plan" was simple and politically effective. Geddes would take over as First Lord, and Carson would be elevated to the War Cabinet from where he could also assist Bonar Law in controlling an increasingly difficult House of Commons. Lloyd George quickly accepted the plan, though Bonar Law and Curzon agreed to it only on condition of Carson's full approval. Neither relished a Tory rebellion headed by the Ulster leader. The same fear held Lloyd George in the grips of indecision for the next two weeks. But for Milner's steadying hand, he might well have backed off altogether. Milner finally intervened on July 16 emphasizing the urgency of the situation; further hesitation would only play into the hands of the Government's critics. The changes were announced the following day. "Lord Milner's resolution," his biographer writes, "had determined the issue. Where Lloyd George, Bonar Law, Curzon and the others had refused to proceed, he caused decisions to be taken."[41]

Some of that willingness to chance the political consequences of Carson's removal was conditioned by the evidence and proddings of the Young Turks. Admiral Henderson consciously tried to impress a sense of urgency on Lloyd George, even going so far as to suggest "a line of least resistance" with respect to Jellicoe's future. He could be promoted into honourific insignificance as C-in-C of all Anglo-French naval forces in the Mediterranean. or as the first chief of a combined Admiralty-War Office "Imperial" war staff.[42] His advice to Milner was somewhat more frank:

> there is no absolute necessity to find a line of least resistance as I suggested in my letter to Mr. Lloyd George; it partakes too much of the whitewashing order . . . .
> If difficulties are encountered, they can be met by a threat to immediately investigate the causes of the failure at Jutland.

In fact, Henderson continued, the list of instances on which the Admiralty had suppressed information from the Cabinet and public was a lengthy one: " 'the Goeben,' 'Cressy,' 'Hogue,' . . . 'Audacious' whose name is not I believe even now allowed to be mentioned by the censor, Coronel, Jutland, the secret C.M. on Troubridge, *ad infinitum.*"[43] But Milner politely declined this form of blackmail and, from this point, kept his distance from Henderson.[44]

in Paul Guinn, *British Strategy and Politics 1914 to 1918* (London: Oxford University Press, 1965), pp. 249-56.

41 Gollin, *Proconsul in Politics*, pp. 438-40.

42 HEN/2/9, Henderson to Lloyd George, June 23, 24, 1917.

43 Ibid., Henderson to Milner, June 29, 1917 (two separate letters on same date).

44 Ibid., Henderson to Milner, July 1, 8; Milner to Henderson, July 9; Major Hugh C. Thornton (Secretary to Milner) to Henderson, July 2, 1917.

These exchanges did at least result in an invitation for Dewar to meet the Prime Minister on July 10. Whether or not such a meeting took place is unknown. Nor is there any direct evidence that Dewar's written comments affected the final form of the new Planning Section when it was established on July 16. In any case, the Admiralty sensed his influence, for as a result of these activities and his submission to the War Cabinet (at Geddes' invitation) of an uncensored Weekly Appreciation, Jellicoe ordered his immediate posting to H.M.S. *Sapphire*, a cruiser then lying in Colombo harbour with her boilers out of action. Dewar blocked this side-tracking only by appealing (via his wife and Sir Herbert Lewis) to the Prime Minister's good offices.[45]

That Lloyd George held back from an immediate assault on Jellicoe following Carson's removal reflects his determination to forestall further controversy which could undermine Geddes' prospects as the new First Lord. "Geddes knew," Lloyd George wrote in his memoirs, "that Jellicoe had the confidence of the senior officers in the Navy, and that it would therefore be a distinct advantage to secure his cooperation if that were at all possible."[46] For the moment, further change was limited to those areas where Geddes' reputation for businesslike efficiency ensured the willing, if not entirely enthusiastic, support of the whole service.

On arrival at the Admiralty, Geddes was astonished at the casualness of the Board's methods. Richmond's father-in-law, Sir Hugh Bell, a director of the North Eastern Railway and close friend of Geddes, reported the First Lord's impressions of "vagueness, the lack of preparation and the absence of minutes, the amateurishness of the whole concern."[47] Much of this he corrected by such basic and long overdue innovations as regular meetings, printed agenda, recorded minutes, and the routine circulation of information. Personnel changes included the appointment, as Controller, of Sir Alan Anderson formerly of the Orient Line. Graham Greene, the Permanent Secretary of the Admiralty since 1911, was replaced by his Assistant, Sir Oswyn Murray. Lloyd George had been long convinced that Graham Greene's power, "the enervating influence of the secretariat," far exceeded his constituted authority and accounted for much of the Admiralty's administrative inertia. The Prime Minister was heavily influenced in this by Hankey, and by Richmond and Henderson who, considering the *Naval Review*'s earlier misfortunes, had no difficulty in documenting their case. Carson had resisted the pressure to remove Graham Greene. Geddes did not hesitate. He simply requested the Secretary's resignation without offering any reasons.

45 DEW, 7, Dewar to Richmond August 19, September 12, 1917. Also, DEW, 13, Diary, August 15, 1917.
46 Lloyd George, *War Memoirs*, vol. 3, pp. 119-20.
47 RIC/1/15, Diary, August 16, 1917.

Whatever misgivings Jellicoe had about Graham Greene's treatment, he saw in it the seeds of his own destruction, for Lloyd George's eyes were also turned towards his own immediate supports—the Second Sea Lord, Admiral Sir Cecil Burney, and the D.C.N.S., Henry Oliver. Since Burney's successor was to be Admiral Wemyss, whom Richmond had been pushing as Jellicoe's replacement, it is difficult, as Jellicoe's biographer suggests, "to avoid the suspicion that the Premier was now making a preliminary move that would at least facilitate his taking that advice if in due course he decided to do so."[48] Unable to defend Burney, Jellicoe was forced to let him go with great reluctance. He was totally unsuitable as Second Sea Lord and as acting First Sea Lord in the event of Jellicoe's absence: "no single flag officer afloat supports him," Geddes reported.[49] But Jellicoe dug in his heels in Oliver's case, threatening to resign if his D.C.N.S. was relieved. Since this was something neither Lloyd George nor Geddes were willing to risk, for the moment, a compromise was reached. Oliver stayed on while Burney was removed (in October he was appointed C-in-C, Rosyth, Coast of Scotland) to make room for Wemyss who took up his new duties in September. By then, external events altered the situation drastically, necessitating a new look at the whole question of Admiralty management.

Throughout the summer and autumn of 1917, public criticisms of the anti-submarine campaign and the impossibility of preventing isolated enemy raids on Allied shipping brought on a new round of the naval strategy debate. Once again, various pet schemes were trotted out by professional and amateur strategists alike. Even Winston Churchill re-entered the field with his well-worn plans for a close blockade and the capture of advanced bases in the Heligoland Bight. With Lloyd George's backing, he also pushed for naval bombardments of Germany's naval bases. And again, they met the same fate. Jellicoe simply refused to countenance any scheme which might jeopardize the fighting strength or freedom of manoeuvre of the Grand Fleet. In his view, there was simply no scope for offensive options beyond providing the necessary covering forces to ensure the maximum efficiency of the mine barrages. That even these were extended during this period owed a great deal to American pressure and resources.

An interesting example of the Admiralty's response to such suggestions was its handling of a widely discussed proposal for containing the U-boats in their bases by blocking the main German rivers and Baltic exits. On Jellicoe's instructions, Section 16 (Plan-

48 Patterson, *Jellicoe*, p. 190.
49 *Jellicoe Papers*, vol. 2, no. 76, Jellicoe to Beatty, August 4, 1917; no. 78 as quoted by Madden to Jellicoe, August 7, 1917; and no. 87, Burney to Jellicoe, September 6, 1917.

ning) was constituted as a special committee under Sir Henry Jackson's chairmanship to consider the project's feasibility and to draw up detailed plans.[50] This was the "special project" for which Kenworthy was temporarily assigned to the Planning section. But from beginning to end, the entire effort was a deliberate exercise in futility. A detailed projection of vast proportions involving some four hundred ships was submitted on August 18. Beyond noting that success would depend heavily on "favourable weather and good luck," Admiral Jackson concluded that the scheme was entirely impracticable. German defences and the risks to Britain in ships and command of the North Sea, should it fail, made it too risky. Kenneth Dewar came to the same conclusion, but for very differend reasons: "I do not say it is impossible but I don't think we have the capacity to carry it out. The Admiralty and Staff are the weak links in the chain." As he reported to Richmond, Jackson's dilettantish approach to the whole investigation gave cause for scepticism: "I am under the impression that J.R.J. [sic] asked Jackson to take a part in it because he can be absolutely depended upon to come to no decision."[51] Admiral Beatty confided to Richmond that this was also his impression of the First Sea Lord's purpose:

> their object . . . was purely negative . . . to prove the impossibility of doing anything. J. had said they had to produce something to shew that the matter had been considered, but to B. it was evident that they were proceeding upon a scale they knew to be impossible in order to demonstrate its impracticability.[52]

This attitude was also revealed in Jellicoe's request for a separate Grand Fleet committee under Admiral Sir Charles Madden (his brother-in-law and former C.O.S. in *Iron Duke*, then commanding First Battle Squadron) to study the same question. When this group reached conclusions almost identical to Jackson's, Beatty was moved to call in Richmond for an entirely different approach, about which more will be said presently.

The whole affair served only to reinforce the misgivings which many held about the Jellicoe regime. By late 1917, unrest amongst senior officers of the Grand Fleet mounted until there was, in Professor Marder's words, "a distinctly revolutionary atmosphere at Scapa and Rosyth." Richmond and the Young Turks no less than many others were utterly frustrated by the Admiralty's imperviousness to

---

50 Adm. Ms., "Blocking the German Harbours to Effectually Prevent the Exit of Their Submarines to the Sea." See also Jellicoe, *The Crisis of the Naval War*, pp. 172-73. Admiral Jackson, the former First Sea Lord, was then Admiral President at Greenwich.

51 DEW, 6, Enclosure, Dewar to Richmond, September 12, 1917. Original, Dewar to Bellairs is dated July 19, 1917. Also, DEW, 12, Diary, (Cabinet Appreciations, Summer 1917), and (Anti-Submarine Campaign, 1917), September 1917.

52 RIC/1/15, Diary, August 25, 1917.

suggestion. But they were equally uncomfortable about the increasingly vociferous though not always enlightened chorus, mainly from outside the Navy, which demanded offensive action whatever the risks.

Much of this ill-defined uneasiness with the war at sea can be traced to a general failure to appreciate the extent to which convoys had already begun to cripple U-boat operations, and indeed, Germany's ability to wage war anywhere. The Young Turks were no different in this respect. Although they had been in the forefront of the convoy advocates, they nonetheless considered it a defensive means. They, too, wanted offensive alternatives by which pressure could be relieved and the enemy's submarine and surface forces destroyed or stifled at the source, their home bases. Indeed the central feature of their thinking was this awareness of the extent to which the U-boat threat was hamstringing offensive possibilities everywhere else. It was this which led Richmond to reiterate his plans for Syrian coastal operations. In addition to aiding the Palestine campaign by drawing off Turkish troops, they would also have the effect of "defending the Mediterranean trade by drawing submarines to defend the Syrian coast." Ironically, this latter effect was the very point which Jellicoe used in rejecting the plan; "such an operation was very hazardous owing to submarines." It made little difference that Beatty and the War Office considered the project worthy of further study.[53] Beatty also supported Richmond's proposals for an Adriatic offensive designed to curtail U-boat actions in the Mediterranean and possibly force Austria to redeploy forces away from Italy. Again the Admiralty's reception was cool, although the subject was inconclusively discussed by Jellicoe during a Grand Fleet conference in August and an Allied Naval Conference early in September.[54] Richmond blamed not only "the timid British school of strategists" but the Allied War Council whose obstinancy and "moral cowardice" was blinding them to any maritime alternative to their army generals' collective commitment to attrition and more land offensives.

> The average man sees nothing but a clash of two fleets—in line ahead of course—in the North Sea, and imagines this to be the one and only aim of naval war. . . .
> What hay the Germans would make of us if they had our superiority and united all the navies of the world in their own hands![55]

53 Ibid., "Proposal for the Employment of a Detached Force on the Coast of Syria," April 26, 1917. (Also parts included in his conversation with the Prime Minister, June 5, 1917). See also Diary entries, March 14, September 16, 1917.
54 Ibid., September 16, 22, 1917. *Jellicoe Papers* vol. 2, no. 83, "Notes of Conference held on board H.M.S. *Queen Elizabeth*, 24 Aug. 1917"; no. 86, "Report of the Naval Conference of Powers united against Germany, 4 & 5 September 1917."
55 DEW, 6, Richmond to Dewar, December 7, 1917; also November 1917.

One of Richmond's offensive schemes (drawn up in part with the assistance of Captain Murray Sueter of the Royal Naval Air Service [R.N.A.S.]) deserves some explanation, for it reveals just the conceptual originality and daring which he criticized the Jellicoe regime for lacking. The plan also demonstrates a highly adaptive ability with respect to recent technology, a trait which Richmond's own critics accused him of lacking in later years. The concept was simple. It involved a massive surprise attack by torpedo-carrying aircraft and flying boats against the ships of the High Seas Fleet at anchor in their home bases. With these major surface forces immobilized it would be possible to move against the U-boats at their sources. The High Seas Fleet was the U-boats' strategic umbrella. It tied down British destroyers to protect the Grand Fleet, and it provided local German superiority in the Bight making Allied blocking and mining operations there risky and only temporary in their effect. Thus, immobilization of the High Seas Fleet was the key to successful trade defence and offensive operations alike.[56]

When Beatty invited Richmond to undertake an investigation into possible blocking operations separate from those of the Jackson and Madden committees, he drew up a mining plan which was then expanded into a comprehensive scheme including the suggestion of an air attack.[57] This was shown to Jellicoe during a conference aboard H.M.S. Queen Elizabeth on August 24. Aware that Richmond's name was anathema at the Admiralty ("I shan't tell him [Jellicoe] you had anything to do with it as your name stinks at the Admiralty"), Beatty presented the paper as the work of another Grand Fleet committee. But the idea fell flat; both Jellicoe and Rear-Admiral George Hope (Director of Operations) had doubts about torpedo aircraft capabilities and the likelihood of ever finding the enemy fleet in Schillig Roads. Moreover, they argued, the requisite materiel was simply not available.[58] Richmond flatly rejected all these arguments: "As to the air attack, J. had said they couldn't get there. I told Beatty this was rubbish—escort them, and they can get there. Send them by night—good Lord! Can the Fleet do nothing?"[59]

Working with Flight Commander Frederick J. Rutland of the R.N.A.S., an ardent advocate of similar schemes since the early phases of the war, Richmond set out to make his case.[60] The result was an

56 RIC/1/15, Diary, "Additional Notes on the Naval Offensive, August 1917."
57 Ibid., August 16, 21, and 23, 1917.
58 Adm. 137/1420. Also, *Jellicoe Papers*, vol. 2, no. 83.
59 RIC/1/15, Diary, August 25, 1917.
60 Adm. 137/1938. Proposals for Attack on the German Fleet at its Base (1915-1917), undated unsigned document (pp. 10) with Ms. heading "*Rutland cum Jutland*: Considerations of an attack by Torpedo Planes on the High Seas Fleet." Also, RIC/1/15, September 4, 1917. Copy of letter, Richmond to Bellairs, with notes for Commander-in-Chief.

outline plan for a combined offensive aimed at "blocking by mines and obstacles, and preventing the enemy from removing the obstacles by using aircraft against the ships in his harbour which we cannot otherwise attack." Successful sea-plane attacks against Cuxhaven in December 1914, against ships in the Sea of Marmora in September 1915, as well as Germany's successful use of aircraft against Riga and Oesel Island in the Baltic satisfied them that the plan was technically feasible. In detail, it involved the use of 121 of the newest type of torpedo aircraft (90 mph, 3-1/4 to 4 hour radius of action). Transported to within an hour of Wilhelmshaven by eight merchant vessels, each fitted with equipment to carry and launch the aircraft, and blisters and paravanes (against U-boats and mines), they would attack their targets in three waves of forty machines each. The fact that the Fifth Sea Lord (Director of Air Services) endorsed the plan—"An attack at dawn on ships at anchor in Cuxhaven, Schillig Roads, or other enemy bases could hardly fail to have results"—suggested that the plan merited at least further study.[61] Beatty agreed and forwarded it to the Admiralty on September 11 with his admonition that "every endeavour should be made to be ready for operations by the Spring of 1918." He repeated this advice to Geddes a fortnight later and to the Admiralty on October 7 and 10.[62]

Predictably, nothing came of the scheme. The Admiralty argued that neither the merchant vessels of the type required nor facilities for their conversion were available. There were also doubts that the Air Service had the necessary skills and that the torpedoes then in use had sufficient range and destructive power. Fundamentally, the Admiralty did not believe that "under existing circumstances, the air presents the greatest facilities for conducting an offensive against the enemy's vessels and bases."[63] This was a strong argument, for those "existing circumstances" included only one aircraft carrier (H.M.S. *Argus*) capable of carrying twenty torpedo aircraft. Of sea-plane carriers, only *Furious* and *Campania* had decks sufficiently long. Between them they could accommodate eleven aircraft armed with thirty-three 112-pound bombs. The fact was that the problem of naval air materiel was one whose roots went back to the first years of the war, or earlier. There was simply no way that these problems of policy and foresight could be remedied overnight. Moreover, and perhaps not insignificantly, the Beatty-Richmond scheme coincided with one of the Admiralty's own plans involving a bombing attack by thirty

61 Adm. 1/8486. "Considerations of an Attack by Torpedo Planes on the High Seas Fleet," C.-in-C. Grand Fleet to Admiralty, September 11, 1917. Adm. 137/1936. Grand Fleet to Admiralty, August 26, 1917; Paine's minute of August 30, 1917.
62 Adm. 116/1805, Beatty to Geddes, September 25, 1917. Adm. 1/8486, Beatty to Admiralty, October 7, 10, 1917.
63 Ibid., Admiralty to Beatty, October 20, 1917.

machines on the Bremen submarine pens.[64] But even this modest number proved impossible to attain because of the Admiralty's own reluctance to divert sea-planes from coastal anti-submarine patrols. The point was that the same defensive mentality which tied an excessive number of escort vessels to the Grand Fleet undercut even this suggestion. Improvisation, on the lines suggested by Richmond, Rutland, and Beatty may well have succeeded. Risks were definitely involved, but not to the Battle Squadrons of the Grand Fleet. It was this important distinction which suggests that Richmond's proposals for more aggressive use of air-power, as well as his Adriatic and Mediterranean schemes, deserved much more serious treatment than they received.

Not all of the Young Turks' proposals fell into this category. When Dewar presented a plan for a broad-front sustained naval offensive which involved the inshore positioning of light craft and submarines supported by heavier units of the Grand Fleet—in effect, a close-blockade for raising the rate of U-boat kills—Beatty was understandably sceptical both of the idea and Dewar.[65] Drax agreed and did not pull his punches when Beatty asked his opinion. The plan *was* impracticable, at least at first glance. It reflected Dewar's usual enthusiasm ("I think Dewar being a Scotsman, has gone too thoroughly at his problem"). Still, Drax was prepared to support his general ideas; they were bold and needed more careful analysis insofar as they rested on his personal assessment that by late 1917 it seemed highly unlikely the High Seas Fleet would ever come out again. He was convinced that the Germans appreciated only too well the deterrent value of their fleet and the freedom of manoeuvre it gave their U-boats. Drax counselled for distinctions between "impossible" schemes and those which would be "very difficult." "We have allowed the cancer to grow for so long," he told Beatty, "that nothing short of the very difficult can be hoped for. It is a case of desperate need and desperate measures."[66]

Drax's response is interesting particularly as it illustrates Beatty's encouragement of even unorthodox views from his younger officers. Also, by that time, Drax had come to believe that Beatty was the Navy's (and the Young Turks') only hope.[67] "No doubt Providence will save us," he wrote to Beatty's secretary, Paymaster Frank T. Spickernell, "We need hardly hope the Admiralty will." Beatty alone,

64 Cab. 27/9. First Meeting of the War Cabinet Air Raids Committee, October 1, 1917. Paper submitted by Jellicoe, "Offensive Bombing Operations from Seaplane Carriers."
65 DEW, 4, "A Naval Offensive Against Germany," September 20, 1917; DEW, 2, Drax to Dewar, September 22, 1917; DEW, 3, Dewar to Churchill, November 1, 1926.
66 R. Bellairs Papers, Drax to Beatty, September 20, 1917.
67 RIC/7/4, Drax to Richmond, July 5, 6; August 16; September 20, 28, 29, 1917. Also RIC/1/7, Drax to Spickernell, August 11, 1917.

as C-in-C, had the power for "recommending (or demanding) the selection of those men who alone can save the situation." Spickernell went even further by suggesting that no solution would come until Beatty was made First Sea Lord. Richmond tended to agree:

> in Beatty we have the makings of a real statesman. The question of whether he should not be at Whitehall intrudes itself more than ever upon me. The second rate man we have there now will never see further than his own interests, nor than the purely naval defensive operations. He cannot see things on a big scale.[68]

Others were coming to similar conclusions. From August on, the press, led by Northcliffe's *Daily Mail*, mounted a steady assault on the Admiralty and Jellicoe. Writing to Admiral Henderson in late August, Drax reported that he and Richmond were convinced that "salvation" would only be possible when the Admiralty, once cleared of all "the old gang," was put under the charge of the "Intellectuals." "It is a pathetic thing," he wrote, "to have to descend to the lowest forms of journalism in our efforts to save the country from disaster."[69] Once again, Admiral Henderson acted as the link between the editorial writers and the voices of dissent in the Fleet. He was supported by other retired officers, notably Admiral Custance in the press and Commander Carlyon Bellairs in Parliament. Criticisms of the Admiralty, such as that carried by the *Daily Mail* of October 23, bear the unmistakable imprint of Richmond's language and ideas. More evidence was needed, the Editor suggested,

> that caution is not the cover for lack of wisdom, absence of inspiration, failure to think in terms of war. It is not pleasing to reflect that the Baltic has become a German lake and that the submarine cannot be attacked at its source. We are lulled to sleep with assurances that the submarine menace has been got under. It has not been got under, and we are dwelling in a fool's paradise if we think it has .... And the question we have to ask is the question we have asked repeatedly. Is the best genius and are the best methods at our command being employed?

In late October the Press campaign reached a climax. The almost total destruction on October 17 of a Bergen-to-Lerwick convoy and two escorting destroyers produced a series of *Daily Mail* diatribes so vindictive in their assaults on Jellicoe that he contemplated legal action under the Defence of the Realm Act.[70] Even Beatty called the attacks villainous and "against all fair play." The First Sea Lord could not reply, he wrote, "and as long as he occupies the important and

68 RIC/1/15, Diary, September 22, 1917.
69 DEW, 2, Drax to Henderson, August 29, 1917.
70 *Daily Mail*, October 19, 22, 23, 25, 30; November 2, 1917. *Jellicoe Papers*, vol. 2, no. 93, F. E. Smith, Attorney General to Geddes, October 31, 1917. Adm. 116/1805, F. E. Smith to Jellicoe, November 5, 1917.

responsible position he does, he is entitled to some measure of protection against the Press."[71] Moreover, if Jellicoe fell victim to press and political pressures, public confidence in the higher command of the entire navy could be undermined. If the press campaign continued, he added, "nobody is safe and nobody will be trusted."

Richmond was no less disturbed by the *Daily Mail's* excesses. He drew a sharp distinction between his own desire for reform and the motives of men like Custance and Carlyon Bellairs who sought to attack Jellicoe personally as a Fisher man. Nor did he mince words in expressing his uneasiness about Henderson's contribution to the incident. He was highly critical of his older colleague's indiscretion:

> Candidly, I thought your D.M. letter was a mistake and would have been better unwritten. The facts about the North Sea convoy weren't sufficiently known for any criticism to be passed upon it, and the references to the battle of Jutland don't seem to me apposite. Your position as a sober critic has been so well established, that I think an outburst like that weakens it.[72]

The ultimate effects of the press agitation are difficult to measure with any precision. It could only have confirmed what Lloyd George and Geddes already knew. An awareness of the breakdown in Admiralty-Grand Fleet communications, and the handicapping effects of "personal factors" (meaning the basic lack of sympathy between Beatty and Jellicoe) had already convinced Geddes to make Wemyss Deputy First Sea Lord as a means of improving "cooperation between the Grand Fleet, the Harwich Force, and the Admiralty."[73]

Wemyss' appointment, however, was only one aspect of a wider programme of vitally important organizational reform through which Geddes hoped to decentralize the Board's business and strengthen the Naval Staff by specifically fixing responsibilities and procedures.[74] Basically, the Admiralty was restructured under two new governing bodies—the Operations and the Maintenance Committees. In addition there was to be a Naval Plans Division, a Training Division, and a Mercantile Movements Division. Superficially at least, Jellicoe accepted these changes, though he was very unhappy to see these new Divisions (particularly the elevation of Plans from a Section under the

71 Chalmers, *Beatty*, p. 321.
72 RIC/7/1, Richmond to Henderson, November 7, 1917. Corbett had the same opinion; "He will be marked as a man with grievances and will carry no weight." RIC/9/1, Corbett to Richmond, October 28, 1917.
73 Lloyd George, *War Memoirs*, vol. 3, p. 120.
74 *Jellicoe Papers*, vol. 2, no. 89. Memorandum on Admiralty Organization with Attached Chart, by Sir Eric Geddes, September 10, 1917. The Operations Committee consisted of the First Sea Lord, Deputy First Sea Lord, D.C.N.S., A.C.N.S., and Fifth Sea Lord. Directors of Trade, Mercantile Movements and Minesweeping, and Anti-Submarine Divisions were placed under its supervision. The maintenance Committee consisted of the Second, Third, Fourth Sea Lords, Controller, Civil Lord, Financial Secretary, and Fifth Sea Lord if required.

control of Operations) especially since it was Geddes' intention to place them all under Wemyss' direct control. Geddes' further decision, made without any reference to Jellicoe, to appoint Rear-Admiral Roger Keyes (a personal friend of Wemyss) as the new Director of Plans (D. of P.) did nothing to ease the tension between the two men.

In the end Jellicoe had his own way, for although the Plans Division was formed, it was placed under Oliver's general supervision. On Jellicoe's instructions, Keyes' terms of reference provided that he consult closely with the Director of Operations before any proposals were submitted to Oliver and the First Sea Lord. Wemyss retained control of only the Training and Staff Duties Division. As Deputy First Sea Lord, he also carried the Second Sea Lord's responsibilities for personnel matters. On the basis of his own suggestion, these duties were taken over on September 27 by Vice-Admiral Sir H. Leopold Heath, thereby supposedly allowing Wemyss to concentrate exclusively on staff work. But Jellicoe's refusal to transfer any real powers made the position of Deputy First Sea Lord largely meaningless, and Wemyss' efforts to smooth out relations by personal talks with Jellicoe achieved nothing.

By December 1917 their relations were strained to the limit over the question of the Dover Barrage and its obvious porosity to enemy submarines. Strongly backed by Keyes and Dewar, and by evidence from Intelligence, Wemyss proposed that Admiral Bacon, chief architect of the Barrage and then commanding at Dover, should be relieved. Jellicoe, ever loyal to his old friends, simply refused, raising for Wemyss the inevitable question of whether or not he could stay on at the Admiralty.[75] By then, however, Geddes had made his decision to remove Jellicoe and, on December 22, offered Wemyss the opportunity to take his place.[76]

Obviously, the decision was neither abruptly nor easily arrived at. Geddes' relations with Jellicoe had been strained for months. Jellicoe's pessimism and obstinate circumvention of the First Lord's attempts at Admiralty decentralization were now compounded by evidence of his serious physical and mental exhaustion.[77] Finally, the tragic sinkings of two Scandanavian convoys, the disappointing re-

75 Lady Wester Wemyss, *The Life and Letters of Lord Wester Wemyss* (London, Eyre and Spottiswoode, 1935), p. 367.

76 Dewar believed that the immediate cause of Jellicoe's dismissal was the Bacon question. DEW, 6, A. C. Dewar to K. G. B. Dewar, October 27, 1917; November 17, 1960. "Archie" Dewar received his information from the Director of Statistics (Beharriel), a close associate of Geddes.

77 Jellicoe's run-down condition was in Newbolt's view the decisive factor. See *Naval Operations*, vol. 5, p. 203. Also Lord Salter, *Memoirs of a Public Servant*, p. 89; Hankey, *Supreme Command*, vol. 2, p. 66. For fuller discussions of Jellicoe's "condition" see Captain S. W. Roskill, "The Dismissal of Admiral Jellicoe," *Journal of Contemporary History*, 1 (October 1966), 69-93; Marder, *Dreadnought to Scapa Flow*, vol. 4, pp. 329-31; Temple Patterson, *Jellicoe*, pp. 177-80.

sults of Vice-Admiral Napier's action in the Heligoland Bight on November 17, and the question of Bacon and the Dover Barrage all combined to shatter what was left of Jellicoe's public image. Still Geddes hesitated to sack him; "it was a matter which could only come disagreeably to him, however it was put," Wemyss wrote in his memoirs, "and I know that Geddes, hating the job, did it in a manner which sudden though it was, he considered the best for him and all others concerned." Jellicoe also detected the First Lord's deep reluctance; he saw the guiding hands of Northcliffe and Lloyd George behind the decision.[78] Though Geddes, in a statement prepared for the Commons, explicitly denied the influence of outside pressures, it nevertheless seems clear that prolonged press criticism was a powerful element in forcing the pace of the whole process.

The Young Turks had reason to be pleased. Richmond's observation that "One obstacle to a successful war is now out of the way" proved largely correct. Jellicoe's firing was quickly consolidated by the removal of most of his colleagues, including Oliver and Bacon. But while the Young Turks and the press rejoiced, the Navy generally was shocked. Jellicoe was deluged with expressions of sympathy and concern including a short-lived threat by the other Sea Lords to resign *en masse*. Even Beatty and Wemyss, like others who understood why Jellicoe had to go, were agreed that the manner of his removal was highly distasteful in the final event. Few aspects of modern British naval history make for such appallingly unpleasant reading; it is hardly surprising therefore that the Young Turks, as important catalytic agents in the entire process, were viewed as pariahs in the years to come. Those who rose to the top in the aftermath of the storm that ruined Jellicoe knew the most about the part played by the Young Turks. Once the crisis of 1917 had passed, it was their methods and not their motives that were best remembered.

78 *Jellicoe Papers*, vol. 2, no. 102. "Jellicoe's account of the circumstances leading up to his dismissal from the post of First Sea Lord."

5

The Wemyss Regime: Great Expectations Unfulfilled (1918-1919)

If Geddes' choice for the new First Sea Lord needed justification, it lay in the fact that Wemyss survived the upheavals of December 1917 virtually unscathed. The appointment of this "Court sailor," an officer of undoubted charm and grace but otherwise not possessed of unusual abilities, occasioned more surprise, perhaps, than any deep anxiety or widespread concern in the Navy. Some senior officers accused him of being too eager to assume Jellicoe's mantle. Others, worried about his possible indebtedness to the politicians, doubted he could ever be his own man. Beatty spoke for many when he wrote to Jellicoe: "What experience Wemyss has to run the complex and great machine I do not know but I fear for the future."[1] Wemyss had never held a principal command afloat or any senior administrative post; nor was he a gunnery or torpedo specialist. Nothing in his record suggested outstanding qualities as a thinker or strategist. What did, however, interest Geddes was Wemyss' reputation as a manager of men. His close friend, Roger Keyes, advised the First Lord that "if he wanted someone who could get the right sort of people about him, back them through thick and thin, accept any amount of responsibility, and never get rattled or worried, Wemyss was his man."[2] The trauma of Jellicoe's dismissal demanded a successor capable of quickly healing sensitive wounds and resurrecting the Admiralty's status in the eyes of the public, the Government, and the

1 Jellicoe Papers, vol 2, no. 105(i), Beatty to Jellicoe, December 27, 1917.
2 Admiral Sir Roger Keyes, The Naval Memoirs of Admiral of the Fleet Sir Roger Keyes, 2 vols. (London: Butterworth, 1934-1935), vol. 2, pp. 108-109.

82

Grand Fleet. A naval statesman was needed and Wemyss, by virtue of his background and temperament, was the man of the moment.

As a relative newcomer to Admiralty politics, he was untainted by binding loyalties to any faction. Lady Wemyss records that she had accepted his initial Admiralty appointment in 1917 with apprehension and foreboding: "she dreaded the Admiralty, which during the war had proved the grave of so many reputations, and the spirit of intrigue which ever since Fisher's reign had clung to its walls."[3] But Wemyss was a man of the world. A member of one of Scotland's oldest aristocratic families and an old and trusted friend of King George V, he moved easily in London's political, diplomatic, and court circles. His fluency in French and extensive contacts with officers in the French and Italian navies were important attributes at a time when Allied naval cooperation was increasing. Popular, polished, and casually at ease with seniors and juniors alike, he was willing and able to talk with his civilian and Army counterparts. In this respect, Wemyss' performance in daily War Cabinet sessions contrasts markedly with his predecessors'. Compared to their more exclusive professional perspectives, Wemyss' instinctive feel for the workings of the political mind almost suggests that he was cast in the mould of an eighteenth-century sailor-statesman.

The same was true of his relationship with his closest professional advisers. By carefully defining responsibility and delegating authority, he instilled a new sense of confidence and initiative in the Board and Naval Staff. Under the terms of the organizational changes announced on January 14,[4] all responsibility for administrative work was removed from the First Sea Lord, the D.C.N.S., and the A.C.N.S., and handed over to the Deputy First Sea Lord. Wemyss was left free to concentrate on naval policy and operational planning. For the first time, the First Sea Lord was C.N.S. in every sense. "Teamwork," Wemyss later wrote, was the basis of his success:

> The Staff Lords and their various Directors of Divisions very soon realised that I trusted them and expected them to assume responsibility, and they "played up" accordingly. I myself avoided all detail. The results were better and quicker even than I had hoped for, and decisions were now reached quickly and with everybody's knowledge, whereas before the rage for secrecy had resulted in confusion, overlapping and clumsy work.[5]

3   Wemyss, Wester Wemyss, p. 362.
4   Wemyss Papers (Selections contained in A. J. Marder Papers, D. History, Ottawa),
    MS, "Account of Admiral Wemyss' Career in the Admiralty from September 1917,"
    n.d. Under these arrangements, duties were distributed as follows: C.N.S.—the
    Intelligence, Training, and Staff Duties, and later in June 1918, Naval Artillery and
    Torpedo Divisions. Deputy First Sea Lord—Operations (Foreign) and general pol-
    icy. D.C.N.S.—Operations (Home), Air, Signals, and Plans Division. A.C.N.S.—
    Anti-submarine, Mercantile Movements, Minesweeping, and Trade.
5   Wemyss, Wester Wemyss, pp. 369-70.

Generally, this expression of self-satisfaction was warranted: a decidedly improved atmosphere at the Admiralty was evident to many contemporary observers. But Wemyss's success was also less complete than he claimed, particularly when it came to his thinking on strategy and operational policy. His record here was much less impressive.

By January of 1918, the major policy decisions of the war had been taken and, in that, Wemyss was fortunate to reap what others had sown. As Deputy First Sea Lord, he had actively supported Keyes and the work of the Plans Division on the Dover Straits problem. His continued backing of Keyes and personal commitment to the preparations for the famous raid and blocking operations against the German submarine bases at Zeebrugge and Ostend (April 23, 1918) contributed to its success, such as it was. But Zeebrugge aside, Wemyss was as strategically unadventurous as his predecessor and this had a direct bearing on the effectiveness of Plans Division as a "thinking" body after January 1918.

The Division produced useful studies on convoy problems and considered possible counters to innovations in the enemy's attack methods. Friendly relations were also established with the American Planning Section in London and joint schemes for the defence of Atlantic convoys were developed. Much of this work was precautionary in nature and never put into effect; its usefulness is therefore difficult to assess.[6] What is clear, however, is that far too much of the Division's time was devoted to the problem of its own survival. Dewar, who was Assistant Director of the Division for two years, conceded that its performance throughout 1918 was considerably improved over the previous year; "but better than bad is not necessarily good, and right up to the end of the war it seemed almost impossible to obtain these rapid decisions on which success so largely depends." The Division's newness was part of the problem. "Reorganising the fire brigade in the middle of a fire has never been an easy task."[7] Time was needed to establish effective channels of communication and to accustom staff personnel in their use. Dewar had pinpointed this fault soon after his arrival at the Admiralty in June 1917.[8] Even under Wemyss, senior staff officers, particularly Fremantle (D.C.N.S.) and Duff (A.C.N.S.), kept to their accustomed ways and virtually ignored Plans in their decision making.

6 DEW, 2, Papers relating to Plans Division and Admiralty Business (1918). Also, Adm. 137/2708, Papers on Anti-Submarine Policy in the Immediate Future, by Plans Division March 28, 1918. Joint Appreciation by the British and American Planning Divisions, March 23, 1918.
7 Dewar, *Navy from Within*, p. 248.
8 DEW, 6, Dewar to Richmond, June 20, 1917. Also, DEW, 13, "The Problem of Naval Command" n.d., from an unpublished Ms for a book on Naval Reform.

Many of the Plans Division's submissions were simply ignored. Decisions, if taken, were often made without further reference to the Division. Frequently they were simply endorsed and sent to file. Insofar as this was an organizational problem, Richmond as Director of Training and Staff Duties (D.T.S.D.) would iron out many of the defects during the summer of 1918. But his investigations showed that out of sixty-four Plans submissions, twenty-four were approved, eight disappeared, and four remained in circulation. Of the other twenty-eight, Plans remained completely in the dark about their final fates.[9] There were other factors—what Dewar called "pseudo-disciplinary inhibitions—which blocked "advisory channels of communications between the First Sea Lord and members of the War Staff."[10] Richmond was more specific. His examination revealed an "almost incomprehensible" situation.

> The attitude of Duff, Fremantle and Hope towards proposals made by Plans is invariably one of self defence or of opposition to suggestions—a sort of resentment that anyone should suggest that there remained any way of improving upon the current measures. There is no attempt whatever to examine the proposals, to seek in every quarter for help which will further our ends in this war. The spirit is a petty, departmental, jealous one.[11]

These criticisms of the Naval Staff's senior members as well as other similar indictments contained in Richmond's diaries of the period are unfair and overly severe. More than anything, they reflect his utter frustration with the fact that in the essential areas of strategic policy, the Wemyss regime was as conservative as Jellicoe's. The fact was Wemyss had accepted the basic position of the distant blockade. Offensive proposals, whatever their source or however brilliant, would never be sanctioned so long as they jeopardized the Grand Fleet's numerical superiority. According to Admiral Fremantle:

> much as we at the Admiralty, and the officers and men of the Grand Fleet and the Harwich and Dover forces, desired them, neither they nor we could devise any practical measures and we had to content ourselves with following the practice of our predecessors in the fleets of Earl St. Vincent, Nelson, Cornwallis, and Collingwood by retaining our principal naval strength in the best strategical positions available and in a state of continuous readiness for action, always hoping that the effect of our blockade might be to tempt the

9 DEW, 2, Papers Relating to the Work of Plans Division (1918). These included "The Anti-Submarine Campaign of 1918," "Deep Minefields in the Kattegat," "Raids in the Downs, Dover Straits, etc.," "Holland and the War," "Scandinavian Convoys and Covering Force." Also, RIC/1/15, July 3, 1918. Adm. 1/8524, Memo by J. R. Fremantle for Re-organization of Plans Division, May 3, 1918; Richmond's Minute, May 8, 1918.
10 DEW, 13, "The Problem of Naval Command."
11 RIC/1/15, Diary, July 3, 1918.

enemy to come out and try conclusions with us, as it did at the Battle
of Trafalgar, and, in the meanwhile, resting assured that the control
of the sea communications was in our hands.[12]

Professor Marder has endorsed this general view; "judged by the
ultimate and decisive results," the Royal Navy was completely successful in performing its basic tasks. Those who opposed it, he
suggests, were victims of a general misreading of British naval history
and tradition which glorified the concept of decisive action. Yet, he
adds, "It is difficult to see where the Fleet could have done more,
within the confines of the accepted strategy [Marder's emphasis],
except perhaps, as the Young Turks had continually urged, in a more
aggressive and imaginative use of aircraft and in amphibious operations in the Mediterranean theatre."[13]

This latter point bears emphasizing for it sets the Young Turks
apart. They argued their case on a sound historical basis, and *within
the parameters* of this "accepted strategy." They advocated
supplementary or complementary offensive schemes in those areas
where they were possible and of positive advantage and, it should be
added, at a time when Germany's collapse was far from obvious.

As soon as Wemyss took office, Richmond resubmitted his
Mediterranean proposals including one for limited amphibious operations on the Adriatic coast aimed at tying down Austria in the south
and alleviating pressure on the western front where all the signs
pointed to a German spring offensive. Command of the Adriatic
would be established through torpedo-plane attacks and the use of
mines, nets, and bombardments to neutralize the Austrian fleet's
main base at Pola. U-boat operations in the Mediterranean would be
interrupted as would the Austrians' lines of communications across
the Venetian Plains. Once again, the Admiralty rejected these plans
because of the high risks to personnel and materiel. Richmond was
convinced that risks of another kind were feared. Wemyss and company were evidently content to ride out the war letting time and the
blockade bring the Central Powers to their knees. "The fact is they're
determined to do nothing . . . ," he noted, "I begin to think that though
we have changed names we retain all the characteristics of the old
gang of do-nothings."[14] Fremantle was the main obstacle, although
Richmond also blamed the Air Service's senior spokesmen—
Commodore Godfrey M. Paine and Rear-Admiral Mark Kerr—for their
lack of vision. "Both of them seem more intent on holding on to their

12 Admiral Sir Sydney Robert Fremantle, *My Naval Career, 1880-1928* (London: Hutch-
    ison, 1949), pp. 245-46.
13 Marder, *Dreadnought to Scapa Flow*, vol. 5, pp. 299, 307.
14 RIC/1/15, Diary, March 4, 1918.

jobs, keeping Churchill out, and not risking anything that might compromise themselves than on forcing the pace of the war."[15]

The Air Council delivered similar arguments against a Plans Division submission on "Aerial Operations Against Ships and Bases" which was developed by Dewar and Wing Commander Malone of the R.N.A.S.[16] The authors conceded that materiel deficiencies had indeed killed any chances for air strikes in 1918. However, if their "tentative programme" of careful preparations was begun by the end of March, some openings for major aerial offensives in the spring of 1919 might be found. The argument of materiel shortages which had prevented any serious exploitation of earlier British air initiatives at Cuxhaven in 1914 and in the Sea of Marmora in 1915 could not be repeated indefinitely.[17]

Beatty supported this reasoning and added his voice to the demand for naval air strikes in the spring. His optimism rested largely on the newly designed "Cuckoo" torpedo whose quick development and procurement he urged on grounds that it "might profoundly influence the whole campaign and especially our ability to carry out an active offensive on the High Seas Fleet." The Admiralty disagreed. Geddes, Wemyss, Fremantle, and Duff replied that materiel shortages—specifically insufficient carriers and aircraft to maintain sustained bombings of enemy targets—prejudiced any likelihood of success. Beatty accepted this point insofar as it pertained to bombing operations. He was not convinced, however, that the requirement for "sustained" pressure applied in the case of airborne torpedo attacks.[18] As it turned out, this disagreement was largely academic. Contracting and developmental problems, as well as foot-dragging by the Air Staff itself, so delayed delivery of the "Cuckoos" to Grand Fleet units that hope for their use before the war ended was thoroughly destroyed.[19]

15 Ibid., March 14, 1918. Refers to Commodore (later Rear-Admiral Sir) Godfrey M. Paine, Fifth Sea Lord and Director of the Naval Air Service (1917-18). Rear-Admiral Mark E. F. Kerr. In January 1918, with the amalgamation of the Royal Naval Air Service and Royal Flying Corps, he became Deputy Chief of the Air Staff (temporary rank, Major-General).

16 Ibid., "Memorandum prepared by Plans Division, by Commander Dewar and Wing Commander Malone. Rejected by Air Council." Wing Commander (later Lieutenant-Colonel) Cecil L'Estrange Malone. He had served as the air representative on Richmond's Grand Fleet committee on the blocking of German harbours.

17 Adm. 137/2709, Proposed Operations for Torpedo Planes, by K. Dewar, October 8, 1918. RIC/1/15, Diary, March 14, 1918.

18 Bellairs Papers, "Notes on [Beatty's] Conversation with Captain Dewar, Assistant Director of Plans," March 7, 1918; "Discussion at Admiralty on Occasion of Visit to C.-in-C. Grand Fleet, on 2nd-3rd January, 1918." Also, Fremantle Papers, Beatty to Admiralty, March 7, 1918 with enclosure, "Notes on Conference with the Deputy Chief of the Naval Staff," February 25, 1918.

19 Adm. Ms., Memorandum D.C.N.S. (Fremantle) to C.N.S. (Wemyss), March 1, 1918.

Not surprisingly, Plans Division was the only Admiralty department which received Beatty's ideas enthusiastically. Since the summer of 1917, relations between Dewar and the C-in-C's personal staff,
particularly William Chalmers and Roger Bellairs, were very close.
Prompted by Drax, Chalmers had written to Dewar, just before his
appointment to Plans, to suggest how they might open new channels
of communication. "It will now be a great relief to know there is
someone at Whitehall with whom we can exchange views....by
acting as a lever you may be able to diminish the vast amount of
correspondence which accumulates before we succeed in getting the
most obvious things through."[20] This suggests that Chalmers was less
interested in Dewar's ideas than in using him to forward the Grand
Fleet's influence, or more precisely, that of the C-in-C's staff. Indeed,
Drax warned Dewar that Beatty and Bellairs were not altogether
impressed with what they knew of his thinking, especially his
schemes for using Grand Fleet destroyers more offensively in North
Sea anti-submarine roles. But Drax's intercessions evidently removed
most of Beatty's doubts and, by early 1918, Dewar was working in
close step with Bellairs and Chalmers.[21]

In March, Dewar took the opportunity of a visit to the Grand Fleet
to further disarm the Commander-in-Chief. The immediate reason for
his visit was the problem of the Scandinavian convoys and the constant threat of a major German raid. Earlier conferences had revealed
serious differences between Wemyss, Fremantle, and Beatty on this
issue. The Naval Staff, determined to maintain maximum traffic,
favoured direct sailing routes across the North Sea. They argued that
chances of German interception could be minimized by alternating
intervals between convoys. Beatty disagreed. Moreover, the Admiralty plan entailed a steady drain on Grand Fleet covering forces. Two
or more escort groups were required at sea on many occasions. Plans
Division advocated rerouting the convoys further north. This would
reduce the volume of traffic though, as Dewar and Fuller showed, by
only two per cent. But there would be a significant reduction in the
risks to Beatty's covering forces while the chances of isolating and
intercepting enemy raiding forces would be increased. The Admiralty
solution also presupposed the receipt of accurate and timely intelligence about the High Seas Fleet. Beatty simply doubted the Admiralty's ability to provide it. Dewar's warning that insufficient attention
had been given to the fact that "the High Seas Fleet could go to sea
without making any wireless signals" seems to have convinced him

20 DEW, 2, Admiral W. S. Chalmers (H.M.S. *Lion*) to Dewar, May 25, 1917.
21 Ibid., Papers Relating to Plans Division and Admiralty Business (1918), "Use of
    Grand Fleet Destroyers on the Northern Patrol," June 13, 1918; "Memorandum on
    Anti-Submarine Operations in the North Sea," July 27, 1918. Also, Chalmers to
    Dewar, March 14, April 18, 1918; Drax to Dewar, March 3, 1918.

to support Plans' suggestion that once the Northern Barrage was finished all convoys should sail behind its protection. This would also permit the withdrawal of the battleship supporting force. But the plan was rejected by Fremantle. As Beatty told Dewar, the Naval Staff had decided "that the vital question was the quick carrying on of trade across the North Sea to and from Scandinavia, and that this must take precedence, the risks to the supporting forces being accepted."[22] It was against this background that Scheer's April 24 sortie of the High Seas Fleet—the last of the war—took place. Bad intelligence on both sides and a serious mechanical breakdown in the German battle-cruiser *Moltke* resulted in an indecisive action. It was enough to confirm Beatty's misgivings and to substantiate Plans Division's logic.

The whole affair illustrates the gulf that separated the Admiralty and the Grand Fleet. Beatty's back-door approach undoubtedly contributed to the suspicion with which Plans Division's schemes were received. The fact is Beatty never did establish a sympathetic understanding with the new First Sea Lord nor a sound working relationship with his senior staff officers.

It has been assumed that just the opposite was the case; that a vast improvement in Admiralty-Grand Fleet relations followed Jellicoe's sacking and that Wemyss' connection with Beatty was one of overall cordiality and friendliness; that they were on a "My dear Rosy"—"My dear David" footing at least until the latter stages of the war. These superficial indications notwithstanding—the meanings of these salutations can be taken several ways[23]—a state of tension and personal rivalry did exist between the two men which even Wemyss' careful efforts could not overcome. Beatty had ambitions. As Commander-in-Chief Grand Fleet he saw himself as the predominant influence in the making of naval policy and as such the *de facto* executive head of the Navy.[24] In effect, he sought to extend the practice which, since Jellicoe's days, had seen final control of operational policy, the power of ultimate veto, exercised from the bridge of *Iron Duke* or *Queen Elizabeth*. Certainly this accords with Chalmers' perception of the relationship between Beatty's staff and the Plans Division. Later, the bitter disappointment of not meeting the High Seas Fleet in a major

22 Bellairs Papers, "Notes on Conversation with Captain Dewar," March 7, 1918.
23 Wemyss Papers. More often than not, Beatty's letters began, "My Dear First Sea Lord," or "My Dear C.N.S." Wemyss usually resorted to "My Dear C-in-C G.F." Taken in context, "My Dear Rosy" usually prefaced a less-than-cordial exchange.
24 Ibid., Confidential Minute: A III 79, Question of Combining Office of First [Sea] Lord and Commander-in-Chief, February 6, 1918, sgd. O.M. [O. Murray]. Also RIC/1/15, Diary, January 30, 1919. "I told Bellairs to warn Beatty against such ambitions. It was impossible. The Comr-in Ch [*sic*] of the Army had been got rid of, we had never had a C.-in-C. at the Adty [*sic*] and it was impossible to suppose that such a constitutional innovation would be listened to."

action would exacerbate the problem, as did Wemyss' subsequent involvement in the Armistice and Paris Peace Treaty negotiations. These prolonged Wemyss' tenure of office thereby bringing the tension out into the open in the summer of 1919. From the beginning, Beatty had considered Wemyss' appointment a temporary measure.[25] Wemyss, on the other hand, was determined to resurrect the Admiralty's status. He resented Beatty's popularity and the assumption that the Admiralty was responsible for all the mistakes of the war. He was not prepared to account for his predecessors' actions, nor was he convinced that Beatty and the Grand Fleet held a monopoly on the answers to existing problems. In response to agitation to have Beatty appointed First Sea Lord, Wemyss complained bitterly to Eric Geddes that "the Grand Fleet is not the only pebble on the beach." Wemyss' determination to exercise his full powers as C.N.S., particularly in the area of Admiralty, Naval Staff, and Grand Fleet appointments, was the real basis of Beatty's feud with him.[26]

The implications of all this for the Young Turks and their crusade for naval reform were clear. Wemyss displayed considerable moral courage in employing them at all, but his willingness to exploit their ideas and talents was always tempered by his distaste for their methods and their connections with Beatty. Like it or not, the Young Turks' futures were very much hitched to Beatty's. Until such time as he became First Sea Lord, their position within the Admiralty was one of sufferance only.

Richmond was recalled to the Admiralty in April 1918 to serve as Director of the Training and Staff Duties Division. Few other posts could have suited his talents so well or offered such wide scope for reform in the areas of Staff organization and service education generally. But the promise was never fulfilled, at least not in 1918. Richmond's talents were unequal to the task. He would achieve highly significant results in rounding out the organizational flaws in the Naval Staff. However, his efforts to improve officer education brought him face to face with the realities of Admiralty politics. Conflicts of personality and ideas, and the natural resistance of the Admiralty system to radical change brought him opposition, suspicion, and eventually, a return posting to the Grand Fleet.

The Training appointment resulted from Beatty's and Geddes' interventions only two weeks after Jellicoe's dismissal. Beatty unsuccessfully tried to get Richmond appointed Director of Overseas Operations.[27] His failure probably had as much to do with Wemyss' resist-

25 RIC/1/15, Diary, January 17, 1918.
26 Wemyss Papers, Wemyss to First Lord, March 10, 1918. "Ms Account of Admiral Wemyss Career in the Admiralty from Sep. 1917" n.d.
27 RIC/1/15, Diary, January 4, 17; March 25, 1918. Also, Adm. 116/1804, Admiralty Section of Private Correspondence of Sir Eric Geddes, First Lord of the Admiralty,

ing attempts to pack the new structure with men not of his own choosing as with any mistrust of Richmond's ideas. Richmond attributed it to the latter: "Evidently, all the folk at the top are against my views. Dewar tells me that there seems to be an opinion that I have wild offensive schemes." Kenworthy also warned him

> that the allegations against myself were due to Roger Keyes as much as anyone, and amounted to saying that I was a visionary and unpractical. This amuses me. A "visionary" is habitually antagonistic to the dull, unimaginative creatures who know nothing of war.[28]

Nevertheless, Richmond continued to hope that he would eventually receive a major Operations appointment. Assured of Beatty's support and, like him, convinced that Wemyss' administration was transitional, he preferred to bide his time with the Grand Fleet, preparing for his recall. He was, therefore, understandably hesitant when it was suggested that he head Training Division. Unwilling to cut himself off from active duty "for a job of that kind," he was equally aware that his room for manoeuvre would be severely curtailed. If anything, his ideas on educational reform were considered even more revolutionary than his strategic ones.

> My views are not the views of the All-Highest. They would not hear of Osborne being shut down, or older entry as a permanency. And finally (and what is sufficient by itself), the Admiralty haven't the least intention of having me there, whether I ask or not. They don't want "visionaries," "revolutionaries," "paper men" and so forth.[29]

This was the nub of the problem. While Geddes and Beatty viewed Richmond's appointment as a mandate for greater things to come, especially with respect to postwar developments,[30] Richmond recognized that the post would be both difficult and dangerous. He knew that Fremantle, Everett (Naval Secretary to the First Lord), Sir Oswyn Murray, and probably Wemyss, were all opposed to his coming.[31] It is difficult to say how much this opposition was related to

1917-18. Correspondence with Sir David Beatty, files A/232/s (Beatty's attitude towards Admiralty Organization), and A/441-447 (Correspondence November 1917-June 1918).

28 RIC/1/15, Diary, February 7, 1918.

29 Ibid., March 14, 1918.

30 Ibid., March 31, 1918. During the course of an interview with Beatty, Richmond was informed of the intention to send him to Training. "He [Beatty] was very pleasant, and said he had hoped I should have got on to the operations side, particularly Mediterranean work, on which I had concentrated so much attention. That I had no choice but must go where I was wanted, and that he thought I should do useful work there in the Staff Directorship. It looks like a bigger business than it appeared on first sight."

31 Ibid., March 14, 15, 1918. His primary source of information and encouragement within the Naval Staff, in addition to Dewar, was Commander (later Captain) Guy P. Bigg-Wither, a member of Training Division and from June 1918, its Assistant Director.

Richmond's personality and reputation, and how much to inside knowledge of his part in upsetting the Jellicoe regime. But certainly, his strong views on the existing educational system—in particular his opposition to Osborne and the principle of "early entry"—were sufficient grounds for many senior officers. "With such opposition," Richmond asked himself, "what good could I do. If 1st Sea Lord is agin [sic] me, I am helpless."[32]

Wemyss had cause to keep Richmond at a distance. Richmond had, after all, been a key factor in Wemyss' own appointment. Moreover, he strongly opposed Richmond's ideas on education, and was, as he told Beatty, prepared to employ him only on certain conditions:

> I shall be on the lookout and shall not let him run off the rails. This will be all the easier as I intend him to work directly under me. Now that I have withdrawn all opposition and got him here, I realise that there are things in which he will be of the greatest value in helping us.[33]

Richmond's chances for success were therefore prejudiced from the start. Neither Geddes nor Wemyss pulled their punches in warning him of the circumstances. The First Lord advised him "to walk like Agag." Wemyss warned that both his "wild-cat" schemes and the efforts of his supporters to bring him back had "put everyone's back up." Richmond at least appreciated their honesty:

> [Wemyss] was most admirably open and shewed what a thorough gentleman he is in telling me everything about his own attitude towards me, his opposition to my appointment and his final decision that I should come—for, he said, "I felt it was rather small to oppose your coming because a lot of people wanted you to come, and ridiculous to be afraid of you: if I could not keep you in hand, I should not be worth much."[34]

Wemyss' apprehensiveness was understandable, for Richmond was not one to compromise his principles. That is, he was too straight, even naïve, in his conceptions of what was right and what was possible. He had "influence" with Beatty, and tried to use it to gain "power" under Wemyss. His failure to make the distinction between the two led, inevitably, to a steady deterioration in his relationship with his Admiralty superiors.

32 Ibid., March 27, 1918. Richmond suspected that Everett's opposition was based not only on their opposing views on education: "I feel pretty sure Everett connects me with Henderson's letter to the *Daily Mail* and credits me with wishing to get rid of Jellicoe. If he does the former, he's wrong, but he's right in guessing my views about the victory of Jutland. Carson is such an untrustworthy individual that he (C.) may have told Ev all about my conversation."
33 Wemyss Papers (1918-1919), Wemyss to Beatty, March 26, 1918.
34 RIC/1/15, April 15, 1918.

In one highly important area at least—the consolidation of Naval Staff reorganization—Richmond's single-mindedness was indispensable. His investigations of the work of Plans Division allowed him to penetrate the morass of petty jealousies and departmentalism which continued to plague the Admiralty. He produced a comprehensive set of proposals for the organization, training, and operation—in peace and in war—of the Naval Staff and also for staffs afloat.[35] The principles which he enunciated formed the basis of all subsequent staff structures, including those used in World War Two. Basically, the reorganization centred on the Operations Committee which was to include the First Lord, First Sea Lord, D.C.N.S., and A.C.N.S. The Naval Staff worked under the Operations Committee and was restructured into eight divisions: under the D.C.N.S. were Intelligence, Plans, Training and Staff Duties, and Trade; under the A.C.N.S. were Communications, Operations, Local Defence, and Gunnery and Torpedo. The most significant aspect of these changes involved the extent of the Staff's responsibility. In matters of policy and training, the Staff's view would be paramount. Previously, each Sea Lord had been considered the final authority in matters within his area of competence. Throughout his own period as First Sea Lord, Beatty energetically defended this system of concentrating all aspects of policy under the D.C.N.S. and A.C.N.S. to whom he delegated his general responsibility. Despite postwar pressures for economies and reductions in staff personnel, he resisted any departures from these principles.[36] "In essentials," Captain Stephen Roskill has written, "the Naval Staff of 1918 has lasted to this day. Though not generally realised by present-day naval men, it is in fact another monument to Richmond's insight and clear thinking."[37] It was an outstanding accomplishment the significance of which Chalmers noted in July 1918:

> The CIO on Staff organisation is a great advance particularly the paragraphs directing that Chief Staff Officers shall be chosen for their ability not their social qualifications. Richmond deserves great credit for this and appears to have considerable influence, otherwise such an epoch making memorandum would never have been issued.[38]

35 The detailed proposals together with the Board's and Beatty's comments and amendments are contained in Adm. 1/8501, /8524, /8536, /8546, and /8558.
36 Adm. 116/1803, Adm. Office Memo. No. 67, March 13, 1920. Also, "Instructions for Naval Staff," Office Memo No. 187, August 2, 1919. This carefully describes the duties of each division: "Notes on Procedure" also laid down the rules of correct procedure. Adm. 116/2683, Keyes Committee on Economies in the Naval Staff, Terms of Reference, dated November 17, 1922; Adm. 1/8638. Report dated January 17, 1923. Also Adm.167/67, Board Minutes of February 1, 1923 (No. 1578) and May 10, 1923 (no. 1640). Other files on Naval Staff Reorganization, see: Adm. 116/1803 (1917-1921), Adm. 116/2105 (1920-1923), and Adm. 116/3683 (1928).
37 Captain S. W. Roskill, "The Richmond Lecture," Naval Review, 57 (April 1969), 140.
38 DEW, 2, Chalmers to Dewar, July 1, 1918.

But Richmond's "influence" was much less than Chalmers supposed. He had succeeded on the organizational question only because Wemyss supported the changes. Education was another matter, and on this score, Richmond's views ran counter to the mainstream of contemporary professional thinking.

He realized that very little would be done in 1918. "It is simply heart breaking. I knew that it w^{d} be useless to try and reform anything in education while the war is on."[39] That he nevertheless made the attempt underlines his abiding conviction that educational mismanagement was the root cause of all the Navy's ills. As D.T.S.D., Richmond campaigned to broaden the basis of the existing system by widening the sources of officer entry and by concentrating on the advantages of a "general" education which emphasized the development of the individual's reasoning and intellectual capacities. He opposed the practice of trying to carry on midshipmen's scholastic training simultaneously with the performance of duties as officers. As he wrote almost a year later to Haldane,

> This is in contradiction to the opinions of every committee that has sat upon naval education since 1870, the reports and recommendations of which have in every case drawn attention to the incompatability of the position of an officer and a schoolboy.[40]

This was the main theme of his dissenting minority report to the Goodenough Committee on Midshipmen in February 1918. He also favoured expanding the system of special entry from public schools which had been started in 1913. This was one of his favourite themes which led into the whole question of early entry and the value or otherwise of the Osborne-Dartmouth training system. It was an issue which would continue to occupy men's minds for years to come. As D.T.S.D., however, Richmond had to confine his indictments to a first draft of his book *Naval Training*, which was eventually published in 1933.

In the summer of 1918, these questions brought Richmond into headlong conflict with Wemyss and Heath, the Second Sea Lord. Richmond had previously encountered Heath's hostility for advocating a settled scheme for opening cadetships to suitable men from the lower decks. The previous D.T.S.D., Rear-Admiral J. C. Ley, had tried, early in 1918, to expand the so-called "Mate Scheme" (introduced in 1912) by offering cadetships to suitable ratings and allowing them to join the "Special Entry" cadets. Heath had vehemently opposed the whole idea, arguing that "to be a good officer it is necessary to be a gentleman." Richmond's direct approaches to Wemyss on the same question only hardened Heath's position. Indeed, it was not until the

39 RIC/1/15, Diary, July 6, 1918.
40 Ibid., Richmond to Haldane, February 15, 1919.

late 1920's that, under Mr. A. V. Alexander, the Labour First Lord, the Naval College's doors were finally opened to lower-deck personnel. In the interim, Heath's policy of placing "no obstacles in the way of really suitable candidates ... but on the other hand to afford no special facilities or encouragement" was the one followed.[41]

On the question of staff training, Richmond reiterated his long-held views that the scope of both the junior and senior officers' staff courses had been far too constricted. Wartime experience had reinforced his conviction that more emphasis on education as distinct from training was essential; that lecture hours at Greenwich should be cut to allow more time for thinking, writing, and discussion; that the curriculum, by focussing on the "art of war" through the study of history, strategy, tactics, international relations, the conduct of war by sea, land and air, and the theory and practice of staff work, should encourage the development of future C-in-C's and senior Naval Staff officers from a much earlier age. He was also convinced that the course should be located separately from other naval establishments as a self-contained and residential institution preferably within reach of the Army's Staff College at Camberley. Given his own staff experience and persistent interest in combined operations-strategic policy, the need for close working relations between the two colleges seemed natural enough to him. To that end, he suggested on November 15, 1918: "A house known as Penneyhill Park, Bagshot, with 100 acres of land attached is now on the market and could be secured if it is decided to institute a Staff College for the Navy. The house is within two miles of the Military Staff College at Camberley."[42] For the moment however, nothing came of these suggestions and Richmond, as will be seen, had to wait until his own appointment as President of the War Course after the war to see his ideas bear fruit.

Wemyss' declared intention of restraining Richmond was clearly successful. Training Division was by-passed in the formation of education policy and even in the consideration of various reports brought in by special committees.[43] Denied the decisions he needed, and infuriated by what he felt was a total want of system in the formulation of overall policy, Richmond approached Geddes directly, knowing that the First Lord's views on staff reforms and education were very much in line with his own.

41 Adm. 116/1734. Adm. 1/8550, Report of Sir Alan Anderson Committee, dated February 12, 1919; Adm. 1/8567, Report of a Committee under Vice-Admiral A. D. Ricardo, dated November 7, 1919.

42 RIC/12/4, Staff Work and Staff Training.

43 Viz. the so-called Jellicoe Committee on the status of Engineer Officers. Actually chaired by Mr. R. McKenna, the former First Lord (1908-1911), Adm. 1/8541, Report of October 1918. Richmond's counter proposals are contained in RIC/1/15, August 25, 1918.

It is the only way I can see to get my views considered. Wemyss
blocks everything. He has thrown out my proposals for a Staff College at Camberley, but he is cunning enough not to minute the paper,
so that no record may exist of his decisions. I therefore write down
what he said to me and leave it on the paper. Fuller tells me he has to
do the same.[44]

Evidently, however, even Geddes' patience had worn thin. Richmond
had ruffled too many feathers, and in this instance had touched a
particularly sensitive nerve. Captain Rhys Williams, the Deputy
D.T.S.D., was convinced as Richmond noted that Geddes' hostility

was developed to cover his own sense of not having supported us. He
knows—and Williams made it clear to him—that I had been brought
here to perform a very difficult task in the face of supreme opposition; that I could only do it if my superiors supported my principles
and me and saw me through. This they—Geddes and Wemyss—have
not done.[45]

Richmond was summoned on December 20 for another of
Wemyss' frank interviews and told he was to leave the Admiralty. In a
curious postscript to their relationship, Richmond recorded in his
diary:

We said goodbye in a friendly manner. I thanked him for what he had
done; for with all his weakness I know he has really protected me
against Heath and his mob, and, in the end, against Geddes.
Wemyss has the inestimable advantage of being a gentleman.[46]

Richmond's efforts as Director of Training had produced disappoint-
ingly few concrete results. One of these enabled young officers whose
education had been interrupted by the war to be sent to Cambridge, a
system which lasted from 1919 to 1923, when Treasury parsimony
brought it to an end.

Richmond was disheartened when he left to return to the Grand
Fleet. But others who had worked closely with him were more hopeful that some useful beginnings had been made. In a letter which
clearly illustrates the warmth and loyalty Richmond invariably received from his immediate subordinates, Captain Rhys Williams
explained his mixed feelings of relief and regret on his own departure
from the Admiralty. Relief, because for all their "high hopes," the
results of their nine months of "earnest and painstaking brainwork"
were "depressing." Regrets for the reforms so "absolutely necessary"
but still left "unsanctioned," and "great regret," he wrote, "that I
leave you for I could not wish for a better master to serve." Still,
despite all the disappointments, Williams was hopeful

44 RIC/1/15, November 28, 1918.
45 Ibid., December 17, 1918.
46 Ibid., December 20, 1918.

that the ideas which we have put forward will sooner or later be
adopted, and that the time we have spent here as "Sowers" will not
have been wasted; that the fruits of our sowing will be reaped by a
Board of Admiralty of the future.[47]

Roger Bellairs also sensed that ultimately the importance of Richmond's work would be recognized; that despite "the impossible position you found yourself in trying to make headway against the combined forces of obstruction, ignorance and reaction" he had, in fact,
laid the foundations for the naval staff system and officer education in
a way no one else could have.

> Nothing now can extinguish what has actually become an ac-
> complished fact, and since this present regime must finally give way
> to the younger school of naval thought, a school which intends to
> make itself felt, I am absolutely certain that before very long progress
> will be made right along the various lines you have mapped out.[48]

If Richmond drew any consolation from these expressions of
hope, he did not record it. However, his appointment to command the
battleship *Erin*, at a time when postwar economies and reductions in
personnel were sweeping many other officers off the Active List,
suggested that he had not been entirely shelved. On the other hand,
Bellairs' optimism must have had a hollow ring for there were, by this
time, indications that any moves to "give way to the younger school of
naval thought" would not materialize in the immediate future. The
most obvious was the Admiralty's attitude to the *Naval Review* which
resumed publication early in 1919 and immediately ran into difficulties.

The first suggestion that the *Naval Review* might resume publication came in early February 1918. Still flushed with his initial
enthusiasm for the new Admiralty regime, Richmond had advised
Admiral Henderson to approach Wemyss privately, providing him
with an outline of projected numbers to sound out his receptiveness.
Whether or not Henderson acted on this suggestion is unknown,
although an approach was made at the end of September, and with
pleasing results. Henderson was informed that revival had been approved, and most significantly, as Richmond emphasized in an ecstat-
ic reply to the good news, with "no censorship."[49]

Interpreting Admiralty approval as the mandate for which they
had waited so long, the Young Turks set out to use the *Review* as their
platform for setting the war record straight and for exposing the
Navy's failures of which the service and the public were generally

47 RIC/7/4, Rhys Williams to Richmond, December 20, 1918.
48 Ibid., Bellairs to Richmond, January 11, 1919.
49 RIC/7/1, Richmond to Henderson, February 6; September 30, 1918.

ignorant. The central theme, Richmond urged, should be one of fearless re-examination and criticism:

> find out where we went wrong and why; Trace errors to their source and put right that which we find wrong.
>
> This is the supreme effort of the next few years. Most dangerous attitude we could take w^d be one of complacent contentment with our achievements; no war, even in our best times of the past has been conducted without mistakes: it w^d be presumptuous in us to-day to imagine ourselves free from the weakness of the men of the past. To do so w^d be to bury our heads in the sand & refuse to see what there is to be seen & to learn what there is to be learned.[50]

Richmond understood the dangers of using the *Review* this way; his experiences as D.T.S.D. should have left few doubts as to what the Admiralty's reaction would be. That he was willing to proceed can only be explained in terms of his overly optimistic notion that somehow truth would prevail. This was the same dogged determination and courageous following of his own convictions that had earlier led him to oppose Churchill and then Wemyss. Moreover, he was convinced that the time was ripe for direct action; that the war had created a will for and an atmosphere favourable to reform which he was not prepared to let slip by. "We are at a most critical moment," he confided to Henderson, "If reactionary people make it their business to support the fiction that the conduct of the naval war is beyond criticism, we shall make no reforms." Any attempt to cover up mistakes on the grounds of protecting the navy's prestige would be, in his view, "more than preposterous. It is disloyal to the Country, it is preference for a personal or departmental loyalty to the wider loyalty we all profess with our mouths."[51]

It is worth emphasizing that Richmond's determination to bring about a postwar British naval renaissance was not simply a response to his immediate frustrations. The idea had been there since the early months of the war when he had drafted his "Need for Enquiry" articles. By early 1916 he was writing more essays in the same vein—a "Profit from the Past" series which he always hoped to publish sometime after the war. Henderson, in discussing how and where they might be published—as a pamphlet, or in periodicals such as the *Fortnightly Review, Nineteenth Century*, etc.—had recommended caution: "I do not think the psychological moment has arrived yet for any form of publication of this order. The thing is to first get such ideas impregnated in the Service and the Naval Review is the only means of doing it."[52] There was thus a consistency of several years'

50 Ibid., November 19, 1918.
51 Ibid., February 11, 1919.
52 RIC/7/4, Henderson to Richmond, February 24, 1916.

standing in Richmond's suggestion that the "Profit" series should be developed in the resuscitated Review and used to sustain a broad front assault on the Navy's shortcomings.[53]

Richmond has been criticized for failing to accommodate his personal views to what was realistically possible in the circumstances. Marder, for example, accuses the Young Turks of contriving "to put people's backs up by their conviction of the absolute correctness of the positions they espoused."[54] They also clearly misjudged the real interest of a war-weary population in investigating past blunders, in Bonar Law's words of "washing dirty linen in public"[55] at a time of more pressing national and international matters. Still it must be said that there is a world of difference between what Richmond and his supporters said in private amongst themselves and what they published. Richmond's introductory article in the February 1919 issue of the Review ("The Training of the Mind for Modern War") shows his keen awareness of his superiors' sensitivities. It is a balanced and reasoned case for an examination of British ideas and methods of naval warfare as practised in the preceding four years, and a call for careful analysis of future needs and policies. Above all, he spelled out, in terms obviously calculated to disarm critics, the requirements for the future education of officers and the fostering of those intellectual disciplines which would make it all possible.

In the event, no objections were raised to Richmond's article. Nor were there any observations on Henderson's somewhat puerile attempts at revenge contained in his article "A Simple Lesson in Censorship" in which all the earlier excisions of November 1915 were printed. However, exception was taken to an account of the 1914 escape of the German ships Goeben and Breslau in which the author implicitly criticized the Commander-in-Chief, Admiral Sir Archibald Berkeley-Milne. The latter's complaint to the Admiralty brought an immediate reimposition of suspension, and an order forbidding all Active List Officers from contributing articles to the Review without prior Admiralty approval.[56] To present-day readers of the Goeben article, the criticisms of Admiral Berkeley-Milne must seem reasonable and innocuous to say the least. However, presented as excerpts from the log of H.M.S. Indomitable, they did imply that a real chance to destroy the German ships had been missed. Admiral Henderson's attempts to protect the author's identity failed. The Admiralty, without difficulty, correctly surmised he was Captain J. W. Kennedy, Cap-

53 RIC/7/1, Richmond to Henderson, February 11, 1919.
54 Marder, Dreadnought to Scapa Flow, vol. 5, p. 299, note 4.
55 Marder, Dardanelles to Oran, pp. 57-58.
56 Admiralty Weekly Order (A.W.O.), 1663/19.

tain of the *Indomitable*. He was duly reprimanded, and subsequently retired without further employment. This, in Dewar's view, was a prime example of "pseudo-disciplinary restrictions" by which "consciously or unconsciously, valuable lessons were evaded or suppressed in order to support the absurd myth of their [the higher authorities'] infallibility."[57]

Richmond was also singled out and explicitly forbidden to publish anything that did not have official approval. "Wemyss said that anything I write must first go to the Admiralty for censorship."[58] Thus he was forced to turn down an invitation to write for Brassey's *Annual*. For someone of his character and seniority, it was an impossible position:

> I feel so strongly about being regarded as if I were an irresponsible person who does not know what to say or what to leave unsaid, and at the implication that I am unfit to write except under supervision, that I feel it impossible to submit to such an indignity. Old Admiral Vernon said that an officer who doesn't value his own honour is not the likeliest man to defend the honour of his country. I value my own honour and my position in the Service; and am not disposed to have either it or my sense questioned and put at the jurisdiction of the fleet paymasters who would do the business of censoring.[59]

When, however, it became obvious that an attempt was being made to force Henderson's resignation, Richmond retraced his steps and adopted a somewhat less arrogant posture. Loss of the Editor would do the *Review* irreparable harm. "Let us hold on," he advised Henderson:

> I am sure we can keep articles going. I am prepared even to submit some harmless historical stuff of mine to the Admiralty for permission to include it, and to write other stuff which I do not submit.
>   When the end of the war comes we can see how we stand; or when a new administration comes to the Admiralty. It is possible that we might make advances to new men but I would make no more to those people now in power.[60]

It was unlikely that the Society would find young serving officers willing to write under the new conditions, but it was still possible for them to read the *Review*. Until a working relationship with the Admiralty could be established, the *Review* would have to depend on outside contributions, notably from Lord Sydenham, Haldane, Carlyon Bellairs, and A. C. Dewar. But Richmond also knew that pro-

57 DEW, 13, "Naval Reform."
58 RIC/7/1, Richmond to Henderson, March 7, 1919.
59 Ibid., February 18, 1919.
60 Ibid., June 13, 1919. This refers to a letter from Admiral Sturdee which convinced Richmond that "the Board's attitude is governed largely by a spirit of revenge—a petty and wretched desire to 'pay you out' for your letter about Jutland."

longed application of this restrictive order would eventually kill the *Naval Review* and the ideas for which it had been founded.

Throughout the summer of 1919 Henderson fought to have the order rescinded or modified. By August, however, the Admiralty's delays had produced deadlock and Richmond began to feel that the Society's only hope lay in a display of resolution, "a strong show of fighting" and a willingness to see it through. He was prepared even to enlist the support of Curzon and Bellairs in Parliament, and even to threaten publication of the Society's correspondence with the Admiralty in a forthcoming issue of the *Review* or elsewhere. It was essential that the authorities appreciate the Society's determination to make the whole issue public and to lay the blame squarely at the Admiralty's door.[61] The following excerpts from a letter of August 26, 1919, vividly demonstrate Richmond's position and his awareness of where the main point of leverage was:

> All we can do is to try and keep the [*Review*] going till the end of the year, bringing pressure through Curzon and others to frighten the Admiralty. Then, if the whole thing comes to an end, to write an article in the "Nineteenth Century" or the "Times" giving the history of the *Review* and shewing up this whole Admiralty action in the matter. What however is our greatest asset is that the Admiralty should know that this or something of the sort is our intention . . . . Once they know what a storm is brewing and that the matter will be raised in Parliament and the actual Goeben article circulated, I think they will find they have exposed themselves to such a charge of stupid bureaucratic action, and of secretiveness in matters of unimportance, that they will give way.
>
> I propose therefore that we should now proceed to work up our case. We need do nothing if they give way; but if they do not, and the *Review* is to die, I propose it should die like Samson and bring down the pillars of the temple with it in its fall.
>
> I feel sure Wemyss will be afraid of being accused of short sighted and narrow views. He prides himself upon being a man of the world, upon his liberal and progressive sentiments. To be exposed as a narrow minded bureaucrat would be a great blow to him.[62]

No evidence has been found to suggest that the threat was actually carried out, but Richmond had clearly struck a responsive note. Almost immediately, a compromise was worked out. The previous Fleet Order was cancelled and a new one approved under which Henderson, as Editor, assumed full responsibility for obtaining permissions to publish.[63] These arrangements helped mitigate the highly restrictive intent of the earlier order. But the *Review* was still subject

61 Ibid., August 19, 1919, together with Richmond's draft of a reply to Their Lordships, n.d.
62 Ibid., August 26, 1919.
63 A.W.O. 3937/19. Also Adm. 1/8708, Henderson to Secretary of the Admiralty, December 1925.

to final Admiralty censorship and remained so for another six years. This generally unrecognized fact had a profound influence on the *Naval Review* as an effective vehicle of reform during these critical years of adjustment from war to peace.

The postwar volumes of the *Review* (1920-25) are of interest more for the articles they do not contain than those they do. There were lengthy discussions and exchanges of views on the future uses and control of aircraft, the future of the battleship, and of submarines. While there were a number of articles on education and training—some of which are the best in these issues—they still took second place to the wartime reminiscences and reviews of autobiographies that began to flood the market. Few papers were devoted to the wider issues of strategy and tactics, and none of these were on the hard-hitting lines the Young Turks had hoped to develop. Richmond lamented these tendencies. The *Review* was becoming an outlet for people who wanted only to air grievances and complaints. "They deserved an airing and have had it," he wrote early in 1921.[64] But with Admiralty censorship still enforced, there was little else to be done. Even the opportunity of reviewing Jellicoe's book, *The Crisis of the Naval War* (1920), involved risks which Richmond was not prepared to take. "No—Jellicoe's book is *not* worth reviewing," he warned Henderson: "If anyone should volunteer a critique on it we shouldn't refuse it: but I foresee storms if we do touch it. The Admiralty w^d be sure to be very tender about any criticisms. It's a sleeping dog at present and my advice is to leave it alone."[65]

Membership in the Society rose after the war, reaching a peak of 1,437 in 1922. For the next decade, it dwindled somewhat, levelling off at just over 1,000. Fewer junior officers joined and many of these were drawn from Commonwealth and reserve forces. This led to a heavier concentration of senior and retired members, a trend which was reflected in the contributions. This may have been attributable to the younger officers' apathy or lack of time, though a more likely cause was fear of their seniors' attitudes and some well-founded doubts that even anonymity of authorship offered sufficient protection. These tendencies prompted Henderson to negotiate first in 1921 and again in 1925 a less stringent censorship arrangement.

In a brief, submitted in early December 1925, Henderson spelled out his reasons for wanting censorship removed, or at least left to the discretion of the *Review*'s own editorial committee. Admiralty restrictions on subjects to be discussed ("articles on questions of material are barred") and the requirement for prior official censorship had given the impression "that the Admiralty does not like junior officers

64 RIC/7/1, Richmond to Henderson, January 19 and June 20, 1921.
65 Ibid., n.d.

expressing their ideas in print." Referral to the Admiralty also gave the *Review* a "kind of official status and appears to necessitate the suppression of articles which would be quite innocuous in an unofficial and wholly private review."[66] Furthermore, Henderson argued that Battenberg's support in 1913 suggested that writing for the *Review* did not necessarily contravene the provisions of King's Regulations and Admiralty Instructions (K.R. and A.I.) the point on which the Admiralty's position had largely rested through the war and after. Since the *Review* was privately circulated, Henderson argued, "it is not a publication in the technical sense of the word, but is in the same category as a privately circulated pamphlet." This latter point had always been a source of debate.

Generally, Henderson's appeal was favourably received by the Admiralty Board. Apart from some observations about the practice of publishing censored *Review* articles in the *Canadian Defence Quarterly* (a "public" journal), the Directors of the Intelligence, Operations, Plans, and Staff Duties Divisions all supported his claims.[67] Opposition came, as it had in 1915, from the civilian side of the house. The Permanent Secretary, Sir Oswyn Murray, objected on several grounds. First, the *Review* was, in his and the Solicitor General's opinions, a "publication" as defined in K.R. and A.I. The Editor's assurances and the Society's rules offered no guarantee that the *Review*'s contents would not fall into outsiders' hands. Removal of censorship, Murray suggested, would put the Admiralty in the position, should further questionable material be published, of having always to shut the barn door after the horse's escape. Murray was prepared, however, to go part way in meeting Henderson by requiring that an Admiralty representative (he suggested the D.N.I.) should sit as a member of the *Review*'s editorial committee. In these views he was supported by Vice-Admiral F. C. Field, the Deputy Chief of the Naval Staff.[68]

At this point, Beatty's more enlightened influence broke through. Posing the rather obvious questions, "Is the Review of value to the

---

66 This, in fact, was the case in 1920 when Henderson submitted an article "The Navy in the Red Sea, 1916-17." It had been rejected on grounds of "present unrest in the Near East." Adm. 1/8708, Henderson to Secretary of the Admiralty, December 1925; also April 26, 28, 1920. This had been the occasion for Henderson's attempt in February 1921, to have censorship removed (NL 1609/21). The application was denied: "It was pointed out that in the short time since the institution of the censorship consequent on the 'Goeben-Breslau' article, several articles had only been conditionally approved, and although the Board had no desire to impose vexatious restrictions on the Editor's work, they were unable to modify their decision." Adm. 167/74, Memorandum attached to Board Minutes, February 25, 1926. The contentious Red Sea article was finally published in *Naval Review*, 13 (1925), 648-66.

67 Adm. 1/8708, Minutes dated December 23, 31, 1925, and January 6, 13, 1926.

68 Ibid., January 18, 1926.

Service?" and "Does the censorship adversely affect the Review?" he concluded the answers to be a resounding "yes." He therefore recommended the removal of all restrictions. As an obvious sop to those who disagreed, he concluded:

> By the imposition of censorship, and the use of the Admiralty power of suppression, the Review has been taught a lesson which should prevent any further indiscretion. I am satisfied to leave the matter in the hands of Admiral Henderson, whose discretion in such matters is not less than that of an Officer in the N.I.D.[69]

Henderson was informed that in future questions of censorship and editorial policy would be left to a "Committee of Naval Officers" which the Society would appoint, and that when Henderson was succeeded as Editor, these arrangements would be reconsidered.[70] These were the arrangements under which the *Review* continued to operate. With one or two minor exceptions, no further difficulties were encountered.[71] Henderson's successors, Admiral Sir Richard Webb (1931-1950) and Admiral Sir Gerald Dickens (1950-1954), agreed to continue under the same provisions. The question of Admiralty interference was never raised again.

In 1919 none of these later developments could be foreseen. For the Young Turks it was a critical year. Admiralty censorship had emasculated the *Naval Review*. This, together with the restrictions on their extra-service activities, would affect both the development of their ideas as intellectuals and to some degree their group identity as reformers. The war's end undermined the sense of urgency which bound them together, and which had given relevance to much of what they had to say. In a world grown weary of war, there was little room

69 Ibid., February 5, 1926. Adm. 167/73, Board Minutes, February 25, 1926, Minute 2169.
70 Adm. 1/8708, O. Murray to Henderson, March 10, 1926; Henderson to Murray, April 1926; Sir Charles Walker to Henderson, May 19, 1926. The editorial Committee as recommended by Henderson and approved consisted of: Henderson, Richmond, Drax, K. G. B. Dewar, and Captain Geoffrey Blake.
71 The first of these arose almost immediately with the publication of the May 1926 number. A complaint was received about the article "The Fleet Air Arm," *Naval Review*, 14 (1926), 315-17, on the grounds of its "scurrilous nature" and criticisms of conditions in that branch of the service. Sir Owsyn Murray and the D.C.N.S. also took exception to the wording of Henderson's explanation of the recent change in censorship policy, particularly his assumption that the *Review* was not subject to Article 14 of the King's Regulations. In fact no decision was ever made on this point. Apart from a mild warning, the incident was quickly smoothed over. Adm. 1/8708.
   A similar situation occured in 1937 when it was noted by the editorial committee that the April 24 number of the *New Statesman and Nation* contained a reference to a *Review* article on the Spanish Civil War. A letter to Kingsley Martin explaining the predicament in which the *Review* might be placed seems to have solved the problem. The Admiralty, if it had noticed the reference, had turned a blind eye. Nothing more was heard of the incident. Sainsbury Papers, Webb to Thursfield, April 26, 1937; Thursfield to Webb, April 28, 1937; Thursfield to Editor, *The New Statesman and Nation*, July 27, 1937.

for those who preached the gospel that the war at sea had not been an overwhelming success. Postwar retrenchments and economies also meant that prospects were far from bright for many officers and, in this respect, the Young Turks had more to fear than most.

Richmond returned to the Grand Fleet in January 1919 to assume command of the dreadnought H.M.S. *Erin* of the Second Battle Squadron. For the next ten months he remained there awaiting the return to favour he hoped would come once Beatty became First Sea Lord. Unaware as to why that event was so long delayed, he could only chafe at the slow passage of time. His impatience reached a peak by early summer when he toyed with the idea of leaving the Navy for a position in the oil business. Admiral Edmund Slade, then representing the Admiralty on the board of the Anglo-Persian Oil Company, had offered him a job which Richmond noted

> would suit me down to the ground. Work in London and probably travelling to the Persian Gulf, etc. I should enjoy it and it would be useful . . . Beatty *may* go to the Admiralty at the end of the year and *may* want me. But whether he would let me do what I think necessary is another question, and I don't think he would. No real reform is possible until people know what blunders have been made, and everyone is afraid—or against—shewing them up.[72]

But Richmond was too committed to the Navy, and to the idea that reform was ultimately possible, to stray very far in the direction of voluntary retirement. His deep professional commitment also prompted him to write off the opportunity of a new chair of history at Cambridge with the glib but illustrative remark: "I think I can do more than that with my life."[73] This opportunity had arisen in January 1919, when Corbett, who had been originally offered the chair, had turned it down and recommended Richmond in his place. The fact is, Richmond did take the idea seriously and it was only after much thought and discussion with Sir Julian that he decided to take the chance that his talents would be properly utilized by the navy.[74]

Despite his impatience, Richmond's time aboard H.M.S. *Erin* was important for his own future. Aided by Corbett, he saw his *History of the 1739-1748 War* through the final stages of publication. He spent much of his time exchanging letters and ideas with a widening range of personalities, and was thus able to keep in close touch with the main threads of postwar development. These exchanges also helped to broaden his horizon and they were an important part of the process by which he gradually broke free of the constrictive circle of the Young Turks over the next few years. Richmond, it seems, was begin-

72 RIC/1/15, Diary, June 18, 1919.
73 Ibid., May 18, 1919.
74 Ibid., January 23, 1919. CP Box 13(a), Richmond to Corbett, January 24, 1919.

ning to appreciate that too close a relationship with Beatty and his supporters bore a heavy price in terms of his own integrity and intellectual independence. If his time at the Admiralty had shown him anything, it was that disengagement would be difficult.

Like Richmond, Dewar was also having second thoughts about the Navy in 1919. Apart from a spring sojourn to Paris as a member of the Admiralty's contingent to the Peace Talks, the year was generally uninspiring for him. With the cessation of active operations, much of Plans Division's work was finished. One bright spot was Drax's appointment as Director of the Naval Staff College at Greenwich. Dewar grasped at Drax's invitation to join the staff there as his assistant. But the move was blocked; by whom and for what precise reasons is not known. He was simply informed by Drax that "difficulties had arisen and it would be better if I first went to sea and relieved him later."[75]

Returning from Paris in April, Dewar temporarily replaced Captain Fuller as Director of Plans Division (D. of P.). Almost immediately he ran afoul of authority once again, in the person of the Second Sea Lord, on a question of finding a replacement for Major G. P. Orde, R.M., who was then leaving the Division. Petty though the disagreement was, it resulted in another attempt to have Dewar posted out— this time to command the obsolete cruiser *Grafton*, a depot ship at Novorossiisk on the Black Sea. Only the intervention of his immediate superiors, Captain Fuller and the D.C.N.S., saved him from going. But the incident, taken in conjunction with what was happening to Richmond and to the *Naval Review* in 1919, suggested to Dewar that there was little cause for optimism concerning his future. Beatty's arrival at Whitehall brought no immediate changes. And so, in February 1920, a completely disillusioned Dewar left Plans Division and asked for half-pay and leave to consider his future. Before the year had ended, however, Beatty would bring him back, along with his brother, into the very centre of postwar naval affairs.

75 Drax Papers, "Fifty Years in Search of Ideas," (June 1966). DEW, 3, Drax to Dewar, January 15, 1919.

6

Postwar Readjustments: The View from Greenwich (1920-1923)

Within two months of Beatty's appointment as First Sea Lord on November 1, 1919, Richmond was recalled from H.M.S. Erin, promoted to Rear-Admiral, and assigned to Greenwich to reopen the Senior Officers' War Course. Few posts could have suited his talents and ambitions better. A new generation of officers was rising and he was convinced they could be reached.[1] The fact that he was given a free hand by Beatty also implied something more than just a chance for serious educational innovation; friendship with the new First Sea Lord opened up wider possibilities for reform at any number of levels—perhaps even that postwar naval "renaissance" for which the Young Turks had campaigned so persistently.

Less than a year would pass, however, when Government economies in the form of the "Geddes Axe" sent nineteen out of twenty-four students and staff members to early retirement. Richmond had to face the unpleasant reality that Beatty's confidence held no special guarantees. He regarded the cuts as proof that the authorities still considered the College to be of marginal value. By the end of his term as President of the College in February 1923, he was even less optimistic about the future. By then, of course, a great deal had happened. The transition from war to peace was complete, and after the 1921 Washington Naval Conference, the main outlines of future naval developments were more or less discernible.

In terms of naval policy development, these were years of uncertainty and, not unnaturally, of considerable extemporization. Four years of war had completely altered the international power structure. Extra-European interests assumed a renewed, though undefined im-

1   RIC/1/15, Diary, November 20, 1919; February 16, 1920.

107

portance for Britain following the collapse of Germany and the rise of Japan and the United States. America's potential for outpacing Britain in naval construction alone demanded new assessments of the Anglo-American relationship. This diffusion of Britain's global defence responsibilities, especially when related to her losses in economic strength, increased the need for more clearly defined relations with the various Dominions and equilibrium closer to home. Successive British governments, all supporting the ideals of the League of Nations, the peaceful settlement of disputes, and disarmament in specific areas, encouraged Europe's reconstruction as part of Britain's while avoiding wider commitments which would overextend her own resources.

These considerations lay at the root of the infamous "Ten-Year Rule" which, reviewed annually, became the secret yardstick for calculating defence expenditure until 1932-33. In politico-economic terms, there was a strong case for the rule's introduction; but in relation to sound defence policy formulation, there was not. It was an insidious and unjustifiable rule of thumb. Too often it led the service hierarchies to assume that financial constraints absolved them from thinking too deeply about their most fundamental problems.

Technological advances further complicated the situation. The war had gradually revealed the possibilities of submarines, torpedoes, mines, and aircraft, all of which challenged the continuing value of battleships which, as the chief units of the Fleet, constituted the index of British naval supremacy. Not since the introduction of the *Dreadnought* had technological change demanded such a fundamental rethinking of basic naval doctrine.

The cumulative effect of all these factors was that Beatty was forced to play for time, to strike compromises in the name of preserving as much material naval strength as possible. The absence of a generally accepted and coherent national strategic doctrine forced all three services into an internecine struggle in which the object, apart from mere survival, was never very clear. Budgetary restrictions and the fluidity of the international situation abetted this tendency; though equally important were the attitudes of the men who held the senior positions in these years. In the same way that the Army was controlled by veterans of the Western Front, so the Admiralty was dominated by the Grand Fleet family—a family deeply divided within itself by the Battle of Jutland and its long aftermath of bitter argument and personal recriminations. The "Jutland Controversy" of the 1920s, quite apart from its divisive and energy-diverting side effects, induced a backward-looking mentality in senior naval circles which bore little relationship to postwar issues or the way they were being argued by the country's political leaders.

As President of the Naval War College and as one of Beatty's confidants, Richmond was able to observe these developments with a well-informed though increasingly independent eye. To some extent, his time-consuming duties preserved him from any direct involvement in the Jellicoe-Beatty feud. But his vantage point also opened up a widening spectrum of contacts outside of the service. The fact is Richmond's horizon was expanding; these were the years of his maturation as an intellectual. Gradually, as his scholarly talents became more widely recognized, and as he turned his mind to the broader problems of national policy, his disillusionment with Beatty grew. Unlike the Dewar brothers whose central role in the Jutland "Controversy," as will be seen, virtually destroyed their credibility as constructive reformers, Richmond preserved his integrity and independence. This is not to suggest that Richmond was becoming a closeted academic. Quite the opposite, his attempts to influence the Beatty regime constitute some of the few instances where originality, rationality, and a sense of deeper perspective entered postwar naval discussion.

Even before the war ended, Richmond had expressed concern over the Admiralty's hesitation in setting out broad policies for the coming peace. Then, within days of the Armistice, Treasury warnings of drastic spending cuts shattered all illusions of a leisurely readjustment period to follow.[2] This pressure merely confirmed Richmond's conviction that matters of general policy could only be handled by a body of the Naval Staff set free from the pressure of current work. As D.T.S.D. he had been especially critical of this aspect of Wemyss' administration:

> large questions of policy are being dealt with at haphazard. Some go to Reconstruction Committee: a body wholly unacquainted with the events and lessons of the war and in no way competent to express an opinion. Others are dealt with hugger-mugger by Wemyss.[3]

The Reconstruction Committee was established early in 1918 to study such questions as the naval clauses of the Peace Treaty, the League of Nations, armaments limitation, building policy, revision of international law, and the creation of an international intelligence organization. Insofar as it showed Wemyss' awareness of the need for careful planning, the Committee was a step in the right direction. But that apart, the Committee's eighteen volumes of deliberations and findings[4] produced few impressive results. Given the uncertainties in the Government's position prior to the Paris talks, much of the work was premature. Moreover, Admiral of the Fleet Sir William May—

2 Adm. 116/1779, Operations Committee Minute No. 105, November 20, 1918.
3 RIC/1/15, Diary, October 19, 1918.
4 Adm. 116/1745-1762.

Vice-Chairman and *de facto* director of the Committee—simply was
not the man to direct such a wide-ranging study and formulate far-
sighted recommendations. In any case, the rush of events overtook the
Committee and prevented serious consideration of most of its findings.

Geddes also had serious misgivings about Admiral May's Committee from its inception,[5] and therefore proposed, in January 1919,
the undertaking of another more critical study:

> a strong, critical and as far as possible independently-minded Com-
> mittee should be appointed to consider and record . . . (among other
> things) the naval position on the outbreak of war and the steps taken
> during the war to remedy defects and meet new requirements.[6]

For the moment, however, nothing further came of Geddes' initiative,
apart from the drafting of some proposed terms of reference. On
January 6 he was succeeded as First Lord in the new coalition government by Mr. Walter Long. A novice in naval affairs who saw his
role as that of "the channel of communication between the Cabinet
and the Board," Long clearly deferred to his professional advisers on
most aspects of naval planning.[7] Not until August, seven months
after Geddes' departure, was the new study group set up.

The Post-War Questions Committee, as it was then constituted
under the chairmanship of Rear-Admiral R. F. Phillimore, was a far
cry from the semi-independent and critical body which Geddes had
envisioned. Under terms of reference which restricted its scope and
sources of evidence, the Committee was directed to examine "in the
light of the experience of the War the military uses and values of the
different types of war vessel" and the future roles of aircraft.[8] In every
respect it was a technical body set up without reference to what, or
against whom, these instruments were to be used. No attempt was
made to assess naval doctrine as such for this undoubtedly would
have involved criticism of wartime decisions and performance. This
much was obvious to Richmond: "Phillimore's Committee is busy . . .
asking us questions about what the speed of a battleship should be,
the calibre of anti-torpedo-bomber and A.A. guns . . . . If that is the line
they are working on they won't do much good."[9] Later, just a month
prior to the submission of the Committee's Interim Report, he added:

5   Adm. 116/1806, E. G. Pretyman (Civil Lord) to Geddes, February 7, 1918; Wemyss
    to Geddes, February 22, 1918. Adm. 116/1809, Geddes to Lloyd George, Novem-
    ber 18, 1918; Lloyd George to Geddes, November 16, 1918.
6   Adm. 167/56, Board Minute No. 566, January 2, 1919; also Secretary's Memoran-
    dum, December 17, 1918.
7   Viscount Long of Wraxhall, *Memories* (London: Hutchinson, 1923), p. 274.
8   Adm. 167/156, Board Minute No. 834, June 19, 1919.
9   RIC/1/15, Diary, October 17, 1919.

The Post-War Questions Committee had merely made statements, assertions: had not examined the war to find out what the influence of the big ship was, or whether she was still in the position she used to be. The thing i.e. the future of the battleship must be approached in a far more scientific manner.[10]

The Phillimore Committee's approach was anything but "scientific." Much of the evidence was verbal, highly opinionated, and selected a priori to bolster the battleship's case. The Committee's composition[11] further vitiated its findings which suggested that nothing in recent weapons developments had undermined the battleship's predominance. On the contrary, the Committee recommended that larger battleships, in excess of 35,000 tons and mounting 15-inch guns, be built. Although the final report was never subjected to a comprehensive review by the Board, it was printed and given limited circulation which suggests that the findings generally accorded with Beatty's.

The conceptual myopia which undermined the work of the Reconstruction and the Post-War Questions Committees continued to restrict strategic and tactical thinking throughout the postwar period, and can be detected at almost every level that the processes of naval policy formulation are studied. The 1920s, Captain Stephen Roskill has suggested, were "a period of tactical sterility"[12] in which the primacy of the capital ship and the Battle Fleet concept dominated to the extent that serious studies in other areas were neglected. An obsessive preoccupation with the battle of Jutland and its "lessons" pervaded all postwar studies carried out by the Naval Staff, the Staff Colleges, and later, the Tactical School. In the words of Admiral of the Fleet Sir Caspar John, "The obsession with Jutland ran through the Navy as a deadening virus."[13] Restrictions on Fleet training and exercises seriously limited opportunities for practical experimentation. In any case, with virtually every major Admiralty and Fleet appointment going to former Grand Fleet officers, it was unlikely that innovative or radical thinking would be encouraged. This was enough to distort the Navy's assessment of its performance in the war. It was also the basis for the highly partisan nature of the Jutland debate which divided the service on the artificial lines of personality and prejudiced the possibilities of detached analysis.

10 Ibid., November 10, 1919.
11 Adm. 1/8586, Interim Report submitted December 19, 1919, and incorporated into the Final Report, dated March 27, 1920. Printed as C. B. 01557. Of its eight members, only Phillimore was an aviator (Admiral Commanding Aircraft in the Grand Fleet) although his previous specialty was gunnery. The Vice-Chairman and three other members were also gunnery men. There was no representation from the sciences, submarines, or construction.
12 Captain S. W. Roskill, *Naval Policy Between the Wars*, vol. 1: *The Period of Anglo-American Antagonism* (London: Collins, 1968), p. 534.
13 Marder, *Dardanelles to Oran*, p. 48.

In 1919 the Naval Staff undertook production of a series of historical studies of the war known collectively as the "Naval Staff History" and the "Technical History." As distinct from the C.I.D.'s *Official History*, being written by Julian Corbett, these Admiralty series were intended solely for the use of senior officers, training establishments, and the Staff College. The "Technical History," as its name suggests, concentrated on the technical lessons of the war. Research was directed by a "civilian engineer" as editor, assisted by officers who had been associated with "certain special operations."[14] Altogether, fifty-one monographs were written between 1919 and 1930. Many are of considerable historical interest but others were so esoteric and highly specialized as to be of little real value.

The "Staff History" consisted of thirty-seven monographs produced by the Historical Section of the Training and Staff Duties Division. Most were completed in the 1920s, though many of the more important volumes dealing with the crucial years of 1917-1918, and especially the convoy period, were not finished by the outbreak of war in 1939. The principal authors were Captain A. C. Dewar, Instructor-Captain Oswald Tuck, and Lieutenant-Commander J. H. Lloyd Owen. All were retired officers hired and paid on a piece-work basis.[15] Taken together, the Monographs are a mine of information covering a wide range of Admiralty operational and intelligence information. But they were not critical or interpretive studies. "The idea," Kenneth Dewar wrote in the 1950s, "was that, eventually, these monographs would provide the material for a proper Staff history of the war."[16] Nor were they an indication of some new-found Admiralty appreciation of the value of detailed historical analysis. Quite the opposite was the case. In view of this, the fact that one of the monographs—the *Naval Staff Appreciation of Jutland* (1922)—was critical, indeed highly explosive and partisan in its tone, is all the more interesting. Beatty was forced to withhold its circulation by members of the Board who rightly feared the controversy it might, and finally did, arouse. Eventually, all but a few of its three hundred copies were destroyed in 1928. But by then, the damage was done; the Jutland "Controversy" was in full swing.

Much of the persistent and emotional debate surrounding the Jutland "Scandal" has been laid to rest at last with the publication of

14 DEW, 2, Ms "Post War Naval Histories," n.d. (written during World War II). The monographs on Minesweeping, Minelaying, and on Atlantic convoys were written respectively by Captain Lockhart Leith (former Commanding Officer, Minelayers), and Paymaster Eldon Manisty (Director, Convoy Section).
15 Ibid., Ms "Historical Section of the Naval Staff," n.d. (written in 1923). Also, see Lieutenant-Commander Peter K. Kemp, "War Studies in the Royal Navy," *R.U.S.I.*, 111 (May 1966), 151-55; and Marder, *Dardanelles to Oran*, pp. 60-61.
16 DEW, 8.

Jellicoe's papers and those of Vice-Admiral J. E. T. Harper which have remained in the custody of the Royal United Services Institute.[17] Publication of Beatty's papers and also Professor Schurman's biography of Sir Julian Corbett will complete the picture. There is, therefore, little need to reopen the issue here except to examine the part played by the Dewar brothers whose historical account of the battle was the centrepiece of all the turmoil.

A monograph on Jutland, as an integral part of the Naval Staff History, should not have raised any special problems had not an account of the battle been prepared prior to Beatty's arrival at the Admiralty. His dissatisfaction with this earlier study, and decision to suppress it, precipitated the controversy that followed, the central issue of which was whether the object in studying the battle was to improve overall naval efficiency or to serve personal reputations.

It was to forestall this latter possibility and, if possible, put an end to the Jellicoe-Beatty schism in the service, that Wemyss originally had commissioned Captain J. E. T. Harper, in February 1919, immediately following publication of Jellicoe's memoirs (*The Grand Fleet, 1914-1916*), to prepare a "Record of the Battle of Jutland." Harper's instructions, as he explained when submitting his draft to the Admiralty Board in October 1919, were "to prepare a Record which would closely define what actually took place, without criticism or comment, no oral evidence to be taken, and no information to be inserted except that obtained from Admiralty records."[18] Harper understood that the "Record" was intended for the Admiralty Board's consideration only. Wemyss intended that the finished product would not be shown to Beatty or Jellicoe until it was eventually printed, probably as a Command Paper.[19] The completed "Record" was submitted in October 1919, a month prior to Beatty's arrival at Whitehall but serious consideration of its contents by the new regime was delayed until the following spring.

At that time, the "Record" was reviewed by Chatfield (A.C.N.S.), Admiral Osmond Brock (D.C.N.S.), and Beatty. All three considered it unfair to the Royal Navy generally and, more particularly, to the Battle Cruiser Fleet which, it argued, had suffered heavy damage from an inferior number of German battle-cruisers. Beatty's reaction

---

17 *Jellicoe Papers* (with Appendix, the Papers of Vice-Admiral J. E. T. Harper), vol. 2, pp. 458-90.
18 Adm. 116/2067.
19 A decision which Jellicoe supported. *Jellicoe Papers*, vol. 2, no. 137, p. 405. Also, Adm. 1/8581. Responding to Harper's submission to proceed with publication (February 12, 1920), Beatty noted that the decision had presumably been made by Wemyss, and that publication should now go ahead "as rapidly as possible." The First Lord (Long) agreed and the suggestion was approved by the Treasury (March 12, 1920).

was the harshest.[20] In a seven-page commentary, he listed various amendments, deletions, and insertions which he ordered Harper to incorporate. While Harper was prepared to accept many of these alterations, there were several that he could or would not. Moreover, by this time, Jellicoe had seen the "Record" and generally approved its contents. Although he preferred to keep clear of further involvement, he nevertheless reserved his right, in correspondence with Long, to pass judgment on any changes introduced by the Admiralty or to comment publicly if necessary.[21] An impasse had been reached. An attempt to break the deadlock by getting Jellicoe or Corbett to write a preface in place of Beatty's failed. Jellicoe refused and advised Corbett to do the same.[22] Corbett, who was concerned that publication of the "Record" would prejudice his own account in the *Official History*, replied that his publishers (Messrs. Longmans) would never countenance it. He wanted Harper's account suppressed and, at the same time, to have access to it himself. Harper, with whom Corbett was in touch during this period and who was "full of Beatty's bullying attitude,"[23] consented. As a result, it was agreed by Beatty, Harper, Corbett, and Longmans that publication of the "Record" would be postponed indefinitely.[24] Corbett was then given access to all the Report's materials.

It was at this point, in November 1920, that Captain A. C. Dewar began work on the *Naval Staff Appreciation*. He was assisted by Lieutenant J. F. Pollen who had worked on the earlier Harper Committee and helped prepare its diagrams. Kenneth Dewar, then on half-pay, was also called in to assist, ironically on Corbett's recommendation. Criticisms of Harper's charts, expressed by senior Admiralty officers (particularly Brock), resulted in the decision to call in another person to re-examine all the diagrams, although Corbett had no idea that a complete re-evaluation was under way.[25] In any event, Dewar's revised charts were submitted in September, and the completed *Appreciation* in January 1922.

That it was a highly partisan account written from the point of view of the Commander-in-Chief Battle Cruiser Fleet, raised serious doubts as to how much its authors were influenced by Beatty. The Dewars have denied any untoward pressure. Yet, if this is so, even more perplexing questions arise, not the least of which is why the Dewars proceeded as they did.

20 Adm. 116/2067. Chatfield's remarks, June 2, 1920; Brock's, June 14, 1920. Beatty's remarks are unsigned and undated, but their content leaves no doubt as to their authorship.
21 Ibid., Jellicoe to Long, July 5, 1920.
22 CP, Diary, August 18, 1920.
23 Ibid., October 5, 1920.
24 Adm. 1/8592.
25 CP. Diary, April 17, 1921.

Richmond was certainly alive to the dangers. When first informed by Harper, in January 1920, that Beatty was pressing for changes in the "Record," he was alarmed:

> I'm sorry. I wish B. [Beatty] w^{d} leave it alone. He has made H. [Harper] alter some things which did "injustice" to the battle cruisers' shooting, also a part of the tract which H. had put in from the evidence; but B. says he doesn't care about all the evidence in the world, as it can't alter *"facts"*. That is to say, his evidence is "facts". A pity this, as it will open the way to controversy afterwards. My opinion, I told H., was that everything should go in—Jellicoe's despatch, Scheer's despatch, and the Admiralty minutes on the paper. Much better put all the cards down, face up; and the narrative should not be interfered with by anyone who was concerned in the action. They are witnesses—not judges.[26]

Later, in November, he repeated this advice to Beatty personally. Summoned to give his views on the intensifying demands of editorial and parliamentary critics for the release of all documents pertaining to Jutland, including most especially the Grand Fleet Battle Orders of 1914, Richmond suggested that full publication risked very little since the tactics of 1916 were by then obsolete. To his mind, the Fleet of the future would consist of far fewer expensive battleships ("We may see a core of heavy ships—a nucleus, with a host of lesser vessels.") and it would employ an entirely new tactical doctrine:

> Smaller formations of great ships will make the torpedo attack a wholly different matter. Torpedo planes will play a part we have hardly thought of, submarines will have a more difficult role, formations will be looser, co-operation of all arms even more important than to-day. To think that the tactical orders of the day of Jutland will be applicable, or will even be guides, to such a situation is to misinterpret the whole meaning of tactics & misunderstand developments.[27]

This wise counsel was given at a time, it should be noted, when Richmond's own views were coloured by his deep personal dislike of Jellicoe.[28] He had not made any detailed analysis of Jutland for himself. It was not until early 1922 that Corbett, then in the midst of preparing Volume III of the *Official History*, first briefed him on the specifics of the battle; "Wh he had never understood before and wh confirmed Jellicoe."[29] Considering Richmond's earlier views, this is a particularly revealing illustration of his historical objectivity and

---

26 RIC/1/15, Diary, January 12, 1920.
27 Ibid., November 10, 1920.
28 Ibid., Richmond to Carlyon Bellairs, February 18, 25, 1919; March 12, 1919. See also Carlyon Bellairs, *The Battle of Jutland: The Sowing and the Reaping* (London: Hodder and Stoughton, 1919).
29 CP, Diary, March 31, 1922. Both Corbett and Richmond were sent copies of the Appreciation, ibid., December 21, 1921. Also Adm. 1/8618, December 22, 1921.

willingness to learn from a knowledgeable expert—qualities for which his critics rarely credited him. Nothing in Richmond's correspondence suggests that he cautioned the Dewars about what they were doing, but there can be little doubt of his views about their integrity as historians. He agreed with Corbett who wrote that Dewar's "facts were, I found, very loose."[30]

In any event, Corbett succeeded in delaying circulation of the *Appreciation* pending the release of his own account. Hankey assisted by placing the matter before the Cabinet to ensure that any future release of the *Appreciation* would require Jellicoe's prior agreement with its contents. But Corbett died on September 22, 1922, before that could be arranged. Fortunately his manuscript was complete, and the conditions under which Volume III had to be accepted were so firmly established that E. Y. Daniel was able to see it through to publication without great difficulty.

Corbett had out-manoeuvred Beatty, but this did not alter the Admiralty's intention to release the *Appreciation* eventually in the form of a restricted fleet issue, along with an expurgated version for public consumption. The latter would require Jellicoe's sanction, since it would amount to a substitute for Harper's account. Accordingly, a draft was prepared and despatched to New Zealand where it reached him in late July.

Well before this, however, the Fleet version encountered difficulties and Beatty clamped tight controls on all copies. Even the authors were denied further access to it.[31] On March 6, A. C. Dewar was informed: "The book in its present form is being withdrawn and held up for the time being and it is not advised that its existence should be generally known."[32] Within two weeks, he was warned that others had expressed reservations:

> There is no question of the accuracy of the book—in fact I understand it is only too accurate and it has been thought better to keep the criticisms unpublished for the present. The only question I have heard raised is that in one or two points it differs from the Tactical Manual—but that is easily adjusted in the next edition of the latter which is not entirely unopen to criticism itself. The real fact is that they haven't the courage to publish it until certain people have passed away.[33]

Serious examination by Admiralty personnel, as well as Corbett and Richmond, revealed that, apart from the anti-Jellicoe bias and several factual inadequacies, the account was so critical of orthodox tactical

---

30 CP, Diary, March 31, 1922.
31 DEW, Paymaster Captain Frank Spickernell (Beatty's Secretary) to Dewar, February 9; March 17, 1922.
32 Ibid., Captain U. H. S. Haggard (D.T.S.D.) to Dewar, March 6, 1922.
33 Ibid., Charles A. Scott to Dewar, March 18, 1922.

doctrine that the Board was not prepared to allow its circulation. The severe roasting which Kenneth Dewar received from the students when he presented the *Appreciation* as a series of lectures at the Senior Officers War Course and at the Naval Staff College undoubtedly increased Their Lordships' reservations at this point.[34] In any case no immediate decisions were made. It was late December when Dewar was finally informed that publication for service use had been decided against. He was advised privately: "when it came to the point they would not take the responsibility of publishing it with the criticisms—but a Fleet Issue will probably be published which will be the original book emasculated with all criticisms removed."[35]

By year's end, however, Jellicoe had seen and commented upon the so-called "public" version. It was, in his opinion, so "full of inaccuracies and misleading deductions" that he took several weeks to study its contents. In late November he replied to the Admiralty, objecting strongly to release as it stood, and attaching a lengthy list of corrections for inclusion in a revised version, or attachment as an appendix. Some of these suggestions were accepted and incorporated into a revised draft which was returned to him after a year's delay. Still far from satisfied Jellicoe replied on December 6, 1923. He cabled his main criticisms directly to London, and sent the remainder by surface mail, requesting that the Admiralty withhold publication pending their arrival.[36] In the end, the expurgated *Appreciation* was published as the *Admiralty Narrative*. Jellicoe's cabled criticisms were included as an appendix, heavily footnoted with counter-criticisms and a prefatory denunciation that : "Where . . . the Appendix differs from the Admiralty Narrative, Their Lordships are satisfied that the Narrative is more in accordance with the evidence available."[37]

Thus, for the time being, matters rested. The unexpurgated version was withheld from circulation even as a Confidential Book. Whether Jellicoe's criticisms were the reason, or the Board's reluctance to distribute a work so critical of a former Commander-in-Chief and of orthodox tactical practice, is not known. Beatty was pleased with the account, and on occasion expressed his satisfaction to intimate associates. He would never allow his own copy to pass out of his

---

34 *Jellicoe Papers*, vol. 2, p. 482, Harper's Narrative. Harper, who was attending the War Course then, wrote: "Not one of the twenty officers present approved of this form of personal propaganda, and, further, the lecturer was severely heckled at the conclusion of each lecture in respect to numerous grossly inaccurate statements made by him, and the wrong conclusions drawn."

35 DEW, Scott to Dewar, December 29, 1922.

36 *Jellicoe Papers*, vol. 2, no. 142, Jellicoe to Frewen, November 6, 1922; no. 143, Jellicoe to Secretary of Admiralty, November 27, 1922.

37 Great Britain, Admiralty, *Narrative of the Battle of Jutland* (H.M.S.O., 1924), Appendix G, p. 106.

hands, but enjoyed reading passages aloud to a limited company. Sir Shane Leslie, one such friend, later wrote in the *Quarterly Review*:

> the difference between these two editions was certainly that between "penny plain and twopenny coloured." He kept the suppressed copy in a locked box. Once he let me read it in his London house but never out of his sight. He returned it to safekeeping murmuring "It will never be published."[38]

In 1928 Beatty's successor, Sir Charles Madden (Jellicoe's Chief of Staff at Jutland, and his brother-in-law) ordered all copies destroyed. Beatty, however, retained his copy despite several attempts by the Admiralty to regain it.[39]

The Jutland Controversy simmered on for some years, periodically fanned to life by such books as Admiral Bacon's *The Jutland Scandal* (1925) and Lloyd George's *Memoirs*. Harper's decision to publish his own version of the controversy, *The Truth About Jutland* (1927) finally provoked the Admiralty into releasing a substantially complete version of his original account, *The Record of the Battle of Jutland*.[40] Of the anti-Jellicoe accounts, the one contained in Churchill's *World Crisis* (Volume 3) is of interest, for while there is no direct evidence to show that Churchill ever saw the Dewars' unexpurgated account, he was strongly influenced by their thinking. Throughout 1926, Kenneth Dewar served as Churchill's main naval consultant.[41] Not surprisingly, many of Churchill's criticisms of Jellicoe parallel—in places, almost verbatim—the Dewars' arguments and diagrams.

Of the protagonists in the controversy, Jellicoe emerges with his reputation the least tarnished. His involvement was restrained and limited to that of a private individual who objected to official tampering with the Harper "Record," and to the obvious bias of the Naval Staff *Appreciation*. Beatty undoubtedly laid himself open to the charge of using his official status to suppress or alter evidence. This is not to say there was anything consciously sinister in his motives, but rather that he, like the Dewars, was subject to the normal biases of his profession, what Captain Roskill calls "that mental arrogance which today we regard as one of the less happy legacies of the Victorian and Edwardian eras."[42] Beatty did work to have his views incorporated

38 DEW, 13, Diary, n.d. (1952), in reference to Leslie's review in the *Quarterly Review* (October 1952).

39 Beatty's Secretary, Paymaster-Captain Sir Frank Spickernell, also retained a copy which, shortly before his death, came into Captain Stephen Roskill's hands. Beatty's copy is in his papers. The Dewar Papers do not contain a copy nor any drafts or notes relating to one.

40 H.M.S.O., Cmd. 2870 (1927). Essentially the disputed Harper "Record" of 1919, but without the diagrams

41 DEW, 13, K. Dewar to Churchill, August 10; November 1, 1926; Churchill to Dewar, October 7, 1926.

42 Captain S. W. Roskill, "Some Reasons for Official History," *The Library Association Records*, 65, no. 3 (March 1963), 96. Reprint copy in CP, Box 7.

into various official accounts of the war. That Sir Julian Corbett, in writing the first three volumes of the *Official History*, successfully preserved his professional and personal integrity in the face of such pressures is one measure of his stature as an academic and as a man.[43] But the cost was high in terms of his already fragile health. For Richmond, whose role in the controversy was peripheral at most, Corbett's death was a tragic personal loss, and an object lesson in the price exacted for anyone who took his stand on historical integrity. Captain Roskill (who as a young Sub-Lieutenant first met Richmond at Greenwich) has recalled how disturbed he was by all that had happened.

> Little did I foresee that what Richmond then told me was to stand me in very good stead when, twenty years later, I was invited to undertake a task analagous to that which Sir Julian Corbett and Sir Henry Newbolt had endeavoured to carry out. I realise now that the treatment accorded to the historians of the earlier struggle had profoundly shocked Richmond's strong sense of integrity.[44]

But Beatty's views on the uses both of history and of historians were not the only grounds for Richmond's uneasiness. By 1921 he found himself at odds with the Admiralty over a more current problem, but one on which the Jutland "obsession" exerted its influence. This was the question of the future of the battleship and its relationship to naval policy development in the months leading up to the Washington Disarmament Conference.

The question of capital ships versus aircraft and submarines had exercised military planners' minds for years and would do so for many more to come. Beatty's appointment as First Sea Lord had pleased many who looked for imaginative responses to the issue. Certainly his reputation as one of the few senior officers who had actively encouraged developments, particularly in naval aviation, suggested possibilities of forward-looking postwar reassessments. Once in office, however, Beatty was faced with other realities that favoured caution and moderation. By late 1920, it was obvious that he would not be rushed into radical policy changes. By then, however, pressure for more positive indications of the Admiralty's thinking was mounting.

In November 1920 Richmond was invited by Beatty to testify before the "Naval Shipbuilding Sub-Committee" of the C.I.D. (the

---

43 In the case of Sir Henry Newbolt's Volumes 4 and 5, Churchill's comment is probably close to the truth: "The able historian has evidently had to submit his chapters to authorities and departments; and important personages in the story have clearly applied their pruning knives and ink-erasers with no timid hand." *Thoughts & Adventures* (London: Butterworth, 1932), p. 123.

44 Captain S. W. Roskill, "Richmond in Retrospect," *Naval Review*, 51 (1963), 26; see also Roskill, "The Richmond Lecture," *Naval Review*, 57 (1969), 135.

Bonar Law Enquiry) which was set up in response to a public outburst that attended the first indications that the new Naval Estimates would involve large additional expenditures. These included the resumption of battleship construction—eight super-Hoods, four to be laid down in 1921, and four more in 1922.[45] Firing the first salvo in a leader of November 29, 1920, entitled, 'The Navy: A Question for the Nation," *The Times* challenged the Admiralty to make known its plans and reasoning. Pessimistically, the Editor suggested that: "In the *arcana* of the Admiralty, plans may already exist for another revolution in naval shipbuilding as important as that effected by the production of the first Dreadnought. But we doubt it." The flood of correspondence that followed, led by naval correspondents who knew something of the internal strife over Jutland, was too reminiscent of the prewar Fisher-Beresford dispute to be written off as the squabblings of proponents of various weapons systems. Significantly, these critics of the big battleships (and by implication, the Beatty regime) included several distinguished officers who had had most to say about their introduction—Fisher, Scott, Jellicoe, and Mark Kerr.

Especially unnerving were the views of Sir Percy Scott. The much-venerated "Father of Modern Gunnery" in the Royal Navy had written only recently in his autobiography: "Some officers say that the battleship is more alive than ever; others declare that the battleship is dead. I regarded the surface battleship as dead before the War, and I think her more dead now, if that is possible."[46] Scott led the campaign in *The Times* to persuade the public that in framing the new Naval Estimates Beatty had not properly "analysed the basis of his convictions." The Admiralty's preoccupation with World War I, the building of bigger ships and guns, and the entire system of professional preferment which was founded on battleship service, appeared to Scott as a mummification of the revolution he had helped foster.

The outcry against the Admiralty's projected building programmes forced the Government into appointing the special C.I.D. Shipbuilding Committee, but it was a body whose purpose was anything but the searching and objective analysis of naval needs which *the Times* demanded and the Government promised. Beatty was the only professional naval member. The others were Bonar Law (Chairman), Sir Robert Horne (President of the Board of Trade), and Churchill, Geddes, and Long—the latter three all former or serving First Lords.[47] But it was not only the composition of the Committee which

---

45 Adm. 167/61, Memorandum for the Cabinet, Navy Estimates and Naval Policy, February 13, 1920. Adm. 167/62, Beatty to First Lord, "Naval Policy and Construction," July 8, 1920. Adm. 1/8602, Memo, July 8, 1920. Adm. 116/1175, "Naval Policy and Construction," Memo for the Cabinet by First Lord, November 22, 1920.

46 *Fifty Years in the Royal Navy* (London: Murray, 1919), p. 332.

47 Adm. 116/3610, "Report of the Sub-Committee of the C.I.D. . . . . on the Question of

prejudiced the possibility of meaningful findings. Beatty made it abundantly clear to his colleagues that the Admiralty's position on capital ships was firm and that further studies would be pointless.[48] Time was pressing in the sense that the nation's armaments firms were finding it difficult to continue armourplate production because of the rapid dispersal of skilled labour that was taking place. Moreover, while Beatty did not want to underrate the significance of new developments in mines, aircraft, and submarines, he was convinced that for the foreseeable future (i.e., the twenty-year life of the ships being requested), they would not supplant the battleship. This was realistic thinking especially insofar as it took into account the effects of either further building delays or demands for new weapons systems on a Government already committed to paring expenses to the bone.

Altogether, fourteen witnesses were called. Of these, all but two—Rear Admirals S. S. Hall (former Commodore of the Submarine Service, 1915-1918) and C. M. de Bartolomé (former Third Sea Lord)—were Active List officers. The more senior of these (especially Brock, Madden, and Chatfield, then serving respectively as D.C.N.S., C-in-C Atlantic Fleet, and A.C.N.S.) were former Grand Fleet officers and predictably pro-battleship in their thinking. Of the many retired officers and knowledgeable civilians whose names appeared in *The Times*, only Admiral Hall was called to testify.[49] Sir Percy Scott refused an invitation to appear arguing that it was a trap to muzzle his activities.

Richmond had not participated in the public debate up to this point although he was involved in the issue from early November 1920, when the First Sea Lord personally solicited his opinions. Beatty was clearly sensitive about public criticism and wanted arguments to bolster his position. With characteristic regard for academic objectivity, Richmond noted at the time, "I thought he was going about the investigation the wrong way round. One should not try to

the Capital Ship in the Royal Navy," C.I.D. Paper N-11, March 2, 1921. Also *The Times*, December 14, 1920, "The Navy: An Ill-Conceived Inquiry."

48 Adm. 116/1775, "Naval Construction," Admiralty Memorandum for the Cabinet and C.I.D., December 10, 14, 1920; "The Retention of the Capital Ship," Memorandum by the Admiralty, "Have Submarines, Aircraft or Mines Arrived at Such a Stage of Efficiency that the Capital Ship is an Obsolete Type?" December 14, 1920 (signed: Beatty), C.I.D. Paper N-5.

49 Of those who signed their names, the most prominent were: Admiral Sir Herbert King-Hall (December 9, 1920; January 7, 1921), Admiral Sir Cyprian Bridge (December 9, 1920; January 15, 1921), Admiral W. H. Henderson (December 11, 14, 1920; January 4, 15, 1921), Captain A. C. Dewar (December 20, 1920), Professor T. B. Abell (December 22), Admiral Sir R. Custance (December 24), and then serving Admiral E. R. Fremantle (January 3, 1921). For Scott's letters see December 9, 13, 15, 17, 21,23, 28, 1920, and January 8, 1921; also, "Sir P. Scott and the Sub-Committee," January 3, 1921.

prove what needed proving in one's own mind, but to find out what was right."[50] When he took this same stance before the C.I.D. Enquiry he found himself uncomfortably straddling both schools of thought.

Like Hall and Bartolomé, Richmond had serious doubts about the continuing dominance of the battleship. But he would not go so far as to say they should be replaced by less expensive submarines and aircraft, or that they were in any way rendered useless for the immediate future by these newer, and still developing, weapons. He agreed with Beatty and the majority of the Active List witnesses that "the capital ship must remain, as it was in the recent war, the main support and cover for the lighter vessel by which sea-power is actively exercised both offensively and defensively." But Richmond was alone in recommending that new construction should be postponed. More time was needed for experimentation and research. The uncertain international situation convinced him that it would be folly to undertake costly building programmes at that time. The monopolistic "command" or domination of the seas once wielded by the Royal Navy was no longer a realistic possibility. In any case, he emphasized, naval mastery had always derived from the judicious exploitation of all of Britain's maritime resources and advantages including geography, bases, and her fleets both merchant and naval. In most of these respects, Britain remained the pre-eminent power, but without a significant strengthening of her international trade and financial position, equality with the United States in battleships would never be enough. Naval security defined in terms of battleships alone had always been, in his view, an "artificial" and "unscientific" standard of measurement.[51]

The immediate effect of these arguments was to split the Enquiry down the middle. As a result, two Reports were submitted to the Cabinet. The first, signed by Bonar Law, Geddes, and Horne, concluded that no adequate evidence had been heard to support contentions that the capital ship was obsolete. However, they added:

> and although it may be true that in the naval warfare of the future squadrons of such ships will play the same vital part as they have done in the past, the Committee feel it their duty to call attention to the evidence of Rear-Admirals Richmond and Bartolomé which points to the doubtful expediency of deciding to build big and costly vessels at the present time.[52]

Churchill, however, came down heavily on Beatty's side. He attacked the Draft Report contending that it misrepresented the gen-

50 RIC/1/15, Diary, November 10, 1920.
51 Adm. 116/3610, "Report of the Sub-Committee on the Question of the Capital Ship in the Royal Navy." Also RIC/10/4, Lectures at Royal Naval War College, autumn 1920.
52 Adm. 116/3610, "General Remarks," para. 21.

eral nature of the evidence heard. He was convinced "that the Admiralty have made out an overwhelming case for the retention of the capital ship as the foundation of sea-power in the period with which we have now to deal." Ignoring the highly restrictive nature of the list of witnesses, Churchill went on to argue that these views "have been supported by the evidence of almost every naval officer in the Service, even those representing the submarines." He singled out Richmond's testimony "the value of which was greatly reduced by the fact that he was mixing up financial and political considerations, of which he was no particular judge, with the matters upon which he has professional credentials."[53] This was not the first time Richmond had encountered Churchill's anger for seemingly exceeding his terms of reference. As for the other witnesses who opposed the capital ship, Churchill uncharitably and inaccurately dismissed their evidence as "the views of officers who have left the service without attaining high command, who are to a large extent not informed on the most recent developments in naval science, and who in some cases are embittered and in all cases without responsibility." In his opinion, the only reasonable arguments against the battleship had been those advanced by the air advocates; namely, those "responsible officers" Trenchard and Sykes. As the Minister responsible for the Royal Air Force (R.A.F.), Churchill's enthusiasm here is understandable. Even so, he maintained that their case was premature; the time had not yet arrived when air-power alone would replace the British battle fleet. For the immediate future, he supported continued reliance on the capital ship and the maintenance of Britain's maritime strength, confident "that the nation has both the means and the will to do so and that it is our duty to make every sacrifice for that purpose." Considering Churchill's subsequent record as Chancellor of the Exchequer when dealing with matters of defence expenditures, this last statement has a particularly ironic ring. Be that as it may, his attack on the integrity and competence of witnesses such as Richmond, Hall, and Bartolomé was unjustified. So, too, was his refusal to consider the very real merits of the arguments advanced. In any event, an alternative Report—which ignored Richmond's testimony or reworded it so as to

53 Ibid., Draft Report (Note by Mr. Churchill), dated February 13, 1921. He added, "I observe that Admiral Richmond has since circulated a paper which is practically a reasoned retraction of his previous arguments. This important fact is not even referred to in the draft report." This probably refers to a paper drawn up at Beatty's request, subsequent to Richmond's original evidence, to state his views on Sir Percy Scott's and Hall's *Times* articles. Richmond replied with a lengthy rebuttal of the Scott-Hall position and showed that submarine successes in World War I were a function of the strategic situation created by the existence of the two main battle fleets. There is, however, nothing contradictory in this. RIC/7/2/2, Beatty to Richmond, January 6, 1921; Richmond to Beatty, January 1921.

de-emphasize its significance or discredit its author—was drafted by Beatty and signed by himself, Long, and Churchill.

The Cabinet was then faced with two conflicting assessments. From the Admiralty's point of view, this was highly disappointing; the case against the battleship had not been made, but neither had the Enquiry justified, in completely unequivocal terms, the need for an immediate and extensive programme of building new ones. By the time of the Washington Conference, firm decisions in this respect had still not been made. Cabinet approval was given for the Admiralty to complete its Super-Hood designs, and orders for two were placed in late October 1921. But within a month, work was suspended, and then in February 1922, cancelled altogether. By that time, events in Washington had altered the question entirely.

The net effect of Richmond's testimony before the Bonar Law Enquiry on these later developments is difficult to assess. Together with Bartolomé and Hall, he had at least ensured that something more than a whitewash of Beatty got to the Cabinet. Clearly, the doubts he expressed played into the hands of those Ministers who were already concerned about increased naval spending and its effects on Anglo-U.S. relations. Richmond's ideas also probably reached the Cabinet by even more direct means than the C.I.D. Report. Hankey had written in December 1920, in a "purely private and personal capacity," asking Richmond for a brief on capital ships which he could show "in strict confidence, if you think fit, to the Prime Minister, Mr. Bonar Law, and Mr. Balfour."[54] Whether Richmond replied is not known, but it was the kind of opportunity he seldom ignored. His correspondence of this period shows that he was anxious to precipitate a full-scale re-evaluation of naval policy in which the influence of the battleship enthusiasts would be placed in reasonable perspective. Had such a study been undertaken, the outcome of the Washington naval agreements may well have been fundamentally altered inasmuch as the British naval delegates would not have been caught so flatfooted as they were.

Throughout the Washington talks, Beatty and his advisers found themselves fighting a defensive rear-guard action instead of a well-directed advance along lines predetermined by thorough assessments of what was desirable and possible. The Admiralty's approach to the Conference was deliberately open and flexible, guided by two general principles: first, that any agreements reached should not jeopardize Empire naval security; and second, that in view of high public expectations, there should be nothing in the British position for which the Admiralty could be held accountable should the talks fail. Beyond that, the delegation followed an essentially opportunist approach of

54 RIC/7/4, Hankey to Richmond, December 20, 1920.

"no concrete proposals." The British representatives were directed to confine themselves to considering proposals put forward by the other delegations, if possible guiding discussion into channels which "the Naval Staff consider the most likely to be productive of a practical solution." On one point only was the Admiralty firm; there should be no extension of the unofficial building holiday which had been in force since the end of the war.[55]

U.S. Secretary of State Hughes' opening remarks to the Conference on November 12, 1921 therefore caught everyone by surprise. Especially disturbing were his proposals for abandonment of all capital ship construction, including the scrapping of Britain's Super-Hoods which had only just been ordered. Suggestions that cutbacks might include post-Jutland ships had simply not been anticipated by the British. The Americans had gained a tactical surprise from which the British naval delegates never fully recovered. Subsequent acceptance of a ten-year building holiday, the system of determining numbers of capital ships to be retained under the 5:5:3 ratios on a Total Tonnage basis, and the restriction of individual battleship displacement to 35,000 tons all ran counter to official naval thinking and owed more to the political assumptions of the so-called "new diplomacy" than to strategic, tactical, or technological considerations. Chatfield, backed by the Admiralty, remained convinced that if such limitations had to be accepted, the minimum tonnage which could guarantee sufficient speed, armour, and armament was 45,000 tons.[56]

In the midst of these discussions, Richmond reopened public debate by asking why even lower maximums were not considered. Using the pseudonym "Admiral," he inquired in *The Times* of November 23, 1921, "why 35,000 tons? What is there in this number of importance? Why not 34,000 or 30,000 or 20,000 or 10,000?"[57] Given the essential artificiality of the limits already accepted, the question was very much to the point. There was, in his view, no valid "military" justification for the 35,000 limit. The rapid growth in battleship sizes—from the 14,000-ton ships of the 1890s to the 40,000 tons and more of the latest designs—was a consequence of international naval competition waged purely on technological considerations. The Washington talks offered a unique opportunity to bring this

55 Adm. 116/3445, C.I.D., "The Washington Conference," Note by the First Lord, October 5, 1921, together with Naval Staff Memoranda.
56 Based on estimate sent to Beatty from the Controller. Adm. 116/3445, November 21, 1921. 45,000 tons was considered the absolute minimum. The Super-Hoods just ordered were designed for 48,000 tons. See Oscar Parkes, *British Battleships* (London: Seely Service, 1956), pp. 650-51.
57 A Ms copy of this letter is contained in RIC/7/2/3, "A letter to *The Times* of November 21, 1921, written after reading the report of the Washington Conference in which the decision to limit the size of the Capital Ship to 35,000 tons was announced," signed "Admiral" and initialled "H.W.R." (Richmond's handwriting).

competition to an end. The argument that armourplate firms would collapse as a result, he felt, was "a case of putting the cart before the horse. Navies do not exist to keep armourplate firms in existence." As to the purely naval reasons for large ships, he concluded:

> There appear to be people who imagine that there is some military reason why a "battleship" should carry 16-inch guns, a mass of armour and so forth. There is none. These guns and this armour have been introduced into the struggle to produce something more powerful than what is possessed by an enemy, or possible enemy. This is not a military but a mechanical reason. Now that our statesmen are sitting round a table and discussing this in friendly fashion they have such an opportunity as has never occurred before. They have the people behind them.
>
> The sole qualifications of a ship of war are that she shall be able to go to sea, and fight. There is a limit beyond which it is quite unnecessary for her to go. I have suggested 10,000 tons but this is guesswork. It may be 6,000 or 10,000. I am sure it is not more.

Richmond's challenge was immediately supported by Haldane and Henderson in *The Times*.[58] Admiral Cyprian Bridge also offered his approval of "Admiral's" thinking, adding: "We have now reached the stage at which naval strategy and naval tactics must be given their rights, no matter what opposition may be offered by the 'material school.'" This support was not entirely fortuitous. Richmond had solicited the backing of these men and others for some time, but had hesitated to have his own name appear in print.[59] There is nothing to indicate that "Admiral's" identity was known to the Admiralty at this time. Eight years later, almost to the day, Richmond's repetition of this stand on big ships would be the immediate cause of his release from the Navy. But in 1921, neither his action nor his ideas had any appreciable effect on events in Washington.

The Cabinet did discuss Richmond's ideas[60] and directed the Admiralty to comment on "the truth" of his contentions that 10,000-ton ships were equal to larger vessels in protecting Britain's interests. After paraphrasing Richmond's *Times* letter, Lloyd George put the question to the Admiralty:

58 *The Times*, November, 25, 1921.
59 RIC/6/4, Keyes to Richmond, November 17, 1921. Clement Fayle, in response to several notes from Richmond wrote: "I quite understand you cannot write over your own name, but if you could get Sir Cyprian Bridge or any other retired officer to do so, it would be much more likely to get in than a letter from a layman." (November 22, 1921), and later, having offered to put Richmond's letter in the *Westminster Gazette*, and having just seen the November 23 *Times*, promised he would still work to get letters elsewhere, including the American Press. "I will, of course, be careful not to let your name be breathed in connection with it. I shall bring up the point as my own and shall not have the slightest idea who 'Admiral' is" (November 23, 1921). See also Fayle's letter in *Truth*, December 21, 1921, "The Big Ship Craze."
60 RIC/7/2/3, Haldane to Richmond, December 4, 1921. This suggests that Hankey was the one who brought them to the Prime Minister's attention.

> If it is held that there is enough in the above considerations to justify
> our advocating a low limit tonnage, it may very likely recommend
> itself to the American Government, since it will go far to solve the
> problem of rapid replacement, presented by the proposed ten year's
> naval holiday . . . . If France and ourselves supported it together the
> appeal to American sentiment morally, as a great further limitation
> of armaments, and materially, as a higher promise of solvency on the
> part of their debtors, would be irresistible.[61]

The Admiralty was predictably unenthusiastic and made no attempt
to meet Richmond's points head on.[62] As a result, they never came
before the delegates at Washington. In any case it was too late. Negotiations were well advanced and a radical change in approach at that
point might well have produced chaos. Had these ideas been carefully
examined by earlier investigative bodies (namely, the Reconstruction, Post-War Questions, and the Bonar Law Committees), it is conceivable that more room for manoeuvre would have been available.
Though his ideas came too late to affect the Washington agreements,
they remained for Richmond a subject for continuing study, reflection, and refinement.

Richmond's time at Greenwich ended in 1923. By then his enthusiasm and optimism for the War Course had been thoroughly
shaken and he left the College filled with a sense of utter futility.
There was precious little to suggest that his superiors were impressed
by what he had accomplished by way of greatly improved course
curricula and teaching methods. The whole question of officer education remained a controversial subject. While staff training was considered by the Army to be an absolute essential in preparing officers for
higher command, it continued to represent in many naval eyes only a
loss of valuable sea-time. There was nothing to indicate that the War
Course was considered anything more than a convenient interim
posting for officers awaiting commands afloat. This was reflected in
the quality of the students who volunteered for or were posted to the
Course and, consequently, in their ability to appreciate Richmond's
efforts. Few were sufficiently well equipped to take full advantage of
his permissive teaching methods, his encouragement of unorthodox
views, or the brilliance of his lectures on strategy and tactics.

His three years, as he told Kenneth Dewar in a long reflective
epistle, were "interesting but saddening." The recent war had had
little impact on the students' comprehension of the principles of
strategy and tactics or their application. "The mind of the average
man is no more advanced than it was in 1914 . . . . One heard able men

61 Adm. 116/3445, C.I.D. 291-B, "Limitation of Tonnage of Battleships," Memorandum received from the Prime Minister, December 1, 1921.
62 Adm. 116/3445, C.I.D. 297-B, Admiralty Memorandum in regard to Note (C.I.D.
   Paper 291-B), December 2, 1921. Copy also in Adm. 116/1776.

talking about tactics as though they were merely a purely mathematical abstraction." The air service students were especially "appalling"
in this respect:

> They are even now crying out that the air should be permitted to
> attack merchant ships with torpedoes and bombs, and that for this
> purpose we require a large air fleet. Sometimes I despair of the
> people who are blind as to where our interests lie, and cannot see that
> sporadic warfare is against our interests.[63]

These private fulminations illustrate the haughtiness of which
Richmond was all too capable and which no doubt helped to undermine his wider efforts to bring home the real lessons of the war in
these difficult years. But they were also the impatient expressions of
virtually the only mind within the Navy which did understand these
connections and recognized the need for a comprehensive doctrine of
war within which questions of policy, strategy, tactics, and education
could be sensibly worked out. Lacking that, he found his time at
Greenwich difficult and instances of student non-appreciation or
outside Admiralty interference only heightened his impatience.

Two instances particularly irritated him. The first was when his
"withers were unwrung"[64] by the Admiralty for failing to obtain prior
approval to invite the President of the U.S. Naval War College (Admiral Niblack) to speak to the War Course. The second concerned the
teaching of history at Greenwich and, more particularly, the kind of
history taught by "that ASS Callender" (Professor Geoffrey Callender). "You never saw such drivel as he pumps into [the students]," he
uncharitably told Dewar. "What would Jervis have said to his crew
before the Battle of St. Vincent and so forth." He raised the question of
Callender's appointment along with the wider issue of "why do you
want to teach Naval History at all" with the Admiralty's Adviser on
Education, Mr. A. P. McMullen. The latter, an unaccomplished
former Assistant Master at Dartmouth Naval College, who had occupied the Admiralty position since March 1919 was directly responsible to the Second Sea Lord for advice on educational policy. This
clearly irked Richmond:

> The "Advisor on Education" apparently is the deciding authority.
> He carries more weight than the President of the War College. And so
> the whole thing is in abeyance and Callender is again lecturing on
> the size of the Henri Grace à Dieu of 1519, and the origins of the
> boatswain. I put to Their Lordships that Naval History to the sea
> officer was what military history is to the soldier—the foundation of
> his knowledge of war. I quoted the writings of Mahan, Henderson,
> Frederick the Great and the great soldiers of all times down to Foch to

---

63 DEW, 6, Richmond to Dewar, July 26, 1923.
64 G. M. Trevelyan, "Admiral Sir Herbert Richmond, 1871-1946," *Proceedings of the
    British Academy*, 32 (reprinted, 1946), p. 331.

shew why these men advocated History as an essential element in a fighting man's education—but apparently it all fell on deaf ears. W. Mullins—or whatever his name is—replied that my view of education was purely *utilitarian*. To which I replied that if it be utilitarian to educate men's minds in such a way as to fit them to perform the highest duties of their profession, I *am* utilitarian; and that I saw no utility whatever in a young officer learning the date at which jibs were introduced.[65]

This was Richmond at his hurtful worst. Whatever his opinion of Callender, he knew only too well, as his own writings attest, that concern for what Jervis said before Cape St. Vincent did not need to stand in opposition to an understanding of why Jervis' fleet was there in February 1797. What did irritate Richmond was outside meddling by lesser bureaucrats while those with real power otherwise ignored his grander visions for the future of the War College.

During his final year at Greenwich Richmond was appointed to the Wood Committee which was set up to examine the possibility of forming a combined War College. Four years would pass before the Imperial Defence College (I.D.C.) became a reality, but Richmond's work with the Wood Committee directly determined that outcome and resulted, as will be seen, in his appointment in 1927 as the College's first President. In 1923, however, the Admiralty was cool to the concept and this, Richmond felt, was tantamount to "Hari Kari." "I put all the weight I could into it," he told Kenneth Dewar, "but Their Lordships don't look favourably on it, they don't see the need." The only other alternative for bringing the three service departments into closer union was, he noted shrewdly, "some damnable Ministry of Defence in which the Admiralty will carry no weight because of its untrained mind."[66] Along with Hankey, Corbett, and others, he favoured re-establishing the C.I.D. and revitalizing its machinery, and any other means short of a unified Ministry that would foster service cooperation and the evolution of a common doctrine for Imperial Defence. Organizational and structural changes alone would not be effective; Richmond's experiences since 1917 had shown him that much. There was nothing in the Beatty regime's handling of affairs to show that the Admiralty's position relative to the other services was inherently stronger than it was in or since Fisher's time.

Increasingly, Richmond found himself out of step with Beatty's regime. The disappointment of Greenwich, Corbett's death, the Jutland "Controversy" and its effect on his attitudes towards Beatty and the Dewars, restriction of the *Naval Review* and indications that Admiral Henderson's health might prevent his carrying on as

65 DEW, 6, Richmond to Dewar, July 26, 1923.
66 Ibid.

Editor,[67] all helped to push Richmond away from and beyond the men and the issues that had been the focus of his world since the prewar years. Growing public recognition of his scholarly abilities assisted that transformation.

On February 21, 1923, Richmond was given the honour of delivering the Raleigh Lecture on History to the British Academy. His subject, "National Policy and Naval Strength, the Seventeenth to the Twentieth Century,"[68] was his first public excursion on a theme which would remain central to all his later writings. In 1928 it was reprinted in *National Policy and Naval Strength*, his first book in the field of what might be called popular history. It contained the fruits of various *Naval Review* articles, and lectures delivered to the Royal United Services Institute, the Royal Institute of International Affairs, Cambridge and London Universities, and to the students of the War Course.[69]

The book is especially valuable as an expression of Richmond's views—consequent to his War Course experience—on the value of the humanities, specifically history, as a medium for military education and preparation for higher command and direction. History, in his view, was not an end in itself, but a direct means to the perfection of the Royal Navy as an instrument of war. The secret lay not in its teaching, but in its study:

> Much of our education is conducted by lectures, in the belief that a person can learn by listening. This idea is fallacious. A lecture can but touch on the fringe of a subject: it can indicate certain points, draw out certain principles, excite interest—or otherwise. But it cannot replace the hard reading, the persistent study, the writing down, and the discussion of views by which alone a professional's knowledge is to be distinguished from that of an amateur.[70]

The essence of Richmond's message was contained in two brilliant chapters—"The Place of History in Naval Education" and "The Uses of History"—which are filled with concrete examples of the bearing

---

67 RIC/1/15, Richmond to Dewar, July 26, 1923. DEW, 8, A. C. Dewar to K. Dewar (August-September, 1923).

68 *Proceedings of the British Academy*, 10 (1923), 339-54.

69 His London University Lecture (1925-1926), "Sea Warfare," is contained in Sir George Aston, ed., *The Study of War for Statesmen and Citizens* (London: Longmans, Green, 1927). Also, RIC/6/2, Lecture Notes and Articles at R. N. College, Greenwich.

70 *National Policy and Naval Strength*, pp. 224-25. Several years later, he reasserted his aversion to the lecture system in an interesting letter to Kenneth Dewar. "My naval history is merely my outside hobby to amuse myself and to develop my instinct in strategy and tactics: but I haven't 'learnt' it by listening to anyone. It is merely a form of mental training which I believe to be useful . . . I am thankful to say that only twice in my life have I given what could be called a historical lecture—and [word undecipherable] bad ones they were." DEW, 7, Richmond to Dewar, n.d. (Written on Imperial Defence College letterhead.)

which the past has on contemporary problems. His own keen aware-ness of the vital importance of sea-power in Britain's history led to a steadily deepening commitment to encourage the serious study of history as a basis of service education and of a broader understanding by statesmen and the public at large of the Navy's role in national life.[71] From this point, Corbett's mantle rested squarely on his protégé's shoulders.

In February 1923 he left Greenwich and for the next eight months went on half-pay prior to taking up a two-year appointment as Commander-in-Chief East Indies Station.

71 "Naval History in Public Education," Address to the Oxford University History Society, June 9, 1942, *History* (June 1942).

7

The East Indies Station: Singapore, India, and Imperial Defence (1923-1925)

Richmond took up his duties as Commander-in-Chief East Indies in November 1923. Compared to other commands, it was hardly one of the more prestigious or influential; only three cruisers and a handful of sloops were involved. Still, it was an immense Station which covered the important waters stretching from the African east coast through the oil-rich Persian Gulf area to India and the giant base at Singapore, the pivot of imperial security in the Far East. In this respect, Richmond's responsibilities epitomized the overall defence dilemma which Britain faced in these years—how to preserve an Empire whose interests and commitments far exceeded its military resources. Thus, in addition to giving him a chance to fly his flag afloat, the East Indies command placed Richmond squarely in the mainstream of naval strategic priorities which, since the Washington agreements and the abrogation of the Anglo-Japanese alliance, were centred on Singapore's development as a major repair and refuelling facility—the key to the policy of rapid reinforcement of the Far Eastern defences.

From 1921, when the Admiralty first recommended the construction of major facilities there, Singapore became the source of persistent professional and political controversy. Labour opposed the base as an unnecessary waste of funds better spent on more pressing priorities for housing and social-welfare programmes at home.[1] In foreign affairs Labour preferred to trust in a new world order based on

---

[1] E.g., "Singapore—Expense and British Slums," *Manchester Guardian Weekly*, 18, May 11, 1923.

the League of Nations and international disarmament. Singapore would affront Japan and might provoke a new navalism in the Pacific. In announcing his Government's 1924 decision to abandon further development, Ramsay MacDonald pointed out that strategic arguments had to be weighed against these broader aspects of Britains's new internationalist foreign policy: "to continue the development of the Naval Base at Singapore would hamper the establishment of this confidence [in the League, and the possibility of a comprehensive limitation of armaments] and lay our good faith open to suspicion."[2] Similar pleas were echoed by the Liberal leadership in the Commons and Press.[3] Conservative reasoning suggested that Singapore would reduce defence costs in the long run. Singapore was a sound investment: "Empire Insurance" in the words of Mr. W. C. Bridgeman, the First Lord.[4] The Conservatives, who reviewed the project immediately after returning to power, refuted Labour's charges of dangerous diplomacy by asserting (somewhat incongruously) that they did not see any real danger in the Pacific, that relations with Japan were not strained, and that the measure was primarily one of naval economy and efficiency. Notwithstanding this, their case did rest on the premise of a perceived threat to British interests, and the underlying economic and political logic of protecting the very considerable sources of trade, investment, and raw materials east of Suez, and of commitments to the Dominions and Empire unity.

The Admiralty's assessment of the effects of the Washington agreements—especially the non-fortification provisions of the Quadruple Treaty and consequent removal of effective American influence west of Hawaii—showed that Britain's strategic position had definitely declined. Beatty had therefore urged that base facilities and the buildup of fuel-oil reserves which would permit rapid concentration of the Fleet in the East be proceeded with at once.[5] These considerations led the Standing Defence Sub-Committee, on December 14, 1922, to reaffirm the decision to go ahead with development of the base at the Johore Strait site. The Overseas Defence Committee was then directed to undertake studies of possible scales of defence re-

---

2   Adm. 116/3149, Cabinet 18(24), Extracts from Conclusions of a Meeting of the Cabinet, March 5, 1924, with Appendix setting forth the Government's policy in regard to Singapore.

3   E.g., Sir John Simon, 5 *Parliamentary Debates* (House of commons), 171, March 25, 1924, 1284; Viscount Grey, *The Times*, May 23, 1924; Asquith, *The Times*, November 19, 1924.

4   *The Times*, March 29, 1924.

5   Adm. 116/3615, Committee of Imperial Defence (C.I.D.), "The Washington Naval Conference and Its Effects upon Empire Naval Policy and Cooperation," C.I.D. Papers 131-C, 138-C (1921); 166-C and 176-C (1922); also, S.S./26th Minutes, C.I.D. The Standing Defence Sub-Committee, Draft Minutes of the 26th Meeting, Thursday, November 30, 1922.

quirements and to work out an annual construction programme. The
Staff Colleges were also requested to consider joint exercises on the
problems of attack and defence.

These studies, as well as those carried out by the three service
staffs throughout 1923 and 1924, revealed a serious divergence of
views even on such requirements as coastal-defence and anti-aircraft
guns, the role of aircraft, and accurate estimates of costs. Public
discussion was equally divided and ranged over the questions of
Singapore's value as a realistic guarantee of Britain's Asiatic interests,
the feasibility of defending the base, types of docks and facilities, and
the usefulness of the capital ships for which they were being built.[6]
The fact was, so long as the three services pursued their separate
interests—the War Office with its eyes on Imperial duties in the
Middle East, and the R.A.F. preoccupied with European considerations and strategic bombing—no fully coordinated study of Singapore
was likely. The lack of a commonly understood national strategic
doctrine made any consensus on Singapore, as well as most other
defence issues virtually impossible.

Richmond first spoke out on this deficiency while he was at
Greenwich. In a thoughtful lecture entitled "Cooperation," which he
delivered to the Royal United Services Institute in February 1923, he
pleaded the cause of closer service harmony based on doctrinal
unanimity. Only when the separate services saw themselves as a
"single instrument" of state policy would true cooperation develop.[7]
And that, he suggested, could be fostered by first establishing a
doctrine of war "in conformity with the interests, needs, and natural
capacities in all their forms of the Empire," and then employing it as
the basis of all officers' education from the earliest stages of their
careers, and in all phases of Staff and Government strategic planning.
His own views on Singapore and his approach to more immediate
problems of the East Indies command and later efforts to create the
Imperial Defence College were coloured entirely by this basic conviction.

Of all the many themes which he championed in the inter-war
years, Richmond's Imperial Defence ideas were the least well under-

6   Kenworthy and K. G. B. Dewar contributed some of the most interesting and com-
     prehensive speculations concerning Singapore's deterrent value and its relation-
     ship to trade protection in time of war. See: 5 *Parl. Debs.* (H.C.), 171, March 25,
     1924, 1228-29 (Statement by Lieutenant Commander Kenworthy); K. G. B. Dewar,
     "Singapore Naval Base," *Contemporary Review* (July 1930), 27-28 (originally writ-
     ten in 1924). Of those arguments favouring the base, the following are worth noting:
     "Lord Sydenham (*The Times*, March 24, 1924); his running debate with Sir Ian
     Hamilton on naval defences vs. military defences (*The Times*, March 24, 25, 27,
     1924).
7   H. W. Richmond, "Co-operation," *R.U.S.I.* (1923), 68, 391-404; republished in his
     National Policy and Naval Strength, pp. 185-203.

stood or appreciated. This was unfortunate for they were the capstone of his general strategic philosophy and, as such, the key to his thinking on many other questions such as disarmament, the limitation of warship sizes, and strategic bombing. In general terms, he visualized his "British doctrine of war" in terms of maritime communications linked by a network of bases whose defence (or acquisition) would be the joint responsibility of all three services. This implied a strategic distribution of resources (not concentration for home defence as R.A.F. doctrine suggested in what Richmond saw as a replay of the old invasion and "Fortress England" bogey) and mobility over secured lines of communication. It was a concept firmly rooted in the writings of Captain Sir John Colomb and more especially those of Julian Corbett. This helps explain why some of Richmond's specific suggestions were generally out of touch with what was politically feasible, particularly when it came to Dominion agreement and participation. Throughout the war and after, Richmond had endorsed the Admiralty's unpopular efforts for a unified Imperial navy or, at least, centralization of control. But despite the postwar facts of extended British imperial commitments and declining defence capabilities, the 1920s would show that a common foreign and defence policy for the Empire was impossible to achieve. From this perspective, Richmond's ideas—though strategically compelling—were politically unpalatable in the postwar atmosphere of evolving 'Commonwealth." Like most of his British contemporaries, Richmond was not altogether sensitive to the forces of developing Dominion nationalism (what he derisively called "State Patriotism") and the changing nature of the whole Empire connection.

Imperial Defence was also an amorphous concept and Richmond was sometimes ambiguous about its precise implications. His views did not flow from any comprehensive or systematically developed theory of international relations. Rather, they evolved in a piece-meal way in his various lectures and essays, some of which were published in his *National Policy and Naval Strength* (1928). Lord Sydenham of Coombe, in the introductory remarks to this volume, suggested that Richmond had produced "a considered philosophy of 'British Warfare' in which the 'major strategy' of the sea, the land and the air is welded into a national policy of Imperial Defence." This was overstating Richmond's achievement, for neither these essays, nor his later (1931) University College, London, and Lees-Knowles, Cambridge, lectures on the subject (published in 1932 as *Imperial Defence and Capture at Sea in War*) were primarily scholarly or historical in their purpose. They were exhortations to look to Empire trade defence at a time when naval policy makers were preoccupied with disarmament and the future of battle fleets. They were significant more as examples of special pleading in the context of contemporary defence discussions than as evidence of a fully developed philosophy. A far more profound expression of Richmond's thinking at that level was to be found in his *The Navy in India, 1763-1783*, which was completed during his command of the East Indies and published in 1931.

This was Richmond's last attempt at a detailed history as such and was, as he told Admiral Henderson, "much the best I have ever written—at least, so I think."[8] Released eleven years after his first major work, *The Navy in the War of 1739-1748*, it bears the imprint of his own experience of how policy tends to be subordinated to materialistic and administrative factors. He set out to analyze the maritime strategy of the Hughes-Suffren naval duel in Indian waters and to show its connection to the American Revolutionary War as a whole. His aim was "to indicate the policy, the causes affecting the strategy, and the influences governing the tactics employed by the commanders; and to bring out the many circumstances of weather, of supplies, of health and of material which played so large a part in the campaigns."[9] Drawing on primary source material in India, Colombo, South Africa, Holland, Paris, and London, he developed a theme from which the problems of British power in the Indian Ocean and Pacific in the twentieth century were never very far removed.

He began by asking why the East had become an important fighting ground in a war whose major issues were American independence, the loss of Gilbraltar, or even the invasion of England. What were the keys to the situation, he wondered:

> was there a strategical object, or was the object purely political, in this fighting on the Coromandel and Malabar coasts? How could a battle between some 7,000 British seamen, in a dozen ships of war, and a similar number of French seamen in about the same number of ships, affect the questions of whether the colonists in America should be free from the British Crown, France should reoccupy Gilbraltar or Holland obtain the licence to supply belligerents with contraband of war? Is there any link which unites a struggle in India with the main object of the war?[10]

For the French, India was an area for distracting and stretching British resources in order to produce a temporary superiority in the English Channel as a pre-condition of invasion, the primary French object. The danger was clear for the over-extended British and after 1778 their major purpose shifted from that of suppressing Americans to defence against the more menacing enemy.

> Thus France was now the principal enemy and the principal object of the war had now become to distress France ... the only way by

8   RIC/7/1, Richmond to Henderson, September 9, 1930.
9   *The Navy in India, 1763-1783* (London: E. Benn, 1931), p. 5.
10 Ibid., p. 18.

which France could be distressed was by the use of force in those parts where it was possible for Britain to bring superior force to bear; that is to say, in her oversea possessions or her commerce.[11]

In this context, an expedition such as the unsuccessful attempt to take Cape Colony in 1781 was, as Richmond showed, "not a mere excentric operation, an attempt to profit by the occasion and add new territory to the Empire," but an essential feature of Howe's plans to secure a base controlling French communications with Mauritius, and to relieve British over-extension in Indian waters.

Communications, bases, and the extent to which their fleets were tied to land operations also affected naval operations between Hughes and Suffren in the Indian ocean. This was particularly true of Hughes, whose prime concern at all times was the French squadron. But what was insufficiently understood by his East India Company associates was that, with the British presence in southern India threatened simultaneously by the French on land (Hyder Ali) and at sea (Suffren), it was imperative that the objective on which British sea and land forces should concentrate be selected as quickly as possible. Thus Hughes' ability to exploit favourable advantages was hampered by his superiors' failure to supply troops to take and garrison the naval bases he needed, and their failure to understand how important, indeed vital, they were to his operations. The loss of Trimcomali, for example, produced a critically dangerous situation. The causes were many, as Richmond explained: "but of these far from the least was the failure to distinguish the keystone of the situation and to direct the efforts of the Navy and Army in full cooperation to the attainment of an object common to both."[12]

Richmond's reasons for writing the book were entirely historical and scholarly. It is unlikely that he seriously intended it should possess immediate relevance to the contemporary situation in the 1920s. However, the marks of his own experiences in Indian waters from 1923 to 1925 are clearly discernible in the principal conclusions, particularly his assessment of how maritime power, in close cooperation with land forces, was employed to preserve British trade and power in the Indian sub-continent. That Hughes was able to surmount the difficulties of insufficient ships and almost constant bickering with his East India Company masters owed much to the fact that he and Sir Eyre Coote (the land forces commander) were seldom seriously at variance in their strategic appreciations. Most important, Richmond provided strong historical validation of Colomb's earlier, more pragmatic theories about the role of bases. They were a vital element in Hughes' exercise of naval force, but they were only as

11 Ibid., pp. 120-21; quoted from Lord Howe's "Secret Instructions," March 22, 1778.
12 Ibid., p. 31.

important as naval power itself made them. Their value related directly to actual non-naval security and the extent to which naval units consequently were freed from guarding them. These historical conclusions corroborated Richmond's personal observations of the situation in the Pacific in the 1920s. They emerge as an integral theme of all his C-in-C East Indies submissions which, of all his various staff papers, are amongst his most moderate and far-sighted. His grasp of historical realities was undoubtedly the basis of what were some of the most perceptive arguments and insights in the entire inter-war debate on Far Eastern security.

Generally, Richmond supported the Admiralty's Singapore policy though he doubted the need for heavy fortifications or defences. In company with his old friend and frequent correspondent in this period, Admiral Edmund Slade, Richmond had no doubts that war with Japan was inevitable and that it would be directed not against Australia and the southern Pacific, but against South-East Asia and India where pan-Asiatic or anti-European feelings would be a major consideration. They also agreed on the improbability of a purely naval attack against Singapore. The Japanese would have to accept too many risks from extended and exposed communications, the improbability of gaining a sufficiently safe jump in time over British naval reinforcements from the Mediterranean, and ammunition shortages at the critical moments when they would have to face the main British battle units. And raids without troops—the *coup de main* which the Admiralty planned to forestall with heavy coastal guns and defences—simply would not be decisive from Japan's point of view. A combined operation in which a major ground force could be landed to secure the base and guarantee supplies for the Japanese naval covering forces was another matter. "It is on this latter point that the whole question turns," Slade suggested to Richmond; "They will therefore be driven to the conclusion that the attack of Singapore is a serious operation for which adequate preparation must be made and the lines of communication secured."[13] Singapore's protection, in Slade's view, rested on the proper deployment of light vessels to watch the Japanese lines of approach and threaten her communications until the arrival of the British main fleet. To that end the East Indies forces should be reinforced by at least five or six fast cruisers, and the C-in-C given primary responsibility for organizing the transfer of military reinforcements from India and securing Indian Ocean communications for war and trade purposes. "When one considers the whole situation from a broad standpoint," Slade concluded, "the causes which are forcing us to consider an advanced base in the Far East are

13 RIC/7/3e, Slade to Richmond, March 22, 1924.

little different from those which forced us to acquire a similar base in the Mediterranean at Port Mahon in the 18th and at Malta in the early 19th centuries." The analogy was not lost on Richmond, though he took the point a few steps further.

In Richmond's mind, India was the key to the entire problem. Singapore and India were parts of a whole; the defence of the North-West Frontier and the China Station could no longer be compartmentalized as separate problems. Singapore's safety was India's and the Indian Army and Royal Indian Marine (R.I.M.) were the means of defending Singapore. "More and more," he suggested in a letter to Admiral Henderson,

> I am coming to the conclusion that in the present state of naval strength in these waters, the true organisation would be one in which the C. in C. East Indies would be the Senior Admiral [as opposed to C-in-C China Station] because *all* preparations for war in these waters may be summed up in one thing—being able to rapidly reinforce Singapore: and the arrangements for doing that must be made by the C-in-C here . . . .
> . . . To spend millions on Singapore and take no precautions for securing it if war breaks out is pure madness. If there is such a hurry to construct it there is equal urgency to make preparations for holding it.[14]

These suggestions would involve major changes in existing arrangements including reform of the R.I.M. and membership for the C-in-C East Indies on the Council of India.[15]

Richmond's earliest submissions to the Admiralty pointed out that current War Orders gave insufficient emphasis to Singapore's reinforcement "the principal object of the initial British Naval and Military Operations in the Far East, on the outbreak of war, must be to ensure the security of Singapore."[16] Japan could not hope and would not plan for the destruction of the British fleet; but she would attempt to neutralize it by depriving it of its only base of operations. British naval forces permanently located in the Pacific could not hope to intercept a Japanese expeditionary force in passage. Reinforcement of the Singapore garrison offered greater possibilities of holding the base until main fleet units could arrive. With this in mind, Richmond prepared his *Appreciation* giving guidelines for the initial deployment of British Far Eastern Squadrons. In these, Singapore's reinforcement figures as a top instead of as a secondary priority and required that planning for the movement of troops from India "must be as complete and efficient as those employed for the transport of the

14 RIC/7/1, Richmond to Henderson, January 20, 1924.
15 Ibid., May 13; November 21, 1924.
16 RIC/5/1, C-in-C East Indies to Admiralty (Secret), "Strategy of the Forces in the Far East," No. 5001, 917, February 24, 1924.

British Expeditionary Force in 1914." Precise requirements forecasts from the Singapore commands would allow the Indian Army, the R.I.M., and the various naval authorities to prepare plans, allocate ports, and arrange for necessary troop ships and their movements by sea together with covering forces and escorts "utilising the whole force available in Eastern waters."

Richmond followed this with another proposal for drastically reforming the R.I.M. as a proper "fighting force," attractive to officers selected on a competitive basis from men of Indian and British birth.[17] By dropping the force's subsidiary and largely civilian functions, and rearming it with sloops, it could be incorporated as an effective element in the direct defence of India and Singapore. The East Indies Squadron would then be made up of ships of the British and Indian Navies under a single Commander-in-Chief; the latter "to be head of the Indian Navy and Naval Member with a seat in Council as 'Extraordinary Member.'"

These prescient proposals were well received in London. Roger Keyes, then D.C.N.S. (1921-1925), told Richmond that his "criticisms are very welcome and will much help in finally arriving at a really sound scheme." The new Labour Government's decision to abandon further work on Singapore only underscored the importance of his suggestions: "We are trying to get the question of the reinforcements for Singapore settled here as far as it can be and then referred to India so that you will be able to make all necessary detailed arrangements with them."[18] But there was more to the problem than the home government's reservations. It was highly unlikely the Indian authorities would ever countenance such a scheme. Richmond was warned about opposition to the idea of using Indian forces in anything but "local" defence operations by General J. R. Charles, a former Indian Army officer who had been recently posted to Singapore and then, instead, appointed Commanding Officer of the R.M.A. Woolwich. "One has got to face the fact that this view does exist," General Charles cautioned:

> any plans for the employment of the Army in India in Malaya will have to be worked out very much in secret without advertising the fact that we contemplate drawing these reinforcements from India . . . . We had the same difficulty in 1912 when we were working out a scheme for the despatch of two divisions from India to Europe in the event of a European war; in fact Lord Hardinge, who was then Viceroy, categorically forebade A.H.Q. to work this scheme out— Fortunately Douglas Haig had a Nelsonian blind eye which he applied to the order—As a consequence when war broke out in 1914

17 Ibid., C-in-C East Indies to Admiralty, "Remarks and Proposals Concerning the Royal Indian Marine," No. 85/3301, April 10, 1924.
18 RIC/7/3e, Keyes to Richmond, May 19, 1924.

we had a [?] scheme which required very little modification to put into effect.[19]

Richmond recognized the central weakness of his thinking insofar as it presupposed some unanimity in strategic outlook and a genuine possibility of close cooperation between the services and all levels of Government at home and in India. But this, as he told Lord Haldane in a private letter, only underscored the need for comprehensive combined staff studies of the Singapore question. Haldane, who in addition to being Lord Chancellor of the new Labour Government was also chairman of the C.I.D., was impressed by Richmond's suggestions and passed them to Hankey for comment.[20]

Generally, Hankey agreed with Richmond's comments about "the proper handling of war problems" though he qualified this with some "observations" of his own. Richmond, of course, had seen only Admiralty files on the issue. Hankey had seen all of the C.I.D. papers and indeed written many of them. Hence, he suggested, "I naturally see the matter from a different standpoint to him."[21] Richmond had criticized the Admiralty for basing its Singapore arguments on purely naval grounds; he held that consideration should have been based first on the political or policy side and then on defence. He had suggested a few pertinent questions which the Government might have put to the Naval, Military, and Air Chiefs, such as:

(1) What in your joint opinion, should this country do if the Japanese tried to invade Australia owing to remonstrance at the doctrine of a white Australia?
(2) In what manner should this country act if Japan infringed the integrity of China?
(3) What action should we take if Japan exercised an unwarrantable influence in India?[22]

Attacking both Richmond's approach and presumption, Hankey defended the C.I.D.'s position which had been "dominated by one essential factor, namely that it takes 10 years to complete a naval base, and no one inside or outside the Foreign Office was prepared to say what would be the political situation in 10 years in the Far East." In fact, all that had been known in 1921 were Japan's wartime record, Australia's and New Zealand's apprehension, the unpopularity of the Anglo-

19 Ibid., General J. R. Charles to Richmond, May 3 (n.d.), in response to Richmond's letter of April 28, 1924. Richmond's marginal note with respect to the 1912 scheme was, "Most interesting piece of news. The Army had worked out a scheme of transport of which the Admiralty were not informed."
20 Ibid., Haldane to Richmond, June 1, 1924. Richmond's private letter of April 26, 1924 has not been found, but other references leave few doubts as to its general contents.
21 RIC/7/4, Hankey to Lord Haldane (Secret), May 26, 1924.
22 Ibid.

Japanese Alliance in America, and the Admiralty's assertion that without the base it would be impossible to exercise sea-power in the East. Richmond, he countered, was therefore "ridiculous" in saying that "the Admiralty was 'making its own little plans for war on its own reading of foreign policy etc.'"

Refuting Richmond's claims, Hankey went on to summarize the various stages of Staff, C.I.D., and Government studies since 1921. Then, in defence of his own part in the process, he added: "I have done my utmost to see that the Chiefs of Staff Committee does probe the vital problems, and although it is a slow business to get its solutions—the Staffs are rather slow-moving bodies—I do not think there is much that we have overlooked."

Haldane was not entirely convinced that a full investigation had ever been made, and in sending a copy of Hankey's memorandum told Richmond of his agreement with his views. But, he added, in explanation of Labour's general approach to foreign policy and specifically the decision to halt development of Singapore:

> The Singapore base would have put us in a position, not merely to defend ourselves, but to dominate the Pacific. The consequences of this from an International standpoint, were decided to be contradictory of a wider attempt to remodel international relations. A definite attempt to this end has been set on foot [The Geneva Protocol].
>
> If it fails we must go back to the Singapore plan. But I have no reason to doubt the probability of its success, if we do not prepare a possible offensive on a large scale.[23]

Haldane's reasoning bewildered Richmond much as it did others who otherwise rated him one of the C.I.D.'s best chairmen to date. Roger Keyes told Richmond: "Your friend Haldane is really helpful—we carried our oil reserves against bitter opposition with his help. He says he is quite alive to the importance of Singapore—but 'What have we to fear from Japan?' 'Other things are more important.'" Roger Bellairs was equally perplexed: "What is the reason that a brain of such capacity can reach such conclusions and put forward arguments so astounding?"[24] Somewhat later, in the midst of the 1924 General Election, Bellairs suggested that "certainly no one will wish to substitute Lord Salisbury for Lord Haldane as Chairman of the Chiefs of Staff Committee. However, nothing can make up for the attitude he took up in regard to the Singapore question, an attitude which I simply do not understand in him."[25] Lord Sydenham, never a great personal admirer of Haldane's, wrote that "[he is] the vainest man I have ever met, and when he went over to the socialists, he was

23 RIC/7/3e, Haldane to Richmond, June 1, 1924.
24 Ibid., Keyes to Richmond, May 19, 1924; R. M. Bellairs to Richmond, July 21, 1924.
25 Ibid., October 20, 1924.

driven to find arguments which suited their ideas."[26] But whatever
Haldane's convictions may have been, so long as Labour remained in
office, nothing more was done about Singapore. However, he was
sensitive to Richmond's pleas for more combined planning and
analysis in defence matters generally, and urged the C.I.D. to look into
the problem of the wide discrepancies in the political assumptions of
the separate services: "to clear up the apparent divergence in policy
and to give some indication to the various departments as regards the
political assumptions on which they should base their preparations
for war."[27] For the time being, Richmond had to be satisfied that the
Admiralty was at least going ahead with arrangements for him to
communicate directly with the Indian military authorities on matters
concerning his own command.[28]

In October 1924 the Conservatives returned to power with an
unassailable majority. Within three weeks of taking office, Baldwin's
Cabinet approved "in principle" the resumption of work on Singapore, although the new First Lord, Mr. W. C. Bridgeman, did not
announce the decision to Parliament until the following March. This
reversal of Labour's policy did not mean, however, that work simply
picked up where it had been dropped almost a year earlier. A special
Cabinet sub-committee under Lord Curzon, appointed in January
1925 to re-examine the question of the base's site, to report on progress to date, and to make recommendations as to defences, revealed
continuing differences between the services, the C.I.D., and the
Cabinet.[29]

The Committee's interim report, which was approved by the
Cabinet in March, reaffirmed the Johore site, but proposed temporary
restrictions on the rate of development; that is, the floating dock
facilities would be proceeded with, the cost (just over £800,000)
being spread over the financial years 1925-26, 1926-27, and 1927-28.
Defences and works were another matter, however, and on this little
sense of urgency was displayed by either the Cabinet or the C.I.D. The
latter recommended in April that development be "reviewed annually in light of the international situation." This, together with a later
decision in June, resulted in local defences being installed in two
distinct stages: the first, involving anti-submarine defences for the
base and Keppel Harbour, to be completed by early 1929; the second,
which included installation of heavy-gun defences, was to be held
temporarily in abeyance.[30] Modest as these advances were, they did at

26 Ibid., Lord Sydenham to Richmond, October 3, 1925.
27 RIC/7/4, Captain Dudley R. Pound (Director of Plans) to Richmond, August 13,
    1924.
28 RIC/7/3e, Keyes to Richmond, July 8, 1924.
29 C.I.D. 193rd Meeting, January 5, 1925.
30 Cab. 124 (25), Interim Report of the Curzon Sub-Committee; Cab. 12 (25), March 2,

least constitute a reversal of policy and opened the way for continued discussion. Richmond was then finally authorized to deal directly with the Indian military authorities.

Of these, his most important contact was General Lord Rawlinson, the Minister of Defence. He alone appears to have grasped Richmond's message about the importance of overriding the North-West Frontier mentality in Indian defence politics. In mid-December 1924, Richmond was informed that Rawlinson, as a result of an earlier conference at the Admiralty, had accepted most of his recommendations concerning the R.I.M., including the political necessity of opening its officer ranks to Indians.[31] Rawlinson also offered Richmond his full cooperation and promised to provide complete statistics on available Indian military resources. These were needed for a conference of Commanders-in-Chief to be held at Singapore early in 1925. He also informed Richmond that the India Office and the Admiralty had agreed to establish a special committee to pronounce on the value and function of the R.I.M. He regarded Richmond's evidence as an important determinant in the committee's work, and since Richmond expected to be in Singapore during the actual sittings, solicited his advice privately.[32]

It is worth noting at this point that the need for changes in the R.I.M. had been recognized for some years, but specific reforms had been repeatedly frustrated by both the Admiralty and the India Office. During his Empire Mission of 1919, Jellicoe had recommended the replacement of the much-criticized force by a Royal Indian Navy (R.I.N.) manned and maintained by Indians and assisted by the Royal Navy. The suggestion was rejected in 1920 by the India Office, the Commander-in-Chief East Indies, and a year later, by the Viceroy's Executive Council.[33] This led Rear-Admiral Mawbey, the Director R.I.M. and S.N.O. Bombay, to resign in protest. He was succeeded by the force's Deputy Director, Captain Headlam, who with Richmond's and Rawlinson's encouragement was instrumental in keeping reforming zeal alive.

The members of Rawlinson's Departmental Commission were Captain Headlam, the Hon. Sir B. N. Mitra (a member of the Viceroy's

1925. Adm. 116/2416, C.I.D., 199th Meeting, April 2, 1925; 200th Meeting, June 22, 1925.
31 RIC/7/3e, Rear-Admiral W. A. Egerton to Richmond, December 15, 1924. They would, however, be given Viceroy's and not King's Commissions; "The reason for this was that it was tacitly assumed that a demand to send cadets to Dartmouth would arise and that is not acceptable as English parents would not send their boys into the Service. Your suggestion of a scheme analogous to the Public School entry would be far better and overcomes the objection."
32 Ibid., Rawlinson to Richmond, December 14, 1924.
33 Adm. 116/1832, Jellicoe Report on India. Adm. 1/8599, Minutes, July 8, 1920; December 14, 1920. Adm. 116/1831, India Office letter, April 28, 1921.

Council), Mr. E. Burdon (the Secretary to the Marine Department), and Richmond. They came down heavily in favour of reconstituting the force as the Royal Indian Navy and giving it a combatant role. These recommendations were accepted by both the Indian and British Governments; and Baldwin, in addressing the 1926 Imperial Conference, welcomed "the step recently taken by India in establishing the Royal Indian Navy."[34] Nevertheless, several years elapsed before reforming plans were translated into action. In 1928, the Indian Assembly rejected the Naval Discipline Act which was an integral part of the entire scheme. Consequently, the R.I.N.'s official formation was delayed until October 1934.

Rawlinson's death in March 1925, just as the Commission's work was nearing completion, accounted for some of this delay. His passing also broke the cooperation that Richmond so enjoyed and meant that another of Richmond's pet ideas—a scheme for the creation of an Imperial Military Reserve in the East—was vitiated by time and circumstance.

Like Richmond, Rawlinson had recognized that the defence of Singapore and India were inextricably entwined. He characterized the Admiralty's plans to install 15-inch guns at Singapore as "perfectly grotesque." As to the problem of finding sufficient land forces for the defence of Malaya and Singapore, he suggested that the recent withdrawal of British occupation forces from the Rhine offered interesting possibilities. He had therefore proposed to Haldane that a C.I.D. study of the redistribution "of our Imperial Army" along these lines be undertaken. The "big question" of an Imperial Reserve in the East, and the development and defence of Singapore were so "closely mixed up" as to require the most careful consideration; and this, he admitted, could take months or even years to settle. In the meantime, he promised to support Richmond in every possible way, including "priming" the Viceroy and other Indian officials. "I fully sympathise with what you say regarding the defence of India," he told Richmond, "and I am not surprised that, in the talks you have had with all and sundry, their ideas have always turned towards the North-West Frontier." It was an ancient reflex and one based on an hitherto unquestioned assumption of British maritime supremacy. The fact was, Rawlinson continued:

> No one in this country has ever envisaged, or is envisaging to-day, the possibility of the hostility of the Japanese nor has anyone considered the strategical situation in the Pacific, and the vital importance of Singapore to the defence of India. These are world problems, far beyond the ken of both Indians and Europeans here in Hindustan.[35]

34 Cmd. 2768, Summary of Proceedings, 1926 Imperial Conference; Cmd. 2769, Appendices, p. 9.
35 RIC/7/3e, Rawlinson to Richmond, January 1, 1925.

Richmond therefore left for the Singapore Conference assured of Rawlinson's full moral support and the promise that should he need the views of the Secretary or the Viceroy, he would get them immediately,

> for your conference is going to be of first-class importance, not only to India, but to the Empire as a whole. I imagine that your report, if it included, as I hope it may, the general question of the defence of the Singapore Naval Base, will form the basis of important discussions of the Committee of Imperial Defence.

Here Rawlinson had touched upon something which neither he nor Richmond was probably prepared to admit openly; namely, that the C.I.D. was not doing its job. Since there was no substitute body to take the initiative, Rawlinson and Richmond assumed that responsibility themselves. The final report drawn up by the Commanders-in-Chief of the China, East Indies, and Australian Stations, the Australian Fleet, and the New Zealand Division, assumed that Indian troops and military resources would be used in the defence of Singapore and that all other defensive arrangements and dispositions were predicated on this being so.[36]

Following Rawlinson's death, Richmond submitted another paper entitled "An Imperial Military Reserve for the purpose of Maintaining Command at Sea in Eastern Waters." But neither the Indian Commander-in-Chief (Sir Claud Jacob) nor the Viceroy (Lord Reading) were sympathetic. General Jacob informed Richmond that the Indian Government had decided, after talks with the War Office, "that no further steps need be taken at this stage towards the completion of the scheme for the reinforcement of Singapore."[37] Frustrated by this decision, Richmond resubmitted the paper to the Admiralty, along with a number of others[38] concerning his Station's defences. The Admiralty generally supported most of what he had to say, and recommended further discussion in the C.I.D.[39] But nothing was done. By the time Richmond left the East Indies at the end of 1925, the only improvement made in the situation was the approval for installing gun defences at the base. British Governments have never been disposed to erect costly colonial defence works in times of profound peace. This was no exception.

36 RIC/5/1, C-in-C East Indies, Proceedings of Singapore Conference 1925, Covering Letter No. 285/01525 (March 13, 1925) and Enclosures 1-9.
37 Adm. 116/2394, C-in-C India to C-in-C East Indies, August 13, 1925.
38 RIC/5/1, Richmond to Admiralty (Secret), November 5, 1925. Papers: (a) "An Imperial Military Reserve for the Purpose of Maintaining Command at Sea in Eastern Waters"; (b) "Limits of the East Indies Station in the Event of a War in the Far East"; (c) "The Future of the British Interest in Basra"; (d) "Design of Vessels Suitable for Service in the Persian Gulf"; (e) "The Period of Command of the East Indies Station."
39 Adm. 116/2394.

It is tempting to think that more would have been achieved had Rawlinson lived. A substantial beginning had been made. Through Rawlinson's cooperation and friendship, Richmond had lectured at the Quetta Staff College and carried out a combined operations exercise in December 1924. This small and faintly unrealistic exercise was one of very few of its kind to be conducted anywhere in the 1920s and 1930s by the Royal Navy. An island off Bombay was chosen to represent Singapore under attack by a Japanese amphibious assault force. Although Richmond underrated the effects of air-power in such an operation, the trial demonstrated the vital importance of careful beach reconnaissance and specialized self-propelled landing craft for troops and vehicles. Richmond's successor repeated the exercise with similar results. But in neither case did the findings influence Admiralty policy in any appreciable way.

With the notable exceptions of the R.I.M. reforms and the ideas and materials he took away to later incorporate into his *Navy in India*, much the same must be said of Richmond's efforts generally as Commander-in-Chief East Indies. He had worked hard; but, as he told Admiral Henderson:

> Their Lordships don't give one much encouragement. I think I have got a good deal done in the time I've been here, but except for saying that my criticisms of a certain scheme had been considered valuable they have shewn no signs that they care twopence whether one works or does nothing.[40]

During the Second World War, Richmond would take some satisfaction from being able to point to the real costs of ignoring the Japanese threat in the Pacific and Indian Ocean. Although he generally resisted the temptation to gloat, he did write to Gerald S. Graham (later Rhodes Professor at King's College, London), within a few weeks of Singapore's collapse:

> There can be only one solid foundation of security in a thalassic state and that is a powerful navy. Local garrisons can serve a useful purpose . . . . But money spent on forts and garrisons, if it effectually weakens the naval forces, is money wasted. The whole defence will crumble like a house of cards when assaulted . . . . Owing to the unhappy predispositions of successive Governments in London and an absence of any appreciation of the essentials of naval defence in the Dominions and Colonies, the navy is not strong enough to guard either the colonies in the Eastern Seas or the very territory of Australia . . . since expenditure on local defence, once undertaken, tends to spread and to develop into reposing a trust in fortifications and to a reduction in the monies needed for the Navy, the path of local defence is a slippery and dangerous one to pursue.[41]

40 RIC/7/1, Richmond to Henderson, June 5, 1925.
41 Richmond to Professor Gerald S. Graham, April 10, 1942, Papers in possession of Professor Graham, Rye, Sussex.

This is not to judge Richmond as a seer tragically proved right by events, but as an individual who, in practical ways and through a deep appreciation of historical realities, had worked to change policy and then lived to see many of his suggestions being hastily and desperately improvised. But his interest in empire security matters did not stop when he struck his Flag in the East Indies and returned to England. He was promoted to Vice-Admiral in April 1925, and the following year became Commandant of the newly created Imperial Defence College.

8

The Imperial Defence College (1926-1928)

The opening of the Imperial Defence College probably saved Richmond from early retirement. For over a year after returning to England he was unemployed. Once again, his prospects were uncertain, although his recent promotion and the award of a knighthood (K.C.B.) in July 1926 helped ease the burden of half-pay. His friends hoped he would still be given a major Admiralty or Fleet assignment. Hankey even hinted that his chances of becoming First Sea Lord were good. That possibility was raised when, as in 1919, Richmond was considered for another university appointment. This time it was the prestigious Chichele Professorship at Oxford recently vacated by Spenser Wilkinson. As the Prime Minister's representative on the board of selection, Hankey sounded out Richmond's interest, adding his personal hope that he would perservere with the Navy for a while longer; "I have always hoped to see you become First Sea Lord." He knew that Beatty thought highly of Richmond—although it was likely he would look after Keyes and Brock first. Hankey advised Richmond to hold the Oxford appointment as a future option for the moment. He was prepared to recommend someone like Sir George Aston (then age sixty-four) as a "stop gap" for five years, and then bid for Richmond.[1] Hankey's sincerity in raising this tantalizing possibility is, of course, a moot point. His friendship with Richmond was always guarded and conditional.[2] Richmond, for his part, had no illusions. He knew that too many senior officers still regarded him as an "unpractical theorist" for such a lofty prospect to seem real. The

1 RIC/5/1, Hankey to Richmond, March 27, 1925.
2 Suggested by Captain S. W. Roskill in conversation with the author. See also Roskill's *Hankey, Man of Secrets*, vol. 1: *1877-1918* (London: Collins, 1970), p. 42.

Imperial Defence College was another matter. It was a congenial puddle for an intellectual frog whose talents as a sailor-scholar were becoming well known. He had actively promoted the concept of such a college for several years; indeed, these efforts made him the most likely candidate for the new job. To a degree hitherto unrecognized, Richmond's ideas and personality shaped the I.D.C. in its embryonic stages and left an indelible imprint on its subsequent development and that of its sister colleges later set up in Canada and other Commonwealth countries.

Like the Chiefs-of-Staff Committee (C.O.S.), the Imperial Defence College became an integral part of the C.I.D. system of higher defence organization which was re-established in the mid-1920s. No individual or group stands out as progenitor of the I.D.C. Haig had seen the need for a national defence university in some form during the war. In 1920 Haldane had twice suggested in Parliament that a system of greater educational interchange between the various staff colleges should be permanently established. Others have been credited with fostering the concept as well.[3] But the first concrete proposal for a joint college on the lines of the I.D.C. came from the Churchill Committee of 1922 which was set up to review the findings of the earlier Geddes Report.

Churchill's group concluded, amongst other things, that any movement toward a single Ministry of Defence would be premature until adequate staff personnel, fully trained in the problems of all services and therefore qualified to advise such a Minister, were readily available. They recommended the re-establishment of a revitalized C.I.D. which would remain in session year round. It would be strengthened by additional bodies whose creation, they suggested, should be studied by two technical committees—one to look into the setting up of a joint staff college; the other, the integration of all support functions (medical, transport, education, supply, etc.) common to the three services. Here, then, was the genesis of the I.D.C. and the C.O.S. together with the Joint Planning and Joint Intelligence Sub-Committees.[4] Churchill volunteered to head the joint college

3   Viz. R. F. Cottrell, "Plea for National Defence," *The Nineteenth Century and After*, 86 (September 1919), 397-409. Haldane's remarks are in *Parl. Debs.* (H.C.), 126, March 18, 1920, 2543; 127, March 22, 1920, 92. See also Sir George Aston, *The Fortnightly Review* 115 (April 1921), 622-39; Franklyn Johnson, *Defence by Committee*, pp. 174-211; Lieutenant-General Sir Gifford Martel, *Outspoken Soldier* (London, 1949), pp. 362-66, regarding General Fuller's efforts; Air Chief Marshall Sir Arthur Longmore, *From Sea to Sky* (London: Geoffrey Bles, 1947); Admiral Sir Frederick Dreyer, *The Sea Heritage* (London: Museum Press, 1955); Great Britain, Parliament, House of Commons, *Estimates Committee, Eighth Report (1963-1964, Service Colleges* (H.M.S.O., 1964).

4   The C.O.S. which was created in 1923 eventually resulted from a recommendation of the Salisbury Committee (1923), Cmd. 2029. See: Roskill, *Naval Policy*, vol. 1, pp. 339-40, 372-73, 377-78; also Franklyn Johnson, *Defence by Committee*, p. 180,

study and in the new Committee's terms of reference was actually appointed Chairman.[5] By the time the body officially met early in 1923, however, he was replaced by Mr. E. F. L. Wood (later Lord Irwin, and subsequently Earl of Halifax), head of the board of Education.

This was the Committee to which Richmond had devoted so much energy during his last months at Greenwich. In retrospect, it is clear that he was the predominant guiding influence throughout the Committee's deliberations. The other members were Major-General Sir Hastings Anderson of the War Office, Air Vice-Marshal P. W. Game for the Air Ministry, and Mr. E. W. H. Millar from the Treasury. After three meetings, the Committee submitted its final report in early May 1923, concluding that a joint college was "highly desirable in order to create a common doctrine in regard to defence policy and to produce a body of officers trained to look at the problems of war as a whole."[6] To that end they recommended the creation of the "Imperial Defence College," an institution to be superimposed on the existing service Staff Colleges and placed under the supervision, in matters of policy and instruction, of the Standing Defence Sub-Committee of the C.I.D. (later, of the C.O.S. when it was formed). The College would be located in London and offer courses of one-year's duration to British and Dominion officers who had already graduated from the regular service Staff Colleges.

Prior to the Committee's formal sittings, each of the members had introduced written submissions. Of these, Richmond's[7] was the most comprehensive, and it became the basis of all later discussion. He began with a commentary on the functions of the existing staff-training systems. This was necessary since the Committee was originally instructed to consider the joint college as a means of reducing the overall number of officers under training and courses offered. This was not possible in Richmond's view, since the existing staff needs of the services were barely being met. Increased cooperation between the Colleges was advisable, he argued, and could be fostered through more regular interchange postings and visits. The concept of a separate joint college "superimposed" on the existing structure fulfilled

   pp. 193-98. The Mond-Weir Report dealing with Common Services: *Report of the Committee on the Amalgamation of Services Common to the Navy, Army and Air Force*, Cmd. 2649 (April 1923).

5   Cab. 16/45, Committee of Imperial Defence, Sub-Committee on the Institution of a Joint Staff College, Report (C.I.D. Paper 409-B), Proceedings and Memoranda. Memo, S.S. (J.S.C.) 1, Composition and Terms of Reference of the Sub-Committee, dated September 9, 1922; S.S. (J.S.C.) 2, Extract from Minutes of the 159th Meeting of the Committee of Imperial Defence, July 12, 1922.

6   Cab. 16/45, C.I.D. Paper, 409-B, dated May 11, 1923.

7   Ibid., Memorandum, S. S. (J.S.C.) 3, Combined Staff College by Rear-Admiral H. W. Richmond, September 1922.

an entirely larger and hitherto neglected requirement. It was not to be a mere joint version of a single-service war course.

> There is in my mind, a distinct need for what the French call a "centre of higher studies"; or, what I should call a "combined War College." . . . . However much we may attempt to develop the staffs within the walls of the Admiralty, the War Office, or the Air Ministry, I doubt that it is possible to attain the complete detachment from current business, the concentration upon the solution of a problem, the uninterrupted work in common, or the appreciation of the questions in their entirety, looked upon as a common problem in which each service is being employed to its utmost capacity to attain a single end.

As to the "Nature of the Work Required," Richmond suggested beginning on small lines. Highly qualified specialists would be called in to present lectures, followed by free discussions and open debate. "Discussion now takes the form of each protagonist trying to prove himself right; of scientific, cooperative study having as its aim the discovery of what is best." To ensure that the work carried out was not solely academic "and tinged with irresponsibility," he argued for a practical programme; that is, specific policy studies that could be forwarded for governmental and service consideration:

> while every word it writes is going to be subject to criticism from the staffs, the College is going to be in a position to examine that criticism. The staffs must not have the monopoly of criticism; must not be, so to speak, in a pulpit, unanswerable. They must also feel they are going to be answered back. I have seen too many irresponsible staff criticisms of proposals—rejections based upon most slender grounds—which could never have been put on paper but for the fact that the writers knew they were not going to be answered and imagined their word final.

He followed up with a list of current problem areas where combined staff study would be most useful. In the light of his own experiences and strategic outlook, it is worth noting that his examples emphasized the defence of specific bases, sea routes, and trade, the use of convoys and methods of controlling or destroying enemy shipping, and the defining of commanders' responsibilities in combined operations. Most interesting was his suggestion for an examination of "The main strategy of a war against Japan: functions of all three services."

Richmond recognized that many officers would shy away from postponing command appointments to attend the new college if safeguards for their career development were not provided. Increasing the time which an officer spent away from his primary duties could be costly. Therefore serious consideration of the entire officer-education system was needed to ensure that the I.D.C. would "dovetail" into the pattern. The Staff Colleges would be required to prepare officers for advanced work at this new school of combined study. Moreover, Richmond felt that I.D.C. students should be officers not so much of "medium rank" as ones of considerable experience. (His views on the optimum age level for education seemed to rise as he himself aged, though what he wanted taught remained constant.) He preferred students of Captain or Rear-Admiral rank in order to give weight to their work.

> I am ... anxious that certain definite studies should be pursued—studies of specific problems of combined interest: but I am equally anxious that the matter should not end in academic smoke. I want practical results: recommendations that carry weight enough not to be pushed into a waste-paper basket. I do not feel that (human nature being what it is) the recommendations of a body of comparatively junior officers would carry enough weight, even though the President of the College should be, as he ought, a man of standing. If the College does not carry weight it will not be able to do what, in my opinion, should be its principal function—investigation with a view to practical results.

The memoranda submitted by Air Vice-Marshal Game and Major-General Sir Hastings Anderson were little more than commentaries on Richmond's.[8] Although both officers generally accepted his views, Anderson doubted that "practical" policy studies could be carried out effectively. Their production might divert the College staff from their primary academic responsibilities. Moreover, the students would be "raw material, not the finished article." There was also the possibility that the necessary official data and views on such topics might not be sufficiently timely or easily acquired, a view which, judged by later developments (especially since 1945), came very close to the mark.[9]

At the Committee's first formal session on February 20, 1923, discussion was brief.[10] Richmond's ideas were affirmed. One important issue—the higher control of the College—was not discussed and was reserved for the next meeting to which Hankey was invited. It was he who suggested that ultimate authority over the College be vested in the Standing Defence Sub-Committee. Hankey testified that he had originally favoured the creation of a governing body made up of the three service Chiefs. Then, seeing the need for an independent

8 Ibid., S.S. (J.S.C.) 4, Combined Staff College, Note by Vice-Marshal P. W. Game, September 1922; and S.S. (J.S.C.) 5, Proposed Joint Staff College for the Three Services, Memorandum by Major-General Sir Hastings Anderson, September 23, 1922.
9 See comments on I.D.C. in *Estimates Committee, Eighth Report, (1963-1964)*.
10 Cab. 16/45, S.S. (J.S.C.) 1st Meeting, Minutes of the First Meeting, ... February 20, 1923. Note: Anderson and Game were from this point replaced on the Committee by Major-General H. F. Romer and Air Vice-Marshal Sir W. Geoffrey H. Salmond (Controller General of Equipment on the Air Council).

spokesman for this body, he had considered the Chairman of the Standing Defence Sub-Committee. Finally, having considered "the very wide questions that might be raised and therefore a requirement for ministerial representation," he concluded that only the Standing Committee itself would suit all requirements. At this point, Hankey also introduced a justification for the joint college which had not been raised previously, but appeared in all subsequent discussions. This was the suggestion that the C.I.D. Secretariat should recruit its future members directly from the ranks of the I.D.C. graduates.

> Hankey attached real importance to being able to obtain officers who had been trained to think "in three dimensions." He stated he was of the opinion that the training of officers to view questions from a broad standpoint was of sufficient importance alone to justify the institution of a Joint War College.[11]

Hankey had ulterior motives as well. He had smoothly arranged for control of the College to pass to the C.I.D.; that is, to himself. His recommendations were incorporated into the Committee's Report which was drawn up after a final meeting held on May 11. So too were his assumptions; particularly that the I.D.C. would be a means of strengthening the C.I.D. machinery. The Final Report was not sufficiently emphatic on this point, however, to allay Admiralty fears that the College (and its highly trained graduates) was nothing less than a prelude to the creation of a unified Ministry of Defence. Indeed, this was a central feature of Churchill's earlier arguments for setting up the joint college Committee.[12] The Admiralty's initial coolness to the Committee's findings is therefore understandable. It may also help explain why more than two years would pass before they were finally acted upon.

The Committee's Final Report was reviewed by the C.I.D. on December 19, when it agreed in principle to the setting up of the I.D.C., and requested the C.O.S. to further consider the details. This was done in a preliminary way in early January 1924, but the change of Government that same month sidetracked further study for the time being. Not until March 1926 did the C.O.S. resume discussion and submit their findings to the C.I.D.[13] Beatty pointed out that all three service Chiefs were agreed on the desirability of the College on the lines suggested in

11 Cab. 16/45, S.S. (J.S.C.) 2nd Meeting, Minutes . . . , March 1, 1923.
12 Ibid., S.S. (J.S.C.) 2, Extract from C.I.D. Minutes, 159th Meeting, July 12, 1922. At that time, the First Lord, Viscount Lee of Fareham, had approved Churchill's suggestion "subject to the proviso, however, that the institution of a Joint Staff College did not prejudice in any way the question of the establishment of a Ministry of Defence, he was cordially in agreement with the idea of a Joint Staff College."
13 Adm. 116/2273, Minutes of the 178th Meeting of the C.I.D., December 19, 1923; C.O.S., 6th Meeting, January 8, 1924 (Paper No. C.O.S. 8); C.O.S. 27th Meeting, March 11, 1926, (C.I.D. Paper 678-B, March 16, 1926).

the Wood Report, subject only to three modifications. Of these, the most important involved investing supervisory powers in the C.O.S. as opposed to the Standing Defence Committee which had ceased to exist by this time. On the whole, the C.I.D. agreed. Sir George Milne, the C.I.G.S., did express concern that the Wood proposals were "on too elaborate a scale." He also suggested that the instructional staff—three Directors, one from each service—should be headed by a civilian Commandant "to ensure that no one of the three services should have a preponderating weight on the instructional staff."[14] Milne was supported on this latter point by Amery and Sir Austen Chamberlain. Both were concerned that the very best instructional talent would be obtained, and that particular care should be exercised in the selection of a Commandant. Churchill was by far the most enthusiastic in his support of the College. He opposed attempts by Trenchard and Milne to limit student numbers to approximately twelve. He favoured a figure of twenty or more which would ensure that sufficient numbers survived over the next decade to be of practical use to the country. He also preferred a two-year course. Then, digressing somewhat, he went on to suggest that the C.O.S. should be charged as formally as possible—"by Letters Patent if necessary"—with joint responsibility for defence matters as a whole "in order that any one of the three should not feel inhibited from discussing the affairs of the other two Services." This, together with a proposal that each Chief should have a staff officer from the other services serving under him, was not taken seriously by others at the meeting—Churchill's unitary thinking was well known. The Prime Minister reminded the members that these larger issues went well beyond the immediate question of creating a joint college. In the end, the C.O.S. position was accepted and they were then requested to produce specific recommendations as to numbers of students, a revised syllabus, and any other necessary details.

Reporting back to the C.I.D. on May 27, the C.O.S. recommended that the College be established on modest lines and then subsequently expanded to its full capacity. They wanted a one-year course which could be lengthened to eighteen months or two years if experience showed this to be necessary. Initially, the number of students would be restricted to thirty-five from each of the services, twelve from the Dominions and India (two from each), and three from those civilian Departments most concerned with strategic problems (Foreign Office, Treasury, Board of Trade, Home Office, and Colonial Office). The Instructional Staff would consist of a Commandant of the rank of Flag, General, or Air Officer (appointed in turn by each service for a two-

14 Ibid., C.I.D., Minutes of 211th Meeting, March 19, 1926. See also Lieutenant-General Sir Giffard Martel, *An Outspoken Soldier*, p. 125, Martel credits Colonel J. F. C. "Boney" Fuller with putting this idea in Milne's head.

year period), an instructor from each service (rank of Commodore or post-Captain or equivalent), and one from the Civil Service—these latter appointments not to exceed three years' duration—and finally, a Secretary-Librarian. Regarding this arrangement, the C.O.S. decided that: "In order to ensure that the instruction at the College is kept in close touch with practical experience in the carrying out of strategic plans, we consider that the terms of appointment of the Instructional Staff should not be for too long a period."[15]

As to the syllabus and functions of the College, the C.O.S. accepted the recommendations of the Wood Report (all written by Richmond) and was prepared to leave the working out of exact details to the Instructional Staff. The College's functions were briefly defined as: "The training of a body of officers and civilian officials in the broadest aspects of Imperial Strategy." The C.O.S. agreed that studies conducted at the College should focus on contemporary issues; but they baulked at the notion that they should automatically carry weight in the formulation of defence policy. Such interference with the chain of command and the C.O.S.'s prerogatives always invoked hostility. In words far more restrictive than those used by Richmond, they declared that the College's functions "might with advantage be expanded to include the occasional examination of concrete problems of Imperial Defence which are referred to it by the Chiefs of Staff Sub-Committee."[16] While it offered some scope for what he considered the College's major function, this rewording of Richmond's original phraseology left the initiative in such matters beyond the College's control. Denied guarantees that such studies would indeed be undertaken, and that the results would be systematically considered, the I.D.C.'s position and influence within the national policy-making machinery was seriously undermined from the start Despite this, the C.O.S. report marked the point at which the concept of the Imperial Defence College was transformed into a practical reality. Implementation of the scheme was left to a special Joint Committee of the service staffs.

Meeting at the Admiralty under the Chairmanship of the A.C.N.S., Rear-Admiral F. C. Dreyer, the Joint Committee hammered out the final arrangements.[17] It was agreed that the College, for which

15 Adm. 116/2273, C.I.D. Paper 689-B, The Imperial Defence College, Report by the Chiefs of Staff, May 27, 1926.
16 In the Wood Committee Report, C.I.D., 409-B, Richmond had included in the suggested Syllabus, para. (f) as follows: "(f) Investigation of practical problems, with a view to subsequent action being taken on the conclusions arrived at." Exception was taken to this at some point during the C.O.S. review (C.O.S. 38). In all subsequent versions of the Syllabus as they appear in Adm. 116/2273, the original version remains unchanged, except for para. (f) which was deleted.
17 Adm. 116/2273, Joint Committee on Imperial Defence College, Minutes of the First Meeting, May 28, 1926. The other members were Air Vice-Marshal Sir Philip Game

a site in London was to be found, would come under the overall administration of the Admiralty with the other two services contributing their share of the costs and that the Navy, being the senior service, would nominate the first Commandant. Details for the appointment and later rotation of instructors were also settled. The College would open in January 1927, and the instructional and clerical staff were authorized to begin work in the early autumn of 1926. Other technical details, matters of pay, emoluments, buildings, and classroom facilities were left to a second meeting on June 9 to which Treasury representatives were invited. From this point, inter-departmental consultation went on throughout the summer without any serious hitches.[18] The Dreyer Committee's report was discussed and approved by the C.I.D. on June 10. Subject only to Cabinet approval, the Admiralty was then allowed to proceed with administrative arrangements. The Colonial Office was instructed to inform the Dominions and the Indian Government of the College's existence and purpose.[19]

Richmond's appointment as Commandant was approved by the King on July 17, 1926, and he was officially informed a week later that the posting was effective from September 1. At the same time, Major L. A. Clemens, then Assistant Secretary to the C.I.D., was appointed Secretary to the Commandant and College Librarian. The appointment of the other instructors followed: Colonel (later, Field-Marshal Sir) John G. Dill as Army Instructor, Group Captain (later, Air-Chief Marshal Sir) P. B. Joubert de la Ferte from the R.A.F., and Captain (later, Admiral Sir) Gerald C. Dickens from the Navy.[20] Richmond evidently had little say in their selection (except for Major Clemens); all the same, it was an exceptional group with which he was justifiably pleased.

Settling quickly into their new location at 9 Buckingham Gate, they set to work pulling the new structure together. Considering the syllabus, with its far-ranging coverage of everything from higher strategy and administration in the conduct of war to various visits about the countryside, the task was immense. Richmond and Dill spent some of their time countering the natural parsimony of the Treasury and the Works Department, even to the point of searching

(Air Council), Major-General A. R. Cameron (D.S.D., War Office), Captain S. J. Meyrick (Naval Staff), and G. F. Cotton (Admiralty) as Secretary.

18 Ibid., Minutes of Second Meeting, June 9, 1926; Notes of a Meeting held at the Admiralty on July 14, 1926.

19 Ibid., F. C. Dreyer to Hankey, May 28, 1926. Contents of this memorandum were reprinted in Hankey's C.I.D. Paper, 698-B, June 9, 1926. Also, Minutes of C.I.D. 214th Meeting, June 10, 1926.

20 Ibid., Memo, signed Frank Larken, Naval Secretary to the First Lord, July 17, 1926; Admiralty to Richmond, M 01791/26, July 23, 1926; Office Acquaint No. 105, July 29, 1926; H. Greedy (War Office) to Admiralty, August 6, 1926, and September 17, 1926.

personally for suitable second-hand furniture for the College's modest lounge facilities. By January 1927, however, everything was ready and the first course was under way.

Richmond's enthusiasm was tempered by a sense of caution about his new and important responsibilities. A suggestion from Admiral Henderson that he solicit someone to write a public tribute to Richmond's achievement evoked a response all the more interesting for its uncharacteristic humility:

> candidly, I would rather say nothing: and truly I could not bring myself to say anything about what I have or have not done. I do intensely dislike publicity. I have a big job ahead of me, & whether I have the confidence of the Services depends rather upon the way I do it than upon any thing I have written hitherto. I would rather leave it alone & not raise expectations in me in the minds of any one which I may fail to fulfil. The more I work at the problem of merely arranging what we are to do in the twelve months of work allotted to each course, the more difficult does the whole thing appear—not that I am at all afraid of it; but it is the kind of thing one needs to begin with a very considerable degree of caution. Like Agag, I must walk gently: and anything that even suggests that most horrible of all things "puffing", is at all times anathema to me, & at present moment, anathema in a superlative sense.[21]

Clearly this was a very different Richmond from the one who had helped assassinate Jellicoe ten years earlier.

Richmond stamped his methods indelibly upon the College and indeed its success in these early years owed everything to the open atmosphere he instilled. There were nine or ten major exercises each year. Syndicates were set up, with students representing the Prime Minister, service Ministers and Chiefs, and various other appointments. The exercises, based on possible war situations, were then thrashed out, the results analyzed, and a staff paper for each completed. Thus Richmond produced what he wanted at the College, although the results were generally ignored, as had been predicted. They were regarded as unofficial or academic documents, and their circulation was strictly limited. Without specific provision for the direct infusion of these papers into C.I.D. or C.O.S. discussions, there was little chance that the reservations expressed in the Wood Committee's Report or in the C.O.S.'s rewording of the syllabus would be overcome. Some of the war games presaged events of 1939-1945 to a remarkable degree—the examples most often cited were that Singapore would be taken from the landward side, or that Hong Kong was an indefensible liability. But there was no way of demonstrating this at the time. For the students, at least, the experience was of major significance, for arguing their cases in that first course under Rich-

21 RIC/7/1, Richmond to Henderson, September 3, 1926.

mond's and Dill's guidance were men who would figure pre-
eminently in those future events. It was an exceptional group which
included such later-to-be-famous personalities as Field-Marshal Sir
Claude Auchinleck, General Sir Clive Liddell, General Sir Robert
Haining, Admiral of the Fleet Lord Tovey, Air Chief Marshal Sir
Richard Peirse, Marshal of the R.A.F. Lord (Sholto) Douglas, Field-
Marshal Lord Alan Brooke. The programme of lectures, guest speak-
ers, and tours was intensive. Visits to experimental stations and a
variety of industrial and service establishments were interspersed
between talks by such eminent personalities as the King, the Prime
Minister, the Foreign Secretary, the service Chiefs of Britain and
India, Haldane and Hankey. But overriding everything, Richmond's
mind and personality were firmly in control.

Not unnaturally, this produced a mixed response. His Naval
Instructor, Captain (later Admiral Sir) Gerald Dickens, remembered in
1946 following Richmond's death, that: "His general erudition, his
vast knowledge of naval and military history, his powers of analysis
and exposition, first things first, his readiness to hear every point of
view argued, won him at once the attention and respect of all those
working with him."[22] General A. G. L. "Andy" McNaughton (later
Chief of the Canadian General Staff), who attended the first course and
thereafter retained strong ties with Richmond recalled him as "an
extraordinarily well-educated and well-informed man. His presenta-
tions were always well-organized in logical sequence with great
power of expression."[23] One can easily imagine the forebodings of the
students who, as experienced senior officers and Staff College
graduates, were faced with a series of Commandant's Lectures on
such hackneyed topics as "The Object in War," "Concentration," and
"The Offence." To Richmond's credit, he raised their consideration
above the level of platitudes to a realization that a deep understanding
of such basics was the key to sound strategy. From the first, his
emphasis fell on free discussion and the working out of problems
from first principles. Rear-Admiral H. G. Thursfield, who frequently
lectured during Richmond's tenure, noted this characteristic feature
of his technique: "It was not his way to seek to instruct as much as to
guide the studies of those under him in the new College; he never laid
down the law on his own authority in formulating principles or
conclusions, but rather sought to convince by argument—in which he
rarely failed."[24]

Not everyone was so impressed. Some officers were offended by
both his manner and his thinking, strongly predisposed as it was

22 The Times, December 31, 1946.
23 John Swettenham, McNaughton, vol. 1: 1887-1939 (Toronto: Ryerson, 1968),
   p. 231.
24 Marder, Portrait of an Admiral, p. 28.

toward the naval side of things.[25] Professor Marder refers to the dissenting opinion of Richmond's work by "one of his staff officers, afterward a high ranking airman"—most likely, Group Captain Phillippe Joubert de la Ferte—who wrote:

> I formed the opinion that he could only treat history objectively so long as its lessons did not interfere with his preconceived ideas. The man was a mine of information on military history and had a memory like a reference library ... Richmond's cold, academic outlook was repellent to the students, who were all fairly senior officers of great experience. He lectured as though he was living in a world apart, gazing out of the window most of the time, and hence seldom got his message across .... You can sum up his outlook as "Navy first, last and all the time, and damn any history that says otherwise" ... his attacks on the R.A.F. were very much resented by the whole course.[26]

Richmond's overbearing manner had offended in the past and undoubtedly did on occasion at the I.D.C., although in this case it was the R.A.F. officers who seem to have been most sensitive to it.

Richmond was accused of failing to see the real value of airpower and, consequently, of downplaying it at the I.D.C.[27] During the Second World War when he became embroiled in the public debate over the use of air resources, particularly in relation to coastal command,[28] he was brusquely reminded by Sir Wilfrid Freeman, one of his former I.D.C. students who was then Vice-Chief of the Air Staff, that his thinking must have changed in the intervening years. Having checked his old lecture notes, he suggested that Richmond was as responsible as most naval officers for failing to see into the future: "The trouble always was that until war broke out no senior Naval Officer believed that air forces could have an appreciable effect on naval power."[29] Richmond's riposte was sharp and to the point. He admitted his own failure, in the 1920s, to predict the way the war would go in 1939-1940.

> I do not think any of us can boast very much of our prescience ... I have a lively recollection, for instance, of a theory that was constantly proclaimed to the effect that as "offence is the best defence" so we did not need fighters to defend ourselves against bombing: the

25 RIC/2/2, Imperial Defence College, Commandant's Lectures, 1927-1928.
26 As quoted in Marder, *Portrait of an Admiral*, p. 367, n. 8.
27 E.g., see Andrew Boyle, *Trenchard* (London: Collins, 1962), pp. 576-79; Lord Douglas of Kirtleside, *Combat and Command* (London: Collins, 1966), pp. 318-19. Richmond's air-power ideas in the 1920s are best summed up in his "Sea Warfare," Lecture at King's College, March 4, 1926 (*The Times*, March 5, 1926); and *Sea-Power in the Modern World*, pp. 100-17.
28 See his "The Naval Air Arm," *Fortnightly Review* (February 1942); *The Times*, June 25, 30; July 6; August 13, 1942; *Fortnightly Review* "Air Power and Sea Power" (July 1942), "The Air Arm at Sea in 1941-42" (September 1942), "The Primary Object (February 1943).
29 RIC/7/4, Freeman to Richmond, October 6, 1942.

proper defence was to bomb the enemy. But it was the fighters of the R.A.F. that saved England in 1940. We should, I think, be wise to admit that none of us were free from error. Among my own however, I do not include two. I opposed constantly and without relaxation, a view presented to me at the Imperial Defence College that the principles of war do not apply to the Air—a doctrine stated to me categorically by Trenchard at a meeting of the Chief of Staffs [sic] Committee—and another according to which the Air staff would make its own plans for war, irrespective of the other two services. I preached the "oneness" of war. It was that spirit I tried to infuse. We all, of all three Services, worked in the most complete harmony at the College. We were too busy seeking to understand each others needs, to find ways by which we could combine our efforts, to descend to any petty squabbles about the greater or lesser importance of our respective Services.[30]

Like many of his naval and military contemporaries, Richmond had his share of anti-Air Force prejudice. He rated his R.A.F. students' performances lower than the others: "how mentally inferior the Air Force is to either of the other Services. Some of the papers written by them are like the products of a partly educated child."[31] But his differences with the airmen went much deeper than personal prejudice, for he saw in the air-power arguments of the 1920s—based as they were on the use of massive terroristic strikes on large urban and industrial centres—a horrible distortion, both in military and moral terms, of Britain's means of waging war. He sensed that strategic doctrine was being warped by an excessive reaction to technological imperatives without a complete understanding of what that doctrine should be or how the new weapons could be used to carry it out. His efforts to counterbalance this distorting tendency earned him a reputation for short-sightedness on air-power which his record disproves. Whether or not his own ideas as to the best doctrine for Britain were the right ones is of course debatable. That his philosophy was Imperial and maritime (and therefore heavily Navy oriented) does not, however, justify the charge that it was a parochial "Navy first, last and all the time."

There were other obstacles in the way of achieving doctrinal unanimity at the I.D.C. as Richmond discovered when, as part of his Commandant's Lectures series, he drew up a three-part paper to stimulate and guide student discussion leading to "the writing of a clear statement defining the principles of Imperial Defence."[32] In Part I, he argued that previous official studies of this subject had resulted in vague statements and generalizations, which invariably lacked the

30 Ibid., Richmond to Freeman, October 14, 1942.
31 RIC/7/1, Richmond to Henderson, September 15, 1928.
32 RIC/2/1, Imperial Defence College, Commandant's Lecture, no. 8, 1928, "Principles of Imperial Defence.'"

precise definition of governing principles which could guide British and Dominion Ministers in developing their fighting forces. Hoping to achieve a more useful policy statement, he suggested "approaching the problem from the point of view of *what interest we have to protect, and to what* dangers those interests are exposed"; in effect, to start from the particular and move to the general. Part II examined what Richmond termed "territorial interests"; that is, the problem of invasion and raids against overseas interests ("bases, harbours, shipping in port"). Part III focussed on trade protection, or "defence of the extra-territorial interests."

The lecture was passed to Hankey for comment by his staff. The reply, though couched in terms obviously indicating Hankey's awareness of how hypersensitive Richmond was to criticism, was nevertheless brutally blunt. Hankey branded Richmond's ideas as "too iconoclastic."[33] He conceded that the lecture was "not intended as a summary of the principles of Imperial Defence so much as a lecture to stimulate thought on that subject." But he justifiably took Richmond to task for some factual inaccuracies and misrepresentations regarding earlier consideration of the subject by various study groups and Imperial Conferences. He also criticized the lecture's organization and construction, specifically in that it failed to show clearly what Richmond did regard as the "real Principles" of Imperial Defence. He approved of Richmond's approach—of moving from considerations of the particular to the general—but was quick to add that this was the C.I.D.'s usual method. One suspects that the vitality of Hankey's response owed as much to personal pique at Richmond's implied criticism of the C.I.D.'s and his own past record as to any real differences on points of substance. However, Hankey did recognize the central defect in Richmond's Imperial Defence thinking; that is, his blindness to political realities—a tendency to "underrate the Constitutional difficulties in the British Empire." Richmond's assumption that "the Empire is in fact an Alliance for the defence of the interests of all its members" drew the pointed reminder that "Possibly two out of the four Dominions would admit the truth of that, though there were days when Australia did not admit it. Neither Canada nor South Africa would admit it."

Parts II and III of the Lecture were less vulnerable to criticism, apart from some comments on what Hankey felt was an overemphasis on trade protection and the omission of other equally important topics. Hankey's main attack was levelled against Richmond's assumption that the I.D.C. should act as a forum for independent critical examination. He doubted the expedience of openly criticizing the higher authorities there:

33 RIC/7/4, Hankey to Richmond (Secret and Personal), June 19, 1928.

We think that everything possible should be done to maintain the prestige of such bodies as the Imperial Conference, the Committee of Imperial Defence and the Chiefs of Staff Sub-Committee. We do not like to contemplate a Dominions [sic] Officer returning to his Dominion to tell his comrades of all the criticisms of the highest Defence authorities which he heard at the College. We think there are other and more tactful ways of teaching the truth than in picking holes in what is at present laid down.

A major criticism of the I.D.C.'s pre-1939 performance has been that, by its favouring of defence orthodoxy and an unwillingness to generate controversy, it failed to develop an overall concept of defence.[34] Given attitudes such as Hankey's, this is not surprising. Richmond, of all the prewar Commandants, is surely the least vulnerable to this charge. In two years, it was highly unlikely that he could have broken down such barriers in any lasting way. Much more time was required than he had available.

On the eve of his final term at the College, Richmond wrote to Admiral Henderson complaining about how much of the work-load the Commandant had to carry personally. Some of that would eventually be overcome once a trained staff was established at the College. In the meantime, he wrote: "it is essentially the work of the Commandant, who must be the directing mind of the place: it is *his* job to criticize and he must do it." Then, reflecting upon what he had achieved, he continued:

> There is a lot to do. I feel that the College has made its beginning. It has by no means solved any problems; nor did I ever expect it would do so. But I think it has opened up a field for much very profitable study, and that our three services have had new aspects of war brought to their notice.[35]

If Richmond had any illusions about the College's achievements, or official (especially Admiralty) acceptance of it, they were dispelled when it came time for him to step down. A question of finding a replacement for Captain Dickens as Naval Instructor brought him face-to-face with reality in the person of Admiral Sir Charles Madden who had succeeded Beatty as First Sea Lord in July 1927.

Richmond was naturally anxious that the Navy should be well represented at the College following his and Dickens' departures; in the words of Admiral Fullerton (the Naval Secretary), "Admiral Richmond lays stress on the importance of having a good man to combat the possibly extremist views of the Air Officer who will be in command of the I.D.C. in January '31."[36] The Admiralty recom-

34 This was Martel's main criticism in 1935; see *Outspoken Soldier*, pp. 362-66; also Dreyer, *Sea Heritage*, p. 280, and Longmore, *From Sea to Sky*, p. 177.
35 RIC/7/1, Richmond to W. H. Henderson, September 15, 1928.
36 RIC/7/2/1, Naval Secretary to First Lord, August 17, 1928.

mended two names—Captains T. F. P. Calvert and J. F. Somerville—neither of which Richmond or his friends wanted. Calvert was the man, Kenneth Dewar wrote, "who caused all the trouble about the remarks on the Naval Air Wing in the *Naval Review* and nearly had the Admiralty censorship reinstated." And Somerville, while pleasant and affable, was not sufficiently widely read to be of much use. Richard Webb, then Commandant of the War College, echoed Dewar's assessment and suggested Captain Brian Egerton who was then his deputy.[37] Richmond agreed and recommended Egerton to Madden. Egerton was somewhat more junior than the position required, but there was, Richmond suggested, a "shortage of officers of the type wanted."[38]

The First Sea Lord had his own ideas, however. Egerton was marked to become Director of Torpedoes and Mines at the Admiralty. Madden was willing to consider other names, but suggested that Richmond was placing too much emphasis on staff-training qualifications. He considered it more important "that he should be an officer of wide experience and strong character." A few days later, after conversations with Fisher, Pound, and Fullerton, he reaffirmed his faith in Calvert whom he felt was even better qualified than Dickens. An added reminder that Calvert had served on Jellicoe's Staff in *Iron Duke* from 1914-1916 should have left no doubts in Richmond's mind as to which school had reasserted itself in the seat of power at Whitehall.[39]

Hankey's comment on the decision was: "appalling! E. would be first rate." According to his information, Egerton neither wanted the Torpedo job, nor was he even technically oriented. Unable to intervene, Hankey promised Richmond that he would "watch for an opportunity"; he had personally noted Egerton as a possible future I.D.C. Commandant.[40] Roger Bellairs was just as disturbed and "amazed." Madden's decision indicated that he "failed to realize the vital importance of the Imperial Defence College appointment and that pure material considerations must give way."[41]

Richmond took the opportunity of a final parting shot on the subject as he left the I.D.C. in December 1928. In a personal letter to Madden, he laid out his case for the selection and subsequent employment of future naval candidates to the College. The College's purpose was, in part, to introduce officers to the study of war in its broadest aspects in order to create a reserve of qualified officers for employment at the highest levels of instructional, planning, staff, and

37 Ibid., Dewar to Richmond, July 7, 1928; Webb to Richmond, July 9, 1928.
38 Ibid., Richmond to First Sea Lord, July 11, 1928.
39 Ibid., Madden to Richmond, July 13, 18, 1928.
40 Ibid., Hankey to Richmond, July 16, 1928.
41 Ibid., R. M. Bellairs to Richmond, July 17, 1928.

command work. It was essential therefore, he argued, that only those officers who had graduated from Staff Colleges and who showed "exceptional promise and fitness for the higher posts of Staff and Command" should be selected to attend the I.D.C. Similarly, a conscious effort should be made to see that the I.D.C. graduate was employed to the best possible advantage. Going further, he recommended that I.D.C. graduates be posted and promoted without reference to normal seniority and waiting-list requirements. The prestige of the course would be well served once it became known that the graduates were men marked for preferential treatment. "Marked men they should be," Richmond concluded

> for only the very best are worth sending through the course. Any others are only a hindrance, and their presence actively detrimental. They contribute nothing to the advancement of knowledge, and, as they themselves (though possibly good captains) will never assume high offices, the time they spend, and the money spent, are alike thrown away.[42]

Richmond never received a direct reply, although his successor was informed in February by Sir Charles Walker that the Admiralty could not accept Richmond's position. It was pointed out that the selection of naval candidates was carried out on the basis Richmond suggested "so far as previous staff training admits." But preferential treatment in subsequent appointments was another question. In the Admiralty's opinion, "good staff knowledge, though meriting due consideration, is not the only qualification requisite for high commands, nor do they consider that such knowledge should be the chief factor in making selections for these posts."[43]

Richmond was deeply offended by what he believed to be a gross distortion of his views. In a heated reply to Madden, he denied recommending that I.D.C. training should be "the only qualification" or "the chief factor" in future posting and promotion policy. He considered it an "insult" to his intelligence and to everything he had ever said or written on the subject.

> Never in the course of my writing, in conversation or lectures have I done otherwise than preach the Doctrine and preparation for command, as I have learnt it in the writings of all the great Soldiers and Sailors, or from the teaching of their careers. I have most strongly and consistently denied that mere fitness in any specialist branch is a sole, or chief, qualification for high command, whether that branch (following Collingwood's and Kempenfelt's words) be seamanship, gunnery, torpedo, electrical science, administration, or any branch of what is now called "Staff Work." Character and courage, moral as well as physical, I have emphasized as essential first and foremost.

42 Ibid., Richmond to Madden, December 31, 1928.
43 Ibid., Sir Charles Walker (Admiralty) to Commandant, I.D.C., C.W. 115/29, February 14, 1929.

Then, referring to his own historical writings on the subject of command, "which received no notice at the Admiralty," and his conversations with Madden about the need for more sea-time in officers'
training, he went on to show why he felt the Admiralty's letter and its
implied criticism that he was seeking to create an intellectual *élite* in
the service had left him feeling so personally wounded.

> I cannot suppose that you yourself saw the letter, or, if you did, that
> you realised the plain implications: for the Board would never think
> it necessary to write to Major General Bartholomew to inform him of
> an opinion so familiar to every soldier. It can only have been for
> myself that this was intended: it was in comment upon a letter of
> mine; and it therefore suggests that either in that letter, or elsewhere I
> had expressed those views which the Board condemn, and rightly
> condemn.[44]

In subsequent exchanges, Madden attempted to soothe
Richmond's injured feelings. Noting that his original letter had indeed been open to the interpretation given, Madden unequivocally
accepted responsibility for the opposition to Richmond's earmarking
scheme. At the same time, he went to some length to reassure Richmond that his opinions were highly valued and respected. The matter
was finally closed a few days later with Madden expressing regrets for
any annoyance caused: "I truly try to do what's right here with as little
friction as possible."[45] This did not alter the fact that on fundamentals
Richmond and Madden were poles apart and, over the next few years,
that distance widened. Their differences in 1928-1929 were just the
first indications of how much Richmond was out of sympathy with
Beatty's successors.

A dramatic change in the tempo and nature of British naval
politics followed Madden's arrival at the Admiralty. The implications
were particularly important for Richmond, for no longer did he enjoy
the protection of sympathetic superiors. This fact is pertinent to any
assessment of Richmond's I.D.C. achievements. Inevitably, the College was in an exploratory and experimental phase during his period
of command. It survived to become one of the most important
politico-military devices of the present century. Like most schemes
put in train that owed much to a man of character and insight, it would
suffer from the later appointments of lesser men. In Richmond's case,
the wonder is that he was able, in the formative committee stages, and
in two short years as Commandant, to stamp the College so hard that
his successors were firmly cradled in his arms whether or not they
fully appreciated the strength of his embrace.

44 Ibid., Richmond to Madden, January 17, 1929 (incorrectly dated, should read
    February).
45 Ibid., Madden to Richmond, February 21, 23, 1929.

9

Madden, "Royal Oak," and "Belligerent Rights": "The Day of the Politician" (1927-1929)

The late 1920s were years of relative political tranquillity for Britain. Pre-1914 clashes of party and class, temporarily diverted by four years of war, gave way in the wake of the anti-climactic General Strike of 1926 to a new mood of reconciliation which made it increasingly difficult to distinguish the dividing lines between Conservative and Labour policy. The same held true in foreign and defence policy where all parties sought the safety of detachment from European entanglement. The dependence of domestic recovery on tranquility abroad was axiomatic. But League of Nations membership and all-Party support of "collective security" masked an underlying isolationism. Indeed, attempts to make collective security a reality were rejected by political, military, and public opinion at home and in the Dominions because they involved undefined or automatic commitments. The splendid generalities of the 1925 Locarno Pact seemed to promise a final settlement of Europe's problems. It was not an alliance. It was more; a guarantee against aggression in the abstract. Arthur Balfour euphemistically termed it "the symbol and the cause of a great amelioration in the public feeling of Europe."

From this high-water mark of Austen Chamberlain's diplomatic skill, down to the General Election of May 1929 when Ramsay MacDonald pledged Labour to continued efforts on behalf of peace through the League and international action, that isolationist impulse was at work. And so long as the "Spirit of Locarno" prevailed, defence questions received little serious consideration except when debated in terms of reductions or disarmament. But the mood rested on illu-

167

sion. Diplomatic guarantees of the Rhine frontier had not translated pious hopes into specific military precautions. Staff talks between the signatories were forbidden—a highly attractive aspect of the entire arrangement for leaders haunted by the pre-1914 sequence of events. Paradoxically, this Locarno-induced stability cost Britain much of her bargaining power and freedom of action. One indirect result was the move by Chamberlain and Churchill in 1928 to have the Ten-Year Rule applied on a daily sliding basis, a reinterpretation which became the basis for planning until 1932 (when the "no war" period was reduced to five years) and made realistic defence forecasting all but impossible.

Locarno's effects did not extend to Britain's relations with the United States. America's persistent challenge to British maritime and commercial power underlay serious differences and mutual hostilities which, though most obviously expressed in naval competition, extended over a wide range of other areas as well. Failure to reach a settlement on their respective claims for cruiser needs at the abortive Geneva Naval Conference of 1927 brought Anglo-American relations to their lowest level in the inter-war period. Few knowledgeable observers considered war between the two powers a serious possibility; but some did sense that American demands for naval parity, once granted, would inevitably restrict the use of blockade in any future war. Even as a neutral, the United States could challenge a British blockade, thereby limiting her freedom to manoeuvre to a greater extent than Locarno had done. This was the basis of the Admiralty's firm stand on cruiser requirements at Geneva. American inflexibility on the same issue produced deadlock and showed that further progress in quantitative naval disarmament was impossible. The search for alternative approaches led to a re-examination of the whole concept of blockade and its place in international law.

In Britain, the result was an intensive behind-the-scenes struggle against any sacrifice of traditional doctrines of Maritime Rights on the altar of Anglo-American cordiality. At the same time, U.S. non-participation in the League reinforced the views of those who opposed pre-commitments with respect to Britain's League responsibilities and thus made the preservation of good relations with the Americans absolutely essential—even if it involved a sacrifice of British cruiser strengths. In 1930, at the London Naval Conference, the beginnings of a new trans-Atlantic equilibrium would be established. But this was a result of not entirely fortuitous circumstances which permitted the political leadership to override expert naval advice without much fear of serious opposition.

Beatty's retirement in 1927 in the midst of the Geneva Conference directly affected that outcome, as did the selection of Sir Charles

Madden as his successor. Though intelligent and highly experienced in the problems of high command, Madden had none of his predecessor's instincts or personal magnetism. Beatty had dominated British naval politics for seven and a half years. Always conscious of his popular backing, he perhaps had overplayed the threat of resignation to enforce his will. Even so, his personal relations with the other service Chiefs (except Trenchard), the politicians, and the civil servants were generally sound.

Beatty had hoped to be followed by his long-time disciple, Sir Roger Keyes. He had been Keyes' champion, bringing him on as D.C.N.S. (November 1921-May 1925) and then as Commander-in-Chief of the Mediterranean (June 1925-June 1928). But the timing of Beatty's resignation caught Keyes with a full year remaining in this, the most coveted Fleet command. Naturally, he was reluctant to leave Malta where he was very much in his element. Years later, Keyes suggested that it was he who advised Beatty to appoint Madden as an interim First Sea Lord:

> I made one great mistake ... by following the advice of my Chief of Staff—Pound—and urging Beatty (who intended to hold his office until I was ready to succeed him as First Sea Lord), to let Madden in for his last two years, active service, as Pound maintained that this would put an end to the so-called Beatty-Jellicoe controversy in the Navy.[1]

Whatever the deciding consideration in Beatty's choice of Madden, which Bridgeman, the First Lord, sanctioned, it was not the need for forceful and imaginative leadership which led them to reach back some distance to get his services.

Madden had been in semi-retirement in Sussex since 1922 when he had left the command of the Atlantic Fleet. He was nine years older than Beatty and, in July 1927, had only two years left before compulsory retirement. He had spent the war years entirely with the Grand Fleet, first as Jellicoe's Chief of Staff (August 1914-November 1916) and then as Beatty's Second-in-Command and Commander of the First Battle Squadron. His services, Jellicoe noted in his Jutland Despatch of June 18, 1916, were "of inestimable value ... I owe him more than I can say." Jellicoe had even pushed Madden's claims to succeed him as Commander-in-Chief in preference to Beatty's ("an officer with infinitely less experience and many years younger").[2] But Madden evidently experienced no difficulties in transferring loyalties to his new chief. A long-time advocate and interpreter of Jellicoe's thinking, Madden had few strong views of his own. Had he been more

1 Roskill, *Naval Policy*, vol. 1, p. 46; Keyes to Churchill, April 30, 1940.
2 *Jellicoe Papers*, vol. 2, no. 9(d), Jellicoe to Jackson, September 16, 1916; also 9(a), Jellicoe to Jackson, September 11, 1916.

individualistic and ambitious, Beatty's position could have been very difficult. As it was, he was able to avoid serious problems by keeping Madden fully informed and consulted.

Madden had not served at the Admiralty since 1907, when he was Naval Assistant to Fisher, and from 1910 to 1911, when he was Fourth Sea Lord. His experiences in the intervening twenty years in no way prepared him for the world he now entered.[3] His unassuming modesty, difficulty in making friends, and uneasiness in dealing with politicians therefore placed the Navy at a severe disadvantage, particularly after Geneva. Madden was simply not the man to fight the kind of actions Beatty had. Over the next few years, he was forced to accept Cabinet reductions on almost all previously approved construction programmes. By 1930, he could do nothing to forestall the Labour Government's complete *volte face* on the question of cruiser tonnages at the London Naval Conference.

Madden's two-year term was extended beyond 1929 through a special Order-in-Council which kept him on the Active List, supernumerary to establishment, so long as he remained First Sea Lord. This decision to forego Beatty's intentions, and also Keyes' claims, owed as much to Madden's greater amenability as to any serious doubts about Keyes' professional qualifications. The latter's suitability and popular appeal were seriously undermined by his handling of the "*Royal Oak* Incident" of 1928. More will be said about that. The fact is, in December 1929, MacDonald's government was preparing its policy for the London Conference which opened one month later. Committed to further disarmament and conciliating the Americans, the Labour leaders were unlikely to tolerate a new First Sea Lord whose views were intractably formed on such matters.

Keyes, at least, was convinced that his determination to resist such political pressures was the reason for his being passed over. In 1940, he told Churchill that "Madden left no stone unturned in order to keep me out, otherwise I would have been in a position to prevent the London Naval Treaty."[4] Though he clearly overrated his own powers to alter the outcome of the London Conference, Keyes' general argument would appear to be confirmed by the fact that Admiral Sir Frederick L. Field, the most colourless First Sea Lord of the entire inter-war period, was eventually selected as Madden's successor.

3 Madden was confirmed as an Admiral in February 1919, and created a Baronet later the same year. After leaving the Atlantic Fleet, he was appointed first and principal naval aide-de-camp to the King, and then, in July 1924, promoted to Admiral of the Fleet. In 1923-1924, he served as Chairman of a Committee on Royal Marines' functions and training, and in 1925 was a member of a committee (under Lord Chelmsford) dealing with the naval executive officers list.

4 As quoted in Roskill, *Naval Policy*, vol. 1, p. 47, n. 3; Keyes to Churchill, April 30, 1940. See also C. F. Aspinall-Oglander, *The Biography of Admiral Lord Keyes* (London: Hogarth Press, 1951), pp. 313, 323.

The decline in Admiralty influence that followed Madden's arrival must be seen against the wider background of defence politics generally in the late 1920s. It was a hiatus period in which many of the men most influential in the making of defence policy before and since the war—Balfour, Bonar Law, Beatty, Haldane, Salisbury, Trenchard, etc.—began to fade from prominence. Even Churchill would be totally excluded from power for a decade after 1929. As Baldwin's Chancellor of the Exchequer, he served his master's proclivities by lowering Estimates, extending the ten-year rule, and making cutbacks in cruiser building and the Home Defence air force. The veterans were gone, or going, and a newer generation would not make itself felt for some years. In the interim, power devolved into the hands of political leaders uneducated in and largely unmoved by matters of strategy and united by a mutual revulsion to the realities of modern war. These, then, were some of the realities—public indifference, Government ineptitude, and uninspired Admiralty leadership—which set the pace of naval politics and governed the work of defence reformers in these years.

Richmond was promoted to Admiral in October 1929 but, apart from a brief spell as President of the International Conference on the Safety of Life at Sea, was never again actively employed after leaving the Imperial Defence College. This was not surprising, to him at least. All the same, his bitter disappointment at being ignored for senior command led him into propagandist activities which, though they eventually resulted in his enforced retirement, nevertheless successfully surmounted Admiralty obscurantism to influence naval policy in a positive way on the questions of Belligerents Rights and the future of Anglo-American relations. Kenneth Dewar's fate, on the other hand, was sealed much more quickly and dramatically. His role in the notorious "Royal Oak Affair" of 1928 fulfilled a predictably tragic destiny which Beatty's benevolence had delayed since the end of the war. But the affair affected more than just Dewar's career for, like the later Invergordon Mutiny of 1931, it was seen by many contemporary observers as evidence of a general decay in naval morale.

As impartial detailed assessment of the "Royal Oak Affair" and the motives of the individuals involved is virtually impossible. Transcripts of the Courts Martial proceedings are closed under the normal 100-years' restrictions. Dewar's personal papers covering the trials are similarly closed.[5] His treatment of the incident in his The Navy From Within is confined to a general narrative of events and a discussion on the principles of military justice, all of which reveals

5   DEW, 4, Royal Oak Court-Martial. "Not to be available for 100 years, or in accordance with the Public Records rule for Court-Martial Papers."

little other than the highly legalistic bent of his mind and the amount of pain his wounds still inflicted as late as 1939. One published account based on interviews with Dewar shortly before his death in 1964[6] fills in some gaps, although the book's usefulness is severely limited by the total absence of supporting documentation. These restrictions preclude anything more than an attempt to discuss the "Affair" and its effects on the public image of the Navy within the perspective of the late 1920s.

Initially at least, Beatty's retirement made little difference to Dewar's prospects. He was disappointed that he was not given command of the Naval Staff College after his return from the West Indies in 1924. Instead, he spent the next two years as Deputy-Director of Naval Intelligence. Few officers could claim so much time at the Admiralty, but Dewar, by hounding his service chiefs (Rear-Admirals A. G. Hotham and later, W. W. Fisher) and the permanent civilian officials, was able to initiate various organizational changes which helped break up what he called the "paralyzing routine" of constantly circulating dockets. Finally, in 1927, he was offered command of H.M.S. *Royal Oak*, Flagship of the First Battle Squadron, Mediterranean Fleet. Twelve years had passed since Dewar had seen service with a large fleet. He was nearing the top of the Captain's list and needed this command to qualify for promotion to the Flag List. Despite this, he joined *Royal Oak* at Malta in October 1927 with deep misgivings.

He had wanted a private ship, and *Royal Oak* as a flagship presented special difficulties. He was surprised to discover how top-heavy with Admirals and their staffs the Mediterranean Fleet was. For a station consisting of seven battleships, twelve cruisers, and thirty-two destroyers, Roger Keyes carried an entourage of thirty-one officers in the Fleet Flagship, Vice-Admiral John Kelly commanding the Battle Squadrons had twelve, and Rear-Admiral Bernard Collard in *Royal Oak* had four. This would unsettle any Captain with ambition and strong views, but Dewar, aware that he was *persona non grata* with Madden, dared not ask for another ship. More significant, however, was the unfortunate combination of personalities involved.

Rear-Admiral Collard was known to be a "difficult" officer. Impatient, arrogant and possessed of a "gas and gaiters" mentality, he was the archetypical officer Dewar had always detested. He was senior to Dewar by three years and a Rear-Admiral for only a year. He hoisted his flag for the first time in *Royal Oak*, in November 1927. Dewar was not his personal choice for Flag Captain. It is unlikely that a better example of bureaucratic insensitivity to sound personnel selection

6   Leslie Gardiner, *The Royal Oak Court Martial* (London, 1965), p. vii.

could be found than the throwing together of these two officers—a "choleric Admiral" and "an intellectual but legalistically-minded Captain." Here, Captain Roskill has suggested, lay the cause of the *"Royal Oak* Affair" that ruined both their careers: "The outcome was one of those, happily rare, occasions when the Royal Navy has made a public fool of itself."[7]

Within weeks of Collard's arrival, the expected collision took place. A number of separate and, under normal conditions, petty incidents between the Admiral and various members of *Royal Oak's* crew—"A swear word at a dance, an argument about a ladder, a salute not given or not seen to be given"[8]—prompted Commander H. M. Daniel, the Executive Officer, to complain in writing to Dewar. He, in turn, some forty-eight hours prior to the scheduled sailing of the Fleet for combined exercises with the Atlantic Fleet, forwarded specific charges against Collard to the Commander-in-Chief. Keyes postponed the Fleet's departure and convened a Court of Enquiry. As a result, Collard was ordered to strike his flag; Dewar and Daniel were immediately relieved and despatched home to England to await an Admiralty decision for trials by Courts Martial.[9] On March 15, within hours of their arrival in London, Commander Carlyon Bellairs raised the matter in the Commons. His questions prompted speculation that Dewar, as a member of Richmond's clique, and Bellairs as his friend, were deliberately prodding the Press, taking judgment to the public, and generally making trouble for the Admiralty. This was not the case. All the same, the impression remained, to divide the Navy and the country.[10] From this point the "Affair" blazed on, fed by a Press eager for scandal, mutiny, or anything else that sensationalist journalism could uncover.

The Admiralty's hesitancy in meeting Dewar's and Daniel's demands for a full trial, the artificiality of the charges that were finally brought against them, and the strict adherence to the most formalized of procedural methods during the trials suggest that the specific incidents were indeed trivial, and that Dewar's and Daniel's positions were, in principle, justified. The initial Court of Enquiry in Malta found that Collard had been tactless as Dewar charged, and "behaved in a manner any senior Captain might take exception to." He was placed, by Board decision, on the retired list.[11] Daniels, who was

7   Roskill, *Naval Policy,* vol. 1, p. 47.
8   Gardiner, *Royal Oak,* p. 218.
9   Adm. 1/8728-170/28, Findings of Court of Enquiry.
10 Allegations to this effect in Brigadier Aspinall-Oglander's 1951 biography of Keyes resulted in Dewar filing a libel suit in July 1953. The High Court found in Dewar's favour, the offending passages were withdrawn, and public acknowledgment given that Dewar and Daniel had no part in the rumours that had spread in March 1928, that allegations regarding the use of Parliamentary "friends" were unfounded.
11 Adm. 167/77, Board Minute, No. 2461, April 16, 1928.

brought to trial at Gibraltar on March 31, was charged with writing and making public subversive letters. He was found guilty, and sentenced to be severely reprimanded and dismissed from his ship. Dewar was found guilty of accepting and forwarding subversive letters, and was similarly sentenced.

Both Madden and Keyes had resisted the granting of public trials, fearing the publicity that would inevitably follow. But the decision was made by the First Lord. Goaded by Kenworthy and Bellairs from both sides of the Commons, and by the Press outside, Bridgeman saw the trials as a means of protecting his own skin. Court Martial rendered the whole affair *sub judice*, thereby ensuring his immunity to further questioning in Parliament. However, his refusal to enlighten the House concerning the actual charges and details of the issue when he rose on March 19 to announce the convening of the Courts Martial only provoked further demands for explanations. The fact is the Admiralty mishandled the business from beginning to end. Dewar's and Daniel's justifiable demands for trials, and unsuccessful bids for clearly specified charges to which they could hope to offer some effective reply, only added to the confusion.

All this was apparent by the time the trials were concluded. It was a pathetic affair in every respect. The socialist press had followed events in daily pursuit of evidence of revolution, mutiny, and disintegration. With a General Election in the offing, flights of journalistic imagination were to be expected. Dewar and Daniel were the natural heroes of the piece; Collard, Keyes, and the Admiralty the villains. In reality, there was room for blame for almost everyone involved.

Happily the incident died quickly as a newsworthy item. After the Easter recess, Kenworthy attempted a brief *post-mortem* in Parliament by demanding a Blue Book on the incident and questions arising out of the conduct of the trial, the framing of charges, and the timing which severely hampered the defendants in gathering witnesses. One question was never answered to Kenworthy's satisfaction. Bridgeman had assured the House that the two officers' careers were not in jeopardy, providing of course they offered no further trouble. Notwithstanding this, Kenworthy noted what a simple matter it would be to block their future promotion. Daniel saw this clearly, and retired immediately for a position with the *Daily Mail*.

Dewar was back on the active list within a few months. In July, he was informed he would be given command of H.M.S. *Tiger*, a vintage battlecruiser employed in trials and experimental firings at the Whale Island gunnery school. *Tiger* was scheduled to be replaced by *Iron Duke* in March 1929, at which time Dewar would transfer in order to complete three years' sea-time to qualify for promotion. In February, however, he was warned that he was to leave *Tiger* on May 13.[12] A question had arisen as to when his three'year period would be complete. Dewar pointed out the discrepancy to the Admiralty leaving no doubt about his bitter disappointment: "The idea of being placed on half pay some six weeks before the completion of that period and having to hang about for the chance of some small cruiser with my promotion to Rear-Admiral getting closer and closer is humiliating."[13] In the end, he was permitted to complete his time with *Iron Duke* until August, and was subsequently promoted to Rear-Admiral. But he would never hoist his flag. At the age of fifty he was appointed Aide-de-camp (A.D.C.) to the King, awarded a "good service" pension of Ŀ150, and placed on the retired list. Kenworthy's intercessions with the Prime Minister and with the First Lord, Mr. Alexander, a "close personal friend," achieved nothing.[14]

Dewar had openly challenged the Admirals and the Admiralty, and he had lost. Head-on collision in such circumstances was usually costly. All the same, it is difficult to avoid the feeling that his ruin resulted from more than just the immediate circumstances of the *"Royal Oak* incident." He had made many powerful enemies in the past who were no doubt quick to see the implications of his predicament with Rear-Admiral Collard. This would explain much of what appears to have been excessive vindictiveness in the Admiralty's handling of the case. *Royal Oak* was one of those rare occasions when the Navy's inner workings were thrown open to full public scrutiny. Subsequent "incidents" such as the *Lucia* affair and Invergordon Mutiny of 1931 seemed to justify the close watch which the national Press maintained over both the upper and lower decks' activities. But all three "incidents" were responses by individuals to specific circumstances; they were not attacks against established authority or a particular class or social group. Dewar's response was open, if not altogether wise. By contrast, Richmond's method of countering the Madden regime's failings exemplified the virtues of a more subtle and indirect approach. In this instance, the focus was Anglo-American relations which after 1927 turned on the question of Belligerent Rights and "Freedom of the Seas."

The Belligerent Rights debate of 1927-1929 is one of the least well-known facets of inter-war British naval politics, despite the fact that it involved one of the greatest threats to the Royal Navy's real power and strategic potential. This is partly because it was a behind-the-scenes debate, and in the end, did not result in any policy changes. Nevertheless, it was a matter of extreme importance. It also

12 DEW, 3, Rear-Admiral Fullerton (Naval Secretary to the First Lord) to Dewar,
   July 20,1928; February 22, 1929.
13 Ibid., Dewar to Fullerton, February 27, 1929.
14 Ibid., Kenworthy to Dewar, June 8; July 1, 17, and 31, 1929.

illustrates how changes in political and naval leadership seriously undermined the development of sound defence doctrine in these years. But for the efforts of a very few men—Hankey and Richmond in particular—the outcome could well have been disastrous in terms of Britain's international position and power. Their ideas, and the methods they employed to stiffen their superiors' thinking, are in themselves an interesting commentary on the extent to which the "realist tradition"[15] had been superseded in the policy formulation processes.

Anglo-American hostility was always close to the surface in the 1920s. The Washington Naval Agreements of 1921 subdued this tendency with regard to the comparatively simple problem of the two powers' overall numerical naval strengths. But more fundamental disagreement persisted on such issues as interpretations of international maritime law and neutrals' rights in time of war—differences which affected the entire field of maritime commercial enterprise. With Britain struggling to regain markets lost mainly to the Americans, the threat of more serious disagreement was always present.

During World War I, these issues had produced a state of uneasy tension in Anglo-American relations. President Wilson's well-known suspicions of British war motives and, more specifically, his criticism of British blockade practices, had strained the connection almost to the breaking point (over virtually the same issues which had caused the rupture of 1812!).[16] Admiralty hostility, in turn, had focussed on American interference in blockade questions and refusal to react firmly to German submarine actions. The influence of the Foreign Office blockade section "who put American good-will above perfection of the blockade,"[17] only increased the hostility.

At the Paris Armistice talks, these issues threatened to ruin all chances of the Anglo-American accord which was essential to the chances of the proposed League of Nations. "Freedom of the Seas," the second of Wilson's original Fourteen Points, came immediately under fire from the Admiralty, who viewed it as a direct assault on the long-established foundation of Britain's claim to naval supremacy; namely, her "right" to blockade an enemy, intercept neutrals, and search for contraband cargoes which would be condemned in Prize Courts. If the war had taught any concrete lessons, the importance of these practices had been made manifest.

15 D. C. Watt, *Personalities and Policies* (Notre Dame: University Press, 1965), p. 27.
16 For an informative account of later inter-Allied cooperation in maintaining the blockade, see: Marion C. Siney, "The Allied Blockade Committee and the Inter-Allied Trade Committees: The Machinery of Economic Warfare, 1917-1918," in K. Bourne and D. C. Watt, eds., *Studies in International History* (London: Longmans, 1967), pp. 330-34.
17 D. C. Watt, *Personalities and Politics*, p. 29.

Wemyss adamantly opposed any concessions, and bluntly warned that whatever the interpretations placed on "Freedom of the Seas," or agreements reached in international negotiations, the Admiralty would not be bound by them in time of emergency.[18] Fortunately, he was supported by the Prime Minister and a majority of his Cabinet colleagues, including Austen Chamberlain and also the C.I.G.S., Sir Henry Wilson.[19] Unquestionably, this accord was a vital element in Lloyd George's successful stand in the pre-Armistice talks (October 29-November 4, 1918) and the Peace Conference against acceptance of the American position on "Freedom of the Seas" or its incorporation into the Peace Treaty.[20] For the next seven years it remained an unresolved issue, side-tracked or submerged by the Washington Agreements, but nevertheless a source of future antagonism.

The issue resurfaced in 1927 following the collapse of the Geneva Naval Conference. In questioning the real causes of the "apparently unreasonable attitude of the United States" at the talks, Austen Chamberlain concluded that "the difference between us centered in the use which we make of our naval forces to enforce our views of the rights of a belligerent at sea."[21] Expert Foreign Office opinion, corroborated by the Ambassador and Military Attaché in Washington,[22] suggested an urgent need for re-examining British assumptions about the continuing validity of blockade under modern conditions, and investigating the possibilities of an accord with the United States on disputed points of international law. Robert Craigie, head of the American Department, argued that it would be impossible for Britain, in view of America's naval parity, if not superiority, "to establish . . . and to maintain an unquestioned command of the sea untrammelled by any serious menace from neutrals." He understood that British naval and legal authorities would resist any attempts to further codify

18 Adm. 167/55, Memorandum by First Lord, October 13, 1919. Forwarded to the War Cabinet, October 17, 1918 (Adm. 116/1771). The same arguments are contained in Adm. 116/1772, Memorandum, December 21, 1918, and an Admiralty Memorandum dated December 24, 1918, which was discussed by the Imperial War Cabinet.
19 H. I. Nelson, *Land and Power: British and Allied Policy on Germany's Frontier, 1916-1919* (London: Routledge, 1963), p. 67. Chamberlain's reputed reaction to Point Two was: "Freedom of the Seas . . . Go to Jericho." In light of his later position in 1927-1928, this is of some interest. See below, pp. 179, 184, n. 39.
20 Hankey, *Supreme Control*, vol. 2, pp. 858-63. Also, S. P. Tillman, *Anglo-American Relations at the Paris Peace Conference of 1919* (Princeton: The University Press, 1961); L. W. Martin, *Peace Without Victory* (Yale, 1958); and M. G. Fry, "The Imperial War Cabinet: The United States and the Freedom of the Seas," *R.U.S.I.*, 110 (November 1965).
21 Cab. 24/189, C.P. 258(27), Austen Chamberlain, "Belligerent Rights at Sea and the Relations Between the United States & Great Britain," October 26, 1927.
22 Ibid., letters, Sir Esme Howard to Sir William Tyrrell, September 15 and 22, 1927; letter from Colonel R. Pope-Hennessy, September 20, 1927.

or restrict the law and its application, but felt the situation had changed so drastically since 1919 that a new look was essential:

> to leave these problems of prize law in a fluid and indeterminate state is like leaving dynamite lying about loose in a ship which may at any moment encounter a terrific storm. So far as Anglo-American relations are concerned, it is tantamount to keeping in being the one question which might conceivably lead to an eventual explosion. By insisting on keeping our hands free now, the Admiralty would run the risk of seeing our activities unnecessarily circumscribed later by a United States determined to "go the limit" in protecting neutral rights.[23]

Chamberlain frankly admitted that the world situation had changed to Britain's disadvantage; "what was possible in the past may have become impossible for the future." He therefore recommended the creation of a special Committee of the Cabinet or Committee of Imperial Defence to conduct a thorough re-examination of Britain's position on Belligerent Rights. He circulated his views to the Cabinet, along with those of Sir Esme Howard in Washington, Hankey, and Sir Cecil Hurst (Legal Adviser to the Foreign Office), on the need for action with a view to early talks with the Americans.[24] As a result, a special eight-man Sub-Committee of the C.I.D., chaired by Lord Salisbury with Admiral Madden, Hankey, and Hurst attached as "Expert Assessors," was set up in December 1927.[25]

The Salisbury Sub-Committee was charged with reviewing the entire Belligerent Rights question and offering specific recommendations about renewal of the Anglo-American General Arbitration Treaty (The Root-Bryce Treaty, signed in 1908 and renewed in 1913)

23 Ibid., "Memorandum respecting the Possibilities of an Anglo-American Agreement regulating the Exercise by either Power of its Belligerent Right to Intercept Private Property at Sea," signed by R. L. Craigie, October 17, 1927. Robert Leslie Craigie (1883-1959). British Representative Inter-Allied Blockade Committee, 1916-1918. First Secretary, Washington, 1920-1923. Transferred to Foreign Office 1923. Later Assistant Under-Secretary of State 1934-1937; Ambassador to Japan, 1937-1941; U.K. Representative to U.N. War Crimes Commission, 1945-1948. Knighted 1936; P.C., 1937.

24 Cab. 24/189, C.P. 286(27), "Belligerent Rights at Sea," Austen Chamberlain, November 14, 1927; Memorandum by Sir M. Hankey on Blockade and the Laws of War, October 31, 1927; Memorandum by Sir C. Hurst on Sir M. Hankey's Paper on "Blockade and the Laws of War," November 10, 1927; also C.P. 287(27), "Some Observations on Sir C. Hurst's Memorandum of November 10 . . . on the suggestion for an Agreement with the United States in regard to the exercise of Belligerent Rights at Sea," by R. L. Craigie, November 16, 1927.

25 Cab. 21/207, B.R. 82, Committee of Imperial Defence, Sub-Committee on Belligerent Rights, Draft Second Report, dated February 11, 1929. The other members were: Chamberlain, Balfour, Bridgeman, Cunliffe-Lister, Viscount Peel, Lord Cushenden, Sir Douglas Hogg (later Lord Hailsham). Amery was added on October 17, 1928. Sir William Tyrrell (Permanent Under-Secretary of State for Foreign Affairs) and Sir Maurice Gwyer (H.M. Procurator-General and Treasury Solicitor) were added as "Expert Assessors" in January 1928.

which was due to expire on June 4, 1928. Shortly after the Committee's first meeting on January 11, it became evident, as a result of a Senate resolution introduced by Senator Borah, that the U.S. was anxious to initiate a general recodification of international maritime law. Whether or not Belligerent Rights would be included in these discussions thus became a matter of pressing concern.

Chamberlain approached the question with a seemingly open mind. In urging the Cabinet to create the C.I.D. Sub-Committee, he warned "that the question is of immense importance, and that the answer, whether negative or affirmative, is fraught with grave possibilities. I have formed no definite conclusion. I ask the Cabinet for no decision until the question has been thoroughly examined by the most competent committee that we can choose."[26] His Foreign Office advisers were somewhat less objective. They argued that a partial surrender on Belligerent Rights would be entirely justified provided a new American agreement could be reached which would make it possible, in any future war, to exercise most of those claimed Rights without fear of American interference. Reinforced by Churchill's strong backing in the Cabinet, this view seemed likely to dominate the Sub-Committee's thinking. Given the fact that the Royal Navy no longer held undisputed supremacy at sea, it was a difficult position to attack.

Predictably, The Admiralty's response was hostile and Madden lost no time in restating the Navy's case. But something more than a defiant reiteration of Wemyss' 1919 stance was needed in the changed circumstances of 1928-1929. Madden and Bridgeman had neither the abilities nor the personal power and influence to head off such forces alone. That job fell to Hankey and Richmond.

Hankey's dedication to preserving Britain's position on Maritime Rights bordered on obsession. It was one of a very few issues, if not the only one, over which he ever raised the possibility of resignation.[27] His qualifications to speak authoritatively, based on some fifteen years' intimate involvement at the highest policy-making levels, were unique. As Secretary of the C.I.D., he had coordinated the efforts of a host of sub-committees which from 1912 to 1914 had studied the problems of wartime transport, insurance, and associated issues concerned with the shipping industry and preparations for economic warfare. He had seen those policies put to the test in war and then, in 1919, witnessed their successful defence by Lloyd George. In 1927, he laid out his convictions in several lengthy memoranda to the Committee outlining the historical background to the question along with

26 Cab. 21/307, C.P. 286(27), November 14, 1927.
27 Roskill, *Hankey*, vol. 2, pp. 134-35. See also K. Middlemas and J. Barnes, *Baldwin* (London: Weidenfeld and Nicolson, 1969), p. 496n.

numerous references to the memoirs and reflections of eminent wartime figures on the folly of Britain ever agreeing to restrictive arrangements in future. Over the next few months, he focussed his
powerful influence on moving the Salisbury Committee around to his
point of view by bringing Balfour into the deliberations and muster-
ing the sympathies of others like Lord Esher, Lloyd George, and even
the King.

Richmond contributed his talents in several different ways. He
fed Hankey useful historical data and arguments, many of which were
incorporated directly into the text of the Committee's report. He was
also a propagandist. The number of outside experts consulted by the
Sub-Committee was limited. Apart from Sir Cecil Hurst, no legal
specialists other than those primed by Richmond were approached.
Naval opinion was similarly engineered or provided by Richmond to
give the impression of widespread service discussion and a well-
defined professional consensus on the subject where actually none
existed. Of all his sorties into defence politics, Richmond's team effort
with Hankey on this issue is unsurpassed as an example of Machiavel-
lian cunning.

Throughout the whole of 1928, much of the Sub-Committee's
time was spent gathering documentary evidence and technical data.
Hankey deluged the members with materials from the C.I.D.
archives—these included papers on the wartime breakdown of international agreements, details of Lloyd George's and the Imperial War
Cabinet's position on the 1919 "Freedom of the Seas" issue, and the
later work of the C.I.D. on wartime trading and blockade practices.[28]
The highly technical nature of the subject meant that much of this
work was given over to a separate Legal Technical Sub-Committee.
Pressing current issues also necessitated a degree of caution. The
Foreign Office kept the members up to date with recent developments
in the United States. In July, Sir Esme Howard returned to London,
and, along with Craigie, was personally interviewed. By then, American pressure for a conference leading towards renewal of the Arbitration Treaty was reaching a climax. In March, Secretary of State Kellogg had forwarded a draft of a new treaty for British consideration.
The existing Arbitration Treaty with the United States expired on
June 2. Similarly, the one with France expired in October, and those
with Italy and Spain, in February 1929. While all these were under
consideration, the Kellogg Pact for the Renunciation of War was
proposed, thus cutting across the whole question. It was therefore

28 C.I.D. Paper 428-B, Committee of Imperial Defence, "Report on Sub-Committee in
   Trading, Blockade and Enemy Shipping," dated May 30, 1923. A copy of this report
   together with Admiralty memoranda and correspondence for the period 1920-1924
   is contained in Adm. 116/2345.

early 1929 before the Belligerent Rights Committee was able to settle down to the final stages of framing policy recommendations.

By then, Richmond had been officially invited, on Chamberlain's suggestion, to review the Committee's work and offer his own evidence and advice. The initiator here was Hankey who, though partially successful in swinging the Foreign Secretary around to a hardline position, was anxious to add Richmond's weight directly to the proceedings. As Corbett's disciple and an historian in his own right, Richmond was recognized as an authority on maritime law and economic warfare. Moreover, his practical experience of dealing with American moralizing about British blockade practices stretched back to the early years of the war when he had worked closely, though entirely unofficially, with those in Britain who hoped to educate opinion on both sides of the Atlantic. In 1915 and 1916, he had assisted and advised A. H. Pollen and Sir Horace Plunkett (uncle of Reginald Plunkett-Drax) who were then corresponding directly with Wilson's personal adviser, Colonel E. M. House. It was through this personal link as well as Pollen's many American Press contacts that Richmond's ideas penetrated, though never permeated, the inner sanctum of the White House. Richmond's postwar writings and letters leave no doubt that his grasp of the principles and details of international maritime law was of a very high order and much respected by established experts in the field.[29]

Richmond, in fact, had influenced some Committee members before they formally met. His commentaries on Foreign Office reports and memoranda had guided and reinforced Hankey's thinking from the beginning.[30] Then, in early 1929, he submitted a number of memoranda which assisted the Committee in arriving at a careful definition of terms relevant to Britain's real interests. What is particularly interesting about Richmond's contribution, however, is that some of it was made in a curiously roundabout way, via the pages of the *Naval Review*.

The first number of the 1929 volume was almost entirely devoted to articles dealing with international maritime law. All were written by legal experts with whom Richmond was acquainted.[31] The second

29 A. H. Pollen Papers, Pollen to Richmond, February 9, 25; March 2, 1916; Richmond to Pollen, February 20, 29; March 20, 1916. Pollen had been introduced to House in May 1914 by Plunkett. Correspondence covering the period July 1915 to March 1916 also includes letters from Drax, Dewar, J. A. Spender, and Geoffrey Dawson. See also RIC/2/3, Commonplace Book, vol. 3, Misc. materials dealing with Trade in War, Economic Problems.

30 Cab. 21/307, Richmond to Hankey, November 8 and 9, 1927; and RIC/7/3d, Hankey to Richmond, January 25, 1928, with copies of papers sent in by Richmond; "Comments on Sir E. Howard's letter of 29.12.27"; "The Value of the Right of Capture in a Single-Handed War" (n.d.); "Russia" (n.d.); "Notes on Sir Cecil Hurst's Paper" (n.d.).

31 *Naval Review*, no. 1 (1929); A. Pearce Higgins (Whenwell Professor of Interna-

number followed a similar vein, except that most of these articles
emphasized the immediate problem of Anglo-American relations.
Except for the articles whose authors were identified,[32] and one to
which Richmond signed his name, the remainder were lengthy commentaries written anonymously by Richmond.[33] These particularly
"delighted" Lord Sydenham who wrote: "It was wise I think, not to
add your name and to give the impression of the existence of other
sane and thoughtful naval officers."[34]

The keynote article was Richmond's reply to a pamphlet, "The
Freedom of the Seas," by Colonel E. M. House, the persistent in-
stigator of most of the American initiatives since the war. Richmond
refuted, point by point, what he saw as the essential hypocrisy of the
American position based as it was on an assumption that the concepts
of blockade and contraband stood in violation of the natural order of
things, and that international agreement to revise maritime law and
naval practice, if guaranteed by a League covenant, could assure
future peace between the great maritime powers. This was flying in
the face of historical realities which demonstrated that nations' attitudes to questions of trade immunity were determined by specific
conditions and situations:

> National advantage, not a philosophical attitude towards war or
> humanity, was ever the spring of their policy. As neutrals, or bellige-
> rents weak at sea, we see them advocate immunity to its utmost
> lengths. As belligerents allied to strong naval powers, they advocate

tional Law, Cambridge, and Member of the Institute of International Law), "The
Treatment of Mails in Time of War" (reprinted from *British Year Book of International Law, 1928*), pp. 1-11; G. N. Clark (Oriel College, Oxford), "War Trade and
Trade War, 1701-1713" (reprinted from *The Economic History Review*, 1, no. 2),
pp. 34-52; "The Causes of the War of 1812," pp. 76-97; "The Monroe Doctrine,"
pp. 117-28; "The Freedom of the Seas," pp. 129-33.

32 Ibid., no. 2: Professor James P. Baxter (Harvard), "The British Government and
Neutral Rights, 1861-65," pp. 185-212; "The British Commonwealth, Freedom and
The Seas," (reprinted from the *Round Table* March 1929), pp. 256-73; "Mr Walter
Lippman's Proposals," pp. 274-80; "Senator Borah and the Freedom of the Seas"
(reprinted, *Round Table*, March 1929), pp. 297-307; John W. David, "Anglo-
American Relations and Sea Power" (reprinted, *Foreign Affairs*, April 1929),
pp. 308-17; K. G. B. Dewar, "The Freedom of the Seas" (written in 1918), pp. 334-
43; Sir Francis Piggott, "The Freedom of the Sea" (1919 Lecture to the Staff College,
Camberley), pp. 344-73; A. C. Dewar, "Freedom of the Seas and Modern Blockade,"
pp. 374-81; G. N. Clark, "Neutral Commerce in the War of the Spanish Succession
and the Treaty of Utrecht," pp. 384-97; Review of Professor Wilford Garner, *Prize
Law During the World War* (New York, 1927) by A. Pearce Higgins, pp. 398-99.

33 Richmond, "The Freedom of the Seas: Some Comments . . . on Colonel House's
Pamphlet Issued by the National Society for the Prevention of War," *Naval Review*,
no. 2 (1929), pp. 221-36 (Colonel House's pamphlet/article preceded Richmond's
response, pp. 213-20; a copy of House's Pamphlet "The Freedom of the Seas" is
contained in RIC/2/3); "Mr. Arthur Bullard's Proposals, With Some Comments
Thereon," pp. 237-55; "Comments on Mr. Walter Lippmann's Proposals,"
pp. 281-96; "Some Comments on Mr. Davis' Paper," pp. 318-31.

34 RIC/7/4, Sydenham to Richmond, May 30, 1929.

> the strongest measures against commerce .... Circumstances, not philosophy, have dictated the attitude of nations, and it is idle to cite humanitarian motives, or to quote imaginary "Rights of Man" as though some high moral purpose informed policy. It did not ... in so far as immunity is a principle, it rests solely upon national advantage. It can find no support in any philosophy of war, in any natural rights or on any ethical basis. None of the claims will stand examination, nor the test of historical experience.

Britain, he argued, had always maintained her position on High Belligerent Rights not as a "right" but as a matter of policy. There were, in his view, two fundamental methods of enforcing an enemy's compliance in war—direct assault, and investment (i.e., control of his external channels of supply). So long as war remained an acceptable instrument of national policy, he doubted that ethical distinctions could be drawn between the two methods. Moreover, nothing in the record of past international agreements or in the field of technological developments suggested that these facts no longer applied. Indeed, it seemed highly unlikely to him that the Americans themselves would ever agree to the outlawing of naval belligerency practices and the virtual confinement of war to operations on land. Certainly, before Britain abandoned her position on Belligerent Rights, he concluded, she was entitled to know the precise American position on the meaning of "Freedom of the Seas" especially in situations when she would be a belligerent: "They cannot have it both ways, and claim freedom to trade when neutral, but power to prevent neutrals—and the enemy— from trading when they are belligerents."

Hankey read Richmond's article early in the new year and thought it "the finest thing I have ever seen on the subject."[35] He was tempted to submit it directly to the Sub-Committee, but on second thought, wanted it withheld for later publication. In the interim, he showed it "privately" to Salisbury and Madden. He was anxious that Richmond not become overly involved in the Committee's actual work; he wanted to protect his status in the event of a decision to enter into conversations with the Americans:

> my own plan has always been that our delegates and staff should include—
> The Lord Chancellor
> *You*
> Hurst or Malkin
> So I agree that at the moment we must keep you out of public controversy.[36]

Almost a month later, Hankey reported the results of "some very private and confidential talk" with Madden, who had asked

35 RIC/7/3d, Hankey to Richmond, January 25, 1929.
36 Ibid., January 31, 1929.

"whether, in the event of conversations or conference in Washington, I thought you would be a good man to represent the Admiralty. I enthused. I think it is certain that in the said eventuality they will give you the offer."[37]

In the meantime, there was much to be done. Hankey was absolutely determined that there should be no conversations. This would mean British capitulation to American "political blackmail"—the threat to outbuild Britain in cruisers if she refused to bargain.

> Here is a great question of international controversy more than a century old on which we are simply told that we must accept American ruling. And what is that ruling? First acceptance of that odious term "Freedom of the Seas." I will stomach that if it means nothing. But what does it mean? Blockade in its most restricted sense. Well. I agree we can get nothing better. But it also means a very limited list of contraband—something approaching the 17th century list. That is not good enough. But it means more than that . . . giving up the right of capture of private property at sea!

He was prepared to argue all these points "but not with a pistol at my head." The root problem, he confided to Richmond, was "I don't trust any Government nowadays to stand up to American threats." Strengthening the Government's nerves therefore became his main aim. If, however, discussions did take place, he intended that they should not be limited to Belligerent Rights but extended to the whole field of the two countries' relations regarding which he noted "the absence of any solid issue (territorial or political) between the two nations." It was essential to arrive first at some *modus vivendi* on the cruiser problem which would remove all possibilities of threats or pressure. Finally, he warned that Britain should not agree to any treaty respecting Belligerent Rights that did not include a "reasonable" contraband list, and "above all,whether by exclusion or inclusion in the Treaty (preferably the former) I would cling at all costs to the right of retaliation—especially for improper use of submarines or aircraft."[38]

There were the policy lines which Hankey emphasized in drafting the Sub-Committee's two Reports. The main report, dealing with Belligerent Rights, presented no major difficulties. All but one of the members had been brought round to a hard-line position. "Thank God," Hankey informed Richmond," they are all for high belligerent rights now except Cushenden."[39] The other Report, dealing with the

37 Ibid., February 25, 1929.
38 Ibid., January 31, 1929.
39 Ibid., February 8, 1929. Commenting on the Foreign Secretary's views, Hankey noted: "It is a most extraordinary position. Austen Chamberlain has now swung round and is saying all the things I wrote eighteen months ago about the undesirability of a Conference. He has actually sent a telegram to Howard to do all he can to

Arbitration Treaties, did give cause for some concern. Chamberlain favoured the inclusion of Belligerent Rights in any new treaty, and his efforts along this line—during Hankey's brief absence with a recurring bout of flu—split the committee in two. Hankey was therefore anxious that the rift be healed before the final Report was submitted. He warned Richmond: "I may have to send you an S.O.S. next week to come up and help me with this report." Finally, after a flurry of last-minute exchanges,[40] the Reports were completed and submitted—that on Arbitration on February 13, the other on March 6, 1929.[41] On the former, however, unanimity had not been achieved and it was then left to the C.I.D. and the Cabinet to weigh the merits of the divided Report.

The Committee members were agreed at least in their regret that the Arbitration Treaties could not be renewed in their old form—with "vital interests" excluded. The disagreement was not that of maintaining Belligerent Rights at a high level, but of the best method to preserve it.

> Those who support the method of concluding an Arbitration Treaty applicable to Belligerent Rights do so with reluctance and only to avoid what they regard as greater risks. Those who oppose this do so because they consider that the risks of injuring our belligerent rights in the long run are greater than those involved in the alternative course . . . . At best it is a choice of evils that the Committee of Imperial Defence and the Cabinet have to make.

The majority (Chamberlain, Salisbury, Cushenden, Hailsham, and Cunliffe-Lister) were convinced that a cooperative attitude on this question would ease Anglo-American relations generally, particularly on the cruiser question,[42] and could obviate altogether the need for an international conference.

The minority (Bridgeman, Amery, and Lord Peel) backed Hankey's position that there should be no discussion of the question until an international conference had established "what these rights are."

ride Hoover off being committed to a Conference before he gets into office. Most amusing, but rather pitiable! Also probably too late!"

40 Ibid., February 11, 18, 1929; also RIC/7/4, Hankey to Richmond, February 14, 1929.

41 Cab. 21/310, B.R. 62, C.I.D., Sub-Committee on Belligerent Rights, "First Report Dealing with the Renewal of Arbitration Treaties," February 13, 1929." (C.I.D. Paper 943-B); and Cab. 21/207, B.R. 82, C.I.D., Sub-Committee on Belligerent Rights, "Second Report Dealing with Maritime Belligerent Rights, March 6, 1929" (C.I.D. Paper 944-B).

42 Ibid., On this point, the report noted: "the conclusion of the Treaty would tend to ease the situation in the cruiser controversy by removing the argument, which has been used with so much effect during the debates in Congress, that a great American Navy is required in order to prevent Great Britain, when engaged in war, from interfering with neutral trade. The existence of the Treaty would clearly cut away this contention. The Secretary of State for Foreign Affairs indeed believes that this would so far improve the situation that the President might even refrain altogether from summoning a Conference notwithstanding the general attitude of the Senate."

They believed "that to include Belligerent Rights among the questions liable to compulsory arbitration is the beginning of concessions,
which will afterwards make it difficult for any Government to stand
firm." They also doubted that the United States, if the majority
suggestion were followed, would refrain from calling a conference.
Conciliation would only underscore Britain's weaknesses and increase demands for further codification of international law. A conference was inevitable and had to be met head on. In the meantime,
delaying inclusion of Belligerent Rights would leave the initiative in
British hands and allow more time "for a dignified and reasoned
statement of the case for our historic policy. If the Senate refused to
accept the Treaty because of the temporary reservation, the onus of
having caused a breakdown would clearly rest with them." Over and
above both these positions, Madden was allowed to attach his personal objection to agreement to compulsory arbitration under any
condition.[43] Hankey requested that his agreement with Madden also
be formally recorded.

On the central issue of Belligerent Rights, the Salisbury Committee's main report came down unequivocally in favour of preserving
them at the highest possible levels. The Report began with a discussion of historical precedents, followed by a systematic refutation of all
the arguments favouring concessions, an analysis of the value of
international agreements, and again, the desirability of an international conference, the ethics of blockade and a study of British and
American practices,[44] and consideration of the strategic factors. Virtually all of it was pure Richmond. Much of the actual text, as Hankey
admitted to him, was "grossly pirated from your classic work on
Blockade."[45] With the one exception of Lord Cushenden, all the mem-

43 Ibid., Appendix No. 2, "Remarks by the First Sea Lord on the Proposal to Allow
    Belligerent Rights to go to Arbitration if International Maritime Law Becomes
    Codified," February 1929.
44 Research in this area was carried out by a Technical Sub-Committee under the
    direction of Sir Cecil Hurst. Its investigations, working from the provisions of the
    1909 Declaration of London, included the technical aspects of British and Ameri-
    can methods and attitudes on such issues as: Visit, Search, and Detention; Block-
    ade, Contraband; Unneutral Service—Destruction of Neutral Prizes, Transfer of
    Flag—Enemy Character Defined; Prize Courts, Convoys; Examination of Mails,
    Retaliation; Armed Merchantmen, etc. Discovering that the differences between the
    two countries were much less than had been expected, Hurst's group suggested that
    the U.S.A., if indeed it did adopt a policy of low Belligerent Rights, would have to
    drastically revise its existing system and Naval Instructions. This suggested that no
    really insuperable problems would be encountered in reaching an agreement,
    provided discussion was limited to questions dealt with in the 1909 Declaration.
    Beyond that limit however—such as was implied in the U.S. Senate's favouring of
    the concept of the immunity from capture of private property at sea—real difficul-
    ties would exist.
45 RIC/7/3d, Hankey to Richmond, February 11, 1929. The reference is to Richmond's
    30-page memorandum, "High or Low Belligerent Rights" (n.d.).

bers had been brought by Hankey and Richmond to a firm policy recommendation which it was now left to the C.I.D. and the Cabinet to consider.

In the end, nothing was done with either of the Reports. They became casualties of the General Election of May 1929. But the Sub-Committee's findings showed that a different approach to naval disarmament and improved Anglo-American relations was needed. Ramsay MacDonald's immediate overtures to Washington and the calling of the 1930 London Naval Conference were the result. This was hardly a more satisfactory consequence and suggests, perhaps, that the prolonged work of the Salisbury Sub-Committee was of little real benefit. Yet, considering the circumstances which had prompted the discussions, the fact that the Baldwin administration had been successfully diverted from any major concessions or surrenders of British claims and, incidentally, gained a much sounder understanding of the basis of British maritime power, the exercise was meaningful. Little had been gained. But neither had anything been needlessly surrendered.

Hankey was not under any illusions about the future of the Reports when they were sent to the Cabinet. He confided to Richmond:

> If I were a betting man, I would offer heavy odds that they (the Cabinet) will "Wait and see" until after the Election. Meanwhile, such evidence as I have points in the direction that the Americans are beginning to think on this question and that the more they think the less are they likely to raise it. There is just the danger that they may bring it up before they have thought enough, but I am not without hopes, more particularly if we can get some Naval Agreement or modus vivendi, that we shall ride the question off altogether.[46]

The prediction was accurate, although his hopes about the Americans were somewhat misplaced. When in October 1929, during MacDonald's Rapidan talks with President Hoover, it became clear Belligerent Rights might be resurrected, Hankey pulled no punches in warning off the Prime Minister.[47] Richmond assisted again by prodding various writers and editors including Geoffrey Dawson[48] whose Times leader of November 12, 1929 helped produce the bad press that stifled Hoover's proposal. Credit for this, as indeed for the whole campaign against any tampering with Britain's claims, must go first of

46 Ibid., March 18, 1929.
47 Roskill, Hankey, vol. 2, pp. 491-96.
48 Notably Admiral Webb, Archibald Hurd, Phillip Kerr (The Round Table), Captain Clement Jones (formerly of Hankey's staff and then prominent in the Institute of International Affairs), and Geoffrey Dawson (The Times). See RIC/7/3d, Richmond to Dawson, n.d. (1929); and RIC/7/4, Hankey to Richmond, June 6, 1929; Clement Jones to Richmond, June 10, 1929.

all to Hankey's adroit and forceful methods. Richmond's part was also important. Few men even recognized, let alone understood, the issues at stake. That these two did, and successfully made their points stick, was a major reason Britain entered World War II able to impose an immediate blockade free of agreements such as those which had restricted its application in 1914.

On Hankey's and Balfour's advice, Richmond had refrained from any direct public expressions of his own so long as his appointment to a British delegation to Washington at an Arbitration Treaty Conference remained a possibility. That changed when the new Government announced its three-part policy of suspending all ship-building programmes, stepping up the work of the General Disarmament Conference Preparatory Commission, and finally, the opening up of direct talks with the Americans for another naval limitations conference. A return to quantitative limitations alarmed Richmond. Public apathy and what he saw as the Admiralty's inability to defend itself eventually forced him into overt action of his own. Lord Sydenham, then age 81, proffered the advice of one who had played the same game since the turn of the century. Like Richmond, he lamented the "miserable set of writers on naval questions," and recognized all too clearly the Admiralty's weaknesses. The difficulty, he suggested, was that "professional sailors and soldiers were unqualified to deal with their subjects: It is the day of the politician."[49]

49 RIC/7/4, Sydenham to Richmond, September 9, 1929. In another letter (October 10, 1929) Sydenham referred to the naval scares of the 1880s and the role of the press in naval affairs; "I wrote as much as I could, and there was readiness to take any [reasoned?] matter. That is all gone now, thanks partly to this L. [League] of Nations Union. We have no one to fight our battles; and as you point out, only the daily Press would count."

10

"Smaller Navies": The London Naval Conference and Richmond's Retirement (1929-1931)

On November 21 and 22, 1929, the London *Times* carried two lead articles entitled: "Smaller Navies—A Standard for All" and "The Capital Ship." But for the fact that they were signed by Richmond and released only a few weeks before the opening of the London Naval Conference, they might have been seen as little more than the opening shots of yet another round of public debate on the subject of battleships versus aircraft and submarines. But these were more than the jottings of a proponent of the anti-battleship side of that well-worn argument. Written by a senior officer recognized as Britain's foremost naval strategist and an historian of consequence, they were an unmistakable challenge to declared Admiralty policy and an open call for a more radical approach to the whole question of naval arms controls.

Richmond would pay heavily for this intrusion into the finely balanced equation of forces that were coming together for these crucial talks. He would be reprimanded for publicly criticizing the official navy line, denied the senior posts he had always wanted, and forced instead into early retirement. More than that, he was blamed at least in part for the 1930 London agreements which many naval officers saw as a total victory for the United States and the other naval powers. A protesting Admiralty Board was forced to accept a further five-year stoppage in battleship construction, an arbitrary cut in cruisers from 70 to 50, and a complete *volte-face* on cruiser sizes and replacement schedules. This and the Global Tonnage figures so reso-

lutely opposed by the Admiralty at the abortive Geneva Conference of
1927 were then extended to destroyers as well. It has been argued,
both then and since, that Ramsay MacDonald's success in meeting his
Labour Government's commitment to Anglo-American accord owed a
great deal to Richmond's anti-materialist attacks and undermining of
the Admiralty's case. In Admiral Brian Schofield's words, 'Richmond's theories made no impact on foreign governments, but caused
considerable mischief with political thought in his own country."[1]
Others have suggested that his arguments so impressed the Labour
leadership that they seriously considered making him First Sea Lord.
"He influenced Prime Minister MacDonald because the latter cared
not a jot for defence, but did regard the budget and peace with high
concern."[2]

Evidence to substantiate these contentions has not been uncovered. Quite the contrary, Richmond's 1929 "small-ship" campaign
reflected his awareness of how little real influence he wielded with
either his political or professional superiors. Moreover, his decision
to publish his "heresies" was made in the full knowledge that it
would cost him his career. In every sense, it was an act of conscience
made necessary by what he passionately believed to be Madden's
inability to speak for the Navy and to protect the nation's true interests. That Richmond's views influenced Government thinking in
1930 is beyond question, though the fault for how they were used was
not his. That stemmed from the breakdown of effective civil-military
relations, from inadequate policy and indeterminate doctrine, and
above all from Ramsay MacDonald's determination (supported by
President Hoover) that during the London talks "we keep political
and not service hands in control" to prevent any repetition of the
failure at Geneva in 1927.[3]

Though directed to the specific circumstances of the 1930 Conference, Richmond's campaign was also the culmination of all his
earlier reform efforts. He brought to bear the full weight of forty-five
years of practical naval experience, his influence as a writer and
agitator, and his mature ideas as a strategist and historian. His action
was therefore neither rash nor precipitate, but rather a calculated
move by a man well aware of his own value and supremely confident
about the soundness of his ideas.

Richmond's views on the ship-size question had developed over
a long period beginning with his involvement in the Capital Ship

1   Vice-Admiral Brian B. Schofield, *British Sea Power in the Twentieth Century*
    (London: Batsford, 1967), p. 105. Also Admiral of the Fleet Lord Chatfield, *It Might
    Happen Again* (London: Heinemann, 1947), p. 60.
2   R. Higham, *The Military Intellectuals in Britain, 1918-1939* (New Brunswick:
    Rutgers University Press, 1966), p. 33.
3   Roskill, *Naval Policy*, vol. 2, p. 40.

Committee and his anonymous *Times* letters of 1921. Churchill's violent attack on his testimony before the Bonar Law Enquiry had taught him the need for greater precision in his thinking, and over the intervening years Richmond tested and sharpened his ideas against the critical commentaries of his friends, of his War Course and I.D.C. audiences,[4] and in his writings such as his 1923 Raleigh Lecture which, in elaborated form, was published in 1928 as *National Policy and Naval Strength*, and also his *Economy and Naval Security* (1931). But this refinement process also served to emphasize the vast gulf which separated him from the mainstream of current naval opinion. In May 1926, after lecturing at the Royal Institute of International Affairs on the "Limitation of Armaments," he was politely but firmly reminded by the D.C.N.S., Vice-Admiral Sir Frederick Field, that in expressing the opinion "that we could reduce naval armaments by a further limitation in the size of ships," he had transgressed the official line. "I feel sure," the unofficial reprimand concluded, "you will refrain from giving public expression to any views which would embarrass the Admiralty in connection with this question."[5] Even the privileged platform of Chatham House meetings offered no protection for a heretic in this sensitive area. Richmond was therefore fully alive to the dangers involved when, in the summer of 1929, he mounted a concerted attack on the Big Ship advocates and the possibility of yet another misdirected disarmament conference.

By this time, he was convinced that his chances for a senior Admiralty or Fleet post were negligible. His work with Hankey on the Belligerent Rights Sub-Committee had done nothing to alleviate his misgivings about the Madden regime. "I feel rather at loose ends," he confided to Admiral Henderson, "and a little out of spirits";

> All the ideas for which I stand seem to be swamped by the idiot dead weight of the materielists. I have been most unpleasantly impressed lately by the obvious and outstanding prejudice of the present regime against anything which could be called staff work or "theory." The cost to the country which results from this is prodigious.[6]

Kenneth Dewar's retirement in June and his impotence to save his disciple's career only heightened his sense of frustration and isolation.[7]

4   RIC/7/2/3, Admiral Roger Backhouse to Richmond, March 4, 1926; Hankey to Richmond, February 17, 1927; Jellicoe to Richmond, May 5, 1927; Lord Sydenham to Richmond, July 10, 21, 22, and August 1, 1927. See also RIC/6/4, Richmond's paper written at the I.D.C., "The Influence of the Submarine and Air on the Size of Fighting Ships," n.d. (1927) (30 pp.), together with students' responses and Richmond's critical marginalia (20 pp.).
5   RIC/7/2/3, Vice-Admiral Field to Richmond, "Personal and Confidential," May 7, 1926. The Lecture was delivered at Chatham House on May 4.
6   RIC/7/1, Richmond to Henderson, March 3, 1929.
7   Ibid., June 16 and 18, 1929.

Arthur Pollen was another important factor in Richmond's decision. They had become close friends during Richmond's I.D.C. posting and continued to correspond and meet frequently in London,
together with their wives, for what they liked to call "family dinners
of us four." The two men had long held common views on many
issues, although Richmond was always careful to steer clear of Pollen's standing vendetta against Fisher and his school. Since 1916,
Richmond had known something of the Admiralty's handling of
Pollen's prewar invention of a long-range, high-speed gunnery control system that included the earliest known continuously acting
gyroscope and electrically driven mechanical analog computer (the
"Argo" clock and Aim Correction fire control system). He evidently
knew very little about the system's complex technical details, and had
never accepted Pollen's claims for its wider tactical implications most
especially as applied to Fisher's controversial battle cruiser designs
which substituted speed and gun-fire accuracy for their comparative
lack of armour protection. For years Richmond tried to convince
Pollen that failure at Jutland was not mainly the result of inadequate
gunnery but, much more importantly, of defective leadership and
general policy, including a highly inflexible tactical system. In August
1927, after reading a draft of Pollen's *Nineteenth Century* article on
Jutland, Richmond admitted: "I have written, and I intend to write
nothing on this matter unless or until it becomes possible to discuss
the fighting instructions; and I candidly believe that all discussion
which omits them is Hamlet without the Prince of Denmark."[8] This
was revealing, inasmuch as Pollen, for the first time in their relationship, then took the time to explain the history of his earlier dealings
with the Admiralty and to show how the highly secret nature of his
inventions had similarly precluded sensible discussion of wartime
gunnery and tactics. Failure to develop his "helm-free" fire-control
system before the war had left no tactical option open other than the
rigid single line-ahead for deploying the Grand Fleet's guns. The
Admiralty, he pointedly remarked, was not interested in what Richmond called "flexible tactics," "largely because they knew that flexibility in action meant artillery out of action. This single piece of
knowledge stood like a blank wall between them and the kind of
tactics you saw to be essential if a fleet action was to be fought to the
finish." In 1927, "eleven years after the battle," the Royal Navy still
had not generally incorporated a helm-free system, though the U.S.
and Soviet navies had.[9] These revelations involved highly sensitive

8   A. H. Pollen Papers, Richmond to Pollen, August 4, 1927.
9   Ibid., Pollen to Richmond, August 19, 1927. For a full discussion of Pollen's system
    and his dealings with the Admiralty before and after the war, see Jon Tetsuro
    Sumida, "British Capital Ship Design and Fire Control in the Dreadnought Era: Sir

state secrets which could not be used in public discussion, though they clearly reinforced Richmond's basic conviction that bigger ships did not automatically mean greater protection. Richmond, it will be seen, developed his controversial "small-ship" theories entirely from a strategic rationale. But because it was Pollen who acted as his technical adviser throughout this campaign,[10] there can be little doubt that dramatically improved gunnery performances based on computer-directed fire-control systems was a major—though necessarily unspoken—assumption of his "ideal" warship concept.

In June of 1929, Richmond began writing a series of articles entitled, "What is it that dictates the Size of the Fighting Ship?". These, together with supporting articles and letters from his own circle and supporters at the Staff College, War College, and Imperial Defence College and from various influential personalities in the publishing world, he planned to release in the August *Naval Review* as a direct provocation to his professional superiors. "The Admiralty are now going to be put on their mettle," he confided to Admiral Henderson,

> they will have to shew cause for their adherence to large ships and I should not be surprised if this Labour Govt. did not shew a desire to take the lead, and propose something positive in economy instead of being dragged at the heels of America all the time.
> What a position we should be in if we took the lead! And what Kudos a Government which did it skilfully would have![11]

He welcomed the thought of controversy. "The more I am attacked, the more openings I have for dealing with sophistries." He also took the precaution of telling the First Lord, Mr. Alexander, about his articles:

> I should like to be able to see the Admiralty objections. I know one man who will oppose me very strongly—Field. His beliefs are the opposite of mine. Keyes is another. Beatty is another. If, however, the Cabinet will not merely accept the authority of great names like Beatty, Keyes, Field, but will examine closely the arguments in a [?] manner, I shall be satisfied.[12]

As planned, the August number of the *Review* was devoted to debate on the "Size of the Fighting Ship." But the result was less than encouraging. Short supporting contributions from the two Dewars and Henderson in no way represented the broad cross-section of naval opinion they had hoped to enlist. Apart from two articles by retired

John Fisher, Arthur Hungerford Pollen and the Battle Cruiser," *Journal of Modern History* (June 1979), 205-30.
10 A. H. Pollen Papers, Richmond to Pollen, July 16; November (n.d.) 1929; Pollen to Richmond July 17, November 25; December 20, 1939; March 4, 14, 1930.
11 RIC/7/1, Richmond to Henderson, June 4, 1929.
12 Ibid., July 12, 1929.

Admirals, Richmond's papers—the unsigned lead article, and another entitled 'The 10,000 Ton Cruiser''—were the only ones of any substance.[13] They dominated the issue.

His message was simple. He wanted to discover the primary determinant of size: "What is the criterion? Is it not possible to relate the size of the ship to something absolute?" Range, endurance, speed, gunpower, and protection were all relative considerations. The then-accepted criteria, he suggested, were not related to the positive requirements of what a ship had to do, but rather to negative considerations of what she must survive. Defence was the ruling factor, rather than function. Since fighting ships were the units which constitute a navy, their function was directly related to the way naval power is exercised, or more concisely, to the object of naval warfare. And that, in his Corbettian view, was the control of maritime commerce. The employment of naval forces as battle fleets, escorts, carrying forces, blockading forces, raiders, etc., were matters of strategy and tactics—the *means* of achieving the prime object. Thus Richmond advanced his theory that the size of the individual fighting ship was in the final analysis determined by the strength of the merchant vessel, "whose arrest is the final object of war at sea."

There was nothing, he reasoned, in recent technological developments which inherently justified size increases. If anything, the war had shown that the smaller units were the least vulnerable and that they posed most of the offensive threat to the new weapons. Reduced size would also decrease docking and repair costs. Most important, size reductions would open the way for simpler disarmament formulae by removing the classifications in size, calibres, and numbers which had been the principal areas of international disagreement. Specifically, he envisioned his ideal capital ship as having the following characteristics: a displacement of 7,400 tons, endurance of 7,000 miles, a maximum speed of 28 knots, and armament of eight 6-inch guns.

The replies were generally disappointing. None expressed serious disagreement with his logic. Most simply reflected their authors' discomfort in working, as Richmond had, at a purely theoretical level. Not one advanced arguments which he had not anticipated. His lengthy and tightly reasoned responses to each in turn are interesting

13 *Naval Review*, 17 (August 1929), "What Is It That Dictates the Size of the Fighting Ship?": 1 (Richmond), 409-33; 2, 433-38; 3 (Q.D.), 438-40; 4, 440-42; 5, "Historical Survey," 442-44; 6 (A. C. Dewar), "The Size of the Battleship," 444-48; 7 (Admiral B. M. Chambers), "Some Considerations as to the Factors Which Govern the Limit of Size in Battleships," 448-51; 8 (Admiral Sir Douglas Nicholson), "Some Reflections Upon Warships" (reprinted from *Brassey's Naval and Shipping Annual*, 1928), 452-57; 9 (Richmond), "The 10,000 ton Cruiser," 457-63; 10 (Admiral W. H. Henderson), "International Considerations," 464-66.

inasmuch as they illustrate his patience when it came to enlightening
interested correspondents. But they also demonstrate the simple, yet
compelling, logic of his small-ship ideas. The difficulty was how
discussion should proceed if, in his words, it was to be "real discussion, discussion on scientific lines."[14]

Richmond approached the problem on three levels, separately
and successively, beginning with the abstract theory "unaffected by
national advantages and disadvantages" which necessitated a particular size, that is, the strategic and tactical principles which governed absolute size. Next he would examine the advantages and
disadvantages of reductions to this theoretical limit. Finally he would
study the possibilities of international agreements along these lines.
His Review articles were trial balloons related only to that first level.
What he sought, up to that point, was some consensus on his theoretical conclusions. Once their validity was accepted, the other two
stages would follow.

The replies he received convinced him that he was right. This
being the case, he confided to Admiral Roger Backhouse,[15] the Third
Sea Lord:

> it does not become easy for individual nations to oppose a scheme
> which is logically correct, which means a vast saving of money,
> which tends to reduce the jealousies now existing, merely on the
> basis of some supposed national requirements. If, indeed, national
> requirements are adversely affected, what this would shew would be
> that the theory was wrong.[16]

The Americans would be obliged to justify their faith in large battleships and 10,000-ton cruisers, and to challenge Richmond's premises.
"Let them disprove them," he continued, "I think they would find it
difficult, if as you say, the arguments are logical." The American
sailor would be hard pressed

> to admit that he must have an 8" gun to fight a wretched mer-
> chantman: that he must have 35 knots to catch a 15 knot ship . . . . The
> fact is that we have shewn up the nonsense they talk: and we ought to
> do so. Further, it would be awkward for the Americans who cry out
> that their purpose is idealistic, that they desire to reduce the burden
> of armaments, to reject proposals which not only materially reduce
> that cost, but enable them, at a reduced cost, to obtain that "parity"
> which they affect to believe is necessary for their security.

14 RIC/7/2/3, Richmond to Bellairs, August 17, 1929.
15 Backhouse was Third Sea Lord, November 1, 1928 to March 1, 1932. He was later
    appointed Commander-in-Chief Home Fleet (August 20, 1935-April 11, 1938) and
    finally, First Sea Lord (November 17, 1938-June 15, 1939). Poor health forced his
    premature retirement. His death shortly after resulted in the appointment of Admi-
    ral Dudley Pound as First Sea Lord.
16 RIC/7/2/2, Richmond to Backhouse, August 24, 1929.

Expectation of determined American opposition was not sufficient grounds for British hesitation. On the contrary, he argued, it was the very reason Britain should take the initiative.

> Are we to be deterred from making suggestions which we believe to be logical and sound, to injure no one, to profit all . . . I say the sound policy is to put them forward and make the American come into the open and disclose whether all his talk is hypocrisy; and whether his intentions are genuinely to benefit the world or merely to increase his own prestige and strength. I would (having satisfied ourselves, of course, as to what we think) throw this bombshell into their camp, and confront them with a proposal which they will find it difficult to reject because they will have to deal with public opinion. Such a proposal coming from the Admiralty would have an uncommonly good effect. No one, alas, can hide from himself that the Admiralty has not got what is called a "Good Press." The silly picture—caricature—of the Admiralty as a body of old redfaced, white whiskered gentlemen with large bellies, crying out for dominance of the world at sea, is really believed by the foolish people who rule us from GRUB Street. Because of this, the fantastic nonsense talked by the Air people gets support. They will not believe that ships are more important than aircraft. They do not want to believe it. But give them evidence that the Admiralty really means to make a drastic cut in expenditure—and it must be something big and unexpected—confidence would be assured, and with it the support of the country.

Backhouse was clearly impressed with Richmond's reasoning as indeed were a number of distinguished Flag Officers on the active list, including Admiral Sir William H. D. Boyle (in 1934 Earl of Cork and Orrery, and, from September 1933 to August 1935, C-in-C Home Fleet).[17] Others, though they could not embrace all of Richmonds ideas, were reportedly anxious to reverse tendencies which had been set in train by Fisher twenty-five years before, but had their reasons for not wanting their views made public. For one thing, radical change in Admiralty policy would mean public admission of errors in the past. Moreover, it was known that Madden was to be succeeded as First Sea Lord by another Fisher disciple, and this implied "a compliance on the part of others." Captain Bernard Acworth, himself a convert and, from this point, one of Richmond's more outspoken supporters, reported that Backhouse had admitted that the "Juggernaut at the Admiralty, manned by 'Materialists' almost exclusively, is too powerful for him to stop. He, and other officers are convinced that the reform of our terrible war and post-war errors of policy must come from outside."[18]

17 RIC/7/4, Acworth to Richmond, August 16, 1929.
18 Ibid., August 20, 1929; also letters of August 16, 1929. Acworth's contribution to the literature of naval politics came later in the 1930s, but the foundations of his first major work, *Navies of Today and Tomorrow* (1930), which heavily attacked the Fisherite-materialist school, were laid in Richmond's 1929 small-ship articles. Richmond, however, never reciprocated Acworth's admiration. Generally, his

This was the responsibility Richmond accepted when he submitted his *Times* letters of November 1929, challenging the Admiralty, Government, and public alike to speak out on the vital issues which the London Naval Conference was about to deliberate. The following excerpt from a letter to Admiral Henderson leaves no doubt as to Richmond's motives:

> I cannot help it if the Admiralty object; or refrain from doing this. I am so convinced that it is for the good of the nation that this matter should be considered, when it comes to be considered next January, on some higher plane of policy, strategy, and logic than it was at that unfortunate Conference at Washington, that whatever my personal advantages maybe [sic]—or rather, disadvantages—do not matter. My professional prospects are not to be considered. Perhaps I exaggerate the importance of my views. I may. But I hold them very strongly, as the result of long thought—eight years and more—and much discussion. I have invited and received criticism freely and I doubt, I hope not in consequence of any vanity, that there is anyone who has applied himself more to the study of the subject than I. That does not mean that I think I must be right. I believe I am, because no proof has been given me that I am wrong. What I propose is, I know, difficult to put into Execution under the conditions of Timidity that govern our policy and practice. But I am sure that a few strong men could do it. Whether such exists remains to be seen.[19]

Stated simply, Richmond set out to demonstrate that previous international limitations agreements had been political compromises based on quantitative mathematical calculations believed to balance off the "supposed interests" of the various powers. With the London Conference only two months off, he called for an agreement based instead on strategic principles.[20] Naval strength should be sufficient

views on Acworth's ideas and methods were similar to those he held on Kenworthy's work. On several occasions he took Acworth to task for "sloppy work and careless reasoning." (RIC/7/4, Acworth to Richmond, September 2, 1929). See also Higham, *The Military Intellectuals*, pp. 61-64.

19 RIC/7/1, Richmond to Henderson, October 5, 1929.

20 RIC/6/3. Contains the original submissions together with Editorial changes. The original articles were entitled "Limitation of Navies" (4 pp.); "The Functions of a Navy" (6 pp.); "Defence of Territory" (5 pp.); "Defence of Trade" (5 pp.); The Relativity of Naval Strength" (6 pp.); "The Qualitative Element" (6 pp.); "Size in Its Relation to Control" (6 pp.); and "Conclusion" (5 pp.). His implied criticism of past policy presented difficulties enough. In the original draft he was much more explicit, as the following excerpt (omitted by *The Times*) indicates: "Looking back at the periods of the Conferences at Washington and Geneva, with slight alterations of the words one may justly apply to them Disraeli's saying about the Liverpool Cabinet. 'That was not a period when Statesmen cared to prosecute the investigation of principles. It was a period of happy and enlightened practice. A profounder policy is the offspring of times like the present when the original postulates of questions are called into question.' It is not pretended that the practice either at Washington or Geneva can truthfully be described as either 'happy' or 'enlightened' for neither epithet is apposite to those haphazard attempts to solve the matter 'practically,' which remind one of the other well-known remark of the same statesman that 'practical men' are 'those who repeat the blunders of their predecessors.' We do not now wish to repeat the blunders of our predecessors; and we can

to ensure the security of maritime trade and designed to handle the realistic threats to it. Surveying the varying degrees of importance which individual nations attached to this consideration, he concluded that the only "true criterion" of naval limitation should be the strength of the weakest naval power—the one to whom naval defence was least vital. This much established, the greater naval powers could then fix their requirements, thereby satisfying the twin needs of security and economy.

Richmond called for a more rational approach to disarmament than that of simply fixing for individual countries the number of ships of defined categories, and the numbers and sizes of weapons carried. He rejected the system of complicated regulations that had been subject to abuse, had caused friction and, above all, had stifled thought. He sought agreements which would allow each power to fix, in concert with the others, its total requirements, basing them on the weakest power criterion as the minimum measure. Each nation could then build whatever types it preferred so long as they did not exceed the agreed-upon adequate tonnage limit for a capital ship. And that, in his view, should be very much less than had been accepted over the preceding decade. In this case, he suggested 10,000 tons.[21] The key assumption of his "smaller navies" concept was, of course, that international agreement on this reduced upper tonnage limit for capital ships was possible. As the *Times* Editor noted, not everyone would accept Richmond's premises. However, he suggested "The views which he now expresses on what is perhaps the most important question of the day can hardly fail to make for a clearer understanding of the problems which will be set for solution in January."[22]

The Admiralty was not so open-minded. When questioned by Kenworthy and Rear-Admiral Beamish in the Commons as to whether the articles written by "an admiral on the active list" had been seen by the Admiralty, and whether they represented the official view, Mr. Alexander emphatically denied both Richmond and his ideas.[23] Within a week, Richmond received an unpleasant official reminder about the provisions of King's Regulations, Admiralty Instructions, and the Official Secrets Act concerning public expression of views on controversial questions.[24] This was not surprising. The public reaction, however, was.

aim at making 'the policy of the present more profound by calling into question the original postulates.'"
21 In the original draft, Richmond used the figure 6,000-7,000 tons; changed to 10,000 tons in the published version in deference to the Versailles limitation on German ships.
22 *The Times*, November 21, 1929.
23 Ibid., November 23, 1929.
24 RIC/7/2/3, Sir Oswyn Murray to Richmond, November 28, 1929; and Richmond to Murray, December 6, 1929.

To have attacked the *status quo* and received the support of virtually the entire London daily press was no insignificant accomplishment. Even those commentators who challenged Richmond's specific conclusions admitted the timeliness and merit of his ideas, and indeed, the personal implications of his action.[25] As the *Spectator* noted:

> No one could give intelligent attention to Admiral Sir Herbert Richmond's recent articles . . . without having his faith in the big ship as an essential feature in a modern fleet gravely shaken if not dispelled. The great merit of such articles is that they bring the battleship to the bar and throw on its defenders, the onus of establishing their case.

The Editor of *Foreign Affairs* agreed. Referring to Richmond as "the ablest mind in the navy," he considered his case against the big ships to be "overwhelming."[26]

In private, the reaction was much the same. Custance, Webb, and Stanhope rushed their letters of congratulations, and of praise for Richmond's personal courage. Stanhope (who became Parliamentary Secretary of the Admiralty in September 1931, and was First Lord from October 1938 to September 1939) had been sceptical about the substance of Richmond's arguments, but from this point became an increasingly enthusiastic backer.[27] Admiral Beamish, who opposed his ideas and especially his making them public, nevertheless admitted that he had been moved to question the First Lord in the House out of "deep respect" for Richmond's reputation as a student of history, strategy, and tactics. "There is no greater nowadays than yourself," he wrote in explanation of his questions in the Commons:

> I wonder if you realise the immensity of harm you can do, or good! to the unthinking masses and untutored anti-national folk in this House. My dear Richmond I shall always remember with pride and gratitude your work and views during the 1st 3 months of war. You foresaw and foretold dangers when others *slept!* I conceive your views on Freedom of the Seas to be flawless, a guide to such as myself.[28]

But expressions of sympathy from friends, the Press, and others did not mean that Richmond's ideas necessarily affected the outcome of the London Conference. Admiral Chatfield's bitter contention that the MacDonald Government was heavily influenced by Richmond's theories[29] is highly doubtful. Nothing in Richmond's papers indicates

---

25 Letters by Admiral B. Barttelot, and Professor Aston, *The Times*, November 23 and 27, 1929. Also the New York *Herald Tribune*, December 1, 1929; *Truth*, December 4, 1929.
26 *The Spectator*, December 14, 1929. Also *Foreign Affairs* (January 1930), pp. 251-54.
27 RIC/7/2/3, Custance to Richmond, November 22, 1929; Webb to Richmond (n.d.), 1929; Stanhope to Richmond, December 22, 1929, and January 14, 23, 29, 1930.
28 Ibid., Beamish to Richmond, December 10, 1929.
29 Chatfield, *It Might Happen Again*, vol. 2, p. 60.

he made personal contact with the Prime Minister on this question. Moreover, the Agreements themselves bear little resemblance to Richmond's proposals. The fact is MacDonald's broad policy lines were well formulated before Richmond went to the *Times*. Indeed, as early as August 1929, MacDonald had made known his Government's willingness to compromise the Admiralty's long-standing claim for seventy cruisers and to reduce that figure to fifty. By year's end, it was public knowledge that the Conference would also seek agreements to further postpone battleship construction on the assumption that the Americans would not raise the ever-contentious "Freedom of the Seas" issue. The net effect was that the London Conference extended the earlier Washington agreements, the original drawbacks of which reappeared in aggravated form.[30] Battleships were not to be replaced until after 1936, but the vessels themselves were not called into question. The Americans reciprocated Britain's submission to cruiser parity by agreeing to reduce their numbers of 10,000-ton Washington Treaty cruisers from twenty-four to eighteen. In view of France's and Italy's refusals to be bound by any of these limitations, the London Naval Agreements had serious implications which MacDonald and Hoover seemed determined to ignore for the sake of trans-Atlantic tranquility.

Richmond was utterly disappointed with the results. He was hopeful that improved relations with the Americans might out-weigh some of the disadvantages and he saw in the postponement of capital-ship construction some promise that the class might disappear altogether.[31] But there was very little else to commend the Agreements in his view. He lamented the fact that his small-ship theories had not been taken seriously: "an unparalleled opportunity" for significantly reducing expenditures had been missed. He especially regretted Labour's concessions on cruisers and for reasons "that will not bear scientific examination."[32] For years afterwards, he maintained that this decision and the standards established in 1930 were a major cause of the Royal Navy's critical cruiser, destroyer, and flotilla

---

30 See *The Nineteenth Century and After*, 106 (December 1929), Hector C. Bywater, "The London Naval Conference: As Viewed from Europe," 717-30; K. K. Kawakami, "As Viewed from Japan," 731-42. Also 107, K. G. B. Dewar, "The End of the Naval Conference" (May 1930), 606-19; H. Sidebotham, "The Naval Treaty" (June 1930), 754-62; Pierre Lyautey, "After the London Conference: A French View" (July 1930), 25-34.

31 This was one area where Chatfield felt Richmond had influenced MacDonald. He cites as evidence a memorandum sent to Geneva by MacDonald: *London Naval Conference, 1930, Extract from Memorandum on the Position of H.M. Government,* February 7, 1930 (Published at Geneva). Cmd. 3485. The same view is held by Higham, *Armed Forces in Peacetime: Britain 1918-1940* (London: G. T. Foulis, 1962), pp. 133-34.

32 RIC/6/3, "The Naval Conference, I" letter to *The Times*, undated (1930). Richmond's marginal note, "Sent to *The Times* but declined."

problems in World War II.[33] More than anything, he regretted the application of "arbitrary and mathematical bounds" for fixing the size of navies. The ratio system, the "doctrine of material parity," had been useful at Washington as a first step, "a clod to stop a leak in time." But, he suggested

> the merit of this formula, its simplicity and mathematic conclusiveness, has tended to impress itself not only upon all our subsequent negotiations but upon our very way of thinking. The only meaning which the phrase "naval parity" conveys to mose people at the present time is this equation of weight and strength of armament . . . mere mathematical equation in naval tonnage brings only a specious resemblance of naval parity unless it achieves those aims which are the true pacific purpose of the whole negotiations.[34]

His call for a more radical, qualitative approach to disarmament received the enthusiastic support of Professor James T. Shotwell of the prestigious Carnegie Endowment for International Peace and led to an extensive exchange of letters with other American academics, and eventually an invitation to visit the United States to expound his views on naval disarmament.[35] In August 1930, he lectured at the Institute of Politics, at Williamstown, Massachusetts, where he felt his ideas were generally well received. There he had an opportunity to exchange ideas with a number of United States Navy (U.S.N.) Admirals and civilian experts on International Law, in particular, Professor J. P. Baxter of the Harvard Law School. In a revealing comment to Admiral Henderson, reporting on his visit, Richmond noted: "I think I shook them on the matter of the battleship but they could not understand the cruiser question either in relation to size or numbers. It was however possible to convince the more intelligent civilians."[36] An invitation to lecture at the U.S. Naval War College also proved interesting. Again, he remarked on the essential orthodoxy of American naval officers: "They certainly were pleased and their eyes opened to a new outlook. They have some very crude ideas both about battleships and big cruisers. It is absolutely necessary to get to work as soon as we can to educate them, and our own folk, in time for the next conference." These visits and exchanges were the immediate inspiration for his next book on navies and fighting ships which was published in 1931 as Economy and Naval Security.

33 See Richmond's letters to The Times, February 5; March 12, 1930, July 4, 1931. Also "Some Elements of Disarmament," Fortnightly Review (February 1932); "Britain's Naval Policy: Some Dangers and Delusions," ibid. (April 1932).
34 RIC/6/3, "The Naval Conference, II."
35 RIC/7/3c, Shotwell to Richmond, April 26, 1930; May 8, 1930. Also Charles Stewart Davison (Counsellor at Law, New York) to Richmond, August 15, and October 31, 1930; Richmond to Davison, September 24, 1930. Other correspondence with Dr. J. P. Baxter (Harvard), Professor J. Garner (University of Illinois).
36 RIC/7/1, Richmond to Henderson, September 9, 1930.

Of all the bodies which Richmond had hoped to influence, the Admiralty was least affected. Madden's passiveness towards his political masters irritated Richmond to no small degree.[37] But if his small-ship ideas failed to provoke a re-examination of official thinking prior to and during the Naval Conference, his public utterances of them did anger and embarrass Their Lordships as he knew they would. Madden used every means at hand to secure Richmond's resignation. Richmond, however, refused to go down gracefully. Convinced that his case was handled with less honesty and courtesy than his record merited, he stubbornly resisted removal for almost a year. For one who had invoked the heady principles of Edmund Burke in justification of his *Times* intervention, that this was "one of the few moments in which decorum leads to higher duty . . . when any, even the slightest chance, of doing good must be laid hold on, even by the most inconsiderable person,"[38] what followed makes unpleasant reading indeed.

No specific disciplinary action was taken against Richmond despite the menacing tone of the Admiralty's "reminder" and "warning" of November 28, 1929. The intervention of his brother-in-law, Sir Charles Trevelyan, President of the Board of Education, may have had something to do with this. Trevelyan was highly disturbed by this implied threat and promised that he would "enquire into what has happened and talk about it thoroughly to the most important of my colleagues."[39] In early March 1930, however, news that Admiral Field was to succeed Madden as First Sea Lord prompted Richmond to inquire about his own chances of receiving the about-to-be-vacated Mediterranean command. Madden's reply was curt and blunt; Richmond would be considered along with other eligible officers, but he cautioned, "I express no opinions on your chances."[40] Less than a fortnight later, Richmond was informed by the Naval Secretary to the First Lord, Rear-Admiral George K. Chetwoode, that changes in ap-

37 RIC/7/4, Madden to Richmond, February 14, 1930. In response to some enquiries from Richmond regarding cruiser strengths, Madden replied: "Our programmes, I assume, will be framed *after* the Conference *on the results obtained there*, and on a scale sufficient to give security." (Richmond's italics.) Richmond's marginal notation to this is revealing: "No (?) [sic] of what are our programmes. It depends what the Conference decides as to *totals*—not how these totals are reached."
38 "Speech on Conciliation with America," Edmund Burke, March 22, 1775, quoted in Richmond, Preface to *Economy and Naval Security* (London: Ernest Benn, 1931).
39 RIC/7/4, The Rt. Hon. Sir Charles P. Trevelyan, Bart., to Richmond, December 8, 1929. Concerned about the Admiralty's warning, he wrote to find out "how and by whom you have been hauled over the coals. . . . Not because you are my brother-in-law but because I so much respect opinion of your informed judgement and because you would be the ablest assistant which the present Government could have in reducing armaments without frightening national susceptibilities."
40 Ibid., Richmond to Madden, March 5, 1930; Madden to Richmond, March 5, 1930.

pointments resulting from Madden's retirement "make it appear to me impossible that the First Lord will be in a position to offer you any further employment."[41] Since specific reasons were not given, Richmond requested and was granted a private interview with the First Lord.

Mr. Alexander's explanation was somewhat less than unequivocal. He informed Richmond that he was being denied the Mediterranean post or command of a Home Port "for the reason it was necessary in the former to have been recently employed in a great fleet, and it was customary for no officer to be given command of a Home Port who had not commanded one of the larger fleets." This was a distortion of historical facts, and Richmond was quick to refute the argument with examples like Fisher, Wilson, Sir John Hopkins, and Sir Charles Drury who had been appointed without fulfilling this requirement. Clearly, the invocation of custom was not the real basis for the Admiralty's decision. Indeed, Richmond wrote, the recent granting to Sir Roger Keyes of a six-month extension at Portsmouth, additional to an extra year already promised, suggested something quite different. In view of the fact that Alexander had personally assured Richmond that his *Times* articles had not influenced his thinking, nor that any unfavourable reports existed in his personal records, Richmond's argument could not be ignored.[42] Yet, Alexander evaded the issue by suggesting that Richmond's historical examples were no longer valid; they related to a period "when the command of a fleet was not the highly specialised duty it has now become."[43] This merely confirmed Richmond's conviction that: "the Admiralty have lost sight of the fact that there is any other side to war other [than] the technical; and of course explains to the full why officers holding other views are considered unfitted to command such fleets."[44]

Though argument was clearly useless, Richmond hung on. Another attempt to secure his voluntary resignation, supposedly in order to protect Admiral Duff's pension, also failed. At one point Richmond gave his assent, but the matter was quietly dropped when he refused to permit publication of his retirement notice as being "at his own request."[45] Then, in late December 1930, he learned that

41 RIC/7/2, Chetwoode to Richmond, March 17, 1930.
42 Ibid., Richmond to Alexander, April 1930. Again it is probable that Trevelyan's intervention played a part here. He advised Richmond not to accept "the dismissal that has been offered you. At any rate you must do nothing unless you discuss it with me. I am taking all the effective steps I can to prevent the country losing your services." RIC/7/4, Trevelyan to Richmond, March 29, 1930. Also, Admiral Sir Reginald Hall to Richmond, March 22, 1930, "Madden has shewn the white feather and allowed the Board to retire you."
43 RIC/7/2, Alexander to Richmond, April 10, 1930.
44 Ibid. (draft of reply), Richmond to Alexander, April 12, 1930.
45 Ibid., Richmond to Chetwoode, April 20, 1930; Chetwoode to Richmond, April 29, 1930.

Admiral Sir Arthur Waistell was to receive the Portsmouth command. Like Richmond, Waistell had never served "with long and distinguished service" in command of a great fleet. The discrepancy was obvious and Richmond lost no time in pointing it out to Alexander. The response, Richmond noted with utter disgust, was less than considerate: "A reply from his Secretary came about ten days later saying that the First Lord had rec'd my letter but that he had to go to the country for some political speeches and had therefore asked his secretary to acknowledge it! I threw the thing away."[46]

Richmond also wrote at length to Admiral Field who, on July 30, succeeded Madden as First Sea Lord. Carefully he reviewed the events since he was first informed that he would no longer be employed. The inconsistencies in Madden's and Alexander's positions were obvious, and could only mean, he concluded, "that the reason asserted for my ineligibility is not the true reason." With supporting documents he went on to review his record from 1897, detailing his various positions and personal contributions to the Navy in war and peace. These examples, he suggested, were sufficient absolution "from the reproach of want of capacity in matters concerning the conduct of war." Equally, and perhaps even more important, were his writings, some of which had been adopted by the U.S. and Japanese Navies, and for which the R.U.S.I. had seen fit to award him the Chesney Gold Medal—the only other naval recipient of this coveted distinction being Mahan (and later, in 1975, Captain Stephen Roskill). Considering all this, he concluded that the true cause for his non-employment had to be his "misconduct" in writing to *The Times*. The Admiralty's denials notwithstanding, everything pointed to this conclusion: "putting aside all subterfuge," he intoned, "what are the true reasons for the First Lord's opinion of my unfitness for any further service?"[47]

The straightforward sincerity of Admiral Field's replies went some way towards soothing Richmond's resentment at what he termed the "crookedness," the "shuffling, the equivocations and the maneouvres" of Madden and Alexander.[48] Field offered no apologies for his predecessor's decision: unfortunately, nothing could be done at that point to change the situation. Existing circumstances, he suggested, required the retirement of at least fifty per cent of the Admirals' list to open up promotions at lower levels. For one who had fought all his life for rapid promotions for talented younger men, this

46 Ibid., Richmond's marginal note to draft of letter, Richmond to Alexander (n.d.) ("On Seeing Waistell's Appointment to Portsmouth").
47 Ibid., Richmond to the Admiralty, December 22, 1930.
48 Ibid., Richmond to Field, January 3, 1931. Also, Field to Richmond, January 2 and 5, 1931; Richmond to the Admiralty, January 8, 1931.

was an argument which Richmond could hardly refuse. On March 16, 1931, he accepted the inevitable and was placed on retirement as of April 1, almost a year before his compulsory release date.[49]

Richmond's insistence on knowing the "true reason" for his removal does raise the question of who his real enemy was. Few senior officers could have viewed the changes in senior Admiralty personnel following Madden's departure with much confidence as Mr. Alexander's determination to keep difficult or strong personalities off the Board became obvious. The First Lord's refusal to have Roger Keyes and the selection instead of Admiral Field as First Sea Lord offered little hope of any improvement over Madden's singularly undistinguished record. Similarly, Alexander blocked Sir John Kelly's succession of Admiral Hodges as Second Sea Lord. That went, in June 1931, to the clever and charming Cyril Fuller who was out of his depth in the job. Kelly's protests, and accusations of Field having reneged on his promises for either the Second Sea Lord's berth or command of the Atlantic Fleet, go some way in corroborating Richmond's charges of "crookedness." The result of Alexander's policy, Captain Roskill has suggested, "was to produce perhaps the weakest Board of Admiralty of all time; and it is ironical that . . . Sir John Kelly had to be recalled to restore the Atlantic Fleet's morale [in the aftermath of the 1931 Invergordon Mutiny] only three months after Alexander had refused him employment in Whitehall or afloat."[50] So much for Richmond's chances. And for Chatfield's and others' contentions that the Labour Government felt obligated in any way for his views on disarmament and naval economies.

News of Richmond's "voluntary retirement" brought a flood of personal condolences.[51] Admiral Webb was stunned: "Your news grieves me greatly. Though I suppose it was obvious." Later, after reading The Times announcement, he wrote: "I can't say how much I regret your retirement: In the best interests of the Service its [sic] a calamity . . . you will take with you the high esteem of a very great body of Naval Officers who will deplore your treatment as much as I do." Others, including Drax, Dickens, Sydenham, and Professor A. Pearce Higgins (Trinity College) were equally disturbed. From General John Dill came the cryptic comment: "The Senior Service must indeed be rich in young Senior officers of experience and high

49 Ibid., Richmond to the Admiralty, March 16, 1931; Sir Charles Walker to Richmond, March 19, 1931; Sir Oswyn Murray to Richmond, March 27, 1931; Sir Charles Walker to Richmond, March 31, 1931.
50 Roskill, Naval Policy, vol. 2, p. 80.
51 RIC/7/2, Webb to Richmond, March 21, 24; April 1, 1931; Drax to Richmond, April 1, 1931; Dickens to Richmond, April 4, 1931; Sydenham to Richmond, April 30, 1931; A. Pearce Higgins to Richmond, April 1, 1931; Dill to Richmond, April 1, 1931; Dawson to Richmond, March 25, 1931.

military education if they can spare you." Geoffrey Dawson of *The Times* spoke for many in his suggestion that "The Admiralty seem to me to be *extremely* shortsighted in making no further use of your services." Common to all these replies was the feeling, stated or implied, that Richmond had been sacked for challenging Admiralty orthodoxy. As one anonymous writer commented in *The Times*:

> The remarkable unanimity with which the press regretted the retirement of Admiral Sir Herbert William Richmond "at his own request" and the unrecorded but equally general sentiment of the Royal Navy to the same effect must have given rise to some curiosity as to why he should have thus retired nearly a year before he need have done so under the employment regulation.

The real reason, the author went on to suggest, was the Admiralty's desire to be relieved of a thinker—"our English Mahan"—whose doctrines challenged and upset established conceptions. "The disquieting conclusion in connection with the loss to the Service of Admiral Richmond is that there is room in the Royal Navy only for those who hold no views, or who are echoes of the official views, or who carefully conceal their views."[52]

Richmond would always believe that, the Admiralty's denials notwithstanding, his shelving was a direct consequence of his public expressions in November 1929. "If there was one thing more than another that embittered me about my retirement," he later wrote to Admiral Field, "it was the lying reasons given me by the First Lord, at, I have no doubt, the instigation of Madden."[53]

Undoubtedly, Richmond pressed too hard to get what he believed were his due rewards. Unbounded ambition and an over-developed need for visible signs of public recognition had always been an unpleasant part of his nature. In strictly personal terms, his prolonged resistance to early retirement was the climax of a long internal struggle between the two dominant and conflicting features of his psychological dynamics—on the one hand, his ambitions as a professional sailor, and on the other, his incorruptibility as an intellectual and scholar. He had always been a prisoner of these two opposing forces. Retirement, however reluctantly accepted, finally set him free. The distasteful aspects of his final struggles cannot detract from the merits of his position on the more vital issues of the London Conference. The specifics of his small-ship theories were relevant only in the

---

52 Ibid., clipping from *The Times* (March 22, 1931), "Admiral Richmond's Retirement, by One Who Knows Him." Richmond's marginal note: "I was accused of having instigated this letter. I did not. I do not know by whom it was written, but I think Sir Herbert Russell, the editor of *Truth*" (n.d.).

53 Ibid., Richmond to Field, February 9, 1932; also, February 14, 1932; and Field to Richmond, February 12, 1932.

context of the pre-Conference situation, but he was right to challenge the decisions made and the assumptions on which they were based. In the following years, he continued to doubt the adequacy of cruiser and destroyer numbers for Britain's needs and the Admiralty's persistent faith in battleships. On the whole, the broad pattern of World War II proved Richmond correct.

11
Cambridge: The Final Years

Richmond's retirement in 1931 opened the way to an equally productive and in many ways more rewarding phase of his life. It also finished the reform movement he had led for two decades, an unpleasant reality underscored by the tragic coincidence of Admiral William Henderson's death that same year.[1] Henderson's passing at age eighty-five removed what had been the other main cohesive force in the Young Turks' agitations since the founding of the *Naval Review*. His successor, Admiral Sir Richard Webb, would prove no less able or dedicated as Editor (1931-1950), though from this point the *Review*'s message changed. The majority of contributions received no longer came from within the ranks of active-list officers. The Young Turks movement was dead and, within two years of Richmond's release, the careers of most of his other disciples also ended.

Kenneth Dewar finished his stormy career by running as a Labour candidate for Portsmouth North in the 1931 General Election. In the course of a bitter campaign against a Conservative who had held the seat for twenty-one years, Dewar was attacked for a scurrilous pamphlet which depicted the Kaiser and the Governor of the Bank of England under the banner: "The British Navy at Jutland in 1916 beat the ex-Kaiser and at Invergordon in 1931 it beat Mr. Montagu Norman."[2] Less than a month had passed since the Invergordon "Mutiny," and the leaflet undoubtedly cost Dewar some votes in that largely naval riding. When the executives of his London club requested some explanation of his actions, Dewar accused them of outright prejudice: "I have even been told that it was disloyal to the

1 *The Times*, April 30, 1931. Also *Naval Review*, 19 (1931), 199-200, 200-204.
2 DEW, 3, the *News Chronicle*, October 27, 1931.

208

Navy for a retired Admiral to stand as a Labour Candidate for North Portsmouth."[3] As he had shown in the *"Royal Oak* Affair", Dewar's political sense was not finely developed. Naturally he lost. But for his book, *The Navy from Within*, Dewar's claim on posterity might well have been lost altogether. Unfortunately, it was released just at the outset of the Second World War, an accident of timing which reduced its impact. Dewar would spend the war years, along with his brother, once more employed in the Admiralty's Historical Section. After the war, he remained in retirement in a suburb of Worthing, Sussex, where at his death in September 1964, at age eighty-four, his last words on reform—a critique entitled "Jutland to Singapore"— remained unfinished.[4]

Kenworthy and Carlyon Bellairs also lost their Parliamentary seats in the 1931 election. Bellairs withdrew from active politics in order to lecture and write and eventually to full retirement in the Barbados where he died in 1955. Kenworthy succeeded his father as Tenth Baron Strabolgi in 1934. He then entered the House of Lords and, from 1938 to 1942, served as Opposition Chief Whip. He died in 1953.

Henry Thursfield retired in 1932 upon reaching flag rank although he continued to make important contributions to the literature of naval affairs. In 1936 he became editor of *Brassey's Annual* and Naval Correspondent to *The Times*. Always a meticulous and fastidious writer, he was one of the very few naval officers genuinely capable of original thought. He was also discreet, and protected his sources. His close friendship with Richmond seems to have developed only after 1932. To the end of his life Thursfield was an active patron of serious naval history. As a Councillor of the Navy Records Society, a Trustee of the National Maritime Museum, the Society for Nautical Research, and the *Naval Review*, he was a well-known and respected figure to all dedicated students of maritime affairs.

Of the other reformers, Reginald Henderson remained in the Navy as Rear-Admiral Aircraft Carriers from 1931 to 1933, and Third Sea Lord and Controller. He played a leading role in furthering the organization, equipment, and morale of the Fleet Air Arm during the years of rearmament, and was largely responsible for the Admiralty's decisions to build the large carriers of the *Illustrious* and *Victorious* designs which did so much to balance Britain's deficits in naval aviation. His death in 1939, brought on by over-work in this important cause, robbed the Navy of one of its most ardent and knowledgeable air advocates at an especially critical point.

3   Ibid., Dewar to Secretary, U.S. Club, November 6, 1931.
4   Ibid., 13, eight chapters of incomplete Ms, and correspondence with various publishers.

Roger Bellairs and Drax would both see service in the Second World War. Bellairs was attached to Plans Division as an adviser on Anglo-American strategy and naval policy, and also served as Chairman of the British delegation to the secret joint staff talks in Washington. Drax was promoted to Admiral in 1936 and served as C-in-C The Nore from 1939 to 1941. His record with various important education committees throughout the 1930s earned him a reputation as one of the most intellectually gifted officers of the period. As a result, when war broke out, Admiral Pound unofficially pulled him into the Admiralty as an "independent authority" to advise on overall planning.[5] In 1939, he led the British Military Mission to Moscow. In reality, his anomalous Admiralty status, which invites comparison to Richmond's role in 1914-1915 and about which more will be said, was designed to assist the Naval Staff in counter-balancing Churchill's endless quests for offensives in Norway and the Baltic and, later, to help redress the Prime Minister's preoccupations with strategic bombing at the risk of naval needs.

But always, the common denominator linking all these officers' careers as reformers was Richmond. Theirs was always a loose relationship in which friendships or the obvious disparities in their individual intellectual attainments mattered less than their shared experience of official mistrust. Richmond simply drew to himself anyone who shared his faith in the healing powers of study and reflection. This helps to explain his long-standing tolerance of the Dewars within his circle. It also helped the reformers to survive the *Naval Review*'s emasculation and with it their early hopes for a renaissance in naval thought.

Practically speaking, it must be said that their total impact on defence policy was limited. The rearmament programmes of the 1930s with their emphasis on size rather than numbers and versatility of ships suggest that Britain's leaders had not learned as much as they might have from earlier mistakes. That the Young Turks did not have a more pronounced effect on these developments had much to do with the limitations of their own abrasive personalities. Nevertheless, considering the environment in which they worked, their record is remarkable. With but a very few exceptions, they were the only real talent available to the Naval Staff in the First World War. And they had the most to say—before, during, and after the war—about the Navy's needs in terms of an educated officer corps and the lessons of the war. As intellectuals they sensed their responsibilities to seek the truth and to expose defects, and in this respect they became powerful catalysts in later national discussions. Experience softened their voi-

5   Captain S. W. Roskill, *Churchill and The Admirals* (London: Collins, 1977), pp. 93, 136, 146.

ces, and maturity tempered their methods, as each was forced to strike the balance between his own intellectual needs and professional aspirations.

That dichotomy was always especially acute in Richmond's case for he was the most professionally competent and ambitious of the group. Intellectually, he was the most gifted officer of his day. The juxtaposition of these opposing strains made him something of a Jekyll and Hyde personality for whom integrity and incorruptibility were both assets and liabilities at the same time. His tragedy was to work in a period when the Navy's anti-intellectualism was so virulent, when suggestions for change, however well-intentioned, clashed head-on with a bureaucracy more concerned with the comforts of well-ordered routine. The ethics of military professionalism can never fully accommodate the fundamentally subversive tendencies of the academic mind; yet if the profession is to avoid enslavement to unreasoning orthodoxy, there must be room for innovators of Richmond's kind. The vital role of "heretics" in preserving any community from "mental crystallization" was amongst the strongest of his basic convictions:

> that it is they that keep a service alive in peace, that every innovator is an innovator because he has given thought to his subject and nourished it with discussion, and that every great captain in war has owed his success to the fact that he was an innovator to whom tradition was a valuable servant, not a tyrannical master.[6]

Retirement largely resolved these semi-schizoidal pulls in his personality and, as he became more deeply involved in his second career as an academic, the less appealing features of his ambitions as an Admiral gave way to the wisdom, kindliness, and personal warmth his friends had always known.

The transition to civilian life did not produce any particular personal problems. The family left London and from April 1931 until September 1932 lived at Hertingfordbury, Herts. He then bought a "small house" at Great Kimble, Buckinghamshire,[7] where he evidently enjoyed the hard work of planning and planting his own garden. But naval affairs continued to occupy most of this enforced leisure for it was during this period that he guided his books *The Navy in India* and *Economy and Naval Security* through to publication in 1931. The latter, written at the height of the world depression, was a timely summary of his earlier disarmament and small-ship arguments. That same year he delivered a series of papers at University College, London, as well as the Lees Knowles Lectures at Trinity

6 Richmond, "The Service Mind," *Nineteenth Century* (January 1933), 90-97.
7 A. H. Pollen Papers, Richmond to Pollen, n.d. (1932); and September 19, 1932.

College, Cambridge. These were published in 1932 as *Imperial Defence and Capture at Sea in War*. The following year he returned to a favourite theme with *Naval Training*, the original draft of which he had written in 1918 as D.T.S.D. at the Admiralty. In 1932, he extended his ideas in three articles in the *Fortnightly Review* (June, July, and August) and incorporated them into this important book. It was a concise history of officer education and a critical analysis of existing methods of selecting and training new entrants in which he called for the abolition of early cadet entry at age thirteen and replacement by regular public school entry at ages sixteen to eighteen, much as the Army did. Competitive examinations and headmasters' reports would ease the problem of accurate assessments of leadership potential, and capitalizing on the relative maturity and general academic preparation of the students would mean that cadets could undergo a much broader professional education. These ideas became fairly common currency after the war, but in the 1930s they were still strongly resisted by the Admiralty (as indeed they had been by Wemyss in 1918-1919, and much earlier by Fisher and Selborne in 1902) even after rearmament and rapid expansion raised the worrisome problem of officer shortages. One cannot ignore Richmond's own contention that official hostility on this, as on other issues, had a lot to do with the fact that he was their main advocate; that giving in to this 'Renegade and Traitor" would undermine the whole principle of "Papal Infallibility in a Whitehall atmosphere." As he told Pollen, "I have the whole weight of authority at Whitehall against me, and the retired list. Madden loses, I hear, no opportunity of disparaging me and my opinions on all naval subjects."[8] In 1934, at the approach of yet another naval conference, Richmond returned to the theme of security and economies in *Sea Power in the Modern World*, about which more will be said. As evidence of Richmond's status as an historian of consequence, all these books (excepting *The Navy in India*) are much less important than his earlier, more detailed and scholarly studies. They are, however, significant examples of his unending commitment to influence contemporary thinking. "I'm getting rather weary of the business," he wrote in December 1932, "but the daemon drives me on and refuses to allow me to drop it however little success appears above the horizon."[9] Popular in form and didactic in method, these books were intended to focus for laymen the practical implications of his own more philosophical concerns. But as tracts for the time, they were of passing relevance and they lacked the stylistic appeal and readability of a Liddell Hart or Fuller who were

8   Ibid., April 21, 1933.
9   Ibid., December 27, 1932.

often more willing to blur the distinctions between history and pamphleteering.[10]

Richmond's friendship with Captain (later, Sir) Basil Liddell Hart merits some explanation both for the light it sheds on Richmond's retirement and on the ways the two men shaped each other's thinking. Their first contact came in late 1929 following publication of Liddell Hart's biography of William Tecumseh Sherman.[11] A word of praise from Richmond produced an exchange of letters which soon revealed their kindred spirit, a mutual sense of mission about the importance of historical research. "It seems to me," Liddell Hart suggested, "a significant coincidence that the more one pursues real research the closer does one come to coincidence of views with those who likewise never tired of continuing to probe and to test their conclusions by history."[12] From this common outlook on their work of educating the services,[13] they nurtured a mutual respect which led to a number of joint efforts over the next few years.

Richmond briefed Liddell Hart about his *Times* articles and the Admiralty's reasons for firing him;[14] the "real intention," he wrote, was "to punish me for writing to the Times." He was naturally pleased when Liddell Hart offered to use his connections as military correspondent to the *Daily Telegraph* to re-open his case with members of the MacDonald Cabinet of which, "prospectively," Lord Thomson, the Air Minister, was the most promising. He was the only one of the three service ministers who might have raised Richmond's case with much chance of success. Shortly before his own death, Liddell Hart recalled that Thomson was Ramsay MacDonald's "personal adviser on everything from food and good drink, to defence and strategy."[15] Thomson's death in the crash of the airship R101 cut short Liddell Hart's efforts and, with them, Richmond's remaining hopes.[16]

A far more important manifestation of Richmond's and Liddell Hart's "coincidence of views" was the extent to which the latter's interests began to reflect Richmond's preoccupations. Prior to 1930, Liddell Hart's writings had been devoted to the problems of battle-

10 RIC/7/4, Fuller to Richmond, June 11, 1933.
11 B. H. Liddell Hart, *Sherman: Soldier, Realist, American* (New York: Dodd, Mead, 1929).
12 LHP, Liddell Hart to Richmond, July 11, 1930; also, Richmond to Liddell Hart, July 9, 1930.
13 Ibid., July 14, 1930. Richmond wrote: "I do not know whether there is some weakening in the mental make-up of the Services to-day; but it is a fact that they will read little except what is put in an attractive narrative style: they do not like to have to think: and above all—at least with my own people—they cannot bother their heads to think out for themselves problems of strategy."
14 Ibid., September 10, 1930; October 2, 1930.
15 Interview with Liddell Hart at States House, Medmenham, July 3, 1969.
16 *The Liddell Hart Memoirs* (London: Cassell, 1965), vol. 1, p. 148.

field mobility and the development of mechanized forces and tank doctrine. Now he turned to some entirely new and broader themes, the first of which was his famous "British Way in Warfare" with its violent denunciation of any mass continental commitment. This was first publicly expressed in January 1931 in an R.U.S.I. lecture entitled "Economic Pressure or Conventional Victories" and subsequently expanded in his book *The British Way in Warfare*, published a year later. Richmond was the only member of that R.U.S.I. audience who applauded his condemnation of British policy in the First World War as an aberration of traditional strategy. It was an unfortunate gesture in the sense that later critics have tended to tar Richmond with the same brush they use to condemn Liddell Hart's distorted use of history in this case. His attack on the "continental" school was useful in contemporary terms in that it implied some "maritime" option was still open to Britain; but it undoubtedly showed more of the impact of Liddell Hart's own wartime experiences than of any profound reading of the more balanced assessments of the maritime historians, including Richmond himself. Liddell Hart's originality in this instance, as one recent analysis suggests, lay "only in his rather extreme and one-sided statement of the maritime case."[17] Richmond was too much Corbett's disciple and too committed to historical objectivity to let himself be dragged along this path of reasoning which eventually led Liddell Hart into the morass of "limited liability" and personal eclipse later in the 1930s. In *Sea Power and the Modern World* (1934), and all his later works, Richmond took some pains to emphasize his long-held conviction that Britain's "maritime" and "continental" strategies had never been mutually exclusive options, and that now, in the age of railways and aircraft which called into question any isolationist policy based on a purely naval blockade, their interdependence within an overall policy conditioned to specific circumstances was more obvious than ever.

Another question to which Liddell Hart had not given much serious thought prior to meeting Richmond was disarmament. In May 1931, he was asked by Sir Samuel Hoare to act as an unofficial consultant to an all-party C.I.D. Sub-Committee on British policy leading up to the 1932 Geneva Conference. Like Richmond, he came to the conclusion that previous failures stemmed from attempts to equate security and parity to simple numerical standards. In order to minimize bickerings over ratios, he determined that only qualitative standards would work. Specifically, it boiled down to limiting

17 Brian Bond, *Liddell Hart: A Study of His Military Thought* (London: Cassell, 1977), p. 75. Also, D. M. Schurman, "Historians and Britain's Imperial Strategic Stand in 1914," in J. E. Flint and G. Williams, eds., *Perspectives of Empire* (London: Longmans, 1973), pp. 172-73.

weapons such as heavy guns and tanks, which inherently favour the offensive. Abolition of these weapons would reduce the chances of successful aggression, leaving countries free to build whatever "defensive" systems they chose. Referring to this whole mental process, he later wrote:

> It was the hardest test that had ever confronted me in striving to take a completely objective view .... For I soon realised that the obvious solution would entail annulling not only the development of tanks as a military tool but the whole concept of reviving the power of the offensive and the art of war, by "lightning" strokes with highly mobile mechanised forces—thus cancelling out all I had done during the past ten years to develop and preach this new concept. If I propounded the "disarmament" antidote to it, and helped to obtain its adoption at the coming conference, it would mean strangling my own "baby."[18]

Yet, this is what he did. His concept of an "offensive-curbing" method of disarmament got a "favourable reception" in the Cabinet and in many of the delegations at the abortive Geneva talks.

All this suggests that Richmond's ideas had fallen on very fertile soil (though Richmond opposed what he called the "dangerous delusion" that offensive-defensive distinctions between ships and other weapons could be drawn).[19] In 1969, Liddell Hart personally discounted Richmond's influence on his own "qualitative" approach to disarmament.[20] But this denial notwithstanding, their correspondence does reveal their frequent consultations and exchanges of views about each other's writings.[21] Over the next few years this association continued on a completely open and reciprocal basis. In 1931, they collaborated on a B.B.C. series, "The New Way in Warfare."[22] Richmond candidly recounted the results of his various lectures in Berlin, Warsaw, and Prague in November 1931, and at the Sorbonne in January 1933[23] (where, for the first time, he met his French counterpart as historian, strategist, and educational reformer, Admiral Raoul Castex). He also described to Liddell Hart the prestigious Lees Knowles lectures at Cambridge in 1931, for which he was paid £60. The audiences were "very" small, "sometimes not more than half a dozen. It was a most disappointing experience."[24] Of course Liddell Hart influenced Richmond's mind as well. *Sea Power*

18 *Liddell Hart Memoirs*, vol. 1, p. 186.
19 Richmond, "British Naval Policy," *Fortnightly Review* (April 1932); and *The Times*, April 28, 1932.
20 In conversation with Liddell Hart at States House, Medmenham, July 3, 1969.
21 LHP, Richmond to Liddell Hart, October 2; November 24, 1930; January 20, 1931.
22 Ibid., July 31; August 31; September 23, 1931.
23 Ibid., November 29, 1931; and January 12, 1933. A copy of his Paris address, "On the Problems of Naval Disarmament," is contained in RIC/6/5.
24 LHP, Richmond to Liddell Hart, April 30, 1932.

in the Modern World is notable for Richmond's support of an international or League "police" force—a notion he previously opposed. Encouraged by Liddell Hart,[25] he also became an active supporter of the New Commonwealth, a society founded in 1932 by Lord Davies "for the promotion of international law and order through the creation of a tribunal in equity and an international police force." In addition to writing a study on "Policing the Seas" (1934) for the society, Richmond also donated freely of his time and advice to the founding members on matters of organization and editorial policy.[26]

In his recent study of Liddell Hart's military thought, Brian Bond had suggested that the early 1930s were his "philosophical phase" *par excellence*: "the only period in his career when he devoted a great deal of time to writing down abstract ideas and speculations." Speculating himself on this "near obsession" with the need to uncover truth in an objective and detached spirit, Bond concludes that the source of Liddell Hart's jaundiced view of the Army's indifference to, even hostility and suppression of, the truth in the history of the First World War was his personal contact with the official historians such as Sir James Edmonds, Cyril Falls, and Cecil Aspinall-Oglander, and others like Hankey and T. E. Lawrence.[27] Richmond should be added to this list for very little of what Liddell Hart wrote in this "philosophical phase" does not bear the imprint of Richmond's obsessions, even his phraseology, and above all, his own long-nurtured sense of shock about the way Sir Julian Corbett had been misunderstood and ignored. The origins of ideas and their impact on personalities are always difficult to trace with any precision. But here, in these early years of the 1930s, the sudden and brief shift of Liddell Hart's own intellectual focus indicates something more than mere coincidence. It was not the first time that friendship with Richmond had turned a knight-errant into a full-fledged crusader. The Admiral's mind was in no way inferior to the Captain's.

This was evident in Richmond's next appointment, for he was elected in 1934 to succeed J. Holland Rose as Vere Harmsworth Professor of Imperial and Naval History at Cambridge. It was a unique honour for a sailor without any formal academic training at a university. Richmond's naval critics had often doubted that a man with "professorial" interests could also be a competent sailor and executive officer. His Cambridge electors had no such doubts about the obverse situation. Holland Rose noted in the *Cambridge Review* of February 9, 1934, that Richmond "not only possesses a brilliant re-

25 Ibid., January 12, 13, 1933; Liddell Hart to Richmond, January 25, 1933.
26 Information supplied by Georg Schwarzenberger, Professor International Law, University of London, in conversation with the author, April 1971.
27 Bond, *Liddell Hart*, pp. 81-85.

cord during his long period of active service, but he has also studied long and deeply the history of the Navy and the influence which it has exerted on our national and overseas development." Specifically, however, his academic credentials rested solidly on the originality and thoroughness of his two scholarly histories, *The Navy in the War of 1739-1748* and *The Navy in India.*

Since Richmond was then sixty-three years old, the appointment was for two years. G. M. Trevelyan, one of the Cambridge electors, has written: "Our choice was a marked compliment to his eminence as an historian, for owing to the age limit affecting professorships he could only hold it for two years, but we felt that his qualifications were so great that even this disadvantage could be overlooked."[28] The title of Vere Harmsworth Professor of Naval History had been changed in 1932, on the initiative of the Cambridgeshire branch of the Royal Empire Society, to the Chair of Imperial and Naval History. Holland Rose, though not primarily a naval historian himself, applauded Richmond's selection precisely because it would allay fears of the new "Imperial" emphasis pushing Naval History "into the background." Also, through him, Cambridge would be brought "into close touch with the Navy and naval thought." As it transpired, support for moving Naval History into the mainstream of Tripos activity did not long survive Richmond's tenure of the Chair.

Richmond mellowed at Cambridge. His outer shell of toughness and reserve seemed to disappear along with his Admiral's ambitions, and was soon overtaken by the gentleness, sensitivity, and personal warmth that had always lain hidden behind that veneer. At Jesus College, where he spent his terms and was made a Professorial Fellow, he entered unreservedly into the congenial preoccupations of the academic world. The verdicts of colleagues and students overwhelmingly attest to the affection and respect with which he was regarded and how deeply he identified himself with his new life. He was "an excellent lecturer and teacher," according to Trevelyan. He was also remembered for his vitality, wit, and good humour. His extensive knowledge of international affairs, fluency in French and Italian, and love of beauty in literature and art had always made him an exception as a naval officer. This catholicity of taste impressed his many university friends who accepted him as a well-rounded man by no means out of his element and who thoroughly revelled in the joys of good conversation and argument. When his appointment was finished, he was elected, on the suggestion of Sir Sidney Cockerell (Director of the Fitzwilliam Museum), to the Mastership of Downing College where he would remain until his death. It was, as he told

---

28 G. M. Trevelyan, "Admiral Sir Herbert W. Richmond," *Proceedings of the British Academy,* 32 (1936), 334.

Arthur Pollen who had sent his congratulations, an especially satisfying prospect for an old war horse: "I should have been very sorry to leave Cambridge after only two and half years of Professorship and I don't fit in easily to a vegetable life in a village."[29]

Richmond came home at Downing. He made the Master's Lodge the focus of Downing's life. Mr. Whalley-Tooker, then Senior Tutor, remembered him as "a wise and kindly man who took charge of us all with firmness but with outstanding humanity." W. L. Cuttle wrote in the *Cambridge Review*:

> He was known at Downing before he became its Master in 1936, for he twice addressed the Maitland Society; his charm and his affability—no-one could have been easier for anyone to speak to—showed how well he knew how to encourage young men. He took his Mastership very seriously; he thought of himself, I think, as the captain of the ship, concerned primarily with the well-being of the whole ship's company. Of University and College routine he had at the beginning little knowledge, but he made it his business to inform himself. The commanders of British battleships live in isolation . . . and the executive officer of the Royal Navy is at no stage of his career concerned with routine office duties, which are the affairs of another branch. Richmond's modesty quickly yielded to the expectancy which welcomed his company in Hall; and when a matter of business called for his attention he went to great pains to understand it. As the Head of his House, he believed in "a band of brothers" and proved what the infection of such a belief can be. He was impatient of quiddities and taradiddles, but was too good a fighter as his professional and scholarly record shows, to decry honest controversy decently conducted.[30]

His success as Master and his enjoyment of the idiosyncracies of his colleagues and students, made all the more pleasurable by regular contact with George Macaulay Trevelyan (then Regius Professor of Modern History and later Master of Trinity) and by increasing recognition of his scholarly status (in 1934, he had been made a trustee of the newly opened National Maritime Museum in Greenwich; in 1937, a Fellow of the British Academy and an Associate Member of the French *Academie de Marine*; and in June 1939, was awarded an honorary doctorate [D.C.L.] by Oxford), all combined to make his Cambridge years the most satisfying of his life. Still, all this did not bury the "daemon" which, ever active, kept him involved in contemporary defence issues through frequent sorties into the press and various periodicals.

Initially, at least until German rearmament began to clarify defence priorities for everyone, his criticisms contained little that was new. They reinforced his earlier preoccupation with the need for a

29 A. H. Pollen Papers, Richmond to Pollen, November 1936.
30 *The Cambridge Review* January 25, 1947.

common policy for all three services and the dangers of any exclusive reliance on deterrence through strategic bombing. He expanded his challenge of the Admiralty's persistent faith in heavy battleships and the "false standards" of the London agreements.[31] Further limitations based on fixed ratios would be meaningless unless they took into account specific political probabilities and strategic factors such as base locations, trade to be protected, and the vulnerability of individual powers to its disruption.[32]

For some years, Richmond had been concerned about growing indications that German naval doctrine would reject the concept of decisive action between large battle fleets in favour of "direct" attacks against shipping by her heavy armoured cruisers, the so-called "pocket battleships" built under the Versailles tonnage restrictions.[33] Should the Germans ever obtain the bases they wanted in Norway or France, that is, outside the "Wet Triangle" of the Heligoland Bight, the threat to Britain's weakened cruiser forces would force the deployment of her limited number of battleships as convoy escorts. In November 1932, he made these points both in The Times and privately to Simon, the Foreign Secretary, whom he was assured would raise them in Cabinet. He confided to A. H. Pollen,

> I think I explained pretty unanswerably the absurdity of the 2 claims which the Admiralty, now in the last ditch of their defences of bigness, fire off to hold their citadel: 1. that big ships are needed, not as "battleships" to fight enemy battleships in battles, but as reinforcements to cruisers to defend convoys against the enemy's big cruisers: and (2) that big ships are needed because the beam, [?] and decks necessary to render ships unsinkable by bombs and torpedoes can only be provided in ships of the size they demand.[34]

In "The Case Against the Big Battleship" of August 1934, he rejected out of hand all arguments which suggested that larger sizes automatically gave increased protection, fighting power, endurance, speed, and stability. Unless Britain, by her own policy and efforts to convert American thinking, avoided the trend towards bigger designs, the outcome would be another building race she could not afford: "the results of all attempts to 'win victory on the building slips' . . . is [sic]

31 Richmond, "Some Elements of Disarmament," Fortnightly Review (February 1932); "Britain's Naval Policy: Some Dangers and Delusions," ibid., (April 1932). Also, Times letters, March 12, 1930; July 4, 1931, November 8, 1934; April 13, 1935.
32 Richmond, "Naval Disarmament," Nineteenth Century (December 1934); "Naval Rearmament," ibid., (January 1936); "The Minister of Defence," ibid. (April 1937).
33 Vice-Admiral A. Meurer in Militar Wochenblatt (1928), no. 20; Vice-Admiral Wolfgang, The Naval Strategy of World War (1926); E. W. Kruse, Neuzeitliche Seekriegsfuhrung.
34 A. H. Pollen Papers, Richmond to Pollen, November 10, 1932. Also "Big Ships," The Times, November 10 and 12, 1932.

to force the rival to follow suit, with a consequent additional burden to the taxpayer and without any increase whatever in the security of him who started the race."[35]

In 1936, when Richmond was called before another C.I.D. Enquiry—this one to study the capital ship's vulnerability to air attack—he reiterated his doubts of the utility of investigations so prejudiced in their assumptions. The question of whether or not a battleship could be made safe against bombs was meaningless unless it also took into account more wide-ranging considerations of how fleets would be used under modern conditions—"a strategical problem transcending in importance the technical one." The risks to a fleet, which he pointed out also applied to its carriers, flotilla, and supply vessels, would depend on the kinds of operations it had to undertake:

> I do not believe that a fleet, however powerfully the capital ships may be constructed and armoured, can operate, except spasmodically and for short periods, in waters where it is exposed to attacks by aerial torpedo craft with any degree of continuity and in large numbers; any more than a fleet twenty years ago could maintain, for more than a very brief period, a position in an area where it would be exposed to constant attack by surface or submarine torpedo craft - e.g., off Wilhelmshaven, Pola or the Southern end of the Adriatic.
> ... the lesser vessels of the flotilla and the smaller types of cruiser, run no greater danger in such work than the greater armoured ships. This belief necessarily carries with it a denial of the claim that great size is essential in order to provide security against this form of attack.

Until there was a fuller appreciation of the interplay of all the various components of the fleet, the protection of its bases, the proportion of naval resources to be assigned to trade protection from aerial, surface, and submarine attack with consequent reduction in offensive and combined operations capabilities, it was pointless concentrating on the safety of the Navy's fifteen capital ships—some five per cent of the total numbers.[36] Predictably, these sensible arguments seem to have made no appreciable impact on the Enquiry's findings and achieved very little by way of curbing the Admiralty's preferences for even larger battleships. Although the findings of a later study, the "Sub-Committee of Assessors on Bombs versus Battleship Experiments" (ABE Committee), hinted that the new designs in excess of 40,000

35 "The Case Against Big Battleships," *Nineteenth Century* (August 1934).
36 RIC/7/2/2, "Vulnerability of Capital Ships" (1936), "Comments by Admiral Sir Herbert Richmond on the Memorandum of the Committee." Copy also in RIC/5/2; RIC/6/3, "Report of the Sub-Committee of the C.I.D. On the Vulnerability of Capital Ships to Air Attack," Cmd. 5301 (H.M.S.O., November 1936). Richmond's invitation to appear before the Committee seems to have been engineered by Roger Keyes. See, RIC/7/4, Keyes to Richmond, June 4, 1936; RIC/7/2/2, Sir Thomas Inskip to Richmond, June 17, 22, 1936.

tons could well be obsolete before their completion in 1941, the Admiralty persisted in its demands for the heavier types in response to reported Japanese, German, and Italian programmes.[37] Well before that, during the 1935 Abyssinian Crisis, Richmond had already forecast the situation should war break out in the Mediterranean: "the big ships of Italy will go to Venice and of England to Alexandria and Australia. And the fighting for command of the sea will be between the small vessels who fear neither the submarine nor aircraft."[38]

Accurate as later wartime events proved him to be about heavy battleships, Richmond did at the same time grossly underrate the future roles of aircraft carriers. When Captain Bernard Acworth suggested in *Britain in Danger: An Examination of Our New Navy* (1937) that the Admiralty intended to patrol trade routes with carriers escorted by battle-cruisers, Richmond strongly attacked the use of "these costly and very weak vessels" for such purposes: "the idea that commerce destroyers could be dealt with—that is, discovered and destroyed—by aircraft lies outside the range of practical possibility. The proposal recalls Einstein's saying that bombarding atoms with sub-atomic particles was like shooting birds in the dark in a country where there are very few birds."[39] This may have reflected some not unjustified doubts about existing British naval aircraft, the Swordfish biplane, and Skua fighter/dive-bomber. But he also feared that the Admiralty, recently granted control of the Fleet Air Arm (though not of land-based naval air craft), might well employ these carriers in a repeat performance of World War I hunter-patrol operations at the expense of more systematic trade protection and convoys. He supported Acworth's contention of the non-existence of a developed naval policy, especially of a doctrine that came to grips with the problems of long-distance oceanic warfare, particularly in the Pacific. His own experience of the East Indies Command had shown that official thinking about how to conduct a war against Japan went no further than concentrating a Battle Fleet at Singapore. "Ask them," he had warned Haldane in 1924, "what they intend to do once they get to Singapore?"[40] The later fate of *Prince of Wales* and *Repulse* may well have hung on that answer.

The Navy's failure to develop a comprehensive carrier doctrine similar to that of the Americans was partly the result of the R.A.F.'s long control over naval air forces and, more especially, its preoccupation with long-range bombing and strategic deterrence. The Bombs

37 Roskill, *Naval Policy*, vol. 2, p. 420.
38 Ibid., p. 260. Cites letter, Richmond to Admiral Pratt, U.S. Chief of Naval Operations, October 23, 1935.
39 Richmond, "Some Naval Problems: Britain in Danger and Captain Bernard Acworth," *Nineteenth Century* (February 1938).
40 Quoted in D. C. Watt, *Too Serious a Business* (London: Temple Smith, 1975), p. 78.

versus Battleship controversy of 1936, like that over the creation of a Ministry of Defence, was deliberately revived to ensure that the Air Ministry did not lose out in the rearmament budget battles to the Navy's new battleship and carrier programmes.[41] Deterrence or counter-force doctrine had been accepted dogma in the R.A.F. since its beginnings. Now, as rearmament priorities went to building up those bomber forces, it was revealed that the R.A.F. had never possessed the operational capabilities to find or destroy its targets. As Professor Donald Watt recently suggested, "for nearly twenty years the Air Force High Command had been preaching a strategy without reference to its operational possibilities, a strategy of the Emperor's clothes being preferred to one of cutting one's coat to fit the available cloth."[42]

Richmond had always questioned the moral propriety of massive terroristic strikes on large urban centres and the enemy population's will. Moreover, because such a strategy lacked specific military objectives, he doubted it could ever produce defined political results and was therefore wasteful and unproductive. Acceptance of the basic assumption that "the bomber always gets through," and its corollary that air defence measures were therefore useless, even counter-productive, led, he argued, to purposeless cross-ravaging "such as that which used in the Middle Ages to be conducted across the Channel . . . before any scientific thought informed strategy."[43] Passive and active defences were possible in Richmond's view if measures and funds to develop them were provided. He was of course not alone in advocating fighter defences; but unlike Sir Warren Fisher of the Treasury, or Thomas Inskip, Minister for the Co-ordination of Defence, who did play the vital roles in forcing the Air Ministry to accept Fighter Command as part of the price for its own bomber forces, Richmond knew very little of Spitfire or Hurricane developments and nothing of Tizard's and Watson-Watt's invention of radar. His reasoning flowed from a deep-seated fear that the offensive bombing panacea was "Continentalist" dogma reincarnate. When the war did come, he would argue that it was precisely this misuse of airpower at the expense of whole-hearted efforts to establish effective command of the sea which contributed to Britain's heavy shipping losses and early military disasters. Here was the special stamp of the historically trained strategist whose instincts consistently emphasized the distinction between ends and means.

Richmond's role in the Second World War was as complete as his circumstances and the censor would allow. In Mr. Cuttle's words:

41 Robert P. Shay, *British Rearmament in the Thirties: Politics and Profits* (Princeton: University Press, 1977), pp. 67-73.
42 Watt, *Too Serious a Business*, p. 77.
43 Richmond, *Imperial Defence and Capture at Sea*, p. 36.

he wrote and he advised, he and Lady Richmond entertained members of the services, British, Dominion, and Allied; especially those of France, a country for which his friendship was strong and abiding. He eagerly talked with serving members of the College, and was always ready to try to help them if he judged it right. He was first chairman of the Joint Recruiting Board, and was throughout in constant attendance to advise young men about the Navy. It gave him great satisfaction to see the University Naval Division established in his college, and to live again with the white ensign flying.

Still, he was upset by the Admiralty's initial indifference to the universities as sources for much-needed junior executive officers. In 1941, when the Navy was attempting to meet these serious shortages by promoting young warrant officers (by Richmond's estimate, over one hundred per week were being taken from the lower deck) and accepting R.N.V.R. (Royal Naval Volunteer Reserve) and R.N.V.S.R. (Royal Naval Volunteer Supplementary Reserve) officers for extended service, he urged the Admiralty to reconsider its policy which barred entry of undergraduates registered at the Naval Centre, if for no other reason than preventing their loss to the Army and R.A.F. His own prewar proposals for summer training camps similar to those of the other services had been rejected. And when he had raised the idea again in February 1939, the Admiralty replied: "We have at present in the Royal Naval Reserve and Royal Naval Volunteer Reserve a supply of officers sufficient to meet almost all our needs at the outbreak of war apart from a certain number of specialists." Given the obstacles that university applicants faced, "conditions of a totally unnecessary character," it was not surprising Richmond should write to the Admiralty Board stating bluntly that the "Admiralty attach very little value to the University man as a potential sea officer" and advising reconsideration "whatever may be the 'repercussions' which may be feared."[44] It might be noted that Canada, then in the process of re-opening its own Naval College, at Royal Roads, B.C., was more responsive to Richmond's liberal views in this respect.[45]

Naval prejudices towards university men as executive officers did not apply of course to specialist talent. Maurice Hankey, then a Peer and Cabinet Minister (Chancellor of the Duchy of Lancaster), and Chairman of the C.I.D.'s Scientific and Technical Advisory Committees,[46] frequently visited Richmond in search of bright young scientists, linguists, and others so urgently needed as part of the general mobilization of intellectual talent which characterized this war effort. Captain Roskill, who for two years served as Deputy D.N.I., has written: "In every case of a new need arising the Admiralty consulted

44 RIC/7/4, Richmond to Secretary, Board of Admiralty, June 26, 1941.
45 Ibid., J. M. Grant, R.C.N., to Richmond (n.d.).
46 Adm. 116/3704. Roskill, *Hankey*, vol. 3, pp. 487-93.

Richmond, and he generally knew where to put his finger on the right person. Indeed it does not go too far to say that between 1939 and 1945 he acted as the Navy's unofficial, and of course unpaid adviser on staff recruiting."[47]

All these many commitments had a cumulative effect. Richmond suffered a severe heart attack in 1940. Recuperation was slow and frustrating, but steady. In Mr. Cuttle's words:

> he fell back upon his sailor's gift of handiness, and found relief from hard thinking in the making to scale of beautiful little reproductions of period furniture, which were sold for the Red Cross; and from this developed the planning, building, and equipping of a large doll's house for a grand-daughter, the work of art which might rank with the best that have been produced of that delightful domestic kind.

Though in the end his recovery was fairly complete, it was obvious to Trevelyan and other close friends that much of his old stamina had gone. And this only aggravated his impatience at being side-tracked from more direct involvement in the war. "Like you," he told Professor Gerald Graham in the summer of 1941, "I am finding it almost impossible to turn my thoughts to anything except what is happening now, and by the time the war is over I shall only be fit for the scrap heap, if indeed that is not already the right place for men like me without practical experience of the present day warfare at sea. And on these summer afternoons I'm much more inclined to read a book in an easy chair on the lawn than pore over foolscap in my library. But I must get my one bit of work done before I pack up."[48] That "one bit of work" involved a regimen of letters and articles few entirely healthy men would care to contemplate.

From 1939, he was the regular naval contributor to the *Fortnightly Review*. In 1941, he wrote two pamphlets for the Historical Association—*The Invasion of Britain* and *Amphibious Warfare in British History*—which along with several other short works and advice to the B.B.C. were designed as elementary introductions for laymen to current naval problems.[49] At Downing, his informal talks on foreign affairs and the progress of the war became a regular feature in the junior combination room and were later perpetuated as 'The Richmond Lectures." With all this, he still found time for research on what he intended should be his greatest historical work, *The Navy as an Instrument of Policy*. When he had first arrived at Downing, he told A. H. Pollen:

47 Captain S. W. Roskill, "The Richmond Lecture," *Naval Review*, 57 (1969), 145.
48 G. S. Graham Papers, Richmond to Graham, August 12, 1944.
49 Richmond, *The Navy* (London: W. Hodge, 1937); *The Naval Role in Modern Warfare* (London, 1940); *British Strategy, Military and Economic* (Cambridge: University Press, 1941); and *War at Sea Today* (London ,1942). Also, RIC/6/2, Malcolm Darling (B.B.C.) to Richmond, July 23, 1942.

> I am working on an outline of British strategy from Elizabeth to 1918, with special reference to the statesman's problem and how he must use the Sea and Land forces he had at his disposal, and how the strategy worked out in practice—the perpetual clash between the two schools of thought, maritime operations and land operations in the main theatre on the continent.[50]

Time permitting, he also planned a book on strategy "in more or less the abstract," and perhaps even one on Jutland, the subject he had always sworn to avoid but the one also for which he sensed that the market had been too long monopolized by Bacon and the Fisherite school. The latter would never be started, however, and The Navy as an Instrument of Policy which was closest to his heart in these final years remained unfinished, overtaken by his preoccupation with more current events.

In most respects, Richmond had nothing but praise for the Navy's performance in this war, which he considered to be incomparably better than the First. A superior staff organization and much healthier attitudes towards its vital role were in great measure the legacy of his own earlier efforts. He found little to criticize in the Navy's operational record in the opening phases of the war, given the cruel limitations in resources which had to be faced with an ingenuity and flexibility of a kind unknown in 1914-1918. Richmond also found cause for some personal satisfaction in the fact that the blockade and cutting off of Germany's external seaborne supplies, which was implemented immediately and without any serious interference from the neutrals, owed not a little to his campaigns against the doctrines of Freedom of the Seas. At the same time, he was not surprised by Germany's decision to mount an immediate counter-attack using her "pocket battleships" supported by her battle-cruisers (Scharnhorst and Gneisenau, permitted by the 1935 Anglo-German Treaty), and later by her new fast battleships (Bismarck and Tirpitz) in a "direct" attack on Allied shipping.

> Germany was naturally well aware of Britain's weakness, and German naval strategists set themselves to think out a form of warfare suitable to the prospective situation and the new instruments. Accepting the basic principle that the ultimate aim in naval war is the control of sea communications and that it was upon trade by sea that Great Britain and France depended for their existence, and that in the trade routes lay their most vulnerable spot, Germany resurrected the theory of the guerre de course, as it had been promulgated by Louis XIV and his ministers. It was an error to devote the country's efforts to obtaining "command" by concentrations of force and pitched battle of the massed strength; this indirect method of destroying the commerce that supplies the needs of Britain should be replaced by the direct method of attack upon the shipping itself.

50 A. H. Pollen Papers, Richmond to Pollen, November 1936.

Modern construction provided the instruments, the submarine, the
heavy cruiser and the mine. Aircraft do not appear to have been
allowed for in the German calculations, possibly because it could not
be foreseen that so rapid a collapse of France would be brought
about, to furnish bases on the coast from which these comparatively
short-ranged instruments could strike at the trade routes.[51]

When Britain was forced to employ her own battleships in defence of
ocean convoys, Richmond took the opening to reiterate his conviction
that the Navy's needs for these types depended

> not directly upon the number of enemy capital ships but upon the
> number of convoys needing simultaneous defence and the scale of
> probable attack: in other words, when the Battleships became
> "cruisers" the "cruiser standard" of strength had to be applied to
> them on the trade routes, while a definite superiority might be
> needed at the same time to meet the continuous threat of the enemy
> capital ships in the North Sea.

All these demands, in the Atlantic, North Sea, and Mediterranean
could not be met by that "mere mathematical equality" the disarmers
had preached for so long.[52]

The Norwegian fiasco, in addition to confirming his earlier pre-
dictions about the fate of surface vessels unprotected from air attack,
also suggested what impact air-power might have on the assumptions
of those who did possess it. "At first sight," he wrote in September
1941, the German invasion of Norway

> had the appearance of being a most hazardous adventure, an inva-
> sion of an oversea territory without command of the sea. That as-
> sumption failed to take account of the power of the submarine and of
> aircraft, working from bases in close proximity to the objective area.
> The British surface forces, operating from the other side of the North
> Sea at a distance of 600 miles, could not be kept in continuous
> position in the Skaggerak, nor could they have the support of air-
> craft.... In these circumstances it was the enemy who, undeterred
> by the prospect of some fairly high losses, had a sufficient command
> to move his transports. We have to realise that the "command of the
> sea" to-day is no longer a matter in which surface or even submarine
> vessels are alone concerned. He who possesses an instrument which
> can sink merchant ships, whether it be a battery of guns on land or
> flights of bombers in the air, commands the sea within the ranges of
> those instruments.... The success of the German operations was a
> strong reminder of the perennial doctrine of the "liaison of arms."[53]

The implications for the defence of Britian herself were obvious.
Available light cruiser and fast destroyer forces—the traditional first
line of defence against a cross-Channel assault—were stretched peril-

51 Richmond, "Some Aspects of the War at Sea," *Engineering*, September 5, 1941.
52 Richmond, *Statesmen and Seapower*, p. 303.
53 Richmond, "Some Aspects," *Engineering*, September 5, 1941.

ously thin, a situation made infinitely worse by heavy losses at Dunkirk. The solution, in Richmond's view, would only come from a conscious recognition that the R.A.F.'s Fighter Command was in fact an integral part (that "highly formidable reinforcement") of the anti-invasion flotilla whose job it was to deny the Lufftwaffe early command of the vital sea passages. Close inter-service efforts in this area could well mean that the Navy's forces in the Channel and North Sea would not require reinforcements from the already strained Atlantic convoying forces. The conflicting demands on these very limited escort and anti-invasion resources became the source of serious disagreement between Churchill and the C-in-C Home Fleet, Sir Charles Forbes. At the height of the invasion threat, Forbes opposed the War Cabinet's decision to deploy most of the Home Fleet's units around the east and south coasts thereby leaving the convoys exposed. From his own assessment of German naval weakness and his own ability to quickly reinforce threatened areas, provided the R.A.F. and Army fulfilled their defensive roles, Forbes argued that the Home Fleet should be left free to carry out its first responsibility of acting "offensively against the enemy and in defence of our trade."[54] As Captain Roskill has shown, this was far from the last of many disputes over strategic priorities which Churchill's "love-hate relationship" with many of his senior naval advisers would produce. And Richmond, by endorsing Forbes's thinking in this instance, placed himself once more squarely in conflict with the Churchillian viewpoint.

He had always mistrusted Churchill's idiosyncratic notions of strategy, and from this point all his public utterances echo the theme that the failure to give an absolute priority to securing the Empire's sea communications was a serious mistake; that Churchill's obsession with the bombing of Germany, his romantic predilictions for amphibious raiding schemes, and his unwillingness to face the Japanese threat squarely would only serve to dissipate Britain's severely limited resources. Victory through the destruction of Germany alone might well be bought at the price of British ruin.

The contrast between Britain's options in 1940-1941 and the real power she had deployed in 1914-1915 underscored the fact that running risks without first guaranteeing the security of her imperial life-lines would be fatal. The comparison with World War I carried other poignant memories for Richmond as well. From the moment of his return to the Admiralty, Churchill had taxed the Naval Staff with constant pressures for offensive moves such as his notorious Operation "Catherine" for forcing a passage into the Baltic. Again, staff officers who criticized or openly opposed his ideas, such as Captain

54 Roskill, Churchill and the Admirals, pp. 119-20.

V. H. Danckwerts (Director of Plans) and Captain A. G. Talbot (Director of Anti-Submarine Warfare), were quickly replaced.[55] Part of the reasoning for Drax's attachment as a special adviser to the First Sea Lord, it will be recalled, was to help forestall these tendencies which involved so much waste and misdirection of the Staff's energies.

There can be no question that Churchill's dynamism and dogged determination and, above all, his commitment to a great Anglo-American coalition were amongst his greatest contributions to the British war effort. But as Richmond always believed, Churchill had never understood the true functions of the Staff and does not seem to have appreciated that a properly organized and well-trained body of staff officers had indeed gradually developed since the end of World War I. His instincts as a politician and reflexes as an historian had taught him, Professor Marder suggests, that the Admirals would never achieve anything approaching the Navy's full offensive potential except under strong political leadership; and that when he became Prime Minister, "he was determined that the strong political control would never be lacking while he occupied the hot seat."[56] That determination was manifest in his reorganization and strengthening of the central political and military machinery of the higher command—the War Cabinet, the Joint Planning Staff, Joint Intelligence Committee, and the creation of a host of specialist organizations such as the Political Warfare Executive, Ministry of Economic warfare, Special Operations Executive (SOE), and Combined Operations Headquarters (COHQ). His appointment of Admiral Sir Roger Keyes to head the latter, for all its "Gilbertian" possibilities, was an act of some political courage; but it ensured that COHQ came under the Prime Minister's control, independent of the C.O.S. and the service ministries.[57]

Richmond endorsed these moves insofar as they might engender further inter-service cooperation. In private correspondence with Keyes, he offered advice on offensive possibilities and generally encouraged the development of specialized amphibious capabilities.[58] But he was less certain of the ultimate value of the "raids policy" actually initiated by Keyes whose intrepid spirit and instinct for quick blood-lettings did not appear to serve any fully developed assessment of Britain's maritime offensive options. Shortly after Keyes' replace-

55 Ibid., pp. 94-95.
56 Marder, *From the Dardanelles to Oran: Studies of the Royal Navy in War and Peace, 1915-1940* (London: Oxford, 1974), p. 178.
57 See B. D. Hunt and D. M. Schurman, "Prelude to Dieppe: Thoughts on Combined Operations Policy in the Raiding Period, 1940-42," in G. Jordan, ed., *Naval Warfare in the Twentieth Century* (London: Croom-Helm, 1977), pp. 192-93.
58 RIC/7/4, November 21, 1940; March 14, 1941; November 18, 1941; December 3, 23, 1941; January 4, 1942.

ment by Mountbatten in October 1941, and on the heels of increasing pressure for some British "Diversion" in support of her beleaguered Russian ally, Richmond publicly spelled out the dangers of failing to make clear distinctions between the true military and political objectives of various kinds of amphibious operations. Though he did not specifically direct his message to Churchill, the inference was clear:

> Of the many lessons which the grim story of failure at the Dardanelles conveys, three are outstanding—the need for a clear understanding and an accurate definition of the object of an operation or series of operations; for the most meticulous and complete preparation in all the elements, strategical, tactical and administrative; and for unswerving determination in its prosecution; for it was through the absence of these that Gallipoli failed—and also Dakar.

Circumstances had also changed drastically since 1915 when the British and French had exercised virtually total command of the Mediterranean, when merchant tonnage had not at that point been seriously threatened by the U-boats, and no air threat existed.

> The communications of any army directed against any part of the occupied coasts today require defence against surface ships of all types, submarines and aircraft. Except in the Narrow Seas there would be no air-bases close at hand to cover the passage and disembarkation against air-attack, while the enemy's air-forces would be close to the spot. . . . The resources of the Navy in heavy ships, cruisers and flotilla-craft are very fully employed in protecting the sea-routes of commerce and military supply in the carriage of material to Russia via Archangel and the Persian Gulf and in the military operations in North Africa. None of these services can be reduced without detriment to the very Power for whom help is being demanded, and, though a substantial improvement has been made in the shipping-situation, and the losses are reduced to a third of what they were in the spring, they still stand at a figure that must be considerably lowered before we can be satisfied that we are out of the wood.[59]

In Richmond's view, Russia's entry into the war had put the question of Britain's general strategy in its simplest form: whether to reinforce and strengthen her new land ally, or to weaken their mutual enemy. The latter he was prepared to accept as the overriding priority providing the systematic bombing of German industry could be supported by a sustained programme of raids and "true diversions" of Axis resources. But existing commitments of British land forces in the Mediterranean, Middle East, and Asia made that entirely unlikely. That left only naval and air forces with which to strengthen Russia via the northern route to Murmansk and the Cape route to the Persian Gulf. He also saw the deteriorating Mediterranean situation in the

59 Richmond, "The 'Diversion' Controversy," The Spectator, November 28, 1941.

summer of 1941 as being one of major concern to Russia should the
Axis win control there and extend its power to Iraq, Persia, and the
Gulf. The build-up of strong land, air, and sea forces for the Battle of
the Atlantic, the defence of the Mediterranean, and the cutting of
German-Italian communications was therefore the most pressing
priority in Richmond's comprehensive view. Churchill's decision to
give precedence to the bombing campaign against Germany was,
according to this reasoning, a major strategic error. The spread of the
war to the Pacific in December 1941 only confirmed Richmond's
worst fears that Britain's imperial holdings and the entire inter-
locking strategic framework could well crumble long before Germany
was brought to her knees.

The Japanese conquest of Malaya and eventual capture of Singapore came as no surprise to Richmond. No amount of recriminations
about the defences or local commanders' actions could compensate
for the fact that the fleet whose needs the great base was meant to serve
did not exist. And lacking that fleet, Singapore was a hostage to
fortune ("a sentry box without the sentry") for which piece-meal
reinforcements such as *Prince of Wales* and *Repulse* only served to
extend the disaster. Richmond's reading of Japan's options in December 1941,[60] suggested an immediate concentration of the greatest
possible naval and air forces in the Indian Ocean ("even if it should
involve reducing attacks on Germany in order to provide the bombing
and fighter forces to ensure superiority at this vital spot") to cover
Allied communications between the Cape and the Mediterranean and
Persian Gulf. On February 11, four days before Singapore's collapse,
he sent a personal appeal to Churchill to consider the imminent threat
to Ceylon and the entire position westward to the African coast.[61] By
the time of the Prime Minister's polite reply, last-minute efforts to
organize arrangements in Ceylon were under way, though they came
to nought. When a Japanese carrier strike force attacked in April,
Admiral Somerville was fortunate to escape, after heavy losses, to the
East African coast. Only the Japanese decision not to extend their
success in the Indian Ocean but to turn back instead towards the
Americans at Midway prevented the full measure of Richmond's
forecast from materializing. It is tempting to believe that some diversion of R.A.F. units from Germany might well have averted or
ameliorated these disasters in the Far East. And Richmond of course
was not the only observer to make the suggestion. Others, including
Wavell (C-in-C India from February 1942), who were more directly

---

60 *Manchester Guardian*, December 31, 1941. See also, ibid., March 14, 1942; and *The
Times*, February 5, 1942.
61 RIC/7/4, Richmond to Churchill, February 11, 1942; and Churchill to Richmond,
February 28, 1942.

involved would also lament what even a few of the hundreds of bombers then flying daily over Germany might have done.[62] Even so, what was needed was naval aircraft (dive-bombers and torpedo planes) the shortage of which was but another legacy of the R.A.F.'s earlier obsessions. Realistically, even Churchill could not be held responsible for being left with few options on that score. But Richmond was right in arguing that the disasters in the East were not just the result of insufficient resources but also of the failure to employ what there was in a joint way. "The idea of using the national arms in combination with the object of obtaining and maintaining command of the sea was absent from the minds of the War Council."[63]

The spreading tide of failure in the Pacific, the alarming step-up in German U-boat successes in the Atlantic following the United States' entry into the war, and serious setbacks in the Libyan desert in January 1942, brought Britain to her most disastrous period of the war. More than ever, Richmond was convinced that every conceivable effort had to be bent toward winning command of the sea. His own precarious health no doubt aggravated his pessimism and heightened his frustration at the War Cabinet's indifference to this basic fact. The year 1942 would be a "winter of discontent" (much as 1916-1917 had been in the First War) which called forth the most serious challenges to the higher direction of the war effort. For Richmond, it was a year of deep personal agony for he sensed in "this unhappy year," as he called it, that the war was being lost and with it the Empire, the Navy, and Britain's moment as a great power. One detects in a note written on March 1 to explain how the press of events of the previous two years had prevented completion of his Navy as an Instrument of Policy an awareness, too, of his own shortcomings as an historian committed to educating his leaders in the essentials of maritime greatness:

> Now everything is in the melting pot and whether after this war there will again be a Navy, or whether the country will interest itself and take steps to ensure that its people are made aware of the importance of sea power, and taught, not only by our terrible experience of tampering with the Navy in these fatal years since 1918 but also by the long experience of the past, I cannot tell. I greatly fear that what has happened before will repeat itself, and the nation, even if it survives—and the Empire—will again relapse into complacency.[64]

Throughout the summer and autumn of 1942 he added his voice to a growing chorus of criticism of Churchill's leadership by arguing that this was a war of combined strategies in which the interplay of all

62 See Churchill, The Second World War, vol. 4 (Boston 1950), p. 187.
63 Richmond, "The Third Year of the War at Sea," Engineering, September 4, 1942.
64 Richmond, Preface, The Navy as an Instrument of Policy.

the various theatres in the East, the Mediterranean, and the Atlantic rested on a foundation of assured lines of communication.

> The fundamental causes of these great misfortunes are plain: we have not obtained command of the sea in the European and Atlantic waters, and we have lost it in the Far East. While those causes derive ultimately from the policy of neglect of British sea power for the last twenty years, and the direction of our strategy to other objects than the command of the sea during the present war, they arise immediately out of two circumstances: namely, the Japanese attack on the United States and on the British territories in the Far East, and the increasing influence of aircraft on the operations of sea warfare.[65]

The ominous rise in shipping losses that summer to their highest levels so far in the war made clear the urgency of reinforcing the Fleet Air Arm and Coastal Command. He did not doubt that hard blows were being struck against Germany's cities; only that the Germans were striking heavier blows on the Atlantic. Growing evidence that Churchill and Air Chief Marshal Sir Arthur Harris were treating Bomber Command's German operations as virtually "a thing apart"[66] from other priorities finally pushed the so-called "Battle of the Air," which had been raging inside Whitehall, into the full-blown public controversy that resulted in the nearly too late recognition of the menace and reallocation of air-escorts that in 1943 began to turn the tide in the Atlantic in the Allies' favour. Though Richmond played a relatively minor role in the instigation of this challenge to Churchill's policies, his appeals in *The Times* and elsewhere for a clear understanding that command of the sea was the only certain foundation for future major land offensives were consistent with everything he had written thoughout the war.[67] Hankey, who following his dismissal as a Minister in March 1942 did play a leading part and was able to rally the support of virtually the entire Press,[68] certainly appreciated the powerful arguments of "my old Shipmate" and encouraged Richmond to keep up his letters which "have done a lot of good."[69] Hankey of course knew a good deal more of the technical and statistical facts of the case than he could ever tell Richmond. Later, in 1945, he urged Richmond not to hesitate in his forthcoming book, *Statesmen and Sea Power*, to denounce Churchill's retention of aircraft in 1942 when they were so desperately needed for the anti-submarine war:

> What we suspected has now become clear, that the bombing of Germany at that time was absolutely futile. It was improved later of

65 Richmond, "The Third Year," *Engineering, September 4, 1942.*
66 Michael Howard, *Grand Strategy*, vol. 4, p. 20.
67 See *The Times*, June 25, 30; July 6; August 13, 1942. Also *Fortnightly Review*, "Air Power and Sea Power" (July 1942); "The Air Arm at Sea in 1941-42" (September 1942); "The Primary Object" (February 1943).
68 Roskill, *Hankey*, vol. 3, Chaps. 15 and 16.
69 RIC/7/4, Hankey to Richmond, July 17, 1942; also, April 20; August 17, 1942.

> course with the development of Radar for aiming purposes, but in
> 1942 they could not find their targets and often not the cities that
> contained them . . . . I do not believe myself that our night bombing
> ever did much good, except in a few instances. We are still suffering
> to-day from the loss of over 8 million tons of Allied shipping in
> 1942.[70]

The twenty-page analysis which Richmond ultimately included
in *Statesmen and Seapower* remains to this day one of the best
summations of the controversy the accuracy and balance of which
three decades of subsequent research, including access to the official
records, has done nothing to diminish. He knew his views must be
unpopular. "The air enthusiasts aren't going to like it" he remarked to
Professor Marder in 1946. But in this, his thinking was not shaped by
any partisan motives of vindicating his earlier positions. His conclusions were true to the concepts he learned as a scholar and, natural
prejudice aside, had no other purposes than to educate his country-
men in traditional British thought.

Statesmen and Sea Power was Richmond's last book, and his
most widely recognized. It was based on the Ford Lectures which he
was invited to deliver at Oxford in 1943 on the broad theme of British
strategy since the days of Elizabeth I. Expanding those lectures into
final book form, with the help of his daughter, Nora, took all his
failing strength, for they had to take the place of *The Navy as an
Instrument of Policy*, the *magnum opus* he knew would never be
finished. The first volume of the latter, carrying his study up to 1927,
was later edited by E. A. Hughes of Trinity College and published in
1953.

In both books, Richmond set out to paint a broad-brush picture of
the unchanging fundamentals of maritime strategy. Setting aside the
operational detail of his earlier histories, he placed overall British
policy within the wider context of naval, military, economic, political, and international considerations without which the term "Sea
Power" was a meaningless catch word. With his own experience of
twentieth-century naval politics and their terrible legacy in two world
wars pressing in on his thoughts, he showed that it is the statesman
who bears the ultimate responsibility for these developments in peace
and war. Unlike most other strategic theorists who, while endorsing
the Clausewitzian dictum of the primacy of political control, took
rationality in that leadership for granted, Richmond sought to say
something by way of guiding the statesman's uncertain steps. He saw
in Britain's imperial-maritime history a well-tried range for conscious
policy choices within which the complex interplay of politics, evolving technology, and unpredictable circumstance might be balanced.

---

70 Ibid., November 27, 1945.

That *Statesmen and Sea Power* was published in 1946 just a few weeks before his death made it an especially fitting final statement of his work as a scholar and tribute to the navy and nation he served so long and well.

Richmond was seventy-five when he succumbed to another heart attack on December 15, 1946. Cremation took place at Cambridge following a private service in the College chapel at which Dr. Trevelyan eloquently summed up his dear friend's achievement:

> In all relations of life he was as nearly perfect as it is given to man to be, and those who were nearest him knew best what he was. When goodness and beauty of character, greatly superior to what we ordinary men can show, are united to great and well-disciplined powers of mind, we see to what height in the hierarchy of being a brother man can rise.

Retrospective

So it was that Richmond's long struggle to educate the Navy and the nation came to an end. His success as a naval officer and his innovating work as a reformer and intellectual leader were all of a piece with his ultimate achievements as a scholar. In this he completed the work of such pioneering forebears as Clowes, Laughton, Mahan, and Corbett. And if, in the end, Richmond's efforts failed to win the professional and public acclaim still given Mahan's, it is useful to remember that superior scholarship rarely has immediate and widespread impact. Mahan was always the exception. Unlike him, Richmond appealed to a people not about to embrace maritime greatness, but one seemingly bent on forgetting it. Still, his most enduring contribution was to raise public awareness of the importance of naval history as a distinct field of serious academic endeavour and as an educative process for spreading sound concepts of strategy and tactics.

In his final years, Richmond was deeply troubled to see that not a single university chair of naval history survived anywhere in Britain or the Commonwealth. His success in getting naval history included in the Cambridge Tripos unfortunately did not long survive his own tenure there as Vere Harmsworth Professor. Similarly his plea in 1942, before an Oxford audience, "for the arising of a new school of naval historians" and a "more lively and better-founded understanding of what seapower means" suggests that he had some doubts as to his own place in the evolution of twentieth-century naval historiography and strategic thought. He could not claim to have fathered a direct line of disciples, a distinct Richmond "school," but few, if any, of the postwar generation of outstanding naval scholars, such as Arthur Marder, Stephen Roskill, Gerald S. Graham, Paul Kennedy, and others, whose careers touched upon Richmond's in various ways, would deny the influence of his mind and pen which had dominated the field since the First World War.

That most of Richmond's writings are now neglected may have something to do with the fact that his approach to history was in some measure coloured by determinist and utilitarian elements which by modern academic standards seem dated. Like Mahan, Richmond looked to the past for "timeless lessons" and immutable principles. He accepted the argument that while the instruments and techniques of war obviously do change, the basic concepts affecting their purposes do not; that such underlying principles, in Mahan's words, "belong to the unchangeable, or unchanging order of things." This determinism was most pronounced in his more popular books where his purpose was to propagandize on behalf of history-based doctrine to an untutored and largely uninterested professional naval audience. To a lesser degree, it also coloured his last two books, *Statesmen and Seapower* and *The Navy as an Instrument of Policy*. His decision to attempt these broad surveys at a time when academic fashion was moving towards more specialized, less positivistic studies, is understandable in the light of his background and place in an established pattern of British naval writing. Unfortunately, it also laid him open to criticism on specific issues, notably that levelled against his assessments of the strategy of Elizabeth I by Tudor experts such as Dr. A. L. Rowse and Sir John Neale. Thus, while *Statesmen and Seapower* is the most widely remembered of Richmond's books, it is not necessarily his best or most reliable.

Richmond's principal purpose, however, was not to devise a universalist theory of sea-power. On this he had always parted company with Mahan. No Jominian model nor any general theory of international relations shaped his thinking. His objective was not to systematize or codify. His major historical works were motivated by a more straightforward desire to explain British maritime achievements in terms of the men, their ships, and the national policies that determined their actions. In terms of scholarship, research, and originality of interpretation, Richmond owed everything to the standards and intellectual framework established by his British antecedents, most especially Sir Julian Corbett. Unlike the more extreme navalists of the "Blue Water" school of writers who placed so much emphasis on the operations of the battle fleet in establishing command of the sea, Richmond demonstrated that sea-power was more complex and all-inclusive in its workings in both a direct military sense and as an instrument of diplomacy and economic enterprise. Hence his preoccupation with such fundamental concepts as bases and lines of communication, trade defence, blockade, combined operations, alliance politics, and the interplay of continentalist and maritime strategic options. With his realist's eye open to the effects of wind, weather, and circumstance, and of geographic and political specificity, he challenged navalist generalizations as they applied to Britain, the pre-eminent naval power, and also to lesser powers for whom the so-called "heresies" of the *jeune école* and *guerre de course* frequently made more sense.

To a far greater degree than either Mahan or Corbett, Richmond also felt compelled to apply the lessons of his researches to developments in his own time. What he carried over into his activities as a defence critic, however, was not historical experience as analogy, but rather those scholarly habits of reasoning which had uncovered it. Richmond the historian was therefore inseparable from Richmond the reforming admiral. His iconoclasm and objectivity in what he liked to call the search for "truth" was the basis of all his activities from the founding of the *Naval Review* to his call for a postwar renaissance in naval thinking that would counter-balance materialist influences. It determined his approach to practical problems such as improving naval staff organization and methods, as it also conditioned his thinking on wider questions of policy from ship design and tactical matters, to disarmament, belligerent rights, and grand strategy in two world wars. His direct involvement in so many of these important questions led him to spell out the need for a generally accepted strategic philosophy which explicitly recognized the strengths and vulnerabilities of an island kingdom and oceanic empire, and which offered a realistic basis for cooperation between the various services and a framework against which to assess the implications of rapidly changing technology. His own attempts to define such a "British doctrine of war" and to give form and substance to continuing honest discussion of the problem through his work at the Naval War Course, the Imperial Defence College, and Cambridge may in the long run be his most important legacy. It may yet transpire that later generations, for whom the threat of nuclear holocaust and a growing Soviet maritime challenge demand deeper understandings than the doctrinal glosses to which contemporary strategic thought all too frequently is reduced, will profit from Richmond's wisdom and personal example. In an age of increasing doubts about the rationality of war in any of its forms, and fears of a growing military-industrial bureaucracy, some room must exist for his heretic's courage and the power of his scholar's mind.

Bibliography

Primary Sources—Unpublished

1. Archives

Great Britain. Public Record Office. Admiralty Papers.
———— . Public Record Office. Air Ministry Papers.
———— . Public Record Office. Cabinet Office Papers.

2. Private Papers

Bellairs Papers. Redpath Library, McGill University.
Corbett Papers. (The late) W. C. B. Tunstall, Coaters, Bignor, Sussex. Copies in the Douglas Library, Queen's University, Kingston.
Dewar, K. G. B., Papers. National Maritime Museum, Greenwich.
Drax Papers. Churchill College, Cambridge.
Fremantle Papers. National Maritime Museum, Greenwich.
Henderson, W. H., Papers. National Maritime Museum, Greenwich.
Keyes Papers. Churchill College, Cambridge.
Liddell Hart Papers. King's College, Centre for Military Archives, University of London.
Marder Papers. Selections from papers and notes of Professor Arthur J. Marder; copies held by the Directorate of History, N.D.H.Q., Ottawa. Includes notes of Admiralty papers some of which were misplaced or destroyed prior to reclassification by the P.R.O. Also notes from the following collections: Beatty, Bellairs (Rear-Admiral Roger M., Fleet Papers, 1917-1918), Graham Greene, Jellicoe, and Wemyss Papers.
Pollen, Arthur Hungerford, Papers. In possession of Mr. J. A. Pollen, London.
Richmond Papers. National Maritime Museum, Greenwich.
Slade Papers. National Maritime Museum, Greenwich. Copies of Diaries held by Douglas Library, Queen's University, Kingston.
Thursfield, H. G., Papers. National Maritime Museum, Greenwich.

3. Naval Staff Studies (Admiralty)

Technical History Section. *The Technical History.* Fifty Monographs (1919-1920).

Torpedo Division. "Remarks of the Naval Staff on Anti-Submarine Operations" (1927).

Training and Staff Duties Division. Monographs (Historical). Thirty-nine monographs (1919-1939). Principal writers were Captain A. C. Dewar, succeeded by Instructor-Captain Oswald Tuck, assisted by Lieutenant-Commander J. H. Lloyd-Owen. A complete set is held in the Naval Library, Ministry of Defence, London. Monographs marked * below are held by the Massey Library, R.M.C., Kingston.

No.	Title
*6	"Passage of the British Expeditionary Force, August, 1914" (1921).
*7	"The Patrol Flotillas at the Commencement of the War" (1921).
*8	"Naval Operations Connected with the Raid on the North-East Coast, December 16th, 1914" (1921).
*11	"The Battle of Heligoland Bight, August 28th, 1914" (1921).
*12	"The Action of Dogger Bank, January 24th, 1915" (1921).
—	"Naval Staff Appreciation of Jutland" (Withdrawn about 1928. Most copies destroyed.) The Naval Library in London does not hold a copy. Copies have survived in the Harper Papers, British Museum, in the possession of Captain S. W. Roskill, and in the Library, University of California, Irvine.
*29	"Home Waters—Part IV, From February to July 1915" (1925).
*30	"Home Waters—Part V, From July to October 1915" (1926).
*31	"Home Waters—Part VI, From October 1915, to May 1916" (1926).
*33	"Home Waters—Part VII, From June 1916, to November 1916" (1927).
—	"The Naval Staff of the Admiralty: Its Work and Development" (1929).
*34	"Home Waters—Part VIII, From December 1916, to April 1917" (1933).

4. Miscellaneous Papers

Papers relating to the Origin and History of the Naval Society. In the possession of A. B. Sainsbury, London, England.

Thursfield, Captain H. G. "The Washington Treaties and the 1927 Geneva Conference." Lecture delivered April 9, 1929, Royal Naval Staff College, Greenwich. In possession of Professor G. S. Graham, Beckley, Sussex.

Waters, Lieutenant-Commander D. W. "A Study of the Philosophy and Conduct of Maritime War, 1815-1945" (1954). Reproduced in part (Part I, 1815-1918) in *Journal of the Royal Naval Scientific Service* (May 1958) (restricted).

_____ . "Convoy: The Core of Maritime Strategy" (1956). Lecture prepared in conjunction with Commander F. Barley, Historical Section, Admiralty.

_____ . "Notes on the Convoy System of Naval Warfare, Thirteenth to Twentieth Centuries." Part I: "Convoy in the Sail Era, 1204-1874" (1957). Part II: "First World War, 1914-1918" (1960).

Primary Sources—Published

1. Official Histories

Admiralty. *Battle of Jutland, 30th May to 1st June, 1916: Official Despatches with Appendices*. London: H.M.S.O., n.d. (Cmd. 1068).
————. *Narrative of the Battle of Jutland*. London: H.M.S.O., 1924.
————. *Reproduction of the Record of the Battle of Jutland: Prepared by Captain J. E. T. Harper, M.V.O., R.N. and other Officers by direction of the Admiralty in 1919-1920*. London: H.M.S.O., 1927 (Cmd. 2870).
Corbett, Sir Julian S., and Newbolt, Sir Henry. *History of the Great War: Naval Operations*. 5 vols. London: Longmans, 1920-1931. Rev. ed. of 1, 1938; of 3, 1940.
Fayle, C. Ernest. *History of the Great War: Seaborne Trade*. 3 vols. London: Murray, 1920-1924.
Hurd, Sir Archibald. *History of the Great War: The Merchant Navy*. 3 vols. London: Murray, 1921-1929.
Raleigh, Sir Walter, and Jones, H. A. *History of the Great War: The War in the Air*. 6 vols. Oxford: Clarendon Press, 1922-1937.
Roskill, Captain S. W. *The War at Sea*. 3 vols in 4. Vol. 1. London: H.M.S.O., 1954-1964.
Salter, J. A. *Allied Shipping Control: An Experiment in International Administration*. Oxford: Clarendon Press, 1921.
Woodward, E. L.; Butler, R.; et al, eds. *Documents on British Foreign Policy, 1919-1939*. London: H.M.S.O.

2. Parliamentary Papers

Report of the Sub-Committee of the Committee of Imperial Defence appointed to inquire into certain questions of Naval Policy raised by Lord Charles Beresford, August 12, 1909. Cmd. 256 (1909).
Navy: Distribution of the Duties of the Naval Staff at the Admiralty. Cmd. 1343 (1921).
The Singapore Base: Correspondence with the Dominions and India. Cmd. 2083 (1925).
The Eighth Report from the Estimates Committee of the House of Commons, Services Colleges (H.C. 296), 1963-1964; (H.C. 229) 1963-1964 and Session 1964-1965, *Special Report 3; Service Colleges (Departmental Observations . . .)* (H.C. 88), 1965.
Hansard's Parliamentary Debates. House of Commons, 5th series.

3 Papers, Diaries and Letters

Blake, Robert, ed. *The Private Papers of Douglas Haig, 1914-1919*. London: Eyre and Spottiswoode, 1952.
Chalmers, Rear-Admiral William S. *The Life and Letters of David, Earl Beatty*. London: Hodder and Stoughton, 1951.
Kemp, Lieutenant-Commander Peter K., ed. *The Papers of Admiral Sir John Fisher*. 2 vols. London: Navy Records Society, 1960-1964.
Marder, Arthur J., ed. *Portrait of an Admiral: The Life and Papers of Sir Herbert Richmond*. London: Jonathan Cape, 1952.

_____ . *Fear God and Dread Nought: The Correspondence of Admiral of the Fleet Lord Fisher of Kilverstone*. 3 vols. London: Jonathan Cape, 1952-1959.

Patterson, A. Temple, ed. *The Jellicoe Papers*. 2 vols. London: Navy Records Society, 1966-1968.

Roskill, Captain S. W., ed. *Papers Relating to the Naval Air Service, 1908-1919*. London: Navy Records Society, 1969.

4. Memoirs and Autobiographies

Amery, L. S. *My Political Life*. Vol. 2: *1914-1929*. London: Hutchinson, 1953.

Beresford, Admiral Lord Charles. *The Betrayal*. London: P. S. King, 1912.

_____ . *The Memoirs of Admiral Lord Charles Beresford*. 2 vols. 2nd ed. London: Methuen, 1914.

Bonham, Carter V. *Winston Churchill as I Knew Him*. London: Eyre and Spottiswoode, and Collins, 1965.

Brownrigg, Rear-Admiral Sir Douglas. *Indiscretions of the Naval Censor*. London: Cassell, 1920.

Chatfield, Admiral of the Fleet, Lord. *The Navy and Defence*. London: Heinemann, 1942.

_____ . *It Might Happen Again*. London: Heinemann, 1947.

Churchill, Winston S. *The World Crisis*. 5 vols. in 6. London: Butterworth, 1923-1931.

_____ . *Thoughts and Adventures*. London: Butterworth, 1932.

_____ . *great Contemporaries*. London: Butterworth, 1937.

DeChair, Admiral Sir Dudley. *The Sea is Strong*. Ed. Somerset deChair. London: Harrap, 1961.

Dewar, Vice-Admiral K. G. B. *The Navy from Within*. London: Gollancz, 1939.

Fisher of Kilverstone, Baron (John A.). *Memories*. London: Hodder and Stoughton, 1919.

_____ . *Records*. London: Hodder and Stoughton, 1919.

Fremantle, Admiral Sir Sydney R. *My Naval Career, 1880-1929*. London: Hutchinson, 1949.

Haldane, Viscount. *Richard Burdon Haldane: An Autobiography*. London: Hodder and Stoughton, 1929.

Hankey, Lord. *The Supreme Command*. 2 vols. London: Allen and Unwin, 1961.

_____ . *The Supreme Control at the Paris Peace Conference, 1919*. London: Allen and Unwin, 1963.

Jellicoe, Admiral of the Fleet Earl. *The Grand Fleet, 1914-1916: Its Creation, Development and Work*. London: Cassell, 1919.

_____ . *The Crisis of the Naval War*. London: Cassell, 1920.

_____ . *The Submarine Peril*. London: Cassell, 1934.

Kenworthy, Lieutenant-Commander J. M. (Tenth Baron Strabolgi). *Sailors, Statesmen—and Others: An Autobiography*. London: Rich and Cowan, 1933.

Keyes, Admiral Sir Roger. *The Naval Memoirs of Admiral of the Fleet Sir Roger Keyes*. 2 vols. London: Butterworth, 1934-1935.

King-Hall, Commander Stephen. *A North Sea Diary, 1914-1918*. London: Newnes, 1936.

_____ . *My Naval Life, 1906-1929*. London: Faber, 1952.

Leslie, Sir Shane. *Long Shadows*. London: Murray, 1966.
Liddell Hart, Captain Sir Basil. *The Liddell Hart Memoirs*. 2 vols. London: Cassell, 1965.
Lloyd George, David. *War Memoirs of David Lloyd George*. 6 vols. Boston: Little, Brown and Co., 1934-1937.
Long, Viscount. *Memories*. London: Hutchinson, 1923.
Longmore, Air Chief Marshal Sir Arthur. *From Sea to Sky, 1910-1945*. London: Geoffrey Bles, 1946.
Martel, Sir Giffard. *An Outspoken Soldier*. London: Sifton Praed, 1949.
Oxford and Asquith, Earl of. *Memories and Reflections: 1852-1927*. 2 vols. London: Cassell, 1928.
Robertson, Field-Marshal Sir William. *Soldiers and Statesmen, 1914-1918*. 2 vols. London: Cassell, 1926.
Salter, Lord. *Memoirs of a Public Servant*. London: Faber, 1961.
Scott, Sir Percy M. *Fifty Years in the Royal Navy*. London: J. Murray, 1919.
Sydenham of Coombe, Colonel Lord (Sir George Clarke). *My Working Life*. London: Murray, 1927.
Walker, Sir Charles. *Thirty-six Years at the Admiralty*. London: Lincoln Williams, 1934.
Wester Wemyss, Lady. *The Life and Letters of Lord Wester Wemyss*. London: Eyre and Spottiswoode, 1935.

Secondary Sources

1. *Works by Herbert William Richmond*

Papers Relating to the Loss of Minorca. London: Navy Records Society, 1913.
The Navy in the War of 1739-1748. 3 vols. Cambridge: University Press, 1920.
The Spencer Papers, Volumes III and IV. London: Navy Records Society, 1924.
Command and Discipline. London: E. Stanford, 1927.
National Policy and Naval Strength. London: Longmans, 1928.
Naval Warfare. London: 1930.
The Navy in India, 1763-1783. London: E. Benn, 1931.
Economy and Naval Security. London: Ernest Benn, 1931.
Imperial Defence and Capture at Sea in War. London: Hutchinson, 1932.
Naval Training. London: 1933.
Sea Power in the Modern World. London: Bell, 1934.
Naval History and the Citizen. London, 1934.
The Navy. London: W. Hodge, 1937.
The Naval Role in Modern Warfare. London, 1940.
The Invasion of Britain. London: Methuen, 1941.
Amphibious Warfare in British History. London, 1941.
British Strategy, Military and Economic. Cambridge: University Press, 1941.
War at Sea Today. London, 1942.
"The Naval Officer in Fiction." In *Essays and Studies by Members of the English Association*, 30. Oxford, 1945.
Statesmen and Seapower. Oxford: Clarendon Press, 1946.
The Navy as an Instrument of Policy, 1558-1727. Ed. by E. A. Hughes. Cambridge: University Press, 1953.

2. Books

Acworth, Captain Bernard. *Navies of Today and Tomorrow*. London: Eyre and Spottiswoode, 1930.
————. *The Navy and the Next War*. London: Eyre and Spottiswoode, 1933.
————. *Britain in Danger: An Examination of Our New Navy*. London: Eyre and Spottiswoode, 1937.
Alexander, Major A. C. B. *Jutland: A Plea for a Naval General Staff*. London: H. Rees, 1923.
Altham, Captain Edward. *Jellicoe*. London: Blackie, 1938.
Aspinall-Oglander, Brigadier-General Cecil F. *The Biography of Admiral Lord Keyes of Zeebrugge and Dover*. London: Hogarth Press, 1951.
Aston, Sir George, ed. *The Study of War for Statesmen and Citizens*. London: Longmans, Green, 1927.
Bacon, Admiral Sir Reginald. *The Dover Patrol, 1915-1917*. 2 vols. London: Hutchinson, 1919.
————. *The Jutland Scandal*. 2nd ed. London: Hutchinson, 1925.
————, et al. *The World Crisis by Winston Churchill: A Criticism*. London: Hutchinson, 1927.
————. *The Life of Lord Fisher of Kilverstone*. 2 vols. London: Hodder and Stoughton, 1929.
————. *The Concise Story of the Dover Patrol*. London: Hutchinson, 1932.
————. *The Life of John Rushworth, Earl Jellicoe*. London: Cassell, 1936.
"Barfleur" [Admiral Sir Reginald Custance]. *Naval Policy: A Plea for the Study of War*. London: Eyre and Spottiswoode, 1907.
Barnett, Correlli. *The Swordbearers: Studies in Supreme Command in the First World War*. London: Eyre and Spottiswoode, 1963.
Beaverbrook, Lord. *Politicians and the War, 1914-1916*. London: Butterworth, 1928.
————. *Men and Power, 1917-1918*. London: Hutchinson, 1956.
Bellairs, Carlyon. *The Battle of Jutland: The Sowing and the Reaping*. London: Hodder and Stoughton, 1919.
Bennett, Captain Geoffrey. *Coronel and the Falklands*. London: Batsford, 1962.
————. *The Battle of Jutland*. London: Batsford, 1964.
————. *"Charlie B.": A Biography of Admiral Lord Charles Beresford*. London: Peter Dawnay, 1968.
Bond, Brian. *Liddell Hart: A Study of His Military Thought*. London: Cassell, 1977.
Bonnett, Stanley H. *The Price of Admiralty: An Indictment of the Royal Navy, 1805-1966*. London: Hale, 1968.
Bourne, K., and Watt, D. C., eds. *Studies in International History*. London: Longmans, 1967.
Boyle, Andrews. *Trenchard, Man of Vision*. London: Collins, 1962.
Bradford, Vice-Admiral Sir Edward E. *Life of Admiral of the Fleet Sir Arthur Knyvet Wilson*. London: Murray, 1923.
Bywater, Hector C. *Sea Power in the Pacific*. London: Constable, 1921.
————. *Navies and Nations*. London: Constable, 1927.
Callwell, C. E. *Military Operations and Maritime Preponderance: Their Relations and Interdependence*. Edinburgh: William Blackwood, 1905.
————. *Small Wars: Their Principles and Practice*. London: H.M.S.O., 1906.

————— . *Experiences of a Dug-Out, 1914-1918*. London: Constable, 1920.

Chaput, Rolland A. *Disarmament in British Foreign Policy*. London: Allen and Unwin, 1935.

Churchill, Randolph S. *Winston S. Churchill*. Vol. 1: *Youth, 1874-1900*; Vol. 2: *The Young Statesman, 1901-1914*. London: Heinemann, 1966-1967.

————— . *Winston S. Churchill. Companion to Vol. 1, Nos. 1 and 2: Companion to Vol. 2, Nos. 1-3*. London: Heinemann, 1967, 1969.

Colvin, Ian. *The Life of Lord Carson. 3 vols. vol. 1 by Edward Majoribanks*. London: Gallanez, 1932-1936.

Connell, J. *Auchinleck: A Biography of Field-Marshal Sir Claude Auchinleck*. London: Cassell, 1959.

Corbett, J. S. *Some Principles of Maritime Strategy*. London: Longmans, Green, 1911.

Dingman, Roger. *Power in the Pacific: The Origins of Naval Arms Limitation, 1914-1922*. Chicago: University Press, 1976.

D'Ombrain, Nicholas. *War Machinery and High Policy: Defence Administration in Peacetime Britain*. London: Oxford University Press, 1973.

Domville-Fife, Charles W., ed. *Evolution of Sea Power*. London: Rich and Cowan, 1939.

Dreyer, Admiral Sir Frederic. *The Sea Heritage: A Study of Maritime Warfare*. London: Museum Press, 1955.

Edwards, Kenneth. *The Mutiny at Invergordon*. London: Putnam, 1937.

Ehrmann, John. *Cabinet Government and War, 1890-1940*. Cambridge: University Press, 1958.

Fry, M. G. *Illusions of Security: North Atlantic Diplomacy, 1918-1922*. Toronto: University of Toronto Press, 1972.

Gardiner, Leslie. *The Royal Oak Courts Martial*. London, 1965.

Geddes, Baron. *The Forging of a Family*. London: Faber, 1952.

Gibson, L., and Harper, Vice-Admiral J. E. T. *The Riddle of Jutland: An Authentic History*. London: Cassell, 1934.

Gilbert, Martin. *Winston S. Churchill*. Vol. 3: *1914-1916*; Vol. 4: *1916-1922*; Vol. 5: *1922-1939*. London: Heinemann, 1971, 1975, 1976.

————— . *Winston S. Churchill. Companion to Vol. 3: 1914-1916, Nos. 1 and 2; Companion to Vol. 4: 1916-1922*. London: Heinemann, 1972, 1977.

Gollin, Alfred M. *Proconsul in Politics: A Study of Lord Milner in Opposition and in Power*. London: Blond, 1964.

Gooch, John. *The Plans of War: The General Staff and British Military Strategy, 1900-1916*. New York: Wiley, 1974.

Grenfell, Commander Russell. *Sea Power in the Next War*. London: G. Bles, 1938.

————— . *Main Fleet to Singapore*. London: Faber and Faber, 1951.

Graham, Gerald S. *The Politics of Naval Supremacy*. Cambridge: The University Press, 1965.

Gretton, Vice-Admiral Sir Peter. *Former Naval Person: Winston Churchill and the Royal Navy*. London: Cassell, 1968.

Guinn, Paul. *British Strategy and Politics, 1914-1918*. London: Oxford University Press, 1965.

Harper, Rear-Admiral J. E. T. *The Truth About Jutland*. London: Murray, 1927.

Hezlett, Sir Arthur. *The Submarine and Seapower*. London: Peter Davies, 1967.

————— . *Aircraft and Seapower*. London: Peter Davies, 1970.

————— . *Electronics and Seapower*. New York: Stein and Day, 1975.

Higham, Robin. *Armed Forces in Peacetime: Britain 1918-1940, A Case Study*. London: G. T. Foulis, 1962.

_____ . *The Military Intellectuals in Britain, 1918-1939*. New Brunswick: Rutgers University Press, 1966.

Hinsley, F. H. *Command of the Sea*. London: Christophers, 1950.

Hough, Richard. *First Sea Lord: An Authorised Biography of Admiral Lord Fisher*. London: Allen and Unwin, 1969.

Howard, Michael, ed. *The Theory and Practice of War*. New York: Praeger, 1966.

_____ . *The Mediterranean Strategy in the Second World War*. London: Weidenfeld and Nicolson, 1968.

_____ . *The Continental Commitment*. London: Temple Smith, 1972.

Hunt, Barry, and Preston, A. W. *War Aims and Strategic Policy in the Great War, 1914-1918*. London: Croom Helm, 1977.

Hurd, Sir Archibald. *Who Goes There?* London: Hutchinson, 1942.

Hyatt, A. M. J., ed. *Dreadnought to Polaris: Maritime Strategy Since Mahan*. Toronto: Copp Clark, 1973.

Hyde, H. Montgomery. *Carson: The Life of Sir Edward Carson, Lord Carson of Duncairn*. London: Heinemann, 1953.

James, Admiral Sir William. *A Great Seaman: The Life of Admiral of the Fleet Sir Henry F. Oliver*. London: Witherby, 1956.

Jameson, William. *The Fleet that Jack Built: Nine Men Who Made a Modern Navy*. London: Hart-Davis, 1962.

Johnson, Franklyn A. *Defence By Committee: The British Committee of Imperial Defence, 1885-1959*. London: Oxford University Press, 1960.

Jordan, Gerald, ed. *Naval Warfare in the Twentieth Century: Essays in Honour of Arthur Marder*. London: Croom Helm, 1977.

Kennedy, Paul M. *The Rise and Fall of British Naval Mastery*. London: Allen Lane, 1976.

Kenworthy, Lieutenant-Commander J. M. *Peace or War*. New York: H. Liveright, 1927.

_____ . *Freedom of the Seas*. New York: H. Liveright, 1928.

_____ . *New Wars: New Weapons*. London: Matthews and Marrott, 1930.

_____ . *The Real Navy*. London: Hutchinson, 1932.

_____ . *Sailors, Statesmen and Others: An Autobiography*. London: Rich and Cowan, 1933.

Kerr, Admiral Mark. *Prince Louis of Battenberg, Admiral of the Fleet*. London: Longmans, 1934.

Kirtleside, Lord Douglas of. *Sholto Douglas: Combat and Command*. London: Collins, 1966.

Liddell Hart, B. H. *Sherman: Soldier, Realist, American*. New York: Dodd, Mead, 1929.

_____ . *The British Way in Warfare*. London: Faber and Faber, 1932.

_____ . *When Britain Goes to War*. London: Faber and Faber, 1935.

_____ . *Europe in Arms*. London: Faber and Faber, 1937.

_____ . *The Defence of Great Britain*. London: Faber and Faber, 1939.

_____ . *Thoughts on War*. London: Faber and Faber, 1944.

Luvaas, J. *The Education of an Army: British Military Thought, 1815-1940*. Chicago: University of Chicago Press, 1964.

Mackay, Ruddock F. *Fisher of Kilverstone*. Oxford: Clarndon, 1973.

McIntyre, W. D. *The Rise and Fall of the Singapore Naval Base, 1919-1941*. London: Macmillan, 1979.

McKenna, Stephen. *Reginald McKenna, 1863-1943*. London: Eyre and Spottiswoode, 1948.

Marder, Arthur J. *British Naval Policy, 1880-1905: The Anatomy of British Sea Power*. London: Putnam, 1941.

———. *From the Dreadnought to Scapa Flow: The Royal Navy in the Fisher Era*. 5 vols. London: Oxford University Press, 1961-1970.

———. *From the Dardanelles to Oran: Studies of the Royal Navy in War and Peace, 1915-1940*. London: Oxford University Press, 1974.

———. *Operation Menace: The Dakar Expedition and the Dudley North Affair*. London: Oxford University Press, 1976.

Maurice, Major-General Sir Frederick. *Haldane*. 2 vols. London: Faber, 1937-1939.

———. *Lessons of Allied Cooperation: Naval, Military and Air, 1914-1918*. London: Oxford University Press, 1942.

Medlicott, W. N. *British Foreign Policy Since Versailles*. London: Methuen, 1940; 2nd ed., 1968.

Middlemas, K. and Barnes, J. *Baldwin*. London: Weidenfeld and Nicolson, 1969.

Miller, Eugene H. *Strategy at Singapore*. New York: Macmillan, 1942.

Monger, George W. *The End of Isolation: British Foreign Policy, 1900-1907*. London: Nelson, 1963.

Morison, E. E. *Admiral Sims and the Modern American Navy*. Boston: Houghton Mifflin, 1942.

Nelson H. I. *Land and Power, British and Allied Policy on Germany's Frontiers, 1916-1919*. London: Routledge and Kegan Paul, 1963.

O'Connor, R. G. *Perilous Equilibrium: The United States and The London Naval Conference of 1930*. Kansas University Press, 1962.

Padfield, Peter. *Aim Straight: A Biography of Admiral Sir Percy Scott*. London: Hodder and Stoughton, 1966.

———. *The Battleship Era*. London: R. Hart-Davis, 1972.

Parkes, Oscar. *British Battleships*. Rev. ed. London: Seeley Service, 1966.

Patterson, A. Temple. *Jellicoe: A Biography*. London: Macmillan, 1969.

Pollen, A. H. *The Navy in Battle*. London: Chatto and Windus, 1918.

Pratt, Laurence R. *East of Malta, West of Suez: Britain's Mediterranean Crisis, 1936-1939*. Cambridge: University Press, 1975.

Reynolds, C. G. *Command of the Sea*. New York: Morrow, 1974.

Roskill, Captain S. W. *The Strategy of Seapower*. London: Collins, 1962.

———. *Naval Policy Between The Wars*. vol. 1: *The Period of Anglo-American Antagonism, 1919-1929*. London: Collins, 1968. Vol. 2: *The Period of Reluctant Rearmament*. London: Collins, 1976.

———, ed. *Papers Relating to the Naval Air Service, 1908-1918*. London: Navy Records Society, 1969.

———. *Hankey: Man of Secrets*. 3 vols. London: Collins, 1970, 1972, 1974.

———. *Churchill and the Admirals*. London: Collins, 1977.

Schofield, Vice-Admiral Brian B. *British Sea Power in the Twentieth Century*. London: Batsford, 1967.

Schurman, D. M. *The Education of a Navy: The Development of British Naval Strategic Thought, 1867-1914*. London: Cassell, 1965.

Shay, R. P. *British Rearmament in the Thirties: Politics and Profits*. Princeton: University Press, 1977.

Sims, Rear Admiral William S. *The Victory at Sea*. London: Murray, 1920.

Siney, Marion C. *The Allied Blockade of Germany, 1914-1916*. Ann Arbor: University of Michigan Press, 1957.

Sueter, Rear-Admiral Murray F. *Airmen or Noahs*. London: Pitman, 1928.

Sullivan, M. *The Great Adventure at Washington*. London, 1922.

Taylor, A. J. P. *English History, 1914-1945*. Oxford: Clarendon Press, 1965.

Terraine, John. *Douglas Haig: The Educated Soldier*. London: Hutchinson, 1963.

Tillman, Seth P. *Anglo-American Relations at the Paris Peace Conference of 1919*. Princeton: University Press, 1961.

Watt, D. C. *Personalities and Policies*. Notre Dame: University of Notre Dame Press, 1965.

Watt, D. C. *Too Serious a Business: European Armed Forces and the Approach to the Second World War*. London: Temple Smith, 1975.

Wheeler-Bennett, J. W. *Disarmament and Security Since Locarno, 1925-1931*. London: Macmillan, 1932.

Williamson, Samuel R., Jr. *The Politics of Grand Strategy: Britain and France Prepare for War, 1904-1914*. Cambridge, Mass.: Harvard University Press, 1969.

Young, Desmond. *Rutland of Jutland*. London: Cassell, 1963.

3. *Articles and Theses*

Campbell, J. P. "Marines, Aviators and the Battleship Mentality, 1923-1933," *R.U.S.I.*, 109 (February 1964).

Corbett, J. S. "The Teaching of Naval and Military History." *History*, 1 (April 1916).

Dewar, Captain Alfred C. "The Necessity for the Compilation of a Naval Staff History." *R.U.S.I.* (1921).

D'Ombrain, N. J. "The Military Departments and the Committee of Imperial Defence, 1902-1914: A Study in the Structural Problems of Defence Organisation," D.Phil. Dissertation, Oxford, 1968.

————. "Churchill at the Admiralty and the Committee of Imperial Defence, 1911-1914." *R.U.S.I.*, 115 (March 1970).

Fagan, George V. "Anglo-American Naval Relations, 1927-1937." Ph.D. Dissertation, University of Pennsylvania, 1954.

Fry, M. G. "The Imperial War Cabinet, The United States and Freedom of the Seas." *R.U.S.I.* (March, 1966).

Galbraith, J. S. "The Imperial Conference of 1921 and the Washington Conference." *Canadian Historical Review* (June 1948).

Mackintosh, J. P. "The Role of the Committee of Imperial Defence Before 1914." *English Historical Review*, 77 (1962).

McIntyre, W. D. "The Strategic Significance of Singapore, 1917-1942: The Naval Base and the Commonwealth." *Journal of Southeast Asian History* (March 1969).

Moon, Howard R. *The Invasion of the United Kingdom: Public Controversy and Official Planning, 1888-1918*. Ph.D. Dissertation, London, 1968.

Morgan, K. O. "Lloyd George's Premiership: A Study in 'Prime Ministerial Government.'" *Historical Journal* (March 1970).

Reynolds, C. G. "Sea Power in the Twentieth Century." *R.U.S.I.* (May 1966).

Roskill, S. W. "The Dismissal of Admiral Jellicoe." *Journal of Contemporary History*. 1 (October 1966).

Schurman, D. M. "Historians and Britain's Imperial Strategic Stance in 1914." In Flint, J. E., and Williams, G., eds., *Perspectives of Empire*. London: Longman, 1973.

Stanford, Peter M. "The Work of Sir Julian Corbett in the Dreadnought Era."
    United States Naval Institute Proceedings. 77 (January 1951).
————— . "Corbett's Work with Fisher at the Admiralty, 1904-1910." Unpub-
    lished Ms. Copy in possession of Professor D. M. Schurman; also in Naval
    Library, London.
Sumida, J. T. "British Capital Ship Design and Fire Control in the Dread-
    nought Era: Sir John Fisher, Arthur Hungerford Pollen and the Battle
    Cruiser." *Journal of Modern History* (June 1979).
Sumnerton, N. W. "The Development of British Military Planning for a War
    Against Germany, 1904-1914." Ph.D. Dissertation, University of London,
    1970.
Trevelyan, G. M. "Admiral Sir Herbert Richmond, 1871-1946." *The Proceed-
    ings of the British Academy*, 32 (reprinted, 1946), with a naval insight by
    Rear-Admiral H. G. Thursfield.
Wemyss, Lord Wester. "And After Washington." *The Nineteenth Century
    and After* (March 1922).

Index